MEDIATING CULTURAL MEMORY IN BRITAIN AND IRELAND

Mediating Cultural Memory is the first book to analyze the relationship between cultural memory, national identity and the changing media ecology in early eighteenth-century Britain. Leith Davis focuses on five pivotal episodes in the histories of England, Scotland and Ireland: the 1688 "Glorious" Revolution; the War of the Two Kings in Ireland (1688–91); the Scottish colonial enterprise in Darien (1695–1700); the 1715 Jacobite Rising; and the 1745 Jacobite Rising. She explores the initial inscription of these episodes in forms such as ballads, official documents, manuscript newsletters, correspondence, newspapers and popular histories, and examines how counter-memories of these events continued to circulate in later mediations. Bringing together Memory Studies, Book History and British Studies, *Mediating Cultural Memory* offers a new interpretation of the early eighteenth century as a crucial stage in the development of cultural memory and illuminates the processes of remembrance and forgetting that have shaped the nation of Britain.

LEITH DAVIS is the author of *Acts of Union: Scotland and the Literary Negotiation of the British Nation, 1707–1830* (1998) and *Music, Postcolonialism and Gender: The Construction of Irish National Identity, 1724–1874* (2005), and is co-editor of *Scotland and the Borders of Romanticism* (2004) and *Robert Burns and Transatlantic Culture* (2012).

MEDIATING CULTURAL MEMORY IN BRITAIN AND IRELAND

From the 1688 Revolution to the 1745 Jacobite Rising

LEITH DAVIS

Simon Fraser University

Shaftesbury Road, Cambridge CB2 8EA, United Kingdom

One Liberty Plaza, 20th Floor, New York, NY 10006, USA

477 Williamstown Road, Port Melbourne, VIC 3207, Australia

314–321, 3rd Floor, Plot 3, Splendor Forum, Jasola District Centre, New Delhi – 110025, India

103 Penang Road, #05–06/07, Visioncrest Commercial, Singapore 238467

Cambridge University Press is part of Cambridge University Press & Assessment, a department of the University of Cambridge.

We share the University's mission to contribute to society through the pursuit of education, learning and research at the highest international levels of excellence.

www.cambridge.org
Information on this title: www.cambridge.org/9781009018487

DOI: 10.1017/9781009039765

© Leith Davis 2022

This publication is in copyright. Subject to statutory exception and to the provisions of relevant collective licensing agreements, no reproduction of any part may take place without the written permission of Cambridge University Press & Assessment.

First published 2022
First paperback edition 2025

A catalogue record for this publication is available from the British Library

ISBN 978-1-316-51081-0 Hardback
ISBN 978-1-009-01848-7 Paperback

Cambridge University Press & Assessment has no responsibility for the persistence or accuracy of URLs for external or third-party internet websites referred to in this publication and does not guarantee that any content on such websites is, or will remain, accurate or appropriate.

Contents

List of Figures	*page* vi
Acknowledgments	viii
Introduction	1
1 Of Documents and Declarations: Mediating the 1688 Revolution	27
2 Remembering to Forget: Ireland, the War of the Two Kings and Cultural Amnesia	68
3 National Correspondences: Print, Letters and the Company of Scotland's Darien Expedition	108
4 Writing the 1715 Jacobite Rising: Periodical Networks and the Inscription of News	157
5 Reading the 1745 Jacobite Rising: "Transitory News-papers," "Fleeting Pamphlets" and Knots of Cultural Memory	200
Conclusion: "Living On" after 1745: From Cultural Memory to the Memory of Culture	249
Bibliography	270
Index	293

Figures

2.1 Phillip Lea, *An Epitome of Sr. William Petty's Large Survey of Ireland.* Courtesy of the Norman B. Leventhal Map & Education Center at the Boston Public Library *page* 77
2.2 Frontispiece and title page of Richard Cox, *Hibernia Anglicana; or, the History of Ireland* (London, 1689). Courtesy of the Beinecke Rare Book and Manuscript Library, Yale University 80
2.3 Engraving of Rev. George Walker (1618–90), Governor of Londonderry (1689). Courtesy of the National Gallery of Ireland. License: CC by 4.0 89
2.4 "A Survey of the CITY of LONDON-DERRY" from John Mitchelburne, *Ireland Preserv'd* (London, 1705). Courtesy of the British Library 103
3.1 "Arms of the Company of Scotland" (1698). By permission of University of Glasgow Library, Archives & Special Collections, Spencer fol. 51 120
3.2 Robert Drummond to Mr. Hugh Montgomerie, August 11, 1699 (Adv. MSS 83.7.4, fol. 22). Courtesy of the National Library of Scotland 136
3.3 "Entries in the Subscription Book," from John Hill Burton, *The Darien Papers: Being a Selection of Original Letters and Official Documents Relating to the Establishment of a Colony at Darien.* Courtesy of the National Library of Scotland. License: CC by 4.0 154
4.1 *The Speeches of the Six Condemn'd Lords at Their Tryals in Westminster-Hall* (London, 1716?). Courtesy of the National Library of Scotland 192
5.1 Engraving of Simon Fraser, Lord Lovat (c. 1667–1747). Courtesy of the National Library of Scotland. License: CC by 4.0 220

5.2 Effigies of the late Earl of Kilmarnock and the late Lord Balmerino (London, 1746). Courtesy of the National Library of Scotland. License: CC by 4.0 — 228

5.3 Frontispiece from *Ascanius; or the Young Adventurer* (London: G. Smith, 1746). Courtesy of the National Library of Scotland. License: CC by 4.0 — 237

5.4 Frontispiece from *Young Juba: or, the History of the Young Chevalier, from His Birth, to His Escape from Scotland, after the Battle of Culloden* (London, 1748). Courtesy of the National Library of Scotland. License: CC by 4.0 — 239

Acknowledgments

Funding for the research for this book was generously provided by the Social Sciences and Humanities Research Council of Canada and the Department of English at Simon Fraser University. An earlier version of Chapter 2 was published as "Cultural Memory and Cultural Amnesia: Ireland and the 'Glorious Revolution'" in *Studies in Eighteenth-Century Culture* 47 (2017): 185–205. A section of Chapter 4 appeared in a special issue of *Parliamentary History* on "Scribal News and Parliament," edited by Robin Eagles and Michael Schaich (41, no. 1, 2022). Sections of the Introduction first saw light in "Memory Studies and the Eighteenth Century" in *Literature Compass* 16, no. 2 (2019). The theoretical scaffolding for Chapter 5 was presented at the first World Congress of Scottish Literatures in Glasgow in July 2014, and the argument regarding the Company of Scotland's letters and the development of a sense of the Scottish nation from Chapter 3 was presented at the second World Congress of Scottish Literatures in Vancouver in June 2017.

This book was begun back in the heady time when it was possible to work in library archives, travel to conferences and engage in in-person discussions. I'm very grateful to all the colleagues encountered along the way who have listened to, commented on and had a positive impact on the ideas in this book. Also to all the friends who shored me up during the long writing process. The Trinity St. Friday Night Group, The Book Club Without a Name, my bandmates in Conchordance and the Sybaritic String Band, and many other friends – musical and otherwise (thank you, especially, Mary Doherty!) – provided vital fun, food, tunes, talk and emotional cheer; I am so fortunate to be connected to these communities and individuals. I also wish to acknowledge the invaluable support of my writing group colleagues in the Department of English at Simon Fraser University: Michelle Levy, Betty Schellenberg, Kandice Sharren and Diana Solomon; Betty Schellenberg heroically read the manuscript in its entirety at a crucial point and offered inspirational feedback. Members of the

Academic Women's Writing Group at Simon Fraser University also gave me companionship throughout the long writing process, as did Kristen Mahlis and Susan Scheckel. We persevered through many Zoom pomodoros together. I was also lucky to have the help of a number of stellar research assistants: a huge thanks to Alyssa Bridgman, Courtenay Connor, Kaitlyn MacInnis, Emma Pink, Sara Penn and Kandice Sharren. The anonymous readers offered suggestions that helped to better shape the narrative arc of the book, and Bethany Thomas and George Paul Laver at Cambridge University Press have been wonderful as the book has made its way through the various stages of production. I am also grateful to Fiona Little for careful copyediting and to everyone else who helped with the publication process. Needless to say, any inaccuracies or errors are my fault entirely.

The final writing process took place in a challenging environment, as COVID-19 upended the world and shrank the boundaries of everyone's life. I have been fortunate to have been living with the most amazing people during this time: my husband, Rob McGregor, and my children, Ciaran, Devin and Nia (and for a short time we also enjoyed the company of Katya Shyyan under our roof). Your laughter, your conversation, your music, your words of encouragement, your bizarre humour and your enduring love nourish and sustain me always; how much more so over the last year! You are everything to me, and this book is dedicated to you.

Introduction

Mediating Cultural Memory in Britain and Ireland: From the 1688 Revolution to the 1745 Jacobite Rising explores the impact of the late seventeenth-century and early eighteenth-century media shift on the creation and shaping of cultural memory in Britain and Ireland. The period on which I focus represents a time when the political shape of the British archipelago was changing as well as a time when, as in the present day, the material practices of mediation and medial networks were also altering significantly. In this earlier era, however, the "new medium" was print, which was coming to take "center stage" within an "already existing media ecology of voice, sound, image, and manuscript writing."[1] It is the argument of this book that the Anglo-centric cultural memories that have come to dominate the United Kingdom over the past several centuries, and, more generally, the notion of cultural memory itself, have their origin in the consolidation (and contestation) of the late seventeenth- and early eighteenth-century British nation as it was becoming saturated by print.[2]

The chapters that follow offer close examinations of a series of crisis points that took place between 1688 and 1746 at various locations in the British archipelago: the Revolution of 1688 in England; the War of the Two Kings in Ireland (1688–91); the Scottish colonial enterprise in Darien that helped establish the conditions for the Acts of Union in 1707 (1695–1700); the series of conflicts throughout mainland Britain that constituted the 1715 Jacobite Rising; and the 1745 Jacobite Rising that

---

[1] Clifford Siskin and William Warner, "This Is Enlightenment: An Invitation in the Form of an Argument," in *This Is Enlightenment*, ed. Clifford Siskin and William Warner (Chicago and London: University of Chicago Press, 2010), 10. See also Dmitri Nikulin, *Memory: A History* (Oxford: Oxford University Press, 2015) and Raymond Williams, *Keywords: A Vocabulary of Culture and Society*, rev. ed. (New York: Oxford University Press, 1985). I take the idea of "media ecology" from Ronald J. Zboray and Mary Saracino Zboray, "Print Culture," in *The Handbook of Communication History*, ed. Peter Simonson et al. (New York: Routledge, 2013), 181–95.

[2] On the phrase "print saturation," see the Multigraph Collective, *Interacting with Print: Elements of Reading in the Era of Print Saturation* (Chicago: University of Chicago Press, 2018).

was launched in Scotland but that also included areas of England. The eighteenth century was a time when the relationship between "the state and the public" was changing fundamentally,[3] and these selected events represent episodes when the tensions in the nation came to the forefront, episodes that either changed or threatened to change the political organization of the three kingdoms within the archipelago. Jan Assmann suggests that "Events tend to be forgotten unless they live on in collective memory"; the reason for their "living on" lies in their "continuous relevance" in "an ever-changing present" in which they are remembered as "facts of importance."[4] Over time, the five episodes considered in this book came to "live on" in printed discourse, turned into "facts of importance" in "collective memory" because they served to affirm an English-centred sense of Britain as a nation based on individual liberty, parliamentary democracy, a benevolent monarchy – and the incorporation of any troubling elements. These five episodes became sites of memory, or *lieux de mémoire*, to invoke the terminology of the French historian Pierre Nora, while competing counter-memories were frequently silenced, fragmented or pushed to the cultural margins, although not without leaving impressions of their existence, as we will see.[5]

In his influential *Realms of Memory: Rethinking the French Past* (1996), Nora offers the following definition of a *lieu de mémoire*: "any significant entity, whether material or non-material in nature, which by dint of human will or the work of time has become a symbolic element of the memorial heritage of any community."[6] Nora proposes that *lieux de mémoire* "emerge in two stages": first "moments of history" are "plucked out of the flow of history"; then they are "returned to it," but in an altered state so that they are "no longer quite life [*sic*] but not yet entirely death, like shells left on the shore when the sea of living memory has receded."[7]

---

[3] Thomas Poole, *Reason of State: Law, Prerogative, Empire* (Cambridge: Cambridge University Press, 2015).

[4] Jan Assmann, *Moses the Egyptian: The Memory of Egypt in Western Monotheism* (Boston, MA: Harvard University Press, 1997), 9–10.

[5] Michel Foucault describes a counter-memory as a memory that "opposes history given as continuity or representative of a tradition" ("Nietzsche, Genealogy, History," in *Language, Counter-Memory, Practice: Selected Essays and Interviews*, ed. Donald Bouchard [Ithaca, NY: Cornell University Press, 1977], 160).

[6] Pierre Nora and Lawrence D. Kritzman, eds, *Realms of Memory: Rethinking the French Past*, trans. Arthur Goldhammer (New York: Columbia University Press, 1996), xvii. *Realms of Memory* is the abridged English translation of Nora's monumental seven-volume *Les lieux de mémoire* (Paris: Gallimard, 1984–92). See also Pierre Nora, "Between Memory and History: les lieux de mémoire," *Representations* 26 (1989), 7–25.

[7] Nora and Kritzman, *Realms*, 7.

In his original formulation of the notion of *lieux de mémoire*, Nora paid little attention to the material conditions through which this "plucking" and "returning" were enabled. His ideas, however, have since been sharpened by a scholarly focus on the ways in which media "shape cultural remembrance in accordance to their specific means and measures."[8] Aleida Assmann and Linda Shortt assert, for example, that discussions of memory must "emphasize the important role played by the media and the institutions which store, preserve, display and circulate information" connected to those memories. Assmann in particular outlines how memories are stored for later re-activation, noting that different media possess different affordances, affordances that also change over time.[9] As Astrid Erll succinctly observes, "the medium is the memory."[10] In this book, as I describe in fuller detail below, I am interested in the affordances of printed texts, their "specific means and measures," which allow events to be "plucked" and then altered and returned to the "flow of history" so that they retain elements of their initial inscription even when they appear in different contexts. The initial inscription and storage of a site of memory through the medium of print, I contend, increased the possibilities for its preservation, display and circulation as well as impacting the range of its subsequent representations. *Mediating Cultural Memory* argues that the early eighteenth century constituted a unique moment for the intersections between print, memory and the nation in Britain; it was a time period which saw the forging of memories that continue to be drawn on even today to connect certain members – and exclude others – within a national community.

In the case of each of the five sites of memory analyzed in the chapters that follow, printed works were important in the process of memorializing events right from the beginning. Over the period that I examine, however, between 1688 and 1745, the role that printed texts played in articulating sites of memory changed, as the meaning of print itself shifted. During this time, the quantity and availability of printed works grew substantially,

---

[8] Astrid Erll, *Memory in Culture* (Houndmills: Palgrave Macmillan, 2011), 115.
[9] Assmann suggests that "with the changing nature and development of the various media, the constitution of the memory will also be continually changing" (*Cultural Memory and Western Civilization: Functions, Media, Archives* [Cambridge: Cambridge University Press, 2011], 10–11). I use the term "affordances" here to mean "functional and relational aspects which frame, while not determining, the possibilities for agentic action in relation to an object" (Ian Hutchby, "Technologies, Texts and Affordances," *Sociology* 35, no. 2 [2001]: 444).
[10] Erll, *Memory in Culture*, 115.

generating a new understanding regarding the processes of mediation.[11] The focus on mediation that accompanied this expansion of print also translated into a perception about how print could be deployed in the service of creating – or at times contesting – what were increasingly being understood as national memories. In other words, the comprehension by human agents that events would "live on," as Jan Assmann puts it, long after the events themselves were over came to impact the ways in which those events were articulated in the first place.[12] In "Remembering as Reinscription – with a Difference," Catherine Belsey observes that our current sense of memory is in fact future-oriented: "we remember the past not simply as it was, but as it is or, more precisely, as it will turn out to have been, in consequence of our remembering it."[13] *Mediating Cultural Memory* argues that we can trace this new understanding of a future-oriented memory to the time period between 1688 and 1745, because we can observe during this time a growing consciousness regarding the place that sites of memory will occupy in the national future.[14] I begin my examination of this history of national sites of memory by comparing two texts that bookend the era under investigation and that reflect how the changes that took place in the media ecology of the British Isles in the first half of the eighteenth century impacted the way in which national memories were created and shaped. I move from a discussion of these two examples to a consideration of the methodologies informing this book, and then I conclude this introduction with a brief outline of the chapters that will follow.

"Living On" in 1688 vs. 1745

On November 1, 1688, William of Orange's fleet set sail from Hellevoetsluis in the Republic of the United Netherlands to challenge

---

[11] See Alvin Kernan, *Print Technology, Letters, and Samuel Johnson* (Princeton, NJ: Princeton University Press, 1987); Paula McDowell, *The Invention of the Oral: Print Commerce and Fugitive Voices in Eighteenth-Century Britain* (Chicago: University of Chicago Press, 2017); Michael F. Suarez, S. J. and Michael Turner, eds., *The Cambridge History of the Book in Britain*, vol. 5, *1695–1830* (Cambridge: Cambridge University Press, 2010).
[12] Assmann, *Moses*, 9–10.
[13] Catherine Belsey, 'Remembering as Re-inscription – with a Difference', in *Literature, Literary History, and Cultural Memory*, ed. Herbert Grabes (Tübingen: Gunter Narr Verlag, 2005), 4.
[14] Alison Landsberg observes that memory "is not a transhistorical phenomenon ... Rather, like all other modalities, memory is historically and culturally specific; it has meant different things to people and cultures at different times," often changing as a result of "technological innovation" (*Prosthetic Memory: The Transformation of American Remembrance in the Age of Mass Culture* [New York: Columbia University Press, 2004], 3).

the right of the Stuart king, James II/VII, to rule the kingdoms of England, Scotland and Ireland. According to Lisa Jardine, William brought with him a formidable force consisting of "twenty thousand highly trained professional troops" and "twenty thousand mariners and support staff."[15] At the same time as he was preparing for this military invasion, William had also been availing himself of the canny media skills of Gaspar Fagel, his English-trained Dutch advisor, and Gilbert Burnet, an ordained Church of Scotland minister and lawyer in exile at The Hague, in order to produce a pamphlet that would ensure that his "Intentions" regarding this "Expedition" would be "rightly understood."[16] In the *Declaration of His Highnes William Henry*, advertised as an explanation of the *"Reasons Inducing [the Prince], to Appear in Armes in the Kingdome of England*, William asserts that he seeks only to *"Preserv[e] the Protestant Religion"* and to restore *"the Lawes and Liberties of England, Scotland and Ireland"* by calling *"a FREE AND LEGALL PARLIAMENT"* (1). He calls into question the legitimacy of the recent birth of Prince James Francis Edward Stuart and stakes a claim for his right to succeed to the British throne along with his wife, Mary. Although he appears *"in Armes,"* however, his "Expedition" is, he suggests, only focused on securing "the Peace and Happines [*sic*]" of the British nation (1).

In 1746 a different William, the Hanoverian Duke of Cumberland, crushed the Jacobite forces led by James II/VII's grandson Charles Edward Stuart at Culloden Moor. The battle lasted less than an hour, and it effectively ended a civil war that had come within 130 miles of London and had threatened the British state with a return to the Stuart monarchy.[17] Initial news of the victory was delivered to King George II by Cumberland's aide-de-camp, Lord Bury, by express on April 23, 1746, and then, three days later, a more detailed official dispatch from His Highness the Duke of Cumberland was printed "By Authority" as an eight-page pamphlet with a headline reading: *"Whitehall, April 26, 1746: This Afternoon a Messenger Arrived from the Duke of Cumberland, with the Following Particulars of the Victory Obtained by his Highness over the Rebels, on Wednesday the 16th Instant near Culloden."*[18] The pamphlet describes

---

[15] Lisa Jardine, *Going Dutch: How England Plundered Holland's Glory* (London: Harper Press, 2008), 4.
[16] *The Declaration of His Highnes William Henry* (The Hague, 1688).
[17] See Murray Pittock, *Culloden (Cùil Lodair)* (Oxford: Oxford University Press, 2016).
[18] *Whitehall, April 26, 1746: This Afternoon a Messenger Arrived from the Duke of Cumberland, with the Following Particulars of the Victory Obtained by His Royal Highness over the Rebels, on Wednesday the 16th Instant near Culloden* (London, 1746). Referred to hereafter as *Particulars of the Victory*.

the military impact of the conflict at Culloden, comparing the heavy loss of 2,000 "Rebels" with the 300 "kill'd wounded, and missing" of the "King's Troops" (3).

As official responses to specific challenges to the current political leadership, these documents were designed to communicate the importance of the event they describe for posterity ("to all men," as the *Declaration* asserts [1]). Both texts encouraged collective identity at a time when a military conflict was exposing the lack of cohesion at the heart of the nation. The *Declaration* appeals to the "Laws, Liberties and Customes," but "above all" to "the *Religion* and worship of God" as these have been "established" in the nation, and it references previous national events, including the signing of the "*Magna Charta*," in order to unite Protestant readers (2–3). The news pamphlet on the *Particulars of the Victory*, too, encourages collective identification, as it contrasts the "wild Manner" of the "Rebels" with the superior order and discipline of the government troops (2). Most importantly for the purposes of this book, both the *Declaration* and the *Particulars of the Victory* were conveyed through printed narratives which were subsequently re-presented in whole or in part in other printed texts. Both texts "plucked" moments out of the "flow of history" almost at the moment of their occurrence, inscribing them in print and enabling further sharing of their specific content in different contexts.

A comparison of the material circumstances surrounding the initial printing and dissemination of the *Declaration* and the *Particulars of the Victory*, however, reveals essential differences, differences that impacted the possibilities for the recirculation of those texts and that remind us of the importance of considering the issue of mediation in any discussion of cultural memory. Printed works in seventeenth-century England were tightly regulated by means of the Licensing Act that was established by Charles II in 1662. The publication and dissemination of William's *Declaration* therefore had to be carefully arranged to avoid detection by the authorities. The contents of the *Declaration* were initially kept secret even from supporters of William's cause. As Jardine notes, copies were "carried to (and concealed in) key locations across England and Scotland," then released "simultaneously at all these places" as well as locations in mainland Europe as William's fleet set sail.[19] The distribution of the *Declaration* was made easier by the fact that political upheaval after the invasion resulted in a temporary chaos in "the various agencies and

---

[19] Jardine, *Going Dutch*, 29.

procedures for controlling printed matter," as Lois Schwoerer notes.[20] The rapid and widespread release of the *Declaration* was an unprecedented media event in Britain, and once in power, William took pains to make sure that nothing similar would occur again by restoring licensing restrictions and press censorship.[21]

The *Declaration* was widely reprinted throughout 1688 and 1689, in London and Edinburgh as well as places further afield such as Boston. Bundled with additional materials such as proclamations addressed "To all Commanders of Ships and all Seamen that are now imployed in the English Fleet" and "To all the Officers and Souldiers in the English Army" as well as "A Praier for the present Expedition," the *Declaration* was republished at least twenty-one times in four languages during the early period after William's "appearance" in England.[22] It continued to play a significant role in justifying William and Mary's assumption of royal power, as it provided a template for the Declaration of Rights,[23] and was reprinted both in full and in condensed form in numerous works in the early eighteenth century that sought to establish the history of the 1688 Revolution.[24]

Between the time when William planned his assault on the coast of Britain and the period when the Duke of Cumberland was dispatching the account of the victory at Culloden, the material practices of mediation and the media landscape in Britain changed significantly. In 1695, in part because of party conflict in Parliament, the Licensing Act was allowed to lapse, signaling the end of pre-publication censorship and limitations on numbers of presses in England. This easing of restrictions, combined with increasing literacy rates and a steadily developing production and distribution system for printed works, encouraged what Michael Suarez and Michael Turner have referred to as "the efflorescence of a comprehensive

---

[20] Lois G. Schwoerer, "Propaganda in the Revolution of 1688–89," *American Historical Review* 82, no. 4 (1977): 858.
[21] Geoffrey Holmes and Daniel Szechi, *The Age of Oligarchy: Pre-industrial Britain 1722–1783* (London: Routledge, 2014), 194. I draw the term "media event" from William Warner, *Licensing Entertainment: The Elevation of Novel Reading in Britain, 1684–1750* (Berkeley: University of California Press, 1998), 178.
[22] Jardine, *Going Dutch*, 31.
[23] See Lois G. Schwoerer, *The Declaration of Rights, 1689* (Baltimore: Johns Hopkins University Press, 1981).
[24] *A Collection of State Tracts: Publish'd on Occasion of the Late Revolution in 1688*, vol. 1 (London, 1705); Laurence Echard, *The History of the Revolution, and the Establishment of England in the Year 1688* (London: Jacob Tonson, 1725); Richard Steele, *The Crisis, or, a Discourse Representing, from the Most Authentick Records, the Just Causes of the Late Happy Revolution: With Some Seasonable Remarks on the Danger of a Popish Successor* (London, 1714).

'print culture' in Britain."[25] To summarize briefly what I examine more thoroughly in the chapters that follow, after 1695 print production flourished in a growing market system in England. Newspapers expanded onto the scene in the early years of the eighteenth century, their distribution enabled by an effective postal system and their dissemination amplified by a robust coffee-house culture.[26] The trajectory of media change was slightly different in Scotland and Ireland, as I indicate in several of the following chapters, but in general, these nations, too, experienced a marked growth in print productions. By 1746 there were well-established networks of print throughout Britain and parts of Scotland and Ireland, with newspapers and periodicals as well as books and pamphlets being printed at and circulating between London, Edinburgh, Glasgow, Dublin and a number of English and Scottish towns – as well as centres such as Philadelphia and Boston in the American colonies.

As a result of these developments, when the news pamphlet outlining the *Particulars of the Victory* at Culloden was printed in London in 1746, it entered a very different media environment than that through which the *Declaration* spread at the end of the previous century. In addition to being published "by authority" as a pamphlet, the *Particulars of the Victory* was issued in a special "*Extraordinary*" edition of the *London Gazette* and was also reprinted in virtually all of the news periodicals of the day, including daily newspapers like the *General Advertiser*, thrice-weekly newspapers such as the *London Evening Post*, weekly periodicals such as the *Westminster Journal, or, New Weekly Miscellany* and *Old England, or the Constitutional Journal* and monthly periodicals such as *The Scots Magazine, Containing, a General View of the Religion, Politicks, Entertainment, &c. in Great Britain*. Although it was not directly influential on any official parliamentary act as the *Declaration* had been, the text of the *Particulars of the Victory* was reprinted frequently in the subsequent histories of the 1745 Rising. Indeed, I discuss in Chapter 5, as well as being incorporated into pro-Hanoverian popular histories such as *The History of the Rebellion Raised against His MAJESTY KING GEORGE II. From Its Rise in August 1745, to Its Happy Extinction, by the Glorious Victory at Culloden, on the 16th of April, 1746* and *A Journey through Part of England and Scotland. Along with the Army under the Command of His Royal Highness the Duke of*

---

[25] Suarez and Turner, *The Cambridge History of the Book in Britain*, vol. 5, 2.
[26] See Andrew Pettegree, *The Invention of News: How the World Came to Know about Itself* (New Haven, CT: Yale University Press, 2014); Brian Cowan, *The Social Life of Coffee: The Emergence of the British Coffeehouse* (New Haven, CT: Yale University Press, 2005).

Cumberland, material from the news pamphlet was reproduced in works like *Ascanius; or the Young Adventurer, a True History*, a popular retelling of the events of the 1745 Rising which adopts a more sympathetic perspective on the Stuarts.[27] As we will see, traces of the *Particulars* even made their way into Tobias Smollett's description of Culloden in his *Complete History of England* (1757–58).[28]

The expanded availability of print meant that a particular account of an event, once inscribed in printed text, could be circulated more widely and more frequently in 1746 than in 1688 – with implications for the consolidation of national identity. In her influential work *Cultural Memory and Western Civilization: Functions, Media, Archives*, Aleida Assmann divides cultural memory into two categories: "stored" memory, which consists of "an amorphous mass of elements," and "functional memory," which "emerges from a process of choosing, connecting and constituting meaning."[29] I would add to Assmann's argument to suggest that, as print came to dominate the media landscape in the early eighteenth century, those memories inscribed in printed form assumed greater authority and became more likely than others to be "chosen" from the vast array of memories associated with an event and subsequently re-activated. The work of Elizabeth Eisenstein can be usefully applied here. Investigating the implications of the shift from manuscript to print after Gutenberg, Eisenstein argues that "typographical fixity" and "duplicative powers," in particular, lent printed works physical as well as conceptual permanence. In addition, Eisenstein asserts that the increased use of printing in the early modern era had the effect of "amplifying and reinforcing old ones" as authors "jointly transmitted certain old messages with augmented frequency even while reporting on new events or spinning out new ideas."[30] Although Eisenstein is referring to an earlier period in the development of print, I extend her comments to a consideration of the period covered in this book when the expansion of the print marketplace, including the burgeoning newspaper and periodical markets, enabled more frequent duplication

---

[27] *The History of the Rebellion Raised against His MAJESTY KING GEORGE II. From Its Rise in August 1745, to Its Happy Extinction, by the Glorious Victory at Culloden, on the 16th of April, 1746* (Dublin, 1746); *A Journey through Part of England and Scotland. Along with the Army under the Command of His Royal Highness the Duke of Cumberland* (London, 1746); *Ascanius; or the Young Adventurer, a True History* (London: Printed for G. Smith, 1746).

[28] Tobias Smollett, *A Complete History of England, Deduced from the Descent of Julius Cæsar, to the Treaty of Aix La Chapelle, 1748*, 4 vols. (London, 1757–58), 4: 673–75.

[29] Assmann, *Cultural Memory and Western Civilization*, 137.

[30] Elizabeth Eisenstein, *The Printing Press as an Agent of Change: Communications and Cultural Transformations in Early-Modern Europe* (Cambridge: Cambridge University Press, 1979), 127.

"of the identical version" – or nearly identical versions – of texts. In an early eighteenth-century context, the initial printing of "messages" connected with particular sites of memory helped inscribe them in specific ways that allowed more opportunities for their selection and recollection over time.[31]

Reciprocally, as *Mediating Cultural Memory* also argues, the association of those inscribed "messages" with the cultural memories of important national episodes also served to elevate the status of print within the media ecology. In critiquing what he perceives as Eisenstein's technological determinism, Adrian Johns asserts that the characteristics of print that Eisenstein describes had to be developed "over generations and across nations."[32] This book suggests that one way in which human agents developed a consciousness of the affordances associated with print was through reading printed works connected with national memories. As I illustrate in Chapter 1, for example, the narration of the 1688 Revolution through the publication of printed documents issued by James II/VII and William of Orange served to elevate the status of print during a time of media transition. Similarly, as Chapter 3 suggests, in the unfolding saga connected with the articulation of the Scottish colonial venture at Darien, print came to take on the authority previously associated with manuscript letters. Attending to the inscription of cultural memory in print throughout this time period offers a way of bridging the gap between Eisenstein's and Johns's perspectives, between print and the agents who employed it and contributed to its meaning.

As sites of memory could be inscribed and re-inscribed, they came to be seen as "portable," in Ann Rigney's term, able to be reprinted in contexts very different from those in which they originally appeared.[33] But the uncertainty and uncontrollability surrounding the potential uses of printed texts subsequently generated an increasing anxiety over how printed works could be consumed in different contexts. The concern became not just

---

[31] Ann Rigney suggests that cultural memory "is continuously performed by individuals and groups as they recollect the past *selectively through various media* and become involved in various forms of memorial activity" ("Plenitude, Scarcity and the Circulation of Cultural Memory," *Journal of European Studies* 35, no. 1 [2005]: 17).

[32] Adrian Johns, *The Nature of the Book: Print and Knowledge in the Making* (Chicago: University of Chicago Press, 1998), 2.

[33] Rigney suggests that literary narrative texts "help stabilize and fix memories in a certain shape," serving as "portable monuments, which can be carried over into new situations" ("Portable Monuments: Literature, Cultural Memory, and the Case of Jeanie Deans," *Poetics Today* 25, no. 2 [2004]: 381). As those texts are read and reread over time, she argues, the specific "images of the past" that they reflect "are at once re-activated and adapted to the new context in which they function" (388). I extend Rigney's observations beyond literary narrative texts to texts in general.

how to control *what* people read but also *how* they read it. In the classic *Amusing Ourselves to Death: Public Discourse in the Age of Show Business*, Neil Postman suggests that there are different epistemologies associated with different media: "a major new medium changes the structure of discourse; it does so by encouraging certain uses of the intellect, by favoring certain definitions of intelligence and wisdom, and by demanding a certain kind of content – in a phrase, by creating new forms of truth-telling."[34] The epistemology associated with the shift to the "major new medium" of print included a growing concern about how mediation impacted truth-telling. Scholars such as Christina Lupton and Paula McDowell suggest that there was a growing "consciousness of mediation" as more and more mid-eighteenth-century texts had "something to say about print and its proliferation."[35] This "consciousness of mediation" also impacted the inscription of sites of memory, I suggest. As we will we see in Chapter 5, for example, the 1745 Rising generated a self-conscious discourse on the nation's reading practices and the complications of "truth-telling" as a result of print playing a more important role in the shaping of the cultural memory of that event as it unfolded. Although William of Orange had been an enterprising pioneer in using print to create what would become a future memory of his invasion, even he could not have imagined the kinds of ways in which printed texts could be disseminated and discussed – or the concerns regarding reading which they could have encouraged – less than sixty years later.

Mediating Cultural Memory, then, makes a claim for the early eighteenth century as a unique moment during which print was becoming dominant and printed works were being used to consolidate (and sometimes challenge) national memories. The book thus revisits and revises the earlier claims of Benedict Anderson. Where Anderson argues for the importance of specific genres of print – the newspaper and novel – in imagining national communities, this book draws attention to the impact of the changing role of print within a complex media ecology on the articulation of the memories of the nation.[36]

---

[34] Neil Postman, *Amusing Ourselves to Death: Public Discourse in the Age of Show Business* (London: Penguin, 2005), 27.
[35] Christina Lupton, *Knowing Books: The Consciousness of Mediation in Eighteenth-Century Britain* (Philadelphia: University of Pennsylvania Press, 2011), 10; McDowell, *The Invention of the Oral*.
[36] Anderson argues that the development of the newspaper and the novel within an expanding era of print capitalism affected how people came to imagine their connection with other citizens of the nation. See Benedict Anderson, *Imagined Communities: Reflections on the Origin and Spread of Nationalism*, rev. ed. (London: Verso, 2006).

Although the chapters that follow focus on the mediation of particular cultural memories, I also see those mediations as depending on and contributing to a changing underlying epistemological sense of the connection between memory and collective identity between 1688 and 1745. In order to grasp the impact of these epistemological changes, it is useful again to note the differences between the time in which the *Declaration* was published and the time when the *Particulars of the Victory* circulated, this time, however, focusing on differences between conceptualizations of memory. Two years after the arrival of William of Orange in Torbay, the physician and philosopher John Locke, who had lived in exile in the Dutch Republic and had accompanied William's wife, Mary, on her return to England during the Revolution, offered a new model for human subjectivity. In *An Essay Concerning Human Understanding* (1689), Locke notes that "it is an established Opinion amongst some Men" that there are "in the Understanding" certain "innate *Principles*" which are like "Characters, as it were stamped on the Mind of Man which the Soul receives in its very first Being; and brings into the World with it." [37] Locke himself took issue with this perspective, positing instead that subjectivity consisted of a consciousness of the self across time through the perceived recollection of earlier impressions, in essence, through memory. As Locke suggests, "the Power to revive again in our Minds those *Ideas*, which after imprinting have disappeared, or have been as it were laid aside out of Sight" is "*Memory*, which is as it were the Store-house of our *Ideas*" (70). Notably, in describing both the older "Opinion" of the understanding and his new model, Locke falls back upon metaphors of print production, as he describes the formation of both innate ideas and the changing template of memory as stamps and impressions on the mind.

Locke's work brought memory to the forefront in early eighteenth-century epistemology. He himself, however, did not consider the social implications of his notion that individuals develop through their remembered impressions from the external world. But this point would be later taken up by the Scottish philosopher David Hume, who extended Locke's interest in the importance of memory to subjectivity as well as hinting at the social connections involved in memory. In his *A Treatise of Human Nature* (1738), Hume suggested that "impressions" in the mind made their appearance as:

---

[37] John Locke, *An Essay Concerning Human Understanding* (London, 1695), 4–5.

we find by experience, that when any impression has been present with the mind, it again makes its appearance there as an idea; and this it may do after two different ways: Either when in its new appearance it retains a considerable degree of its first vivacity, and is somewhat intermediate betwixt an impression and an idea; or when it entirely loses that vivacity, and is a perfect idea. The faculty by which we repeat our impressions in the first manner, is call'd the MEMORY, and the other the IMAGINATION.[38]

In the wake of the 1745 Rising, as I indicate in the last chapter of this book, Hume began his attempt to knit the nation together with his *The History of Great Britain* (1754–62).[39] At the same time, he developed his ideas of memory and subjectivity further to consider the ways in which individual subjectivities relate to each other within society. In a revised and extended version of *Essays, Moral and Political*, for example, published three years after the Battle of Culloden, he reflects on "National Characters," attempting to dispel commonly held misconceptions about the subject through the application of empirical reason, noting the similitude between individuals of the same nation: "Men of Sense ... allow, that each Nation has a peculiar Set of Manners, and that some particular Qualities are more frequently to be met with among one People than among their Neighbours."[40] Hume articulates his own position regarding the underlying causes of this phenomenon, demonstrating that moral causes (by which he means "the Nature of the Government, the Revolutions of public Affairs, the Plenty or Penury in which the People live, the Situation of the Nation with Regard to its Neighbours, and such like Circumstances") clearly trump physical causes ("those Qualities of the Air and Climate, which are supposed to work insensibly on the Temper, by altering the Tone and Habit of the Body") in determining the character of a nation's people (268). He concludes, "If we run over the globe, or revolve the annals of history, we shall discover every where signs of a sympathy or contagion of manners, none of the influence of air or climate" (268). In drawing attention to the social means through which people of different nations consolidate and replicate themselves (the "sympathy or contagion of manners"), Hume can be seen to be articulating a kind of

---

[38] David Hume, *A Treatise of Human Nature*, 3 vols. (London, 1739–40), 1: 23.
[39] The work would eventually become *The History of England, from the Invasion of Julius Cæsar to the Revolution in 1688*. For the publication history of the work, see John Robertson, "Hume, David (1711–1776), Philosopher and Historian," *Oxford Dictionary of National Biography*, September 23, 2004, https://doi.org/10.1093/ref:odnb/14141.
[40] David Hume, *Essays, Moral and Political*, 3rd ed. (London, 1748), 267.

theory of cultural memory. Hume's observations resonate tellingly in the context of comments regarding the manners of the Scottish Highlanders in the post-Culloden works that I examine in Chapter 5, suggesting that his ideas of national culture both informed and were informed by perceptions of the recent crisis.

The work of Locke and Hume – and of those writers and thinkers who responded to their different ideas about memory – confirms James Ward's suggestion that while memory "may not have been invented during the enlightenment," it was "conceptualized in highly influential and historically enduring ways" during this period, and in ways that were significantly different from earlier conceptualizations.[41] Specifically, as I argue in this book, between 1688 and 1745 memories began to be understood as ways of connecting individuals through shared experiences of the world. The increasing availability of those shared memories through an expanded print marketplace consolidated the idea of national belonging as a feature of shared culture – at the same time making it clear who was excluded from that national culture and those national memories.

In exploring the relationship between print, memory and the nation in the following chapters, *Mediating Cultural Memory* engages with and contributes to several areas of academic inquiry. First, my focus on the mediation of cultural memory in the early eighteenth century provides a unique historical perspective on a time period that is generally overlooked in the growing area of Cultural Memory Studies, offering important correctives to theorizations of cultural and collective memory. Second, by examining the ways in which print gained currency from, relied on and changed other media in the establishment of particular sites of memory from 1688 to 1745, I contribute to studies of Book History a greater understanding of the dynamics of media change in this crucial time period. Finally, *Mediating Cultural Memory* adds to the field of British Studies by considering the interplay of memory and forgetting in the establishment of national *lieux de mémoire* in the British archipelago. In the next section, I situate the book more fully within the discourse of these three fields – Cultural Memory Studies, Print Culture Studies and British Studies – indicating as well the important ways in which I put all three into dialogue with one another.

---

[41] James Ward, *Memory and Enlightenment: Cultural Afterlives of the Long Eighteenth Century* (Houndmills: Palgrave Macmillan, 2018), 8.

Fields of Inquiry

This book is situated primarily within the field of Cultural Memory Studies, an area of research that has expanded exponentially since the 1990s, largely through the influence of Nora, to become what Mieke Bal identifies as a "travelling concept," moving "between disciplines, between historical periods, and between geographically dispersed academic communities."[42] While, as suggested earlier, the field of Cultural Memory Studies has developed in such a way as to recognize the fundamental importance of the materiality of the media involved in the inscription, circulation and selection of memories, scholarship in the area has been heavily weighted toward the twentieth and twenty-first centuries, with some scholars going so far as to claim cultural memory as a strictly modern phenomenon.[43] Within researches on the history of the mediation of cultural memory, the early eighteenth century has received short shrift. Although scholars such as Ann Whitehead, Aleida Assmann and Kurt Danziger include the early eighteenth century in their important longitudinal studies of memory in relation to technological changes, they often do so in limited ways and in such a manner as to obscure the period's distinctiveness. In *Memory*, for example, her exploration of memory from classical times to the twentieth century, Whitehead begins by focusing on the "connection between memory and the means used to record that memory" from the time of Plato up to the fifteenth century. When she reaches the eighteenth century, however, Whitehead shifts away from a focus on media, jumping instead from Locke's theory of memory in the seventeenth century to the "the relation between memory and the self" in the Romantic era.[44] In *Cultural Memory and Western Civilization: Functions, Media, Archives*, Aleida Assmann acknowledges the early eighteenth century as an important time period when literacy rates rose and print culture expanded, resulting in a shift in metaphors of memory and ideas about how it worked. But Assmann also limits her study to representative canonical writers of the era who responded to the changes in

---

[42] Mieke Bal, *Travelling Concepts in the Humanities: A Rough Guide* (Toronto: University of Toronto Press, 2002), 24.

[43] See, for example, Richard Crownshaw, Jane Kilby and Antony Rowland, *The Future of Memory* (New York and London: Berghahn Books, 2010); Michael Rothberg, *Multidirectional Memory: Remembering the Holocaust in the Age of Decolonisation* (Stanford, CA: Stanford University Press, 2009); Richard Terdiman, *Present Past: Modernity and the Memory Crisis* (Ithaca, NY, and London: Cornell University Press, 1993).

[44] Anne Whitehead, *Memory*, The New Critical Idiom (London and New York: Routledge, 2008), 15, 50.

print, such as Jonathan Swift, rather than examining a variety of printed works within the media ecology.[45] More recently, in *Marking the Mind: A History of Memory*, his study of the "techniques and practices" that influence how memory is conceptualized from earliest times to the present, Kurt Danziger laminates "eighteenth- and nineteenth-century mnemonics" together, suggesting that during this period memory was seen both as "a vehicle for the exact reproduction of some precisely defined informational input" and as an opportunity for "the adequate representation of a lived experience."[46] For Danziger, the eighteenth century seems to merge with the nineteenth century as a stepping stone to a modern sense of memory.

In terms of works which consider the mediation of cultural memory in the context of more limited subjects within specific historical eras, the early eighteenth century is also less commonly addressed than other areas such as the early modern period.[47] Harold Weber's *Memory, Print and Gender in England, 1653–1759* is an exception as it examines the impact of media on memory, considering the "technologies of storage and transmission [that] govern both the form and content of what individuals and societies can remember."[48] Weber focuses, however, on the creation of "literary authority," looking at "the aspirations of writers concerned with how a commercial print trade might determine their place in cultural memory" (2). In both works that trace the long history of cultural memory and media and works that consider particular instances of the mediation of cultural memory, then, early eighteenth-century Britain continues to be underrepresented. In an attempt to address that gap, *Mediating Cultural Memory* draws attention to the period between 1688 and 1745 as a crucial era for changes in ideas regarding both cultural memory and mediation – and in the relationship between them. It suggests that there is much more to be studied about media and memory in the eighteenth century within both the longer and the shorter terms, given the fact that the media

---

[45] Assmann, *Cultural Memory and Western Civilization*, 190–92.
[46] Kurt Danziger, *Marking the Mind: A History of Memory* (Cambridge: Cambridge University Press, 2008), 86–87.
[47] See Leith Davis, "Memory Studies and the Eighteenth Century," *Literature Compass* 16, no. 2 (January 17, 2019), htttps://doi.org/10.1111/lic3.12504. Two books that focus on cultural memory in the later eighteenth century and Romantic eras appeared as this book was going to press: Craig Lamont, *The Cultural Memory of Georgian Glasgow* (Edinburgh: Edinburgh University Press, 2021) and Kenneth McNeil, *Scottish Romanticism and Collective Memory in the British Atlantic* (Edinburgh: Edinburgh University Press, 2021).
[48] Harold Weber, *Memory, Print, and Gender in England, 1653–1759* (Houndmills: Palgrave Macmillan, 2008), 2.

landscape of the eighteenth century was undergoing such profound changes.

At the same time as it contributes to the discourse on Cultural Memory Studies, *Mediating Cultural Memory* also serves to extend scholarly understanding of Book History Studies, or Print Culture Studies as it is sometimes known, by presenting a series of focused examinations demonstrating how the media landscape of the early eighteenth century was shifting to accommodate the new role of print. In *Always Already New: Media, History and the Data of Culture*, Lisa Gitelman suggests the importance of considering periods of media transition: "looking into the novelty years, transitional states, and identity crises of different media stands to tell us much, both about the course of media history and about the broad conditions by which media and communication are and have been shaped."[49] Responding to Gitelman's invitation, *Mediating Cultural Memory* directs attention to the period between 1688 and 1745 in order to examine how the authority of print was in part established through the articulation of sites of cultural memory. Drawing on the methodologies of scholars of Book History who work on the intersections of orality, manuscript and print, I look at the ways in which the "identity" of print was, to a large extent, determined by its refraction through other media as works of print were created, disseminated, discussed and consumed through oral and manuscript as well as other print mediations.[50] As I discuss further in Chapter 1, for example, while the publication of the *Declaration* was important, references to the *Declaration* in ballads and oral performance at such sites as Exeter Cathedral also determined its impact. Moreover, the *Particulars of the Victory* was enclosed within handwritten letters to English diplomats in Europe with instructions to make the information about "His Royal Highness's extraordinary valour and conduct and the gallant Behaviour of the King's Forces as publick as possible,"[51] while Sadler's Wells Theatre used the "the latest Intelligence" conveyed by the dispatch to stage its "grand Representation of the compleat Victory, gain'd by his Royal Highness the Duke, over the Rebels in Scotland."[52] It is only by

---

[49] Lisa Gitelman, "Introduction: Media as Historical Subjects," in *Always Already New: Media, History and the Data of Culture* (Cambridge, MA, and London: MIT Press, 2006), 1.

[50] James Chandler, Arnold I. Davidson and Adrian Johns, "Arts of Transmission: An Introduction," *Critical Inquiry* 31, no. 1 (2004): 2. See also Michelle Levy, *Literary Manuscript Culture in Romantic Britain* (Edinburgh: Edinburgh University Press, 2020) and Margaret J. M. Ezell, *Social Authorship and the Advent of Print* (Baltimore: Johns Hopkins University Press, 1999).

[51] British Library, Hardwicke Papers, vol. 541, Add. MS 35889, fol. 346 recto and verso, letter from William Stanhope, Lord Harrington, to Thomas Robinson, Whitehall, April 25, 1746.

[52] *The Penny London Post or the Morning Advertiser*, May 16–19, 1746.

taking into account the entire media ecology that we can properly understand the role that print played in the successful dissemination of the message of national salvation that William conveyed.[53] By considering the connection between the growth of print and the conscious creation of sites of memory, I add to Book History scholars' understanding of the complexities of the changes in the media ecology between 1688 and 1745.

Additionally, by bringing Book History Studies into dialogue with Cultural Memory Studies, *Mediating Cultural Memory* also reflects back critically on Nora's theorization of sites of cultural memory. In *Realms of Memory*, Nora identifies two kinds of "historical events" that constitute *lieux de mémoire*. First, there are "events that may have seemed relatively minor and gone almost unnoticed at the time but upon which posterity has conferred the grandeur of a new beginning or the solemnity of an inaugural break with the past" (17–18). These he refers to as "foundational events." In contrast, he observes, are "spectacular events," those "that are immediately invested with symbolic significance and treated, even as they are unfolding, as if they were being commemorated in advance" (18). The five episodes that I examine in this book can be considered "spectacular events" in Nora's definition. I also use these episodes, however, to challenge the distinction Nora makes between "foundational" and "spectacular" events. I consider in particular what role media play in helping invest events "with symbolic significance" at the time of their unfolding and in making them accessible and reproducible. Robert Darnton observes that "communication systems have always shaped events,"[54] but the question I ask in the chapters that follow is how changes in communication systems affected how events were initially inscribed and subsequently selected for re-inscription. How does mediation impact what is selected out of "stored" memories and what is simply forgotten?

In the process of determining the role of media in creating cultural memory in the first instance, *Mediating Cultural Memory* also adds a critical historical perspective to Nora's theories. Nora makes a crucial distinction between memory in the past and modern memory. For Nora, premodern memory is essentially lived experience, while cultural memory

---

[53] For an example of the importance of a multi-media approach, see Karin Bowie, *Public Opinion in Early Modern Scotland, c. 1560–1707* (Cambridge: Cambridge University Press, 2020). Bowie considers "four modes of engagement and communication that were significant in the early modern Scottish context: protestations, petitions, oaths and public communications in oral, written and printed forms" (4).

[54] Robert Darnton, "An Early Information Society: News and the Media in Eighteenth-Century Paris," *The American Historical Review* 105, no. 1 (2000): 1.

in modern times is a compensatory attempt to return to that prelapsarian state of lived memory: "Societies based on memory are no more: the institutions that once transmitted values from generation to generation – churches, schools, families, governments – have ceased to function as they once did."[55] As Nora laments: *"Lieux de mémoire* exist because there are no longer any *milieux de mémoire*, settings in which memory is a real part of everyday experience" (1). In the modern era, then, memory becomes condensed in sites which "offer a maximum amount of meaning in a minimum number of signs," as Rigney explains with reference to Nora's formulation.[56] Rigney herself has explored the connection between memory and the archive in the context of the nineteenth century, arguing against what she sees as Nora's narrative of implied loss in the modern era.[57] But my examination of the inscription of sites of memory in the early eighteenth century suggests that even at this earlier time there existed a dynamic between living memory and the process of archivization. As the following chapters demonstrate, the inscription of cultural memory was accomplished through a complex interplay of lived and mediated experiences.

Finally, *Mediating Cultural Memory* connects Cultural Memory Studies and Book History Studies with British Studies in order to examine the role that cultural memory – and cultural forgetting – played in consolidating the nation in the early eighteenth century. The starting point of this study, 1688, saw not only changes in the media landscape, but also changes in the organization of the nation-state in the British Isles. As John Brewer suggests, 1688 marked the beginning of the establishment of an interconnected web of military, economic and state interests.[58] The development of the identity of the British state over the next fifty years was fundamentally connected to the expansion of the state's imperial aspirations and the consolidation of its internal government. *Mediating Cultural Memory* examines the way in which the *lieux de mémoire* under consideration helped provide the "images and symbols" that were used to promote the development of British aspirations.[59] It is not "pan-archipelagic," as it does

---

[55] Nora and Kritzman, *Realms*, 2.   [56] Rigney, "Plenitude," 18.
[57] Ann Rigney, *The Afterlives of Walter Scott: Memory on the Move* (Oxford: Oxford University Press, 2012).
[58] John Brewer, *The Sinews of Power: War, Money and the English State, 1688–1783* (Cambridge, MA: Harvard University Press, 1990). See also Kathleen Wilson, *The Island Race: Englishness, Empire, and Gender in the Eighteenth Century* (London and New York: Routledge, 2006) and Linda Colley, *Britons: Forging the Nation 1707–1837* (New Haven, CT: Yale University Press, 1992).
[59] But see Alok Yadav, "Nationalism and Eighteenth-Century British Literature," *Literature Compass* 1, no. 1 (2005): 1–14.

not include Wales in its purview, but it does share the objectives of other works of what has been called the New British Studies in that it considers "a wide range of multiple and criss-crossing impacts and influences that are sourced within parts of the archipelago."[60]

At the same time as it focuses on the consolidation of the nation around particular sites of memory, however, *Mediating Cultural Memory* also considers what is forgotten in the process of that consolidation. As Ernst Renan famously observed as far back as 1882: "Forgetting ... is a crucial factor in the creation of a nation."[61] Chapter 2, for example, examines how the War of the Two Kings has been erased from British memory of the 1688 Revolution, while Chapter 4 considers the way in which the Jacobite threat to the government in 1715 was minimized even as the Rising was unfolding. The work of Michael Rothberg provides a particularly useful way of understanding the complex interplay between dominant memories and counter-memories within the British nation in this crucial period. In attempting to move "beyond the framework of the imagined community of the nation-state," Rothberg proposes "a new model – or models – of remembrance," replacing Nora's figuration of *lieux de mémoire* (sites of memory) with *noeuds de mémoire* (knots of memory).[62] For Rothberg, the metaphor of *noeuds de mémoire* acknowledges that "all places and acts of memory" are "rhizomatic networks of temporality and cultural reference that exceed attempts at territorialisation ... and identarian reduction" (7). Such memory knots, he adds, may be conscripted for particular purposes and may "well have territorializing or identity-forming effects," but "those effects will always be contingent and open to re-signification" (7). I would add to Rothberg's assessment by suggesting that the affordances of print – the "typographical fixity" and "duplicative

---

[60] Marie-Louise Coolahan, "Whither the Archipelago? Stops, Starts, and Hurdles on the Four Nations Front," *Literature Compass* 15, no. 11 (2018): 2. The field of what is called the "New British Studies" has its origins in J. G. A. Pocock's "British History: A Plea for a New Subject," in which he described the great divide he saw between English history and the histories of the rest of the British Isles (*The Journal of Modern History* 47, no. 4 [1975]: 603–04). See also John Kerrigan, *Archipelagic English: Literature, History, and Politics, 1603–1707* (Oxford: Oxford University Press, 2008) and John Morrill, "Thinking about the New British History," in *British Political Thought in History, Literature and Theory, 1500–1800*, ed. David Armitage (Cambridge: Cambridge University Press, 2006), 23–46.

[61] Renan continues: "Indeed, historical inquiry brings to light deeds of violence which took place at the origin of all political formations, even of those whose consequences have been altogether beneficial. Unity is always effected by means of brutality" (Ernst Renan, "What Is a Nation?" trans. Martin Thom in *Nation and Narration*, ed. Homi K. Bhabha [London: Routledge, 1990], 11.

[62] Michael Rothberg, "Introduction: Between Memory and Memory; From *lieux de mémoire* to *noeuds de mémoire*," *Yale French Studies*, nos. 118–19 (2010): 7.

powers" identified by Eisenstein – as well as print's ability to remediate other media – make it particularly effective for the preservation, reactivation and circulation of knotted memories. In the political climate of post-1688 Britain, print served as an important way in which memories could be territorialized and stored in the service of the nation. But, as the chapters that follow suggest, those printed memories were complex, existing in dialogue with and bearing traces of counter-memories expressed variously in oral, manuscript as well as other printed mediations. Chapter 5, for example, explores how Hanoverian-oriented popular narratives borrowed from pro-Jacobite accounts, representing the 1745 Rising as an interwoven knot of memory.

By foregrounding the constructedness and precariousness of sites of memory between 1688 and 1745 through a process of initial mediation and later re-inscription, *Mediating Cultural Memory* also contributes to the question of how the nation state came to be "the natural container, curator, and telos of collective memory."[63] Writing in the 1980s in France, Nora took the relationship between the nation and cultural memory for granted.[64] In contrast, *Mediating Cultural Memory* examines the nation of Britain as both a problem and a project, as each chapter of the book considers how the figure of the British nation both drew on and defined itself against the articulations of other identities: religious collectivities (Protestants and Catholics in Chapters 1, 2, 4 and 5), local identities (Highlanders in Chapters 4 and 5) and economic collectivities (the joint-stock company in Chapter 3), for example. Together, then, the chapters explore how cultural memory helped shape the nation and how the growing focus on the nation helped form ideas of cultural memory during this dynamic time of media change.

Summary of the Chapters

Mediating Cultural Memory takes up the challenge issued by Clifford Siskin and William Warner for eighteenth-century scholars to focus on "the ontological priority of mediation."[65] It is a work of literary criticism as well as media history, as it considers texts that have been frequently ignored by literary critics and examined by historians only in terms of

---

[63] Chiara de Cesari and Ann Rigney, eds., *Transnational Memory: Circulation, Articulation, Scales* (Berlin: De Gruyter, 2014), 1.
[64] For a critique of Nora, see Hue-Tam Ho Tai, "Remembered Realms: Pierre Nora and French National Memory," *The American Historical Review* 106, no. 3 (2001): 906–22.
[65] Siskin and Warner, "This Is Enlightenment," 32.

content rather than form: official documents in Chapter 1; newspaper advertisements in Chapter 2; letters in Chapter 3; manuscript newsletters in Chapter 4; and popular printed narratives in Chapter 5. I examine how each of these kinds of mediations operates within a complex ecology of print and non-print works to create sites of national memory. The first two chapters address the 1688 Revolution in relation to cultural memory and cultural amnesia. Chapter 1, "Of Documents and Declarations: Mediating the 1688 Revolution," explores the invasion of William of Orange in terms of the multi-media environment of the late seventeenth century. I situate William's *Declaration* within the history of the printed official document, suggesting his new strategic use of the genre. At the same time, as suggested above, I examine how the authority of the *Declaration* was in part established through oral and manuscript means. This chapter ends by reflecting on how the initial mediation of the 1688 Revolution impacted its later re-inscription as a site of cultural memory in Britain. The phenomenon known as the "Glorious Revolution," I suggest, represents more than a political change in Britain at the end of the eighteenth century. It is a moment of media change, signalling a shift in the understanding of the way printed works could be used to inscribe sites of memory.

Chapter 2, "Remembering to Forget: Ireland, the War of the Two Kings and Cultural Amnesia," considers the wider archipelagic impact of the 1688 Revolution, examining in particular the conflict in Ireland known in Gaelic as *Cogadh an Dá Rí*, or the "War of the Two Kings." From 1689 to 1691 Ireland was an important focus of attention for the rest of the population of the British Isles, with Irish events mediated in newspapers such as the *Orange Gazette* and the *London Gazette*. As well as providing news of the war in Ireland, the newspapers also included advertisements for other works of print which drew attention to the subject of Ireland. I examine several of these printed mediations, including maps, Richard Cox's *Hibernia Anglicana* (1689) and James Farewell's *The Irish Hudibras* (1689), then focus on the attention given to the first government victory in Ireland, the relief of the siege of Derry on July 29, 1689. The siege shaped English perceptions of the rest of the conflict in Ireland, drawing as it did on articulations of a previous *lieu de mémoire*, the 1641 Irish Rebellion. Representations of the siege of Derry as a site of providential trial and redemption were further reinforced and amplified, I suggest, by the embodied presence of individuals like George Walker, an Episcopalian minister who had served as joint Governor of Derry during its siege and who travelled to London after the siege, and by thanksgiving services held in churches in London commemorating the events of 1641. A focus on events from the "War of the Two Kings" – and on how they were subsequently erased from the memory of the so-called Glorious Revolution in Britain – suggests the way that the inscribing of national memories depends as much on forgetting certain details as on remembering others.

Chapter 3, "National Correspondences: Print, Letters and the Company of Scotland's Darien Expedition," serves as a bridge between the first two and the last two chapters, as it considers a neglected episode of history that led to the union of England and Scotland in 1707. The creation of the Company of Scotland Trading to Africa and the West Indies took place in 1695, the same year as the lapse of the Licensing Act in the English Parliament. The Darien venture was in fact the first colonial enterprise to be constituted in the context of this newly expanding market for print. But the forging of the Company and the narrative of the expedition were facilitated by a combination of old and new media. In this chapter, I focus on how a conjunction of manuscript and printed letters helped shape the ways in which the Darien venture – and its subsequent failure – came to be understood in the imaginations of readers in Scotland, Britain and the American colonies. Letters in both manuscript and printed form helped establish the Company. Letters served to connect the Company directors with the colonists in Darien, and, when published in pamphlet form, they provided information and propaganda about the new colony to the nation back home. After the collapse of the Darien settlement, letters also became the evidence used to shape the cultural memory of the disaster, but, over the course of the eighteenth century, that memory was folded into the bigger controversy surrounding the implications for the Scottish nation of the 1707 Acts of Union.[66]

Chapters 4 and 5 of the book focus on Jacobite attempts to change the government of Great Britain and Ireland in the years following the Acts of Union, examining ways in which the Risings of 1715 and 1745 were inscribed during their respective time periods. In Chapter 4, "Writing the 1715 Jacobite Rising: Periodical Networks and the Inscription of News," I focus on the early mediation of the events of 1715 Rising within the context of a mediascape for news that featured both the older form of manuscript newsletters and an increasing number of printed newspapers and periodicals. I compare reports about the developing conflict found in

---

[66] I use the plural "Acts" here to refer to the fact that separate acts were passed by the parliaments of Scotland and England to confirm the policies of the Treaty of Union that had been negotiated by commissioners of both nations in 1706.

the manuscript newsletters sent to the Newdigate family between May 30 and September 29, 1715, with those printed in five newspapers during the same time period, suggesting that the affordances of the newspaper form amplified the sense of discontinuity in the news about the Rising as it was unfolding. I explore the subsequent treatment of the conflict in two examples of the new genre of the periodical essay that were published in the final months of the conflict: Richard Steele's *The Town-Talk* (December 17, 1715–February 13, 1716) and Joseph Addison's *The Free-Holder* (December 23, 1715–June 29, 1716). These works, I argue, refocused readers' attention on wider issues of social governance rather than the disconnected and chaotic events of the Rising and attempted to unite the nation through a politics of politeness. I conclude by considering popular histories written in the immediate aftermath of the Rising such as *A Compleat History of the Late Rebellion* (1716), Robert Patten's *The History of the Late Rebellion* (1717) and Peter Rae's *The History of the Late Rebellion* (1718). These books reprinted information originally found in newsletters and newspapers within the context of a continuous narrative leading logically to the suppression of the "unnatural Rebellion." Within the periodical essays and the histories, what had been the very real threat of the '15 was minimized, reduced in cultural memory to what Steele referred to as a temporary "absurdity" within a longer history of Jacobite containment. At the same time, as I suggest, these works also helped to circulate some of the counter-memories of the Jacobites.

The newly expanding form of the newspaper played a crucial role in accustoming the subjects of the nation in 1715 to reading about the events taking place around them. In Chapter 5, "Reading the 1745 Jacobite Rising: 'Transitory News-Papers,' 'Fleeting Pamphlets' and Knots of Cultural Memory," I analyze the implications of the further expansion of the periodical press and the print marketplace in general, arguing that the 1745 Rising generated a self-conscious discourse on the nation's reading practices and the complications of "truth-telling" in print within a politically fraught environment. Information about the events of the 1745 Rising was made available to readers in a more continuous and a more pervasive way than during the earlier conflict. Examining pamphlets published in 1745 and 1746 that discuss the periodical press, I explore how this expanding circulation of information also prompted greater concern not just about the trustworthiness of the medium of the newspaper but also about how citizens were consuming information. In the second part of the chapter, I focus on three different genres of printed works produced after the Battle of Culloden that reworked newspaper reports into their narratives. Accounts of the trials and executions of the "rebels," narratives detailing the escape of Charles Edward Stuart after Culloden and popular histories were important not just in shaping the cultural memory of the 1745 Rising, but they also raised further questions about the reading and interpretation of printed sources. They represented a cultural memory of the Rising that promoted the Hanoverian government, but, as items designed for quick sale on a competitive market, they borrowed material from each other and from a variety of other pro- and anti-Jacobite sources, inscribing traces of the counter-memories that they sought to eradicate within the fabric of their texts. With their conscious and unconscious intertextual borrowings, these printed works, like those of the 1715 Rising, embodied "knots of memory."

Finally, in the concluding chapter, "'Living On' after 1745: From Cultural Memory to the Memory of Culture," I briefly trace the afterlife of the knots of memory examined in earlier chapters in two printed genres: the multi-volume histories of the nation that became popular in the late eighteenth century and the historical novel in the hands of Walter Scott. Works such as David Hume's and Tobias Smollett's histories replicate some of the counter-memories that were produced in the earlier printed discourse on the nation. Scott, however, transforms the complicated knots of memories and counter-memories by drawing attention to and framing them. *Waverley*, for example, both acknowledges the power of counter-memories and prevents their re-activation by including them within a narrative that connects a progressive sense of a consolidated British cultural memory with a model of media succession.

In "Travelling Memory," Astrid Erll argues that in the conflicted world in which we currently live, "we cannot afford the luxury of not studying memory."[67] If we want to understand the various crises of the present, she asserts, "we must naturally look at certain mental, discursive, and habitual paradigms that were formed in long historical processes – via cultural memory, as it were."[68] *Mediating Cultural Memory* originated from my interest in the parallels between an earlier age of media and political transition – the early eighteenth century – and the contemporary moment, in which the shift to new digital media is re-presenting and reinforcing fractures both between and within the nations that make up the United Kingdom. The events that unfolded during the writing of this book – the 2014 Scottish referendum on independence, the 2016 "Brexit" referendum and the 2020 protests against systemic racism prompted by the killing

---

[67] Astrid Erll, "Travelling Memory," *Parallax* 17, no. 4 (2011): 5.   [68] Ibid., 5.

of George Floyd – have had an undeniable impact on its ideas. Rather than making explicit connections between past and present, however (and trying to pin down a present which is ever-changing), I have sought instead to to analyze the conditions under which the concept of a unified British nation-state developed its power – as I argue, in conjunction with the development of the print marketplace and an evolving self-consciousness about the concept of cultural memory. It is my hope, however, that by focusing on the initial inscription and later storage and re-activation of these five specific historical episodes, this book will also contribute to contemporary conversations by highlighting the complex, constructed and at times arbitrary nature of national memories.

CHAPTER 1

Of Documents and Declarations
Mediating the 1688 Revolution

The 1688 Revolution has long been considered a pivotal moment in the cultural memory of Britain. In *The English Revolution, 1688–1689*, G. M. Trevelyan asserted that the event was a "turning-point in the history of our country and of the world," a time when the warring political parties in England came together to choose "compromise, agreement and toleration" over despotism.[1] In contrasting England's inclination for "government by discussion" with the "absolutist governments of a new and more formidable type" in existence in Europe (131), Trevelyan was undoubtedly responding to the conflict between nations that would erupt the following year into World War II. But his commentary also re-inscribes a memory that had been circulating for two and a half centuries before his time in annual sermons, statues, works of art and a public centennial in 1788, and in the influential account provided by his own great-uncle Thomas Babington Macaulay in his *History of England from the Accession of James the Second*.[2] Trevelyan's understanding of the Revolution as "that distinctive contribution of Anglo-Saxon civilization to Western political culture" subsequently played a starring role in shaping perceptions of 1688 for decades to follow as *The English Revolution, 1688–1689* provided the standard perspective for history textbooks until well into the 1980s.[3]

Astrid Erll's comments regarding the complicated construction of *lieux de mémoire* offer a useful perspective on the long and layered history of the representation of the 1688 Revolution as a "Glorious" assertion of British exceptionalism which Trevelyan's narrative re-activates:

> What is known about a war, a revolution, or any other event which has been turned into a site of memory ... seems to refer not so much to what

---

[1] George Macauley Trevelyan, *The English Revolution, 1688–1689* (London: T. Butterworth, 1938), 4.
[2] Thomas Babington Macaulay, *History of England from the Accession of James the Second*, 5 vols., vol. 5 ed. Lady Hannah Trevelyan (London: Longman, Brown, Green, Longmans, 1848–61).
[3] See Dale Hoak, "The Anglo-Dutch Revolution of 1688–89," in *The World of William and Mary: Anglo-Dutch Perspectives on the Revolution of 1688–89*, ed. Dale Hoak and Mordechai Feingold (Stanford, CA: Stanford University Press, 1996), 2.

one might cautiously call the "actual events," but instead to a canon of existent medial constructions, to the narratives and images circulating in a media culture.[4]

For Erll, "remembered events" are "transmedial" phenomena whose representation is not tied to one specific medium. Rather, as she suggests, "memorable events are usually represented again and again, over decades and centuries, in different media: in newspaper articles, photography, diaries, historiography, novels, films, etc." (392). According to Erll, it is the repetition of an event across disparate media over time that determines how it comes to mean what it does.

Erll's observations on the transmission of sites of cultural memory raise several crucial questions which this chapter will explore – and which are important to the book as a whole. First, how does the *initial* mediation of an event – the media through which it is articulated when it first enters what Aleida Assmann describes as "stored" memory – affect its later selection and repetition in a "canon" of "medial constructions"? And, second, does the storage of a memory through particular media render it more accessible for re-activation in later contexts as "functional memory"? In the specific case of 1688, how did the initial media inscription of the events of the Revolution impact the way it was "stored" and accessed later as a site of cultural memory? This chapter attempts to address those questions by turning back to the "existent medial constructions" that captured events as they unfolded in 1688. As I will argue, the 1688 Revolution was a transmedial phenomenon right from the beginning, inscribed in a number of different media even as it was unfolding. But its subsequent ability to be "represented again and again, over decades and centuries" and deemed "Glorious" was enabled by its early inscription in printed texts like official documents during a time period when print culture was gaining new authority. Before I elaborate on this argument, however, I want to examine two different ways in which the 1688 Revolution has been conceptualized in terms of mediation up to this point, the first by an eighteenth-century participant in the events and the second by contemporary historians.

"Foolish Ballads" and Printed Declarations

In writing his voluminous *History of His Own Time* (1724–34), Bishop Gilbert Burnet looked back at the 1688 Revolution in order to encapsulate events in Britain from the time of Cromwell to the reign of Queen Anne.

---

[4] Astrid Erll, "Literature, Film, and the Mediality of Cultural Memory," in *Cultural Memory Studies: An International and Interdisciplinary Handbook*, ed. Astrid Erll and Ansgar Nünning (Berlin: De Gruyter, 2008), 392.

Carefully considering events in England in relation to those in Scotland and Ireland as well as on the continent, Burnet's *History* also served as a defense of William's ascent to the throne and of the ensuing Protestant succession in Britain. In describing the success of William during the crucial events of November 1688, Burnet drew attention to what he perceived as the singular media event that precipitated the flight of James II/VII:

> A foolish ballad was made at that time, treating the Papists, and chiefly the *Irish*, in a very ridiculous manner, which had a burden said to be *Irish* words, *lero lero lilliburlero*, that made an impression on the Army that cannot be well imagined by those who saw it not. The whole Army, and at last all people both in city and country, were singing it perpetually. And perhaps never had so slight a thing so great an effect.[5]

The "foolish ballad" to which Burnet refers, "Lilliburlero," references James II/VII's creation of Richard Talbot, Earl of Tyrconnell, as the new Lord Deputy of Ireland in 1687; upon assuming this role, Talbot granted positions of authority to Catholics. Told from the narrative point of view of an Irishman, "Lilliburlero" relies for part of its comic effect on what Andrew Carpenter refers to as Hiberno-English and on mockery of what Burnet suggests are "*Irish* words":

> HO Brother *Teague* dost hear de Decree,
> Lil-li Burlero Bullen a-la;
> Dat we shall have a new Debittie,
> Li-li Burlero Bullen al-a.

The song depicts the Irish as violent and lawless, but also servile, as they require the "Dispence" from "de Pope" in order to hang both "Magna Carta" and "de English." Although one stanza expresses the narrator's unease at the "Protestant wind" that delays the arrival of Tyrconnell, the song ends ironically on a triumphant note for the Catholic forces:

> Now now de Hereticks all go down,
> Lilli, &c.
> By *Chreist* and St. *Patrick* the Nation's our own,
> Lilli, &c.[6]

The power of the song lies in its juxtaposition of the narrator's hubris and the actual events of the Revolution, as the "Nation" did most certainly did not end up belonging to the Catholic Irish. The song mocks Irish and

---

[5] Gilbert Burnet, *Bishop Burnet's History of His Own Time*, 2 vols. (London, 1724–34), 1: 792.
[6] "A New Song," in *A Collection of the Newest and Most Ingenious Poems, Songs, Catches &c. against Popery Relating to the Times* (London, 1689), 9.

Catholic pretensions at the same time as it serves to unite Protestants under William's banner.

We can also read Burnet's claim that "never had so slight a thing so great an effect" in the light of media critic Paula McDowell's comments that ballads in the early eighteenth century were "among the most 'speedy' and mobile discursive forms" because "they were rapidly composed and disseminated by voice, manuscript, and print."[7] In Burnet's *History*, the main import of this media event is not just its speed, but the way in which the ballad connects disparate sections of the "population": not by "manuscript" or "print," but by the act of singing. Soldiers and citizens, urbanites and country dwellers are presented as coming together to sing for William of Orange's cause. Their interest in the popular song is spontaneous, spreading naturally from one person to the next until all are "continually" singing it. Burnet presents a powerful image of an organic, embodied and cohesive nation raising their voices together in support of the new regime.

In his *History of Great Britain* (1754–61), David Hume appears to have relied on Burnet's comments in affirming the importance of "Lilliburlero" to the success of the Revolution: "It may not be unworthy of notice, that a merry ballad, called 'Lilliballero' ... was greedily received by the people, and was universally sung by all ranks of men, even by the King's army, who were strongly seized by the national spirit. This incident both discovered, and served to increase, the general discontent of the kingdom."[8] Later, Thomas Percy would also repeat Burnet's claims in his *Reliques of Ancient English Poetry* (1765), arguing that "Lilliburlero" "contributed not a little towards the great revolution in 1688," and that it had "a more powerful effect than either the Philippics of Demosthenes, or Cicero."[9] According to Burnet, Hume, Percy and the many other eighteenth-century commentators who reproduced their accounts, the Revolution was a testimony to the power of oral culture.

This representation of the oral performance of "Lilliburlero" as the definitive moment of the 1688 Revolution contrasts startlingly with what more contemporary scholarship has suggested about the unprecedented importance of printed works during the 1688 conflict – and, indeed, it also minimizes Burnet's own enormous contribution to the pamphlet discourse at the time. Instead of focusing on orality, Lois Schwoerer, for example,

---

[7] Paula McDowell, "'The Manufacture and Lingua-Facture of Ballad-Making': Broadside Ballads in Long Eighteenth-Century Ballad Discourse," *The Eighteenth Century* 47, nos. 2–3 (2006): 160.
[8] David Hume, *History of Great Britain Volume 2 Containing the Commonwealth, and the Reigns of Charles II and James II* (London, 1757), 430.
[9] Thomas Percy, *Reliques of Ancient English Poetry*, 3 vols. (London, 1765), 2: 358.

discusses the exceptional use of printed tracts, broadsides and prints by William's propagandists, suggesting that these materials "shaped the public image of the prince, interpreted his purposes and policies, and presented events in ways favorable to his interests, while at the same time they blackened the character and policies of King James II."[10] In a more dramatic vein, Jonathan Israel claims that the printing of William's *Declaration* was "one of the greatest and most decisive propaganda coups of early modern times."[11] Other scholars also draw attention to the importance of print culture in promoting the cause of the Dutch Stadtholder and his English wife. In "The Revolution of 1689 and the Structure of Political Argument," for example, Mark Goldie considers "the connexions between doctrines, government and the polemical press" during the crisis of allegiance,[12] while Joad Raymond asserts generally that the use of print was crucial to the success of the Revolution: "By 1688, the year of the Glorious Revolution, it was self-evident that any attempt to generate public support for a political initiative, party or position, would have to exploit the persuasive powers of the press."[13]

Contemporary scholars of 1688 have concentrated for the most part, however, on works that they sometimes identify as "propaganda," limiting themselves to viewing the printed productions of William and his adherents.[14] In this chapter, I bring the focus of contemporary scholars on the print culture of the 1688 Revolution together with mediations such as the song that Burnet describes as I examine how printed texts such as the *Declaration* gained their authority to represent the cultural memory of the event only by interacting with other media within a complex ecology.[15]

I focus in particular on the role of the official document in inscribing the events of the 1688 Revolution. In *Paper Knowledge: Toward a Media*

---

[10] Schwoerer, "Propaganda," 848.
[11] Jonathan Israel, ed., *The Anglo-Dutch Moment: Essays on the Glorious Revolution and Its World Impact* (New York: Cambridge University Press, 1991), 14.
[12] Mark Goldie, "The Revolution of 1689 and the Structure of Political Argument," *Bulletin of Research in the Humanities* 83 (1980): 480.
[13] Joad Raymond, *Pamphlets and Pamphleteering in Early Modern Britain* (Cambridge: Cambridge University Press, 2002), 25.
[14] In "Propaganda," Schwoerer, however, does analyze medals produced in support of William and Mary.
[15] Ironically, Trevelyan also draws attention to some of the multiple mediations – printed as well as sensory and performative – that impacted the Revolution, as he writes, "In the first days of November, William's Declaration, multiplied by secret presses, was in the hands of the English, who stood watching the weathercocks for a 'Protestant wind,' whistling 'Lilliburlero,' or listening to the ballad-mongers' songs" (Trevelyan, *English Revolution*, 58).

History of Documents, Lisa Gitelman describes the characteristics of the genre of the document:

> The word "document" descends from the Latin root *docer*, to teach or show, which suggests that the document exists in order to document. Sidestepping this circularity of terms, one might say instead that documents help define and are mutually defined by the know-show function, since documenting is an epistemic practice: the kind of knowing that is all wrapped up with showing, and showing wrapped with knowing.[16]

Official documents such as proclamations and declarations originally served as "know-show" assertions of political authority, mediations of power designed to "show" and make "known" the relationship between the ruler and the ruled. Situated within a performative context where their oral delivery was important in "show[ing]" their meaning, official documents assumed form as printed broadsides beginning in the Tudor times.[17] Their function shifted when they began to be printed more cheaply for distribution to a wider readership as both Parliamentarians and Royalists used them to assert their authority during the British Civil Wars.[18] As I demonstrate, the genre of the official printed document altered still further during James II/VII's rule, as both James and William used official documents in an increasing effort to generate public approval.

But changes in one medium take place only in relation to other media. In William Warner's words, "While it is conceptually possible to disentangle one media object from the larger aggregation of media, this analytical procedure seems to run counter to the way media actually worked in the seventeenth and eighteenth centuries, where a particular medium acquired its salience within a multimedia buzz of communication."[19] I therefore consider how the power of both James's and William's official documents was to a large extent determined by their refraction through other media as they were created, disseminated, discussed and consumed

---

[16] Lisa Gitelman, *Paper Knowledge: Toward a Media History of Documents* (Durham, NC: Duke University Press, 2014), 1.

[17] According to Elizabeth Foster, there was "stabilization and consolidation of procedure" during the "early Stuart period," as "more and more, parliament, particularly the House of Commons, had come to insist on written, formal communication with the crown." See her "Petitions and the Petition of Right," *Journal of British Studies* 14, no. 1 (1974): 37.

[18] As Kevin Sharpe contends, Charles II also demonstrated an awareness of the rhetorical power of the genre in producing the document designed to win back his kingdom, the *Declaration of Breda*. See Kevin Sharpe, *Rebranding Rule: The Restoration and Revolution Monarchy, 1660–1714* (New Haven, CT: Yale University Press, 2013), 5–7.

[19] See William Warner, *Protocols of Liberty: Communication Innovation and the American Revolution* (Chicago: University of Chicago Press, 2013), 26.

through oral and manuscript sources as well as through other genres of print. While print, including the genre of the printed official document, was gaining "salience" within the "multimedia buzz" of the events of the Revolution, that "multimedia buzz" also determined the impact that specific printed works were able to have. As well as analyzing James's and William's printed documents, then, this chapter also considers the non-print media that played a crucial role in defining the meaning of those printed works. I conclude the chapter by tracing the re-inscriptions of documents in early histories of the Revolution. Appearing only shortly after the conclusion of the military conflicts in Scotland and Ireland, these histories attempted to shape the way in which the 1688 Revolution would serve in the future as a national *lieu de mémoire*. As I indicate, however, even within these histories that were designed to confirm the Williamite succession, counter-memories surfaced to complicate the representation of 1688 as a "Glorious" Revolution.

"Perswad[ing] the World": Print and the "Multimedia Buzz" before 1688

Schwoerer comments on the importance of print in 1688: "By the time of the Revolution, English people were well accustomed to the public airing in print of political and religious commentary and ideas that were sharply critical of the government. This background of experience with the print media was an important part of the context within which the Revolution unfolded."[20] While her observation is generally accurate, it is important to note that, in fact, English people's "experience with the print media" and "the press" had been quite uneven up to that point, having been characterized by years of official proscription broken by two significant periods during which censorship was temporarily suspended: the British Civil Wars (1642–51) and the Exclusion Crisis (1679–81). As critics have noted, the increased desire for information about political events during the British Civil Wars not only led to an unprecedented increase in print productions but also encouraged the creation of new print genres such as the newsbook.[21] Jason Peacey argues that the new availability of more

---

[20] Lois G. Schwoerer, "Liberty of the Press and Public Opinion, 1660–1695," in *Liberty Secured? Britain before and after 1688*, ed. J. R. Jones (Stanford, CA: Stanford University Press, 1992), 220.

[21] See Joad Raymond, ed., *News Networks in Seventeenth-Century Britain and Europe* (New York: Routledge, 2006); Carolyn Nelson, Matthew Seccombe and Maureen Bell, "The Creation of the Periodical Press 1620–1695," in *The Cambridge History of the Book in Britain*, vol. 4, *1557–1695*, ed. John Barnard and D. F. McKenzie (Cambridge: Cambridge University Press, 2002), 533–50; and

printed works also had the effect of sharpening the reading skills of those "members of the middling sort and lower orders" who were consuming information during this time, while David Zaret goes so far as to credit "the 'invention' of public opinion as a political force" to this time period when the expansion of print impacted "traditional forms of political communication."[22]

The Restoration of the monarchy under Charles II, however, was accompanied by a re-introduction, indeed an expansion of the spectatorial and performative elements of court life, along with a renewed distrust of print on the part of the government.[23] As Harold Weber notes, Charles employed "forms and ceremonies, fictions and representations that had sustained the power of his forebears; adapted, however, to a different marketplace and royal history."[24] In an effort to curb the "exorbitant Liberty of the Press," for example, Charles created the Court of Star Chamber and passed the Licensing Act in 1662.[25] But he was also cognizant of the importance of harnessing the power of print. Instead of completely suppressing the news, he attempted to control what was available to the public, supporting newsbook writers like Henry Muddiman and authorizing a network of newsletter writers and information gatherers through the Secretaries of States' offices.[26] In addition, Charles sanctioned the publication of the *London Gazette*, which became "the only printed periodical news source between 1665 and 1688."[27] Charles faced down his own media crisis when his attempts to confirm his brother James as heir to the throne triggered a parliamentary impasse

---

Barbara Shapiro, *Political Communication and Political Culture in England, 1558–1688* (Stanford, CA: Stanford University Press, 2012).

[22] Jason Peacey, *Print and Public Politics in the English Revolution* (Cambridge: Cambridge University Press, 2013), 406; David Zaret, *Origins of Democratic Culture: Printing, Petitions and the Public Sphere in Early Modern England* (Princeton, NJ: Princeton University Press, 2000).

[23] Shapiro, *Political Communication*, 40. Jeremy Black asserts that Charles and James were two of the most repressive monarchs of all time if their attitude to print is considered (*The English Press: A History* [London: Bloomsbury Academic, 2019], 4).

[24] Harold Weber, *Memory, Print, and Gender in England, 1653–1759* (Houndmills: Palgrave Macmillan, 2008), 49.

[25] Zaret notes that the Licensing Act set rigid limits but failed to enforce these rules effectively (*Origins of Democratic Culture*, 143).

[26] See Peter Fraser, *The Intelligence of the Secretaries of State and Their Monopoly of Licensed News 1660–1688* (Cambridge: Cambridge University Press, 1956) and Rachael Scarborough King, "The Manuscript Newsletter and the Rise of the Newspaper, 1665–1715," *Huntington Library Quarterly* 79, no. 3 (2016): 411–37. As during the similar lapse during the outbreak of the British Civil Wars, printed works poured from the press.

[27] Shapiro, *Political Communication*, 81.

leading to the prevention of the renewal of the Licensing Act in 1679.[28] At the same time, other factors such as the development of the coffee-house and the postal service also contributed to the proliferation of printed political commentary at this time.[29]

When James II/VII finally ascended to the throne after his brother Charles II's death in February 1685, he ruled over a population that had more experience with and expectations of print than ever before. Like Charles, James struggled throughout his reign to contain voices of dissent, renewing the Licensing Act in his first parliamentary session. Tony Claydon has argued that James was dependent on "the use of traditional persuaders such as ceremonies, etiquette, visual display, or cultural patronage," which had been appropriate when "the political elite had crowded around the monarch" but which were ineffective in circumstances when it was necessary to convince a general English population of "the virtues of their king."[30] But in fact, James, like Charles, also employed printed resources to promote his political and religious agendas and to fight his political adversaries, even contemplating publishing his memoirs when he acceded to the throne as a means of self-representation.[31] James's employment of and relationship to print changed over the course of his short reign, however, as he turned more and more to using printed official documents to persuade his subjects to accept his policies and to publicize the changes that he sought to institute toward the end of his reign.

An examination of James's response to the uprisings at the beginning of his reign suggests the way he sought both to repress printed opposition and to use print in strategic ways; at the same time, it provides a basis of comparison for James's later uses of print. James's authority was challenged almost from the moment at which he assumed the throne when Archibald Campbell, Earl of Argyll, and James Scott, Duke of Monmouth,

---

[28] Melinda Zook argues that print in the hands of a radical Whig press became more powerful during and after the Exclusion Crisis: "Whig exploits and propaganda combined to make a powerful impression on the English public" (*Radical Whigs and Conspiratorial Politics in Late Stuart England* [University Park: Pennsylvania State University Press, 1999], xxi). Peter Fraser argues that it is at this period, rather than the British Civil Wars, that "journalism first entered the political arena as a considerable force" (*Intelligence*, 7).

[29] See Ian Atherton, "The Press and Popular Political Opinion," in *A Companion to Stuart Britain*, ed. Barry Coward (Oxford: Oxford University Press, 2007), 88. The institution of the government-run public postal service in 1660 and the Penny Post in 1680 (subsumed in 1682 within the General Post Office) also provided an important network for the distribution of printed as well as manuscript materials.

[30] Tony Claydon, *William III and the Godly Revolution* (Cambridge: Cambridge University Press, 1996), 4.

[31] On James's memoirs, see Sharpe, *Rebranding Rule*, chapter 5.

co-ordinated uprisings in Scotland and the West Country against the new king.[32] Significantly, both men issued printed declarations to justify their acts of rebellion, drawing upon and adapting a genre that was associated with opposition to the established monarchy during the British Civil Wars.[33] The fact that both Argyll and Monmouth chose to publish and disseminate their aims through printed declarations indicates the recognition of the genre at this time as a document generated by subjects but designed to appeal to a popular audience rather than to be directly presented to a monarch or Parliament.

The declarations of Monmouth and Argyll also bear examination for later comparison with William's more famous *Declaration* issued in 1688. Argyll in fact produced two declarations which were printed together. The first, *The Declaration and Apology of the Protestant People*, was presented in the name of "the Noblemen, Barons, Gentlemen, Burgesses and Commons of all sorts now in Arms within the Kingdom of Scotland"; and the second, *The Declaration of Archibald Earl of Argyle*, was issued in Argyll's own name.[34] *The Declaration and Apology* was designed as a manifesto to appeal to the Presbyterian population of Scotland.[35] Like William's later *Declaration*, it claims that its adherents are acting out of a desire to restore "the Protestant Religion" (2). It focuses on abuses of law and conscience in Scotland, but it also makes a more pointed comment regarding the "*common Wealth*" of the British Isles, noting that adherents from the various stations will support each other as well as "their persecuted and oppressed *brethren* and *friends* in England and Ireland who shall pursue the same end" (6–7). *The Declaration of Archibald Earl of Argyle* also asserts its concern with the "*common Wealth*," but it serves as an official order to Argyll's "Friends and Blood-relations" to join his cause as well as a threat to his "Vassals" that they will be punished for not obeying his "particular Orders" (3). Where the *Declaration and Apology* deploys the rhetoric of the Covenanters in its representation of a British

---

[32] Archibald, ninth Earl of Argyll, had been living in exile in Friesland, having been "outlawed for high treason in 1681, at the direction" of James, who was Duke of York and "royal commissioner to Scotland at the time" (Zook, *Radical Whigs*, 128). The Duke of Monmouth, the illegitimate son of Charles II, had also gone into exile in Europe after the Rye House Plot.

[33] Stephen E. Lucas, "The Rhetorical Ancestry of the Declaration of Independence," *Rhetoric & Public Affairs* 1, no. 2 (1998): 150.

[34] Archibald Campbell, Earl of Argyll, *The Declaration and Apology of the Protestant People* and *The Declaration of Archibald Earl of Argyle* (Campbell-Town, 1685). The work was reprinted as *The Declaration and Apology of the Protestant People* and *The Declaration of Archibald Earl of Argile* (Edinburgh, 1685).

[35] Tim Harris, *Revolution: The Great Crisis of the British Monarchy, 1685–1720* (London: Penguin, 2006), 77.

commonwealth consisting of representatives of all the estates, Argyll's personal *Declaration* draws on the ideology of clanship to assert his right to command the loyalty of his clan members.

Monmouth's *Declaration*, like Argyll's, condemns James for undermining both the political and religious interests of the nation. Whereas Argyll's *Declaration and Apology* focuses first on James's abuses of religion, however, Monmouth begins by accusing James of crimes against the state, suggesting that he has compromised the ancient political "Constitution" of England that was established to ensure the "peace happiness & security of the *Governed*, & not the private Interest, & personal greatness of those that Rule."[36] Instead of promoting the interests of his people, the document claims, James is attempting to turn England's "*limited Monarchy* into an *absolute Tyranny*" (2). Significantly, like William later, Monmouth indicates that he will refrain from asserting his own title to the throne, leaving it up to a restored, legitimate Parliament to determine his claim, and he asserts that he will "in conjunction with the People of *England*" work to establish laws to limit the power of the monarchy in the future (7). Monmouth's *Declaration* ends with a promise of a more extensive "*Manifesto, & Remonstrance*" that will be written for "our Country men, & Foreigners" that will lay out the particulars of the "*Grievances, Persecutions, Crueltyes & Tyrannies*" perpetrated by James (8).

As propaganda, the declarations were not terribly effective. Tim Harris suggests that, despite its claims to preserve the Protestant cause, Argyll's *Declaration* failed to engage either radical Cameronians or more moderate Presbyterians.[37] Similarly, Steven Pincus argues that, although Monmouth's *Declaration* was "a powerful and sophisticated statement of radical political aspirations," it "poorly describes the ideology of his rebellion," under-emphasizing the religious reasons that prompted most participants to engage in rebellion.[38] Neither Argyll's nor Monmouth's declarations was widely circulated, nor were their statements referred to by their followers. Monmouth, in fact, contradicted the claims of his *Declaration* as, after indicating that he would let a free Parliament decide

---

[36] *The Declaration of James Duke of Monmouth &; the Noblemen, Gentlemen & Others, Now in Arms, for Defence & Vindication of the Protestant Religion, & the Laws, Rights, & Privilieges of England, from the Invasion Made upon Them & for Delivering the Kingdom from the Usurpation & Tyranny of James Duke of York* (London, 1685), 1.

[37] Harris, *Revolution*, 77.

[38] Steven Pincus, *1688: The First Modern Revolution* (New Haven, CT: Yale University Press, 2009), 106.

on the monarch, he had himself proclaimed king on June 20, 1685, nine days after he raised the standard of his rebellion.

The symbolic importance of the declarations, however, is indicated by the fact that James took decisive action against the documents of Argyll and Monmouth, suppressing access to and symbolically discrediting them at the same time as he brutally suppressed the risings. Argyll's troops were soundly defeated by the government army under the Earl of Dumbarton, and Argyll himself was captured on June 18, 1685. Monmouth's forces were crushed at the Battle of Sedgemoor on July 6, 1685, and Monmouth was taken prisoner shortly after. Both leaders were executed as traitors. At the same time, the "traitorous Paper, entitled, *A Declaration of James Duke of Monmouth*" was ordered to be "burnt by the Hands of the Common-Hangman."[39] James also issued a proclamation on June 15, 1685, warning his subjects not to "Receive and Entertain the said Traterous Paper or to publish the same to others their fellow Subjects" and requiring them to "Apprehend and Cause to be Apprehended, all and every Person and Persons, who shall Publish, Disperse or Entertain without Discovery thereof to the Justice of the Peace, the said Traiterous Paper."[40] In his public response, James employed his own proclamation as a "know-show" document designed to reaffirm the loyalty of his subjects and counteract the authority that his opponents were claiming in their printed manifestos.

At the same time as James officially condemned Monmouth's and Argyll's declarations, however, his government also authorized a pamphlet which drew further attention to Argyll's documents. The author of the pamphlet, which was printed by the heirs of Andrew Anderson but which bore the same title as Argyll's original text, lambastes the *Declaration and Apology* for "Impudently and irreligiously" discussing the advantages to the Protestant religion of "the horrid Rebellion against King *Charles* the first."[41] It summarizes with shocked horror the contents of the collective "Canting Declaration" (2). But at the same time, it also reprints the entirety of the *Declaration of Archibald Earl of Argyll*. The author of the pamphlet was following a protocol established during the British Civil

---

[39] Ibid., 166.
[40] James II/VII, *By the King, a Proclamation against Spreading of a Traiterous Declaration* (London, 1685).
[41] *The Declaration and Apology of the Protestant People* (Edinburgh: Printed by the heirs of Andrew Anderson, 1685), 1.

Wars of republishing original documents along with arguments against them. According to David Zaret, this practice encouraged a "dialogic" form of political thinking in the early public sphere.[42] But at this historic moment, the reproduction of the original document created a paradox; at the same time as James was attempting to dissuade dialogic debate by issuing edicts against the reading and dissemination of the "Traiterous Papers" of Monmouth and symbolically executing documents, his government was authorizing the dissemination of one of the offending texts to a wider public. James's government was caught between two paradigms: an older one in which print had been employed in order to represent opposing points of view to a readership who had access to numerous documents and the other of re-intrenched authoritarianism including the careful control of printed works.

Two years after the suppression of the two uprisings, James turned to the genre of the printed declaration himself in order to promote his unpopular political and religious agenda of toleration, issuing *His Majesties GRACIOUS DECLARATION to All His Loving Subjects for Liberty of Conscience* on April 4, 1687, without approval of Parliament.[43] The *Declaration . . . for Liberty of Conscience* asserts that the King's interest in establishing his "Government on such a Foundation, as may make Our Subjects happy, and unite them to Us by Inclination as well as Duty" has convinced him to offer them "free Exercise of their Religion for the Time to come."[44] It provides a double justification for freedom of religion, noting not only that toleration is the King's personal "Inclination," but also that enforced religious conformity is contrary to the interest of the government because it destroys the nation by "Spoiling Trade, Depopulating Countries, and Discouraging Strangers" (2). The *Declaration* lists the numerous changes James is planning to introduce in order to ensure "liberty of conscience," including abolishing penal laws and the oaths of supremacy and allegiance as well as pardoning those who are currently being punished under the penal laws. The *Declaration*

---

[42] Zaret, *Origins of Democratic Culture*, 14.
[43] James had issued an earlier *A Proclamation for a Toleration in Scotland, February 12, 1687*, that eased laws against Roman Catholics, moderate Presbyterians and Quakers as well as established the King's dispensing powers. He subsequently prorogued Parliament before issuing the declaration aimed at establishing religious toleration in England in 1687. See Richard Boyer, "English Declaration of Indulgence of 1687 and 1688," *The Catholic Historical Review* 50, no. 3 (1964): 332–71.
[44] James II/VII, *His Majesties GRACIOUS DECLARATION to All His Loving Subjects for Liberty of Conscience Establishing Religious Toleration in England* (London, 1687), 1.

includes only brief reference to the fact that the King is exercising "Our Royal Prerogative," as James indicates his confidence regarding "the Concurrence of Our Two Houses of Parliament, when We shall think it convenient for them to Meet" (2). This latter comment both reminds his subjects of the King's power to decide when to summon the elected body and also foreshadows the great lengths to which he would go in order to find parliamentary representatives who would validate his policies. The *Declaration . . . for Liberty of Conscience* was printed by Charles Bill, Henry Hills and Thomas Newcomb, "Printers to the King's Most Excellent Majesty." It was also reprinted in the official government newspaper, the *London Gazette*, providing another means through which James was able to circulate his position without parliamentary approval.[45]

James also availed himself of the affordances of other genres of print to widely circulate the policies of his *Declaration* as he supported the publication of pamphlets that praised his policies.[46] *Reasons Why the Church of England, as Well as Dissenters Should Make Their Address of Thanks to the King's Majesty, for His Late Gracious Declaration for Liberty of Conscience*, for example, draws readers' attention to the political tumult of the recent past in order to make the argument "that it's not *Liberty*, but *Restraints* laid on Conscience, that has been most prejudicial to the Nation and its Government."[47] James's *Declaration* was also promoted in printed works that did not receive official government sanction. *A Pindarick Ode upon His Most Sacred Majestie's Late Gracious Indulgence*, for example, referring to the document in its title, employs the metaphor of different religions being like "various Instruments" as it praises James for bringing together his subjects "to joyn in one harmonious Quire":

> So we at length, Great *James*, compos'd by thee,
> Like different Notes agree
> To make up one melodious Harmony.[48]

---

[45] On the practice of printing declarations as "instruments of government" such as declarations in the *London Gazette* see Michael Twyman, "Printed Ephemera," in *The Cambridge History of the Book in Britain*, vol. 5, *1695–1830*, ed. Michael Suarez and Michael Turner (Cambridge: Cambridge University Press, 2010), 74. Whereas the broadsheets used what was referred to as "proclamation-print," the newspapers reprinted them in Roman font.

[46] Scott Sowerby, *Making Toleration: The Repealers and the Glorious Revolution* (Cambridge, MA: Harvard University Press, 2013), 3.

[47] *Reasons Why the Church of England, as Well as Dissenters Should Make Their Address of Thanks to the King's Majesty* (London, 1687), 6.

[48] *A Pindarick Ode upon His Most Sacred Majestie's Late Gracious Indulgence* (London, 1687), 7, English Broadside Ballad Archive (hereafter EBBA), http://ebba.english.ucsb.edu.

A Loyal Paper of Verses upon His Majesties Gracious Declaration also promotes the king's political agenda. The poem lauds the *Declaration* as the inspiration both for written verses and a celebratory soundscape:

> Ingenious Poets! can your Pens lye still
> On such a Subject, as might Volumes fill:
> Hark! How the Declaration sounds our Joys,
> None but great JAMES could chime such Heavenly Noise.[49]

For the poet of *A Loyal Paper*, the *Declaration* cancels out the need for the expression of any opposition, as James's "Gracious Mercy" anticipates his subjects' desire so much that it is no longer necessary to "send Petitions": "What would you have! You now can ask no more, / Here's Mercy strew'd at every Subjects Door."

On a more popular note, the broadsheet ballad *The Manifestation of Joy, or, the Loyal Subjects Grateful Acknowledgment* celebrates the religious tolerance of the King through a song to the tune of a popular jig, "The Country Farmer."[50] The ballad reframes the King's lack of consultation with Parliament, praising James for being a "great Moderator" who has decided to abolish "those laws / Which Conscience restrain'd" and allow subjects now to "partake" of "freedom of Conscience." It hints at the subject of the royal prerogative, suggesting that "In Mildness and Mercy," the King "does dispence" his power, and it reworks the language of the *Declaration*, indicating that the King wishes liberty of conscience so that "trade may increase and more plenty abound" and subjects can "joyfully sing" the monarch's praises. Significantly, *The Manifestation of Joy*, like the other non-official printed works *A Loyal Paper of Verses* and *A Pindarick Ode upon His Most Sacred Majestie's Late Gracious Indulgence*, deploys a representation of orality, of singing and music-making, to further the *Declaration*'s message of religious tolerance.

James also went out of his way to promote his *Declaration* using non-print means available to him. In August 1687, he embarked on a progress which took him to Portsmouth and Bath, up to Chester and back to Windsor via Oxford.[51] Lucile Pinkham indicates that James's progresses "through the western shires" were met with "coolness by the gentry and

---

[49] R.P., *A Loyal Paper of Verses upon His Majesties Gracious Declaration* (London, 1687).
[50] *The Manifestation of Joy, or, the Loyal Subjects Grateful Acknowledgment. Occasionally Written upon the Publication of His Majesties Most Gracious Declaration, Allowing LIBERTY of CONSCIENCE* (1687), EBBA.
[51] George Agar Ellis, ed., *Letters Written during the Years 1686, 1687, 1688, and Addressed to John Ellis, Esq.*, 2 vols. (London: Henry Colburn and Richard Bentley, 1831), 1: 337.

aristocracy," but were enthusiastically greeted by the general population.[52] The commencement of the assizes also provided an opportunity for James to see his policies disseminated. As a "system by which judges from Westminster visit[ed] some fifty provincial towns to deliver gaols and try civil cases,"[53] the assizes provided, as Shapiro notes, "a concrete, readily observable fact of royal authority ... Delivered at the opening of each assize, the assize sermon was a vehicle by which political meanings could be assigned to the spectacle about to unfold."[54] Judges were reminded of their duties and urged to bring juries in line with official policies.

Despite what can be seen as a concerted multi-mediated propaganda effort, however, James faced unprecedented non-compliance with his directive. Scott Sowerby notes that when James "instructed the bishops of the Church of England to organize addresses from the clergy thanking him for his edict," the "clergy of the diocese of Oxford refused to sign such an address, creating a public scandal, which was magnified when the reasons for their refusal were printed in a widely circulated pamphlet."[55] Accordingly, James republished the *Declaration ... for Liberty of Conscience* on April 27, 1688. The new version of the *Declaration*, however, differs significantly from the first. The original version of the *Declaration* stated the King's intentions with a brief explanation of the reasons behind them. The new version, however, includes paratextual material that consciously and directly engages James's subjects as readers. In the short preface, James attempts to assert his absolute authority, indicating that he will hold steadfast in his commitment to liberty of conscience. He suggests that his actions in the past should indicate his intention to remain resolute: "Our conduct has been such in all times, as ought to have perswaded the world, that we are firm, and constant to our resolutions." But he also indicates an awareness of ways that his subjects can be misled, and he suggests that it is due to this awareness that he repeats his message: "yet that easie people may not be abused by the malice of crafty wicked men, we think fit to declare, that our intentions are not changed since the fourth of April 1687."[56] The second version of the *Declaration* shows the King actively attempting to persuade his subjects through the reading process rather than just directing them in their duty.

---

[52] Lucile Pinkham, *William III and the Respectable Revolution: The Part Played by William of Orange in the Revolution of 1688* (Cambridge, MA: Harvard University Press, 1969), 50.
[53] J. S. Cockburn, *A History of English Assizes 1558–1714* (Cambridge: Cambridge University Press, 1972), ix.
[54] Shapiro, *Political Communication*, 185. [55] Sowerby, *Making Toleration*, 6.
[56] James II/VII, *His Majesties Gracious Declaration. James R. Our Conduct Has Been Such in All Times* (London, 1688), 1.

The conclusion of the reprinted *Declaration* also shifts its mode of address, as James now urges his subjects to "reflect" on their present "Ease and Happiness" (4). He acknowledges the power of the opposition's rhetoric in casting him in a negative light but attempts to counter it with affective rhetoric of his own: "We have not appeared to be that Prince, Our Enemies would have made the World afraid of" (4). The revised *Declaration* indicates James's interest in "Conjuring" a response from his subjects and requests them to "choose" representatives in the upcoming elections who will support his policies (4). In its new form, the *Declaration* rhetorically shifts from informing subjects of the monarch's will to engaging with them, from "commanding" to "recommending." In its reprinted form, the *Declaration* appears to acknowledge the importance of printed mediation in "perswad[ing] the world," as it also suggests that half of the "know-show" equation involves readers' reception.

While it was important in its printed form, the impact of the *Declaration*, like that of other official documents, depended not just on its printed circulation but on its oral delivery. On May 4, 1688 the King issued an order that his *Declaration* be read out loud in all churches and chapels,[57] attempting to assert the monarch's dispensing powers and to signal official approval of his policies despite the fact that they had not been passed in Parliament.[58] Although some clergymen, including the Bishops of Durham, Rochester, Lincoln and Hereford, complied with the request to read the *Declaration* out loud, the Archbishop of Canterbury and six other bishops did not, and on May 18, 1688, they presented a petition to James expressing their "great Aversion," not to the *Declaration* itself, but to its "Distribution and Publication in all their Churches."[59] Although they indicated that they had "many other Considerations," the chief objection that they voiced was the fact that the *Declaration* was "founded upon such a Dispensing Power, as has been often declar'd Illegal, in Parliament" (5). The seven bishops were arrested and imprisoned in the Tower after the publication of their objections.[60]

A key issue in their trial was the question of what constituted "publication." Sidestepping the issue of whether or not the bishops had arranged

---

[57] Boyer, "English Declaration of Indulgence," 364.
[58] See Esther S. Cope, "The King's Declaration Concerning the Dissolution of the Short Parliament of 1640: An Unsuccessful Attempt at Public Relations," *Huntington Library Quarterly* 40, no. 4 (August 1977): 326.
[59] Henry Care, *An Answer to a Paper Importing a Petition of the Archbishop of Canterbury; and Six Other Bishops* (London, 1688), 3.
[60] *The Petition of William Sancroft, Archbishop of Canterbury and Six Other Bishops* (London, 1688).

the publication of their petition, however, Lord Justice Wright asserted that in this case "publishing" constituted presenting their petition to the King. The question then concerned whether they had "maliciously, seditiously, and slanderously made, contrived, and published, a false and seditious libel against the King, which tended to diminish his regard, authority and prerogative" or whether they were merely pointing out to the King the legal limits of his authority.[61] The jury eventually decided on a verdict of "not guilty." In fact, although the printing of the *Petition* had not been the focus of the bishops' guilt or innocence, the appearance of the *Petition* in print generated a new stream of printed debate that "tended to diminish [the King's] regard, authority and prerogative."[62] In addition, the mediation of the bishops' case served to further reflect on the limits of monarchical authority. Narcissus Luttrell describes the "Medalls" of the bishops that were "lately made" with the motto: "Wisdom hath built her a house, and chosen her 7 pillars; with the reverse, a church undermining by 2 Jesuite with a pickaxe and shovel, and a hand pointing out of the cloud, with this motto, The gates of hell shall not prevail against it."[63] The bishops also gained popular support through the circulation of ballads such as "A New Catch, in Praise of the Reverend Bishops":

> True English men, Drink a good health to the Mitre:
> Let our Church ever Flourish, tho' her Enemies spight her:
> May their Cunning and Forces no longer prevaile,
> And their Malice, as well as their Arguments, faile,
> Then Remember the 7, which Supported our Cause,
> As Stoute as our Martyrs, and as Just as our Law's.[64]

The ballad pits the bishops against the "Enemies" of the Church, suggesting that they have successfully outwitted the evil machinations against "our Cause" as well as "our Law's." As the circulation of the ballad suggests, it was the general knowledge that the bishops had defied the King's orders rather than the text of the petition itself that proved important. But the fact that the petition was circulating in print in tandem with these other mediations like the medals and ballads made their intervention more tangible and easy to "Remember."

---

[61] Dover, *Letters to John Ellis*, 2: 8, 10. See also Harris, *Revolution*.
[62] See, for example, *An Address to His Grace the Lord Archbishop of Canterbury, and the Right Reverend the Bishops* (London, 1688) and Care, *An Answer*.
[63] Narcissus Luttrell, *A Brief Historical Relation of State Affairs from September 1678 to April 1714*, 6 vols. (Oxford: Oxford University Press, 1857), 1: 458. Luttrell was himself a numismatist.
[64] "A New Catch, in Praise of the Reverend Bishops," in *A Collection of the Newest and Most Ingenious Poems, Songs, Catches &c. against Popery Relating to the Times* (London, 1689), 20.

As indicated earlier, scholars examining the mediation of the 1688 Revolution have focused largely on the role of that William's propaganda played in impacting how the Revolution played out. In this section I have suggested that by examining James's and his government's increasing focus on printed productions we can see how the shift in attitudes to print was occurring prior to William's propaganda efforts. Changes in the official documents reflected both the fact that subjects in England were primed to receive printed political information and the fact that the King and his government were becoming increasingly aware of the possibilities of print and the necessity of its use. This awareness of and self-consciousness about the efficacy of print that was growing during James's reign came to a head in the unfolding crisis as the texts of William's advisors, schooled in the persuasive uses of printed works in the Dutch Republic, began circulating works in English communication networks. At the same time, as the cases of James's *Declaration* and the bishops' petition indicate, the impact of those printed works was still very much determined through their dissemination by non-print means.

The "Prints" of Orange: William's *Declaration* and Transmedial Circuits of Opposition

Despite James's attempts to promote his views and to suppress opposition, oppositional voices clamoured to be heard as James's pro-Catholic policies elicited more and more concerns. The author of *A Pindarick Poem* suggests that the subject of liberty of conscience had been "bandied about by all parties; not an useless Pen in Town but has consumed both Ink and Paper in Defence or Opposition of it."[65] Lucile Pinkham comments that the summer of 1687 saw "a regular pamphlet war" as "hot words and exaggerated accusations" for and against James's policies "flew wildly."[66] Many of the pamphlets circulating in London originated in the Dutch Republic. *A Letter Writ by Mijn Heer Fagel, Pensioner of Holland to Mr. James Stewart, Advocate, Giving an Account of the Prince and Princess of Orange's Thoughts Concerning the Repeal of the Test and the Penal Laws*, for example, was "translated into four languages, printed, and scattered in broadsheet form throughout England and western Europe."[67] Although Fagel's letter supported religious toleration, it argued against the repeal of

---

[65] *A Pindarick Poem*, 3.   [66] Pinkham, *William III*, 44.
[67] Ibid., 54; *A Letter Writ by Mijn Heer Fagel, Pensioner of Holland to Mr. James Stewart, Advocate, Giving an Account of the Prince and Princess of Orange's Thoughts Concerning the Repeal of the Test and the Penal Laws* (London, 1688).

the Test and Penal Laws, and, more importantly, it served to broadcast the fact that William and Mary also supported this view. The diarist Narcissus Luttrell confirmed the impact that printed works from the Dutch Republic had been having in England, writing in March 1688 that "Several Libells and pamphlets have been lately printed and sent about; many are come over from Holland."[68] Luttrell also commented on the government's attempt to curb oppositional voices, observing that "Some booksellers, as Mr. Clavell, one Wild, &c., were taken up for selling libelous papers" (1: 472).

Despite the measures taken to suppress anti-government pamphlets, these oppositional works circulated widely, and, moreover, the messages that they conveyed were amplified by being delivered through other media. A broadside of popular "Lampoons" from 1687, for example, includes "A Dialogue between a Loyal Addresser, and a Blunt Whiggish Clown" that casts aspersions on the King's official position. The "Loyal Addresser" in the ballad is presented as gullibly believing James's "Proclamation" promising that he would "rule by Law," chastising the "Clown" for not trusting the king:

> Ungrateful Wretch! Canst thou pretend a cause
> To fear the loss of Liberty and Laws?
> Has not the King been at a vast expence
> To raise the Gallant Troops in thy Defence?
> Did he not promise in a Proclamation,
> To rule by Law ats Coronation?[69]

The wise fool, on the other hand, asks whether the king has "not already damned the Test" and suggests that a "Princes Word is but a jest / Who Rules an Army and Obeys a Priest." Because the King is Catholic, argues the ballad, his "Solemn Oath" is insubstantial; although his "Sword is Steel," "his God is but a Wafer." The birth of a son to James II/VII and his Catholic wife, Mary of Modena, in June 1688 generated further suspicion of the King and opposition regarding the supposed illegitimacy of the new Prince of Wales.[70]

---

[68] Luttrell, *Historical Relation*, 1: 484.
[69] "A Dialogue between a Loyal Addresser, and a Blunt Whiggish Clown," in *Lampoons* (London, 1687), EBBA.
[70] See John Pinkerton, *The Medallic History of England to the Revolution, with Forty Plates* (London, 1790), 107–09. See also Frederic George Stephens, ed., *Catalogue of Prints and Drawings in the British Museum: Division 1. Political and Personal Satire*, vol. 1 (London: Printed by order of the Trustees, 1870), 714–17.

Speculation in the form of rumour and hearsay compounded opposition to James. As Adam Fox suggests, "oral exchange and tradition, however derivative from textual sources, remained a vital and innovative force throughout [the early modern period] and beyond."[71] In his *The History of the Desertion*, Edmund Bohun, a Tory-leaning apologist for William, comments retrospectively on the place of rumour in establishing the conditions for the Revolution: "The nation was by this time exasperated and fermented to that height against the Court and Popish party, that all places were fill'd with Reports and Whispers to their Disadvantage, many of which were false, and some ridiculous and impossible, which yet were then greedily swallowed, and industriously spread and promoted."[72] Luttrell also indicates the role of hearsay in casting doubt on the Prince of Wales's legitimacy in particular: "People give themselves a great liberty in discoursing about the young prince, with strange reflections on him."[73] Contemporary manuscript newsletters, too, recounted the "surmises and uncertainties" that were "industriously spread about the coffee-houses of our town, touching his Majesty's ministers and his affairs."[74] Such newsletter reports themselves carried speculation further, as they circulated along with private letters to individuals.[75] James attempted to put a stop to this growing multi-mediation of news and rumour, giving an order "for the suppression of news letters at coffee houses and other publick places" on October 6, 1688.[76] The only newsletters that were allowed to be published were those that were compiled and distributed by the Secretaries of State.

It was within this multi-media questioning of monarchical authority that the Prince of Orange planned his foray into England. Warned by one advisor that if he wanted to keep England "in humour," he "must entertain it by papers," William and his advisors opted to publish a document that

---

[71] Adam Fox, "Remembering the Past in Early Modern England: Oral and Written Tradition," *Transactions of the Royal Historical Society* 9 (1999): 233.

[72] Edmund Bohun, *The History of the Desertion* (London, 1689).

[73] Luttrell, *Historical Relation*, 1: 449. Luttrell notes that they were "not fitt to insert here." John Evelyn suggests the impact of this rumour and hearsay on the King, reporting on the King's calling a council and seeking testimony from "all the ladies and lords who were present at the Queen Consort's labour": "This procedure was censured by some as below his Majesty to condescend to, on the talk of the people" (John Evelyn, *Diary and Correspondence of John Evelyn, F.R.S.*, ed. William Bray, 4 vols. [London: Henry Colburn, 1850], 2: 282).

[74] Dover, *Letters to John Ellis*, 2: 27.

[75] See Leith Davis, "Mediating the 'Sudden & Surprising Revolution': Official Manuscript Newsletters and the Glorious Revolution," in *After Print: Eighteenth-Century Manuscript Cultures*, ed. Rachel Scarborough King (Charlottesville: University of Virginia Press, 2020), 148–74.

[76] Luttrell, *Historical Relation*, 1: 467; Schwoerer, "Propaganda," 859.

would consolidate the grievances against James, defend William against accusations that he was invading England in order to make himself king and capitalize on the dissatisfaction circulating throughout James's three kingdoms.[77] *The Declaration of His Highnes William Henry* was the product of a combination of Dutch and English advice. Originally drafted by Gaspar Fagel in consultation with members of the English expatriate community at The Hague, it was abridged and translated into English by Gilbert Burnet. Having borne witness to the events of the British Civil Wars and then the Exclusion Crisis during the subsequent Restoration, Burnet was acutely aware of the power of print to shape cultural memory of an event. In his *History of His Own Time*, he comments frequently on the impact of printed works, suggesting, for example, that the public memory of Charles I was influenced both by the dignified comportment of the King at his execution and by the publishing of the *Eikon Basilike* in 1649; Burnet acknowledged that, as the work was universally believed to be written by the King himself and that, "coming out soon after his death, [it] had the greatest run in many impressions than any book has had in our age."[78] According to Burnet, it was the affect generated by the printed account, the "compassionate regard" for the beheaded King, rather than any political rationale that was "the true occasion of the great turn of the nation in the year 1660" (1: 50). Through his translation, advertisement and editing of the Prince of Orange's *Declaration*, Burnet attempted to create such "compassionate regard" for William at the same time as including rational arguments for the Prince's cause.[79]

The choice of genre for the document, the declaration, was strategic, not only connecting the Prince's struggle against James with a pedigree of previous protests against absolute monarchy, including the recent declarations of Argyll and Monmouth, but also inviting a negative comparison with James's own unpopular *Declaration*.[80] Whereas Argyll's and Monmouth's declarations had been incidental to their campaigns, however, William's *Declaration* was carefully integrated into his plans. The publication of the *Declaration* was indeed a unique media event in the history of political communication in Britain in terms of the sheer size of

---

[77] Schwoerer, *Declaration of Rights*, 107. [78] Burnet, *History of His Own Time*, 1: 50.
[79] Eveline Cruickshanks suggests that William's "very successful propaganda campaign" was "masterminded by Burnet in 1688" but that after this, he "did not bother to conceal his dislike of and contempt for his British subjects" (*The Glorious Revolution* [New York: St. Martin's Press, 2000], 66).
[80] See Asa Briggs and Peter Burke, *A Social History of Media: From Gutenberg to the Internet* (Malden, MA: Blackwell, 2001), 48.

the print run and the document's carefully planned dissemination. The collaborators on the *Declaration*, Fagel, Burnet and their co-creators, were attempting to use the document to shape the interpretation of the events to come. They were establishing the conditions for the creation of the kind of event that Nora would later label "spectacular" as they consciously "invested" the Revolution "with symbolic significance" even as it was unfolding.[81]

Aware of rumours about the Prince of Orange's imminent invasion, on October 26, 1688, the King issued a proclamation against the "divers evil disposed Persons" who "make it their business by Writing, Printing, or Speaking, to defame Our Government with false and seditious News and Reports."[82] The proclamation drew upon the language of the ancient constitution in order to defend the practice of punishing those who published anti-government material, referencing "the ancient Laws and Statutes of this Realm" that allow for "great and heavy Penalties" to be "inflicted upon all such as shall be found to be Spreaders of false News, or Promoters of any malicious Slanders and Calumnies in their ordinary and common Discourse, or otherwise." Like the proclamation against the Duke of Monmouth's *Declaration*, this proclamation suggests that James was at least as much concerned with the consumers of seditious material as with the producers of it. Negative representations of the government and court, the proclamation asserts, are intended "to amuse Our loving Subjects as far as they are able, to create in them an universal Jealousie and Discontent." The arousal of such emotions threatens subsequently to "alienate the Hearts of such of Our loving Subjects from Us, who otherwise would readily yield unto Us that Aid and Assistance which by their Natural Allegiance they are bound to do." Negative representations would thus sever the "Natural" bonds between monarch and subjects. This affective danger is especially acute in the present time of "publick Danger threatned by the intended Invasion upon this Our Kingdom," suggests the proclamation. At such a time, it is not enough just not to publish anti-government material; punishment, the document suggests, also needs to be meted out to those who consume such material: "bold and irreverent Speeches . . . and all malicious and false Reports" are "punishable not only in the Speakers, but in the Hearers also, unless they do speedily reveal the same unto some of Our privy-Council, or some other of Our

---

[81] Nora and Kritzman, *Realms*, 17.
[82] James II/VII, *By the King. A Proclamation. To Restrain the Spreading of False News* (London, 1688), no page number (hereafter n.p.).

Judges or Justices of the Peace." Echoing the earlier proclamation, all media – manuscript, print, oral and aural – are included in the proscription.

James was able to see William's *Declaration* for himself when, on October 31, 1688, Colonel Langham, one of the men selected to circulate the *Declaration* at the time of the invasion, was arrested with copies of the *Declaration* on his person.[83] Accordingly, on November 2, 1688, James issued another proclamation specifically condemning the spreading of the *Declaration* of the Prince of Orange.[84] This time, he noted the particular way in which the documents were distributed through an established network: "a very great Number whereof being Printed, several Persons are sent and employed to disperse the same throughout Our Kingdoms." Again, James focused on the dangers of consuming the material in question, which, he suggested, was designed to "seduce our People and (if it were possible) to corrupt our Army." The November 2, 1688, proclamation targeted public dissemination as well as private and public consumption, admonishing subjects not to "Publish, Disperse, Repeat or Hand about" or "Read, Receive, Conceal or Keep" the "Treasonable Papers or Declarations." James's intent here was both to make opposition disappear by ending access to material that would foster that opposition and to prevent his subjects from reading or listening to any such material that found its way into their hands.

James's intentions backfired, however, as prohibition served only to increase desire to see the *Declaration*. Writing in 1702, the ex-patriot French Huguenot writer Abel Boyer comments on the negative effect the proclamation had on the population: "The greatest part of the Nation were already so prepossess'd of the good Intentions of the Prince [of Orange], that this Proclamation ser'vd only to exasperate their Minds against King James; but His Majesty and his Counsellors were now giddy with Resentment, and incapable of following those wise Methods which are only suggested by cool and sober Thoughts."[85] In his account, Bohun, too, suggests that this proclamation "had the same effect with all the rest of their Counsels, for men suspected thereupon, that there was much more in the Declarations and Papers than they afterwards found, and accordingly became more desirous by far to see it."[86] Boyer's and Bohun's retrospective

---

[83] Abel Boyer, *History of King William the Third. In III Parts*, 3 vols. (London: A. Roper, 1702–03), 1: 229. Luttrell also discusses James's reaction to the *Declaration* (*Historical Relation*, 1: 472).

[84] James II/VII, *By the King, a Proclamation. Whereas the Prince of Orange and His Adherents* (London, 1688), n.p.

[85] Boyer, *History*, 1: 240.   [86] Bohun, *History of the Desertion*, 35.

accounts, although certainly biased, are confirmed by media at the time that suggested that as rumours circulated about a planned invasion, interest in William's *Declaration* in particular was generated even before its release. The author of *Private Occurrences* anticipates printed confirmation regarding William's plans, for example:

> A strong Fleet and Army they hither are bent,
> We know well the cause that there is something in't,
> And we doubt not, e're long we shall see it in print.[87]

Notably, the actual content of William's *Declaration* was less important at this stage than its role as a symbol of opposition. Although a printed document, it also served as a sign whose significance was augmented through manuscript, song and hearsay.

The *Declaration* was crafted to complement existing oppositional works, and it subsequently became the focus of William's propaganda campaign, its ideas circulating in transmedial networks after William landed on November 5, 1688. As with James's earlier *Declaration*, ceremonial performance of the document was considered necessary in order to lend legitimacy to the *Declaration*. The author of *An Account of the Proceedings and Transactions That Have Happened in the Kingdom of England* tracks events from the time of "*the Arrival of the Dutch Fleet, and the Landing of the Prince of Orange's Army*" and confirms the importance of the reading of the *Declaration* during the Prince's ceremonial entrance in Exeter:

> He entering that City in much Splendor, and with the loud Huzza's and Shouts of the People, the Bells Ringing, and the Bonefires at night flaming in every Street . . . And here it was that His Highness's Declaration, relating His Intentions for the preservation of the Protestant Religion, and Redressing the Grievances of the Nation, by removing Evil Counsellors, &c. was published, more especially publickly Read.[88]

Boyer also describes the pomp and circumstance accompanying William's entry into Exeter and comments on the public reading of the *Declaration*:

> After the Collects were ended, Dr *Burnet* began to read His Highness's Declaration, at which the Ministers of the Church there present were so surpriz'd, that they immediately left their Seats, and went out; however, the Doctor continued reading, and the Declaration being ended, he said, *God*

---

[87] *Private Occurrences, OR, the Transactions of the Four Last Years* (London, 1688), EBBA.
[88] *An Account of the Proceedings and Transactions That Have Happened in the Kingdom of England, since the Arrival of the Dutch Fleet, and the Landing of the Prince of Orange's Army* (London, 1688), 2–3.

save the Prince of Orange, to which the major part of the Congregation answer'd, *Amen*.[89]

The *Declaration* was also read out publicly at Bath on November 20, 1688, and at Oxford on December 6, 1688.[90]

Other printed works helped spread the word about William's arrival and the claims he was making in his *Declaration*. Some of these works, like Burnet's *The Expedition of His Highness the Prince of Orange for England*, were composed by William's advisors and were designed to amplify the message of the *Declaration*.[91] *A Letter from a Gentleman in Exeter to His Friend in London* reproduces text from Burnet's longer account, noting the providential aspect of the date of the Prince's arrival, as November 5 was the date on which the plan of Guy Fawkes and his co-conspirators to blow up the Parliament of James I/VI had been foiled.[92] Pamphlets such as these became increasingly common as censorship channels broke down.[93] As John Evelyn noted on December 2, 1688, "Every thing, till now concealed, flies abroad in public print, and is cried about the streets."[94]

Ballads circulating at the time also encouraged interest in the Prince and his *Declaration*, echoing its language as well as its sentiments. *A New Touch of the Times, OR, the Nat[i]ons Consent, for a Free Parliament* encourages "English hearts" to "uphold the Prince in the way of Right."[95] The ballad lists the "Lords and Gentry of high Renown" who have gone over to the cause of the Prince, celebrates the anticipated execution of the "Jesuit-Council which the King had of late" and also makes an affective connection between the Prince and the earlier Protestant hero, "brave Monmouth." The ballad repeats the phrase "Free Parliament" four times in the first four stanzas, building it into the scansion and rhyming it with positive terms such as "content," "consent" and "government" as it envisions William as the instrument "To maintain the Protestant Religion" and the "Rights and Laws" of the land:

> Since Popery from our Nation must depart,
> For the Prince will have a Free Parliament,
> And they bravely will settle our Government.

---

[89] Boyer, *History*, 1: 240.   [90] Ibid., 1: 252.
[91] Gilbert Burnet, *The Expedition of His Highness the Prince of Orange for England* (London, 1688), 3.
[92] *A Letter from a Gentleman in Exeter to His Friend in London* (London, 1688).
[93] A number of accounts praising William were also printed during the deliberations of the Convention. See, for example, Robert Ferguson, *A Brief Justification of the Prince of Orange's Descent* (London, 1689).
[94] Evelyn, *Diary*, 2: 296.
[95] *A New Touch of the Times, OR, the Nations Consent, for a Free Parliament* (London, 1689), EBBA.

The ballad entitled *A Full Description of These Times; or the Prince of ORANGE's March from EXETER to LONDON* similarly promotes the causes which William embedded in his *Declaration*: "The Brave Prince of Orange has been our best friend / And routed all Popery out of the Land."[96] Significantly, neither *A New Touch of the Times* nor *A Full Description of These Times* anticipates William's assumption of the crown. Rather, in keeping with the *Declaration* itself, they imagine a future that only goes as far as the "secur[ing]" of "Our religion," the "settl[ing]" of "the Laws" and the establishment of peace and profitable "trading again."[97] *A Full Description* does go so far as to provide an account of the celebration surrounding the Prince of Orange's arrival in London, however, suggesting the "joy" with which he was greeted:

> Now he is in London with his Noble Train,
> The Bells they did trowl it again and again;
> The Bone-fires did blaze, and the People rejoice,
> For joy of this Prince they did strain up their voice:
> The Lord he did bless him along in his way,
> To save and secure our Religion this day.[98]

Along with printed descriptions of the reading out of the *Declaration*, such remediations ensured that, although people might not have read the *Declaration*, they had a sense of what it contained. William and his advisors had crafted the printed *Declaration* to articulate fears regarding the threats to the nation's "law, liberties and customs" and to justify the legal basis of his invasion. For those ideas to become truly persuasive to the nation, however, they needed to be disseminated through means other than print.

Fighting Words: Debating the *Declaration*

Faced with the increasing popularity of his son-in-law and nephew's arrival, James's strategy changed over the month of November 1688 as he began to issue printed documents with more frequency in response to developments. Attempting to beat William at his own game, James published his own declaration the day after the Prince landed. *By the King, a Declaration*, like James's earlier *Declaration … for Liberty of Conscience*, focuses on affect and persuasion. It expresses James's "Horror" at the

---

[96] *A Full Description of These Times; or the Prince of ORANGE's March from EXETER to LONDON* (London, 1689), EBBA.
[97] Ibid.   [98] Ibid.

"Unchristian and Unnatural ... Undertaking in a Person so nearly Related to Us," and it attempts to brand William's undertaking not as an intervention but as a hostile intrusion of a foreign power.[99] Claiming that William's appearance is "an Invasion of Our Kingdom," the *Declaration* warns of the "many Mischiefs and Calamaties" which "an Army of Foreigners and Rebels" will bring upon the English. James's *Declaration* also calls attention to the "specious and plausible Pretences" of William's remarks, suggesting that despite all William's attestations, he plans no less than "*an Absolute Usurping of Our Crown and Royal Authority.*" At the same time as it calls William's claims in his *Declaration* into question, James's *Declaration* also serves another purpose: to inform his subjects that he has restored the Ancient Charters of Cities and Burroughs and to reassure them that he will call an actual "free Parliament" as soon as the nation is "delivered from this Invasion." Drawing from William's own rhetoric of restoration, the *Declaration* ends with an appeal to his subjects to join with him to restore the "Peace and Tranquillity of these Our Kingdoms."

In the developing conflict of 1688, James also sought to stifle enthusiasm for William's cause by authorizing other printed works designed to question the claims of the Prince's *Declaration*. In fact, however, such works authorized by the government served only to further increase perceptions about the power of the *Declaration*. As Joad Raymond notes in relation to controversial pamphlets and newsbooks in the British Civil Wars, writers who "alluded to them" and "attacked them" only confirmed "their literary potency."[100] The pro-government *Some Reflections upon His Highness the Prince of Oranges Declaration*, for example, addresses the "Particulars" of William's document, attacking it paragraph by paragraph. Unlike the pamphlet that James authorized regarding the Duke of Argyll's rising, *Reflections* does not reprint the *Declaration* in whole or in part. But the author nevertheless performs a careful close reading of the *Declaration*, noting, for example, that William wrongfully employs the language of kingship in the document. William's use of "the Style of WE and US" and of words like "*Commanding, Preferring, Advancing, Rewarding, Punishing, having of Parliaments* and *setling the Nations*," argues this pamphlet, betrays the fact that his "Design is to be King."[101]

[99] James II/VII, *By the King, a Declaration. As We Cannot Consider This Invasion of Our Kingdoms without Horror* (London and Edinburgh, 1688).
[100] Joad Raymond, *The Invention of the Newspaper: English Newsbooks, 1641–1649* (Oxford: Clarendon Press, 1996), 20.
[101] *Some Reflections upon His Highness the Prince of Oranges Declaration* (London, 1688), 1, 3.

Moreover, *Reflections* comments self-consciously on the genre of document that William employs, claiming that the Prince's employment of a "declaration" betrays his actual plan to seize the monarchy: "Had his *Highness* only pretended to come to deliver the *King* from *Evil Counsellors*, and to engage Him further into the Interest of *England* and *Europe*, that he might not seem a Property to a few ill Men for narrow ends, The *Prince of Orange* had less needed an Apology with some others" (1). The author of *Reflections* draws on the historical association of declarations with challenges to royal authority during the British Civil Wars in order to warn James's subjects about William's hidden agenda in the present day.

The Dutch Design Anatomized, subtitled *or the Discovery of the Wickedness and Unjustice of the Intended Invasion*, also authorized by the government, similarly rebuts the *Declaration* but avoids reprinting specific content. *The Dutch Design* blames the current crisis on English and Scottish "*Male-contents*, who had setled themselves in the United Provinces" and by their "correspondences here" have managed to keep up the suspicions against the King.[102] The author notes in particular the effect of the "subtile and well-Penned Treatises" which these "*Male-contents*" distributed to their "Correspondents" in order to alarm both "Church-men and Dissenters" (4). Where the *Reflections* employs only subtle anti-Dutch commentary, the author of *The Dutch Design* alludes to the recent Anglo-Dutch Wars (1652–74) for a more pronounced affect, suggesting, for example, that "The Dutch" have "wormed us out of the Trade of the *East-Indies*; and ... their unjust dealing hath heretofore occasioned great Wars betwixt *England* and the *United Provinces*" (7). Borrowing the rhetoric of slavery, *The Dutch Design* further warns against the "slavery and misery" that will come with William's invasion. If the English are permitted to live at all after conquest, asks the pamphlet, what "can they expect, but to be Hewers of Wood, and Drawers of Water; to be Slaves to every *Swedish* or *Dutch* Pedee, or Rot in Loathsome Prisons, or Pine in Desarts, Forest and Woods" or be "sent to their Plantations as Slaves to make room for their own people to possess what they had."[103]

Like James's earlier proclamations, *The Dutch Design Anatomized* attempts to counter the effect of the Prince of Orange's *Declaration* by suggesting that its claims are fictitious and arguing that it was "framed on purpose to amuse the People" and to make them believe that "the setting us at Rights is the only design of the *Dutch*" (29). The author points out

---

[102] True Member of the Church of England, *The Dutch Design Anatomized* (London, 1688), 4.
[103] *The Dutch Design Anatomized*, 19.

how the Prince's propaganda machine actually works, claiming that writers who are the "King's enemies" are "working Night and Day to Pile one Story upon another; and when one is found false, or that the King grants any thing they wish, then a new one must be substituted and some fresh demand made" (30). The invective against William also serves to disparage the business of news in general, as news-mongering is dismissed as a cowardly and false activity: "of all the Trades in England, that of a News-monger is most numerous; and it is a most easie thing for one person to give birth to an hundred sham-stories that have not a syllable of Truth in them, while he keeps himself *Incognito*, and is not bound to prove what he says" (32). In an attempt to circumvent such "*False News and Reports,*" James also increased the frequency of the *London Gazette* from two to three issues a week.[104] The *Gazette* promoted James's cause by minimizing the Prince of Orange's activities at the same time as it republished James's proclamations.

The "sham-stories," however, continued to circulate. Bohun observes that because neither *Reflections* nor *The Dutch Design Anatomized* was "suffered to print the Declaration it self," then "what they said of it, was neither regarded, nor believed by any of the Protestants, and served only to exasperate the Nation the more against them."[105] Finally, however, finding that his attempts to counter the "sham-stories" were still proving ineffectual, James authorized the printing of the complete text of the *Declaration*.[106] The author of *The Prince of Orange His Declaration Shewing the Reasons Why He Invades England: With a Short Preface, and Some Modest Remarks on It* confirms the way in which the suppression of the document has added to its appeal: "nothing could be more eagerly desired, than a Sight of the Prince of *Orange's* Declaration; For the Expectations of most Men are, That some Extraordinary Secrets, some hidden Works of Darkness should be reveal'd, and brought to Light; as generally those, who yet never saw the Prince's Declaration, do still believe."[107] He suggests that he has chosen to print the *Declaration* so that the reader can see that it contains no "Extraordinary Secrets" that would justify "so Bloody an Enterprise" as the invasion of Britain (3). As the author argues, "if others impartially Peruse the Declaration, we doubt not but 'twill Convince them, that they give no Reason powerful enough

---

[104] *London Gazette*, November 15, 1688. [105] Bohun, *History of the Desertion*, 36.
[106] Schwoerer, "Propaganda," 860.
[107] *The Prince of Orange His Declaration Shewing the Reasons Why He Invades England: With a Short Preface, and Some Modest Remarks on It* (London, 1688), 3.

to Justifie so Bloody an Enterprise, as this."[108] It was indeed a gamble to further disseminate the text of the *Declaration*, but James and his advisors were hoping to dampen down the emotional appeal of the document. In spite of such hopes, the printing of the actual words seems to have only further contributed to the *Declaration*'s potency as it was also answered by more printed works defending it. A number of these defenses were produced by the skilled team of writers working for William. Pamphlets such as *A Review of the Reflections on the Prince of Orange's Declaration*, authored by Burnet and published "By the Prince of Orange's special command,"[109] as well as *An Answer to a Paper, Intitled, Reflections on the Prince of Orange's Declaration*, countered the *Reflections* paragraph by paragraph.[110] In combination with the other mediations referencing the *Declaration*, these pamphlets worked to reinforce an oppositional media "buzz" through which it was impossible for James's messages to penetrate.

James's authority was further undermined by the publication of more official documents objecting to his policies. On November 17, 1688, the Archbishops of Canterbury and York Elect and the Bishops of Ely and Rochester presented a petition to the King indicating that "the only visible way to preserve Your Majesty and this Your Kingdom, would be the Calling of a Parliament, Regular and Free in all its Circumstances" and beseeching his Majesty to "use such means for the preventing the Effusion of Christian blood."[111] On November 20, 1688, James published his response, promising "UPON THE FAITH OF A KING" that he would call a parliament when the Prince of Orange had "Quitted this Realm" and protesting, "How is it possible a Parliament should be Free in all its Circumstances, as You Petition for, whil'st an Enemy is in the Kingdom, and can make a Return of near an Hundred Voices."[112] The two documents were published together for Thomas Pyke in Pall-Mall as *The Petition of the LORDS Spiritual and Temporal for the Calling of a Free Parliament Together, with His Majesty's Gracious Answer to Their Lordships*. Finally, on 30 November 1688, James issued another proclamation, his final one as monarch, calling for a parliament and offering commissioners to treat with the Prince of Orange.[113] The increasing frequency of

---

[108] Ibid., 3.
[109] Gilbert Burnet, *A Review of the Reflections on the Prince of Orange's Declaration* (London, 1688).
[110] *An Answer to a Paper, Intitled, Reflections on the Prince of Orange's Declaration* (London, 1688).
[111] Bohun, *History of the Desertion*, 44.
[112] *The Petition of the LORDS Spiritual and Temporal for the Calling of a Free Parliament Together, with His Majesty's Gracious Answer to Their Lordships* (London, 1688).
[113] James II/VII, *By the King a Proclamation for the Speedy Calling of a Parliament* (London, 1688).

publication at this point suggests that official documents were being issued by James not out of any predetermined policy but out of desperation to reach his subjects. Such reactivity proved hollow. In a burst of subjectivity uncommon in his diary of the times, Narcissus Luttrell remarked regarding these last-minute concessions: "O rare invasion! To occasion so many gratious acts in restoring things to their old legall foundation, which hath been the work of some years past to unhinge!"[114] James's concessions came too late, as, amid the ongoing desertion by the government armed forces and the growing support of nobles, the Prince of Orange made his way to London.

As William's forces gained ground, even the government-authorized *London Gazette* began to change its policy of providing very little commentary on William's movements. On November 19, 1688, for example, the *Gazette* noted "That the Prince of *Orange* does every day go out to view the Country with the Mareschal *de Schomberg*, and last *Saturday* he went to *Autry*, 12 Miles from thence, and returned thither at Night."[115] It also added that "The Prince of *Orange* had forbid Praying for the King, who is now left out both by Churchmen and Dissenters in their Prayers. The new Prayers made on the occasion of this Invasion are lay'd aside, and Burnet's Prayer for the Prince of *Orange* is used by some." On December 13, 1688, the *Gazette* marked the change of regime by publishing the *Declaration of the Lords Spiritual and Temporal* asking the Prince of Orange to call a free parliament because the King had now "withdrawn himself."[116] (James had, in fact, attempted to leave England on December 11, 1688, but was apprehended and ignominiously escorted back to London before fleeing again a week later.)[117]

On December 18, 1688, William arrived at St. James's Palace, James having left London early that morning and successfully crossed over to France via Rochester. The last official document printed on English soil with James's name on it represents the final diminishing of the authority of the King.[118] The *Kings Letter TO THE Earl of Feversham*, his General, was published December 11, 1688, and represents James not as the royal monarch, but as a desperate man whose plans have been thwarted and

---

[114] Luttrell, *Historical Relation*, 1: 468. [115] *London Gazette*, November 19, 1688.
[116] *London Gazette*, December 13, 1688.
[117] Newsletter to Edmond Poley, December 14, 1688, British Library, Add. MS 45731, fol. 83.
[118] A manuscript newsletter sent to John Ellis indicates: "The King is said to have left a paper behind him, directed to the Earl of Feversham, for him to disband the army; which his Lordship read at the head of most regiments, and accordingly disbanded them, some with, others without their arms" (Dover, *Letters to John Ellis*, 2: 352–53).

whose only recourse is to fly with his wife and child beyond the borders of the nation: "Things being come to that extremity, that I have been forced to send away the Queen, and my Son the Prince of *Wales*, that they might not fall into my Enemies Hands, which they must have done, if they had staid; I am obliged to do the same thing, and to endeavour to secure Myself, the best I can."[119] James's letter suggests that he has lost any official agency he once had and can only at this point admit the truth of the advice of his commanders: "though I know there are many Loyal and brave Men amongst you, both Officers and Soldiers, yet you know, that both you, and several of the General Officers, and Men of the Army told me, it was no ways advisable for Me to venture Myself at their Head, or to think to fight the Prince of *Orange* with them." The King's final official words were not delivered via a proclamation or declaration but as a letter of personal thanks and nostalgia. In the end, he writes not as a monarch issuing directives, but as a man scribbling before he flees for his life: "And now there remains only for Me to thank you, and all those both Officers and Soldiers who have stuck to Me, and been truly Loyal. I hope you will still retain the same Fidelity to Me." The letter abruptly breaks off: "Time presses, so that I can say no more."

A manuscript newsletter sent to John Ellis in Ireland describes the riots that broke out in London in the midst of James's departure and the subsequent regime change, commenting that, having burned and destroyed several Catholic chapels, the mob "carried all the trumpery in mock procession and triumph, with oranges on the tops of swords and staves; thus victoriously passing by the Guards that were drawn up."[120] As Boyer would later indicate, the next site of attack was the King's printer, as the mob made its way to "Harry Hill's Printing-house, which they served in like manner."[121] Boyer writes that in the midst of the conflagration, "all the Paper" that was found in the printing-house, "whether printed or not, serv[ed] only for a Bonfire" (1: 271). In the end, James's attempts to "perswade" his subjects of his case through his official printed words were consumed in their fires of celebration at his departure.

"Knowing-Showing" the Revolution in Cultural Memory

Whereas James's printed words literally went up in flames, William's *Declaration* enjoyed a long afterlife and proved an important marker in

---

[119] *The Kings Letter TO THE Earl of Feversham* (London, 1688).
[120] Dover, *Letters to John Ellis*, 2: 351.   [121] Boyer, *History*, 1: 271.

the contemporary shaping of cultural memory of the 1688 Revolution and its later reshaping by commentators like Macaulay and Trevelyan. The *Declaration* was utilized to support competing positions during the Convention Parliament held in January and February 1689. Arguing against offering William the crown, for example, *An Honest Man's Wish for the Prince of Orange* refers to the Prince's assurance in his "own most Gracious Declaration" that "He came to preserve the Right of Succession," not to seek kingship himself.[122] On the other hand, William himself continued to refer to the *Declaration* during the Convention, suggesting that the claims of the *Declaration* were not in opposition to his adoption of monarchical authority.[123] William's *Declaration* eventually served as a template for the *Declaration of Rights* and the subsequent Bill of Rights, the foundation of the new regime.[124] As Schwoerer notes, the *Declaration of Rights* was read out to William and Mary in a carefully choreographed ceremony in the Banqueting Hall on February 13, 1689. The House of Commons subsequently "requested a written copy of William's speech" after the ceremony, and the House of Lords "upon receiving the official version, ordered William's response to be printed and published with the Declaration of Rights."[125]

In addition to serving as a draft version of the official document known as the Bill of Rights, William's original *Declaration* was also included, along with other official documents, in early histories of the 1688 Revolution. Scholars have examined the use of printed works in the evolution of historiography dating from the British Civil Wars, when popular printed works like newsbooks, newspapers and newsletters began to be used by writers seeking to construct the history of events. Michael Mendle suggests that the "historicity of news" developed when newsbooks began to include dates in the mid-1640s: "What turned one moment into history was the succeeding moment; one needed to collect the record of the story."[126] Writers giving an account of events drew from printed

---

[122] *An Honest Man's Wish for the Prince of Orange* ([London?], 1688).
[123] William himself saw the *Declaration* playing a role in establishing the new basis for the state, as he addressed the Members of Parliament he had summoned on December 26, 1688, asking them to advise him on "the best of manner how to pursue the ends of his Declaration" (Boyer, *History*, 1: 307).
[124] In *The Declaration of Rights, 1689*, Schwoerer explores in painstaking detail the differences and similarities between William's *Declaration* and the *Declaration of Rights*.
[125] Lois G. Schwoerer, "The Glorious Revolution as Spectacle: A New Perspective," in *England's Rise to Greatness, 1660–1763*, ed. Stephen Baxter (Berkeley: University of California Press, 1983), 130.
[126] Michael Mendle, "Preserving the Ephemeral: Reading, Collecting, and the Pamphlet Culture of Seventeenth-Century England," in *Books and Readers in Early Modern England: Material Studies*, ed. Jennifer Andersen and Elizabeth Sauer (Philadelphia: University of Pennsylvania Press, 2001),

ephemera as a source of information. In his *A Short View of the Late Troubles*, William Dugdale, for example, refers to the use of printed papers, including the "*Perfect Diurnal* and the *Weekly Accompt*": "What falleth within my own cognizance, I deliver with my own words: what is beyond my knowledge, in the words of my Authors; most of which I have quoted: the rest being taken from the common *Mercuries*, and other public-licensed Narratives of the chiefest occurrences in those times."[127] Later historians also drew from these sources. In *Memorials of the English Affairs* (1682), Bulstrode Whitelocke gave an account of "*What Passed from the Beginning of the Reign of King Charles the First, to King Charles the Second His Happy Restauration*" by incorporating not only "Messages, Letters, Remonstrances" but also "Petitions, Representations, Addresses, Votes, Conferences, Orders, Informations, Proclamations, Declarations and Proposals."[128]

In the wake of the 1688 Revolution, printed sources again provided the basis for retrospective narratives of events. *An Account of the Proceedings and Transactions That Have Happened in the Kingdom of England* notes that its information is "Impartially Related from the best and most Authentick INTELLIGENCE and ADVICE."[129] It reprints almost verbatim, for example, the notice in the November 2–5, 1688, edition of the *London Gazette* about the first sighting of the Prince's fleet, even reproducing the comment on the weather: "On the third of *November*, about eleven of the Clock, about half Seas over, the *Dutch* Fleet was discovered, and about five in the Afternoon passed by *Dover*, steering a Channel Course Westward, the Wind at East, North-East, a very fresh Gale" (1). Like their earlier counterparts, writers seeking to give an account of the events of 1688 also drew on official public documents, particularly the Prince of Orange's *Declaration*. But the fact that, as Mendle suggests, the collection and reprinting of printed documents had become a common practice by the end of the seventeenth century allowed for more experimentation with the genre. Accordingly, writers constructing the history of the events of 1688 demonstrate a new degree of self-consciousness about

---

202. See also Matthew Neufeld, *The Civil Wars After 1660: Public Remembering in Late Stuart England* (Woodbridge: Boydell Press, 2013).

[127] Quoted in Royce MacGillivray, *Restoration Historians and the English Civil War* (The Hague: Martinus Nijhoff, 1974), 11.

[128] Bulstrode Whitelocke, "The Publisher to the Reader," in *Memorials of the English Affairs* (London, 1682), n.p.

[129] *An Account of the Proceedings*, title page.

the shaping of the narratives they are telling through documentary evidence.

One of the first of such histories, *The History of the Desertion*, for example, was published by Edmund Bohun just after the coronation of William and Mary in April 1689. Bohun originally designed the work to respond to Jeremy Collier's *The Desertion Discuss'd*, which defended James's continuing right to the throne.[130] Where Collier expressed his views through the form of a "*Letter to a Country Gentleman*," however, Bohun reprinted official documents that had been published during the crisis, including the texts of both James's and William's proclamations.[131] Unlike the earlier histories such as Whitelocke's that employed printed documents, however, *The History of the Desertion* skews the reader's perspective by embedding the documents within a narrative that provides a specific interpretation for the reader. In his introductory remarks "To the Reader," Bohun suggests that his aim in his *History* is to address the concerns of those of the Church of England who are "discontented" and who believe that "the Religion, Laws and Liberties of the Nation" could have been secured through "more legal Methods," rather than through decisions made by the Convention Parliament. He promises an objective position, suggesting that "*the matter of Fact*" of the Revolution can be "truly and fairly stated" only "by representing in one View all the Papers which passed on both sides, with the Actions which hapned, the present State of Affairs at home and abroad, when the Revolution began, and the temper of Mens Minds in all the Occurrences as they hapned" (1). But although Bohun punctuates his narrative with official documents from "*both sides*," he also editorializes on the circumstances surrounding those documents. Before inserting James's September 20, 1688, *Declaration* promising to call a parliament, for example, Bohun describes the "Disorder" and "insolence" of the government forces in September 1688, the design to "fill up the English army" with "*Irish* and Roman Catholicks" and the King's anger with the officers in Portsmouth who refused to comply with the orders to take thirty Irish soldiers into their regiment (6–7). His inclusion of these details counteracts any possible interpretation of the *Declaration* as indicating the King's actual interest in the welfare of his subjects. Although he suggests he is aiming for objectivity by including both James's and William's documents, Bohun clearly weighs in on the side of William, weaving the documents into a carefully constructed

---

[130] Bohun, *History of the Desertion*, title page.
[131] Jeremy Collier, *The Desertion Discuss'd. In a Letter to a Country Gentleman* (London, 1689).

narrative which justifies the story of William's intervention on behalf of the English Protestant nation.

Moreover, Bohun differs from his British Civil Wars predecessors in describing the motivations of the creators of the "Papers" that he includes as well as the intended effects on readers. *The History of the Desertion* draws attention to the fact that James's official documents were increasingly deliberately constructed with the response of the readers in mind. For Bohun, this suggests a lack of sincerity on James's part. He notes, for example, that James chose to publish the September 20 *Declaration* because "the Nation had become so distrustful of all the Proceedings of the Court" and the *Declaration* was "thought absolutely necessary to assure them that a Parliament should be held" (6–7). Despite the fact that James designed his *Declaration* to reassure his readers of his good intentions, however, Bohun indicates that the *Declaration* was "after all ... little believed" (9). In Bohun's narrative, James's *Declaration* failed to convince its readers that it represented what they knew to be the truth. Bohun represents the King's downfall in terms of the growing failure of his official documents to function properly. Instead of serving, in Gitelman's terms, a "know-show function," James's documents are presented as personal propaganda efforts, rapid responses by the King to situations which frustrated his plans. The *Declaration* of September 20, 1688, suggests Bohun, "was penn'd with too much Spleen and Passion, to create suitable Thoughts in the Hearts of those who had less Interest in the Defeat of the Prince's Army than the R[oman] C[atholics] had" (38). In a similar vein, the inclusion of information about the birth of the Prince of Wales in the *Declaration* "made Men smile." Eventually, Bohun suggests, the official documents issued by the King stopped eliciting responses from readers. The King's Proclamation of Pardon issued on November 26, 1688, for example, was "regarded by no body" (76). Bohun's account suggests that the "know-show" function of James's documents deteriorated into "no-show."

In contrast, Bohun suggests, the official documents issued by William, including his famous *Declaration*, were "regarded" even before they were read. Interestingly, Bohun chooses not to reprint the Prince of Orange's *Declaration* in its original form; rather he includes it within the pro-government pamphlet that disputed it, just as it would have been read initially by those of the nation's citizens who had been unable to obtain a copy of the *Declaration*. Prefacing the reprinting of this pamphlet, Bohun notes: "The Prince of *Orange*'s Declaration could be no longer suppress'd, and therefore it was suffered about this time to be printed with a short

Preface, and some modest Remarks (as the Author pretends) *on it*: In 4to" (50). Bohun dismisses the pro-government editorial remarks about the *Declaration* as "a spruce piece of Sophistry" and instead concentrates on how William's document, despite not being quite what readers expected, revealed to them what their best "Interest" actually was: "Though there was not all that Men had fondly expected in this Declaration, yet here was enough to satisfie any rational Man, that the Expelling this Prince and his Army before our Religion, Liberties, Properties and Government were effectually settled in Parliament... would certainly end in the ruin of them" (72). For Bohun, it was the argument of William's *Declaration*, not the arms of his soldiers, that secured him the nation: "This and nothing else was the cause that wherever the Prince's *Declaration* was read, it conquered all that saw or heard it" (72). *The History of the Desertion* registers a self-consciousness about mediation which makes it unique in its time, as it reflects generally on the power of print, including its own power to create cultural memory.

Bohun's was just the first of a number of histories of the 1688 Revolution that reproduced William's *Declaration* along with other official documents. *A Compleat Collection of Papers in Twelve Parts Relating to the Great Revolutions in England and Scotland* also reprinted the "*Publick Papers*" regarding the events of the Revolution "*from the time of the Seven Bishops petitioning King James II*" to the time of the coronation.[132] The papers from the *Compleat Collection* originally appeared in twelve separate sections. They suggest retrospectively the inevitability of events, as they represent a chronological unfolding of key moments of contention; the seven bishops' petition, for example, is followed by what appears retrospectively as an inadequate response on the part of the King. The papers also attempt to include Scotland in a vision of unity, incorporating items such as "Five Letters from Scotland, giving Account of expelling Popery from thence" (vol. 6) and "The Scots Grievances: or a Short Account of the Proceedings of the Scotish [*sic*] Privy-Council" (vol. 10). Volume 12 juxtaposes "The Manner of Proclaiming King William and Queen Mary at Whitehall, and in the City of London, Feb. 13. 1688" with "The Scots Proclamation, declaring William and Mary King and Queen of England, to be King and Queen of Scotland," concluding with the "Coronation-Oaths" of both England and Scotland. In the prefatory

---

[132] Gilbert Burnet, *A Compleat Collection of Papers in Twelve Parts Relating to the Great Revolutions in England and Scotland* (London, 1689). Burnet took the opportunity of his preferment by William to reprint works originally printed in pamphlet form in *A Collection of Eighteen Papers Relating to the Affairs of Church & State during the Reign of King James the Second* (London, 1689), including "A Review of the *Reflections on the Prince of Orange's Declaration*."

comments "To the Reader," the compiler indicates that he has reprinted "over a hundred" of the "most considerate" of these "*Publick Papers*" and pamphlets so that they might not "lie buried."¹³³ The codex form served as a way of making permanent what might otherwise be lost in the profusion of paper that was produced over the course of this eventful year. *A Compleat Collection*, like Bohun's *History of the Desertion*, selected particular partisan texts out of the vast numbers of printed works that were produced in the course of the Revolution, ensuring that they were "stored" in print and therefore more easily accessed for later re-activations as what Aleida Assmann refers to as "functional" memory.

William's *Declaration* was also reprinted in works that appeared after his death such as *A Collection of State Tracts, Publish'd on Occasion of the Late Revolution in 1688* and *Princely Excellency: or, Regal Glory*, which advertises itself as "*an Exact Account of the Most Glorious Heroick, and Matchless Actions, of that Most Serene and Potent Prince, William the Third.*"¹³⁴ A number of other works such as Boyer's *The History of King William the Third. In III Parts* (1702–03) and Richard Steele's *The Crisis, or, a Discourse Representing, from the Most Authentick Records, the Just Causes of the Late Happy Revolution* (1714) cited the importance of the *Declaration* even though they refrained from reprinting it directly.¹³⁵ In the process of being reprinted and referenced in these later works, William's *Declaration* shifted from being a document with an official "know-show" function to serving as a key site of a pro-Williamite account of the Revolution as a national cultural memory. In turn, the authoritative collection and reprinting of official documents within such narratives helped produce the 1688 Revolution as a Whiggish *lieu de mémoire* of the nation, plucking William's representation of his intentions from the flow of other mediated events at the time, investing it with authority and storing it for the functional memory of future generations. The self-consciousness of figures like Bohun and the editor of *A Compleat Collection* as they collected and printed official documents indicates the way in which, at the conclusion of the seventeenth century, the perception of living at a time of media change generated a new awareness of the importance of print in the process of constructing future impressions. In the years following his coronation with his wife Mary, William and his advisors and promoters launched into an

---

¹³³ Burnet, *A Compleat Collection of Papers*, 239.
¹³⁴ *A Collection of State Tracts*, vol. 1, and J. A., *Princely Excellency: or, Regal Glory* (London, 1702).
¹³⁵ Boyer, *History*, and Steele, *The Crisis*. Boyer notes that for the second and third parts he "had Recourse" to "Publick and Authentick Records" as well as his own experiences and eyewitness accounts (1: xxii).

unprecedented printed propaganda campaign as they deployed "speeches, sermons, histories, political treatises, panegyrical poems, broadside ballads, and portraits, prints, medals and ceremonies" to support their legitimacy.[136] Underpinning that legitimacy was the *Declaration* as it wound its way through re-activations by means of numerous mediations.

At the same time, as Burnet's anecdote regarding "Lilliburlero" suggests, the 1688 Revolution took place during a time when the medium of orality was still very powerful.[137] Although Burnet suggested how oral performance through singing worked in the service of the government, oral transmission in fact served as an important means of preserving counter-memories of recent events, those which expressed what became known as the Jacobite cause. English-language ballads in support of James circulated orally and in manuscript in Jacobite networks throughout the British Isles. The Stuarts continued to be celebrated in Scots Gaelic oral culture by poets such as Sìleas na Ceapaich (Cicely Macdonald of Keppoch) (c. 1660–1729) and Iain Dubh (c. 1665–1725) and in Irish Gaelic oral culture by Uilliam Mac Cairteáin (c. 1668–1724) and Séamas Dall Mac Cuarta (c. 1647–1733).[138] Jacobite counter-memories also circulated in manuscript works such as the Scots Gaelic *Làmh-sgrìobhainn Fheàrnaig* (the Fernaig manuscript) by Donnchadh MacRath (Duncan MacRae) of Inverinate (d. c. 1700), while James Philip (Philp) of Almerieclose (1656–1713) penned his unfinished Latin poem "Panurgi Philocaballi Scoti Grameidos" in manuscript, retelling in the style of Virgil's *Aeneid* and Lucan's *Pharsalia* the story of Dundee's fight against William's troops in the Scottish Highlands. The Latin poetry of the Scottish Jacobite Archibald Pitcairne (1652–1713), later published as *Poemata selecta*, also first circulated after 1688 in manuscript.[139] The relative devaluing of oral and scribal cultures in relation to print over the ensuing decades, however, would ultimately work to further marginalize the counter-memories of these groups.

---

[136] Sharpe, *Rebranding Rule*, 344.   [137] See McDowell, *The Invention of the Oral*.
[138] See Jack MacQueen, "From Rome to Ruddiman: The Scoto-Latin Tradition," in *The Edinburgh History of Scottish Literature*, vol. 1, *From Columba to the Union (until 1707)*, ed. Thomas Owen Clancy and Murray Pittock (Edinburgh: Edinburgh University Press, 2006), 203. See Steven J. Reid and David McOmish, *Neo-Latin Literature and Literary Culture in Early Modern Scotland* (Leiden and Boston: Brill, 2017) and Vincent Morley, *The Popular Mind in Eighteenth-Century Ireland* (Cork: Cork University Press, 2017). Morley points out that the concerns of Irish Jacobites were unique and different from those of their English or Scottish counterparts.
[139] John MacQueen and Winifred MacQueen, eds. and trans., *Archibald Pitcairne: The Latin Poems* (Assen and Tempe: Royal Van Gorcum and Arizona Center for Medieval and Renaissance Studies, 2009), 1.

This chapter has provided a case study of the way in which print came to be seen as possessing the "persuasive powers" attributed to it by scholars such as Raymond. James's and William's struggles for dynastic control of the kingdoms of England, Scotland and Ireland, as expressed through official documents, both reflected and contributed to an increasing awareness of the role of print in shaping public events for posterity. While James registered this awareness only as he was losing his grip on power, William and his advisors understood how the printed document would not only influence the public in 1688, but also shape the meaning of the Prince's actions in the future. But as I have also argued, the authority vested in print needs to be understood in relation to its changing relationship to other media. Before considering the further development of the role of print in the mediation of cultural memory in the early part of the eighteenth century, the next chapter considers the role of forgetting in the cultural memory of the 1688 Revolution. It focuses on the manner in which events in Ireland, which were so central to the lasting outcome of William's invasion, were omitted in the subsequent re-inscription of 1688 as a site of what Trevelyan would describe as a glorious "turning-point in the history of our country and of the world."[140]

---

[140] Trevelyan, *English Revolution*, 58.

CHAPTER 2

Remembering to Forget
Ireland, the War of the Two Kings and Cultural Amnesia

Although William and Mary were proclaimed King and Queen of England, France and Ireland on February 13, 1689, at Westminster, their status was confirmed only later in other locations in the British Isles. *The Historian's Guide, or, Britain's Remembrancer*, a chronology of events in 1689, indicates the unevenness of the change of regime following the 1688 Revolution as it lists the rippling geographic progress of the dates on which the new monarchs were acknowledged: "on [February] 19th at *Rippon, Beverly, Lancaster, Hartford, Ware, Royston, Baldock* ... St. *Albanes, Stamford, Alesbury, Wendover, Chesham, Beaconsfield, Rewsborrow, Colebrook, Burnham, Ivingo, Marlo, &c.* the 18th at *Bath, Cardigan, &c.* the 23d at *York, Taunton, &c.* March 5. at *Bridgewater, Bristoll, &c.* the 6th at *Sandwich, &c.*"[1] It was not until April 2, 1689, the *Remembrancer* indicates, that "The Convocation of *Scotland* voted the Throne vacant; and on the 4th, voted to settle the Crown on K. *William* and Q. *Mary;* and on the 10th proclaimed them, and declared against Bishops, and made a new Oath of Allegiance to K. *William* and Q. *Mary*" (199). In between these proclamations, however, not everyone was falling into line for William's cause. In April 1689, John Graham, first Viscount Dundee, began mustering followers in the Highlands on behalf of James II/VII, and, crucially, James himself was intent on restoring his kingdom by gaining a foothold in Ireland. As the *Remembrancer* notes, on March 12, 1689: "K. *James* II. arrived at *Kingsale* [sic] in *Ireland*, and on the 24th entred *Dublin* on Horseback" (200). Reflecting on the events of 1688 from the perspective of 1691, the clergyman George Warter Story summed up the situation at that early point: "tho all things succeeded so happily for the

---

[1] *The Historian's Guide, or, Britain's Remembrancer* (London, 1690), 199.

Protestant Interest in *England*; yet there was a Cloud in *Ireland* that seemed to threaten us, if due care was not taken in time to disperse it."²

This chapter focuses on that "Cloud," its threat and its dispersion. The conflict between William and James, known in Irish Gaelic as *Cogadh an Dá Rí*, or the War of the Two Kings, dragged on for nearly three years in Ireland after William's landing in Torbay. During that time, Ireland came into a new focus in England through a combination of print and non-print media. During James II/VII's reign, the concessions granted to Catholics in Ireland had become a source of concern for the English population, but the pro-Catholic inclinations of James's government meant that such concerns were not represented in authorized print sources such as the official government newspaper, the *London Gazette*.³ Following William's assumption of power, however, Ireland moved front and centre into the sights of the English population as Irish events were represented serially, first in the unofficial newspapers that sprung up in the wake of the 1688 Revolution, and then in the now pro-Williamite *London Gazette*.⁴ As the conflict worsened, and England began to experience a flood of Protestant Irish refugees who had escaped, the *London Gazette* also began to advertise printed works that aimed to inform English readers about the territory to the west that was the site of the conflict. The "Cloud" in Ireland was at this point a martial and political storm, but the printed mediations attempted to assert colonial dominance by mapping out the time and space of Ireland. This was, however, an ambiguous sense of control at best.

In the midst of the increasing focus on the disturbances, the relief of the siege of Derry on July 29, 1689, played a pivotal role in shaping the conflict in Ireland for the duration of the war. In particular, Protestant Irish mediations of the siege drew parallels between contemporary events and a previous Irish *lieu de mémoire*, the 1641 Rebellion, which worked to frame the current war as a providential narrative through which to interpret the rest of events in Ireland. This chapter examines those printed mediations but also presents them in the context of the embodied interventions of one of the governors of Derry, George Walker, who came to London to draw attention to the importance of the siege he had just experienced. I conclude by examining how the construction of the

---

² George Warter Story, *A True and Impartial History of the Most Material Occurrences in the Kingdom of Ireland during the Two Last Years* (London, 1691), 2.
³ As the case of "Lilliburlero" examined in Chapter 1 suggests, however, songs and ballads continued to communicate anti-Irish-Catholic sentiments during this time.
⁴ This was the first time since the creation of the *London Gazette* in 1660 that Ireland occupied such a significant place in the English news.

1688 Revolution after the Wars of the Two Kings necessitated the erasure of the inconvenient matter of Ireland from British cultural memory.[5] Instead of appearing as an important theatre of war determining the fortunes of William's Protestant cause, Ireland was decoupled from the story of the "Glorious Revolution" as the Irish nation and its people became a foil to the Anglo-centric British nation-building project. This inscribing, re-inscribing and un-inscribing of Ireland in the context of the 1688 Revolution through various media, I argue, illustrates the complex relationship between remembering and forgetting in the formation of "knots of memory" in a colonial context.[6]

Newspaper Accounts of Ireland in the Aftermath of the 1688 Revolution

Ireland played a crucial part in the events leading up to the 1688 invasion. In discussing James II/VII's "elaborate reform programme across England, Scotland and Ireland" to promote Catholic interests, Tim Harris notes that it was Ireland that saw the most drastic changes under James's rule.[7] The appointment of Richard Talbot, who had been made Earl of Tyrconnell in June 1685, to the position of head of the armed forces in Ireland resulted in the inclusion of more Catholics in public offices and a drastic remodelling of the army to include a higher percentage of Catholics as officers, non-commissioned officers and private soldiers. Tyrconnell, a spokesperson for Catholic land rights who had himself been dispossessed of lands during the Cromwellian period, was subsequently made Lord Deputy of Ireland in January 1687 (as referenced in "Lilliburlero"). Protestants on both sides of the Irish Sea watched the changes with alarm, fearing "a political resurgence of Irish Catholics."[8] According to Edmund Bohun in *The History of the Desertion*, it was the installing of Irish officers in the English army that turned the troops against James and "contributed very much to what followed."[9]

---

[5] On Ireland's complicated role within the British Empire, see, for example, David Armitage, *The Ideological Origins of the British Empire* (Cambridge: Cambridge University Press, 2000) and Kevin Kenny, *Ireland and the British Empire* (Oxford: Oxford University Press, 2004).

[6] For an expansive historical exploration of the relationship between media and empire, see Harold A. Innis, *Empire and Communications* (Toronto: Dundurn Press, 2007).

[7] Harris, *Revolution*. See also Morley, *The Popular Mind*.

[8] Thomas Bartlett, *Ireland: A History* (Cambridge and New York: Cambridge University Press, 2010), 134. Jim Smyth suggests that under Talbot's deputyship, "the Irish kingdom experienced a process of re-'Catholicisation', the rapidity and thoroughness of which may even have outstripped the king's wishes" (*The Making of the United Kingdom, 1660–1800: State, Religion and Identity in Britain and Ireland* [Harlow and New York: Longman, 2001], 51).

[9] Bohun, *History of the Desertion*, 7.

In *The The Declaration of His Highnes William Henry* (The Hague, 1688), William of Orange had played on Irish Protestant fears of Catholics. As the *Declaration* notes, "The dismal effects of this Subversion of the Established Religion, Laws and Liberties in *England*, appear more evidently to us, by what we see done in *Ireland*; where the whole Government is put in the Hands of Papists, and where all the Protestant Inhabitants are under the daily fears of what may be justly apprehended from the Arbitrary Power which is set up there" (1–2). In point 27, the *Declaration* pledges that "We will also study to bring the Kingdom of *Ireland* to such a state, that the Settlement there may be religiously observed; and that the Protestant and British Interest there, may be secured" (3). But to read the *Declaration* in an Irish context is to realize how different Ireland's situation was from that of either England or Scotland at the end of the seventeenth century. William's claim to save the "Protestant Religion" would have been appealing only to approximately one quarter of the population of Ireland.[10] Moreover, his promise to restore "Consciences, Liberties, and Properties" (1) of the population had uneven resonances in Ireland, given the historical conflict between religious groups there around these issues. In short, while the *Declaration* was designed to address the minority population in Ireland who adhered to the tenets of the official Protestant church, it ignored the majority of the Irish people who were Catholic and largely Gaelic-speaking.[11]

Information regarding the conflict in Ireland was initially represented in England within the pages of the six unlicensed newspapers which sprung up shortly after William's arrival in London in December 1688. Of these, the *Orange Gazette* paid particularly close attention to Irish affairs.[12] In *The News Revolution in England: Cultural Dynamics of Daily Information*, C. John Sommerville considers the way in which "the news media helped to create a new kind of reading public, even a new society."[13] He argues that, from the time of the earliest newspapers in England, "the corantos of

---

[10] J. H. Andrews estimates that "Protestants, though only 300,000 in an estimated total population of 1,100,000, owned four-fifths of the country's profitable land" (J. H. Andrews, "Land and People, c. 1685," in *A New History of Ireland*, vol. 3, *1534–1691*, ed. T. W. Moody, F. X. Martin and F. J. Byrne [Oxford: Oxford University Press, 2009], 466).

[11] In fact, the response in Ireland to William's appearance in England did not initially fall along religious lines. See Harris, *Revolution*, 423 and Raymond Gillespie, "The Irish Protestants and James II, 1688–90," *Irish Historical Studies* 28, no. 110 (1992): 124–33.

[12] See R. B. Walker, "The Newspaper Press in the Reign of William III," *The Historical Journal* 17, no. 4 (2013): 691–709.

[13] C. John Sommerville, *The News Revolution in England: Cultural Dynamics of Daily Information* (Oxford: Oxford University Press, 1996), 4.

1621," "newspapers spread the language of fact throughout culture," as "they gave information a precise location in space and in time, they scrupulously identified its sources, and gave it a bogus closure in a developing reality" (11). The newspapers of 1688 shaped the messy confrontation in Ireland into information for a population which was experiencing a new taste for news. But the "language of fact" used to describe Ireland was also heavily inflected with the language of affect. The January 17, 1689, edition of the *Orange Gazette*, for example, included praise for the "Associate [*sic*] Inhabitants of the Northern Counties" at "*Iniskelly*" (Enniskillen) who banded together to take up arms in defense of their "Religion," "Government" and "Laws and Liberties."[14] The newspaper report included the full statement of the association, including their assessment of "*the great Hazards and Dangers threatening . . . this Kingdom of Ireland*" and their warning that "if any attempt be made, by Roman Catholics upon Protestants," they will "with Gods Assistance" prosecute them "with the utmost Rigour and Severity." While it celebrated the bravery of the Protestants in Ireland, the newspaper also ridiculed the Catholic Irish forces. A report from a "Gentleman coming lately" from Dublin described the state of one of the "New Rais'd" companies:

> they had two blind Harpers instead of Drums, their Colours part of a woman's strip'd Petticoat, their Officers such, as had purchased their Commissions. For a Captain at four Cows, and two Sheep. The Lieutenant for Three Cows. And the Ensign two Cows and a Pig. And . . . divers of the Soldiers are such Miserable dispirited wretches, that being drawn up to Exercise, some trembled, and turned away their Faces at the discharging their Muskets. And when Order'd to the *Right*, or *Right About*, would move the Contrary way round, and could hardly be brought to be taught.[15]

Such depictions asserted the superiority of the well-disciplined and masculine Protestant troops and implied that the conflict would be easily won. Despite its ridicule of Irish military prowess, however, the paper also conveyed the danger of the situation, reinforcing the need for "English Succors" and noting that "if the *English* do not hasten their coming, the *Papists* may get into such a body, as to be able to perform Considerable damage."[16] Accordingly, the *Orange Gazette* also included periodic updates reassuring readers that William was in the process of organizing troops and settling a "Fund to carry on the Expedition design'd for *Ireland*."[17]

---

[14] *Orange Gazette*, January 17, 1689. [15] *Orange Gazette*, January 26, 1689. [16] Ibid.
[17] *Orange Gazette*, January 21, 1689.

After William re-established pre-publication control over printed works soon after assuming power, the new newspapers vanished, and information regarding Ireland was available only through the official *London Gazette*. As the conflict deepened and more Irish Protestants fled the country, the *Gazette* began to include more eyewitness reports from refugees who had arrived in the "Western Parts" of England. A report from Bristol dated March 6, 1689, notes, for example, the arrival of a large number of Protestants seeking refuge, bringing with them little except stories about their ill treatment:

> There are arrived in all these Western Parts great Multitudes of distressed *English* Protestants from *Ireland*, whose Condition is most deplorable; From whom we have an account that at *Dublin* the Protestants were all disarmed, and their Horses taken from them, and many of them plundered and cruelly treated by the Soldiers, who had likewise seized both the Cathedrals and the Colledge; and all Ships and Passengers bound for *England* were stopt, and their Goods and Plate that was found on board taken away.[18]

The report indicated that things were similar in "Munster, Leinster and Counnaught [*sic*]" where the Protestants were "disseized of their Inheritances, as well as plundered of their Arms, Horses and Goods, and many of the Chiefest of them Imprisoned." The report concludes suggesting that "the sad and lamentable Condition of the Protestants" in Ireland "exceeds all the Relation that can be given of it," owing to "the Violences of the *Irish*, who not only Quarter upon them, but Rob and Spoil them of their Money, Goods, and Cattle."

The number of Protestants fleeing from Ireland to England was so great that the April 25–29, 1689, edition of the *London Gazette* included instructions to them not to try to make their way to the capital as it was already over-burdened with the influx of refugees:

> These are to give Notice to all Poor distressed Irish Protestants who came lately from *Ireland*, and are at present in several remote parts of this Kingdom, That they keep their respective places of abode, unless other necessary Occasions draw them to *London* then [*sic*] the Charity of the Brief, seeing they may live much cheaper elsewhere, and many of them cannot find Employments fit for them in the City.[19]

---

[18] *London Gazette*, March 11–14, 1689.
[19] *London Gazette*, April 25–29, 1689. On charity briefs, see Thomas Auffenberg, "Church-State Philanthropy: English Charity Briefs and the Relief of Persecuted Continental Protestants," *A Journal of Church and State* 21, no. 2 (1979): 287–303.

The notice indicates that if they comply, "speedy care will be taken to send them Relief out of the Monies that shall be given by virtue of Their Majesties [charity] Brief granted for that purpose." People in the metropolis and other "remote parts" of England read about Ireland, including the "pretended Parliament" that James called in Dublin and his plans to restore "all the Popish Clergy to their Churches and Abbeys" and to confiscate the estates of all who had been in arms against him.[20] But they also encountered Irish refugees who had experienced such confiscation of their possessions and heard at first hand their particular stories of aggrievement. At the same time, after the second week of May, 1688, citizens in London witnessed another shift of population when a proclamation was issued ordering Catholics to remove from the "the Cities of London and Westminster."[21] The Irish situation was not merely imagined through news; it was embodied through repercussions such as fleeing Irish Protestants and displaced English Catholics.

The flood of refugees was not to last long, however, as it became increasingly difficult for people to leave Ireland. The March 21–25, 1689, issue of the *London Gazette* comments, for example, that a "Vessel from Drogheda" had arrived at Liverpool, but it "brought no passengers; For they are so strickt, that they will not permit Man, Woman, or Child, to come away."[22] A report from Chester dated May 1, 1689 indicates: "We have an Account from *Ireland*, that all Masters of Ships are forbid to bring off any Passengers, or Houshold [sic] Goods, unless they have Passes, upon pain of Death."[23] In the absence of people arriving with eyewitness reports of their own experiences, second-hand news filled the void. The master of the ship arriving from Drogheda passed on information that he himself had obtained from "an Express [that] came to Drogheda last Sunday, before he came away."[24] The report gave details about the losses after a battle as well as the general observation that "the condition of the poor Protestants there is most miserable."

The "facts" provided about the Irish situation in the *London Gazette* worked in different ways. On the one hand, information about the desperate situation in Ireland justified William's increase of taxes in order to pay for the campaign to "subdue" Ireland. The May 16–20, 1689 edition of the *London Gazette* featured William's proclamation regarding the "Nominating and Appointing Commissioners for putting in Execution the Act of Parliament lately Passed for Raising Money by a Poll, and otherwise,

---

[20] *London Gazette*, May 2–6, 1689.   [21] *London Gazette*, May 13–16, 1689.
[22] *London Gazette*, March 21–25, 1689.   [23] *London Gazette*, May 2–6, 1689.   [24] Ibid.

towards the Reducing of *Ireland*."[25] In addition, by representing stories suggesting the brave resistance of Protestant Irish groups against the unscrupulous and bloody-minded Catholics, the paper also created a sense of sympathy and common cause between the Protestant Irish and the Protestant subjects of England, drawing attention to Ireland as a vital part of the crusade for the Protestant religion. The *London Gazette* focused the public's attention on Ireland, but walked a fine line between justifying the necessity for English intervention in Ireland and not blaming the government for procrastinating in sending troops there.

In fact, while William had carefully planned the invasion of England since the spring of 1688, his plans for Ireland were much less clear. After becoming king in England, his more immediate worries were the Dundee uprising in Scotland, and, above all, the wars in Europe. Although William was aware of the "Cloud" in the west and the appearance there of James with French forces in March 1689,[26] it was not until June that William ordered troops to Ireland. In the months between William's invasion of England and the transportation of English, Scottish and Dutch soldiers across the Irish Sea, Ireland moved front and centre in the perception of the English population as a result of its regular appearance in the newspapers.

Advertising Ireland in Space and Time

At the same time as Ireland began to occupy more space in the main columns of the *London Gazette* and Protestant Irish refugees were making their way into England, Ireland was also beginning to be represented in the advertisements section of the newspaper as the subject of numerous printed works. Advertisements, as Udo Fries notes, were "an integral and important part of early newspapers."[27] In her study of eighteenth-century "things," Barbara Benedict analyzes the work that advertisements did in early newspapers, noting that that they "could literally 'turn the mind' (*ad + verto*) toward a topic, propel an event or a thing into public notice, and

---

[25] *London Gazette*, May 16–20, 1689.
[26] Story looks back on the situation at the early stage of William's arrival in England: "the *Protestants* in *Ireland* were in daily expectation of Arms, Ammunition, Commissions, and some Forces from *England*" (*A True and Impartial History*, 3). He suggests that, had aid been sent earlier – or had Protestants not been led to "hop[e]" for "succours" – "it's more than probable ... the Business had cost neither so much Blood, or Treasure as since it has" (3–4).
[27] Udo Fries, "Newspapers from 1665–1765," in *News as Changing Texts: Corpora, Methodologies and Analysis*, ed. Roberta Facchinetti et al., 2nd ed. (Newcastle upon Tyne: Cambridge Scholars, 2015), 74. The first issues of the *London Gazette* did not contain advertisements at all.

make it a subject of culture."²⁸ The advertisements of items focusing on Ireland turned the minds of metropolitan readers westward, further shaping the way in which the Irish nation was experienced and explained. While the reports on specific events gave metropolitan readers a sense of the particular details of the war, the advertised items familiarized them with the imagined contours of the space and time of Ireland.

Advertisements for maps of Ireland began to appear in the *London Gazette* soon after the arrival of James in Kinsale, starting with the advertisement of March 21–25, 1689, by Robert Morden for *A Large Map of Ireland, in One Sheet*. In *Bibliography and the Sociology of Texts*, D. F. McKenzie argues that maps "can function as potent tools for political control or express political aspirations."²⁹ Theorists of cartography confirm McKenzie's claims, examining how maps serve as instruments of power in constructing knowledge.³⁰ In Ireland, in particular, maps were historically used as an instrument of English governmental and economic control.³¹ The most extensive mapping of Ireland was done after the Cromwellian conquest, when William Petty organized "the mapping of nearly 8.4 million Irish acres" for the 1656–58 Down Survey, measuring and commenting on each parish in painstaking detail.³² Petty's map was an important tool in the displacement of Irish Catholics and the redistribution of the lands of all those who had been active in the Irish Rebellion to government supporters and the adventurers who had funded the reconquest.³³ Morden capitalizes on the authority of Petty in his advertisement in order to generate interest in his own map, noting that it is "*drawn from the late Survey made by Sir William Pettie*."³⁴ Other mapmakers also exploited the cultural authority of Petty. Phillip Lea, who advertised in the May 13–16, 1689 edition of the *London Gazette*, refers to his map as "An Epitome of Sir Will. Petty's Large Survey of Ireland."³⁵ In referencing

---

²⁸ Barbara M. Benedict, "Encounters with the Object: Advertisements, Time, and Literary Discourse in the Early Eighteenth-Century Thing-Poem," *Eighteenth-Century Studies* 40, no. 2 (2007): 199.
²⁹ D. F. McKenzie, *Bibliography and the Sociology of Texts* (Cambridge: Cambridge University Press, 1999), 47.
³⁰ See Alan M. MacEachren, *How Maps Work: Representation, Visualization, and Design* (New York and London: Guilford Press, 1995) and Jeremy Black, *Maps and Politics* (Chicago: University of Chicago Press, 1997).
³¹ William J. Smyth, *Map-Making, Landscapes and Memory: A Geography of Colonial and Early Modern Ireland, c. 1530–1750* (Cork: Cork University Press, 2006).
³² Adam Fox, "Sir William Petty, Ireland, and the Making of a Political Economist, 1653–87," *Economic History Review* 62, no. 2 (2009): 389.
³³ See "The Down Survey of Ireland: Mapping a Century of Change," Trinity College Dublin, 2013, http://downsurvey.tcd.ie.
³⁴ *London Gazette*, March 21–25, 1689.   ³⁵ *London Gazette*, May 13–16, 1689.

Figure 2.1 Phillip Lea, *An Epitome of Sr. William Petty's Large Survey of Ireland*. Courtesy of the Norman B. Leventhal Map & Education Center at the Boston Public Library

the earlier survey, these mapmakers recall Petty's project of rendering Ireland a product of English measurement.

The maps indicate what English consumers needed to know about Ireland as they read about events taking place there. *A New and Exact Map of the Kingdom of Ireland*, advertised in the April 1–4, 1689, *London Gazette*, for example, represents the nation "*divided into all its counties, Cities, Towns, Castles, Harbours, and Bays, &c*," a perspective that emphasized Ireland's economic and military utility.[36] Phillip Lea provided "the Cross Roads, and number of Miles between the towns" as well as "particulars too large to be incerted [*sic*] in this place" (see Figure 2.1). His map provides a sense of how to navigate across the landscape, despite the appearance of numerous "Bogs" that are scattered throughout the island.

[36] *London Gazette*, April 1–4, 1689.

Lea also marks the Irish terrain with signs of English governmental and religious order, representing the "Archbishoppricks" with a double cross, the "Bishoppricks" with a cross, the "Citty's" with a stroke with a circle on top and the "Boroughs" with a stroke and asterisk on top. In fact, Lea's map attempts to delineate everything about Ireland, providing anglicized nomenclature for everything from towns to counties to provinces, and including drawings of hills and ships sailing upon rivers. At the bottom of the map, an inset confirms the most important message of the map, representing "Brittain and Ireland" as a combined geopolitical entity. Whereas the map proper emphasizes Ireland and England as separated from each other by the "Irish Sea," the inset image also suggests that the two kingdoms are protected together from the rest of Europe, including France, by the "English Channel" and the "British Sea." Such maps created a visual image of Ireland as separate but connected for English readers, allowing them to track the locations of the war in Ireland and providing an illusion of containment by referencing the earlier English conquest as well as Petty's colonial surveying project.

As Ireland was being represented in space by maps, it also became the object of mapping through time as it was rendered an object of history. The May 2–6, 1689 issue of the *London Gazette*, for example, the same edition which announced the arrival of James in Dublin, included an advance notice for the first volume of Richard Cox's *Hibernia Anglicana; or, the History of Ireland, from the Conquest Thereof to This Present Time*, which was "in press" and expected to be available by April 15.[37] The son of a royalist soldier who had been educated at Gray's Inn, Cox had served as Recorder of Kinsale from 1680 to 1687.[38] He left Ireland during its re-Catholicization period under Tyrconnell and took up residence at Bristol, where he became a supporter of William's cause. Cox had presented his *Aphorisms Relating to the Kingdom of Ireland Submitted to the Most Noble Assembly of Lords & Commons at the Great Convention at Westminster* in January 1689 in order to "show the position of Ireland constitutionally, her importance to England, and the measures necessary for her recovery."[39] Like the *Aphorisms*, *Hibernia Anglicana* is designed to encourage

---

[37] *London Gazette*, May 6–9, 1689.
[38] Richard Cox, *Autobiography of the Rt. Hon. Sir Richard Cox, Bart.*, ed. Richard Caulfield (London: J. Russell Smith, 1860).
[39] F. Elrington Ball, *The Judges in Ireland, 1221–1921*, 2 vols. (London: J. Murray, 1926; reprinted Clark, NJ: The Lawbook Exchange, 2005), 2: 5; *Aphorisms Relating to the Kingdom of Ireland Humbly Submitted to the Most Noble Assembly of Lords & Commons at the Great Convention at Westminster* (London, 1689).

the recovery of Ireland by pointing out its relationship to England in the past. The book is dedicated to William and Mary, but it also acknowledges the numbers of Irish Protestants who were then residing in England: it is addressed to both "the People of England" and "the Refugees of Ireland, especially at this Juncture, when that Kingdom is to be re-conquered."[40] In his prefatory remarks to the King and Queen, Cox justifies William's previous inaction in Ireland in flattering terms: "in Truth, the Recovery of *Ireland* was not proper for Your Majesty's Undertaking, until it became difficult beyond the Hopes of others; any Body can do easie things, but it is Your Majesty's peculiar Talent to atchieve [*sic*] what all the rest of the World think Impossible." *Hibernia Anglicana* provides encouragement to William himself to proceed with the military undertaking as well as further justification for the financial support of the campaign in Ireland.

Cox suggests that despite the fact that Ireland is "reckoned among the Principal Islands in the World," it has remained so obscure that

> not only the Inhabitants know little or nothing of what has passed in their own Country; but even *England*, a Learned and Inquisitive Nation, skilful beyond comparison in the Histories of all other Countries, is nevertheless but very imperfectly informed in the Story of *Ireland*, though it be a Kingdom subordinate to *England*, and of the highest importance to it.

Cox asserts that he is the first to provide an "Entire and Coherent" account of Ireland's past. In order to make that claim, however, he has to dismiss previous histories of the nation by "Irish Historians." He suggests that their accounts are "of no Credit" because "the very Truths they write do not oblige our Belief, because they are so intermixt with Impossible Stories and Impertinent Tales." Emphasizing the "the great Pains" he has taken "in collecting and methodizing" the "perplexed History" of Ireland, he suggests that he replaces Irish fiction with English fact (n.p.). Like the maps listed in the *London Gazette*, *Hibernia Anglicana* interprets Ireland from an English point of view; the work is divided into chronological sections based not on Irish events, but on the reigns of the monarchs of England.

In the opening chapter, "An Apparatus or Introductory Discourse to the History of Ireland Concerning the State of that Kingdom before the Conquest Thereof by the English," addressed to William, Cox analyzes the long history of conflict in Ireland, concluding with the assessment that

---

[40] Richard Cox, "To the Reader," in *Hibernia Anglicana; or, the History of Ireland, from the Conquest Thereof to This Present Time* (London, 1689), n.p.

80   Mediating Cultural Memory in Britain and Ireland

Figure 2.2   Frontispiece and title page of Richard Cox, *Hibernia Anglicana; or, the History of Ireland* (London, 1689). Courtesy of the Beinecke Rare Book and Manuscript Library, Yale University

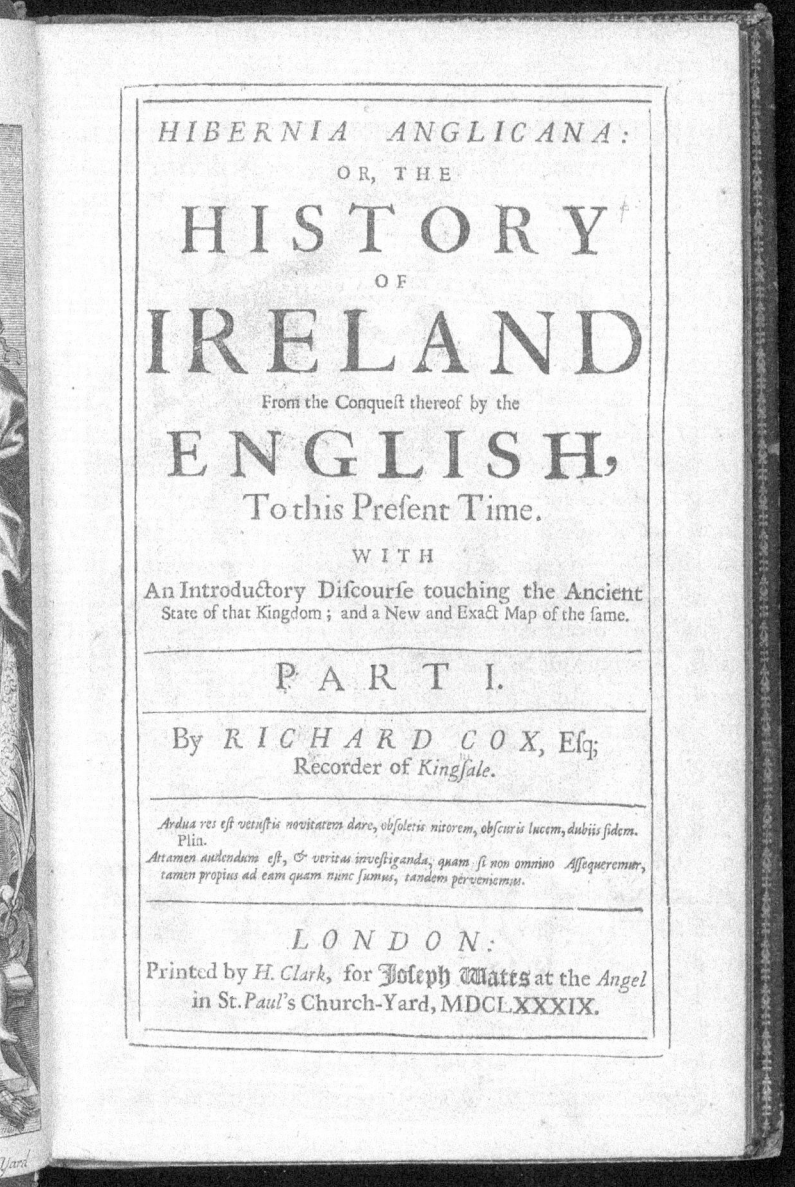

Figure 2.2 *(cont.)*

the Catholic Irish have now "gotten the whole Kingdom of *Ireland* into their Possession; and by wheedling some and frightning others, they have expelled the Body of the English out of that Island." Lest this be interpreted as a deterrent to William's plans to retake Ireland, however, he notes that the Irish can be reconquered: "their *Nature* is still the same, and not to be so changed, but that they will again vail their Bonnets to a victorious English army." Moreover, he asserts that the Irish are indeed worth conquering because they can be taught Protestant ways: "I do avouch, that even the common sort are not only capable, but also very apt to learn any thing that is taught them, so that I do impute the Ignorance and Barbarity of the Irish meerly to their evil Customs" (n.p.). Cox's *Hibernia Anglicana* raises concerns regarding the current state of the conflict in Ireland, but attempts to channel those concerns into support for William's endeavours across the Irish Sea. As well as presenting an English-oriented history of Ireland for those English readers unfamiliar with their nearby colony, the book also appeals to them by featuring "a new and exact Map" of Ireland as well as engravings by Robert White of William and Mary in separate oval frames under a crowned canopy bearing the message "Rex et Regina Beati" (see Figure 2.2). In the context of the book, the two monarchs appear to reinforce English ownership of "Hibernia," staring out at the reader from the left side of the title page and implicitly promising that Ireland will remain part of their domains.[41]

While the maps of Ireland and Cox's history were designed to encourage a sense of knowledge and ownership of Ireland on the part of English readers, another work published during the eventful summer of 1689 provided a much more ambiguous representation of the relationship between England and Ireland. *The Irish Hudibras, or, Fingallian Prince* by James Farewell, advertised in the June 24–27, 1689, issue of the *London Gazette*, was originally a manuscript poem entitled "The Fingallian Travesty" that circulated among Anglo-Irish settler landowners.[42] The poem adapts the story of the sixth book of the *Aeneid* "to the Present Time," setting it in the north of Ireland during the time of the siege of Derry. In Farewell's "adaptation," Nees is a prince of Old Irish stock who lands with his men on the shores of Lough Erin in a fleet of hollowed-out tree trunks because

---

[41] The same engraving had been advertised in the March 21–25 edition of the *London Gazette* as sold by Joseph Watts (*London Gazette*, March 21–25, 1689).

[42] "British Library, Sloane MS 900. See Andrew Carpenter, *Verse in English from Eighteenth-Century Ireland* (Cork: Cork University Press, 1998), 42–44, and Andrew Carpenter, ed., *Verse Travesty in Restoration Ireland: 'Purgatorium Hibernicum' (NLI MS 470) with "The Fingallian Travesty" (BL, Sloane MS 900)* (Dublin: Irish Manuscripts Commission, 2013).

"*the Scotch* ha[ve] burnt" their boats at Culmore.⁴³ Nees is encouraged by a nun and soothsayer, Shela, to redouble his efforts and "march bolder to the Front":

> Humble the Whiggs in *London-derry*,
> The Forlet *Scot* beyond the *Ferry*:
> From *Edinburrow* cross the *Tweed*,
> And make the Heart of *Europe* bleed. (17)

But Shela also indicates that this success will depend on "Fortune" and the hope that "Great *Nassaw*" and "*Schomberg*" will "let our Troops alone" (17). She leads Nees into the underworld at St. Patrick's Purgatory at Lough Erin, and, at the end of the poem, Nees's father, Anchees, chronicles the downfall of the Catholic cause in Ireland, recounting the hubris of Tyrconnell and foretelling the doleful future of Catholicism when the "War-like Prince" William will appear as "*Englands Augustus*" who, "plac'd upon the *British* Throne, / Shall make poor *Nees* to sing, O *hone*!" (133). *The Irish Hudibras* also borrows from the song "*Lilli-bo-lero, lero*" to proclaim that "*Tyrconnel* is no longer K[ing]" (151).

But whereas anti-Irish sentiment in "Lilliburlero" was unremittingly disparaging of the Irish Catholics, the satire in *The Irish Hudibras* is complicated, as it presents a complex alignment of ethnic, religious and linguistic affiliations. Nees and Shela are both Catholic, but they are of different "nations." Nees, as a Fingallian prince, is a member of the Old English, whereas Shela appears as a native Irishwoman. In the comments "To the Reader," Farewell notes, however, that Shela speaks "*tolerable* English" because, as a nun, she was educated at the "English *Court, which something Refin'd*" her "Gibberish." Nees, on the other hand, "*gabble*[s] ... *down-right* Fingallian" because his "*Pride and Contempt of the* English-*Nation*" made him "*despise the Language*" (n.p.). These comments suggest that it is not simple to untangle the threads of native and colonial connection.

The narrative perspective in *The Irish Hudibras* reinforces a sense of the complexity of identity in Ireland. The prefatory comments "To the Reader" announce the author's intention to provide an explanation of "*some Terms and Notions in the following Poem*" "*for the better understanding of the* English Reader" (n.p.). In addition, the poem includes copious

---

⁴³ James Farewell, *The Irish Hudibras, or Fingallian Prince* (London, 1689), 4.

marginal glosses, footnotes that indicate which quotations from the *Aeneid* correspond to passages in the poem and a glossary at the end. The marginal glosses in the text provide not only translations, but also a dizzying array of information ranging from topographical to antiquarian to local knowledge. The narrator demonstrates his familiarity with a wide area ranging from what he calls *"Fingaul"* ("the English Pale") to Donegal, the location of St. Patrick's Purgatory. He cites previous historians' researches as well as providing his own explanations for both mythological and historical Irish figures, including *"Fin-Mac-Heul"* and *"Byran Boro"* (104). In describing subjects such as the music of the "Clarsey" (the clarsach or "Irish Harp"), he includes specific tune names such as "Mageen" (glossed as "Margery Cree") and genres such as *"Ports* and *Portrinkes"* (glossed as "Lessons" and "Jiggs" [103]). He represents himself as an expert on a range of Gaelic practices.

In *Archipelagic English*, John Kerrigan argues that the inclusion of elaborate references for the "English Reader" in *The Irish Hudibras* indicates "a perverse respect for the life and language that are mocked": "the printed version of 1689," he suggests, "attests to a cultural richness in the mix of classical and church Latins, Hiberno-English, Irish, and Anglo-English that the work aims to deride and . . . that it tries vainly to put into hierarchies, and seeks politically to polarize."[44] In fact, the explanations, glossed words and footnotes mock the "English Reader" as much as the Irish people, subtly poking fun at their desire for knowledge about Ireland by offering elaborate and confusing explanations. In his prefatory comments, Farewell explains the title of his work, offering a Latin translation of the word "Fingallian" as "Finis Galliae" and indicating that the term refers to *"the Confines, Bounds and Limits of the* Gauls *in Ireland: It extends from the County of* Dublin, *and part of* Westmeath, *by the Sea-Coast; and is called the* English Pale, *the Ancient Habitation of the* Gauls." Farewell offers further specifics on the Gauls to whom he refers, mocking the antiquarian knowledge of his readers: *"Not Those supposed by* Josephus, *the Gomerians* or Cimbri; *nor Those who were Repressed by* Caius Marius, *mention'd by* Cicero, *and* Appian Alexandrius; *nor Those* Gauls, *who despoiled* Delphos *under* Brennus. *But the* Old English, *called* Gauls, now Fingallians, *to distinguish them from the Native* Irish." The name "Gaul" in this context, he indicates, derives from a Gaelic expression: "Fer Gault, *or* Sessony, *a* Gaul *or* Saxon, *being the Name or Character of an* Englishman *unto this Day"* (n.p.). While "Fingallian" is presented in the beginning of the

---

[44] Kerrigan, *Archipelagic English*, 70.

paragraph as derived from the Latin term for an "Ancient Habitation," Farewell later implies that it has its origins in a Gaelic word. *The Irish Hudibras* draws further attention to the name "Fer Gault" by rendering it and the Gaelic word "Sessony" in Gothic type within the text, using typography to emphasize the strangeness of the Gaelic language. But even as it draws attention to Gaelic difference, the poem itself interpolates the "English Reader" into that Gaelic world.

Farewell also indicates a complicity or at least tacit acceptance on the part of those Irish being ridiculed: "Nor will an ingenious Disposition find any occasion of Affront; it being not only Encourag'd, but carry'd on by the best sort of Gentlemen-Natives of the place, when the Foundation of this Shallow-work was first laid." He further suggests a degree of connection with the subjects of his satire, noting that in order to "find out their Language, Sports, and Customs," he was "often entertain'd" at the "Houses" of these "Gentlemen-Natives" (n.p.). As the poem progresses, the marginal comments also embody the cultural mixing being described as the author begins to provide marginal comments that include Gaelic words and phrases. "Drink is shorter den your Tale" is glossed in the margin by "Skerrit Dough no Skeal" in Gothic type (82). A marginal jest about Irishmen's lack of aptitude for work is accompanied by an approximation of a Gaelic "cry": "*Teague* a Trade! *Il-lil-lil-loo*" (103). No longer do the marginal glosses seem designed to enlighten the English reader; rather, they seem to suggest the author/editor's participation in the culture he is observing. The reversal is evident as a translation of "Suggain" as "Straw" in the marginal gloss (107) shifts later so that the Gaelic word "*Suggane*" appears as the gloss of the word "Straw" in the text proper (110). Just as Nees is led by a native Irish character who speaks perfect English into another world that abounds with Irish history and customs, the text of *The Irish Hudibras* itself provides a multi-lingual narrator who leads readers into a limbo of cultural contact.

During the uncertain period after William assumed power in England in December 1688 and before he finally sent over troops in June 1689, works of print culture circulating in the metropolitan centre made Ireland into an item of consumption for English readers. Morden's map was designed not just "for all Officers" but also for "private Gentlemen to carry in their Pocket-books without damage." It was sold for one shilling, but it could also be "Pasted upon Cloth, with Descriptions &c." for five shillings, according to the taste and pocket-book of the consumer.[45] With

---

[45] *London Gazette*, March 21–25, 1689.

the payment of such sums, Ireland came to occupy a place not just in English readers' minds but on their bookshelves. While the newspaper reports provided a sense of the day-to-day events in the conflict, the maps offered a comprehensive geographical survey of the Irish nation for English readers, and *Hibernia Anglicana* represented the historical and cultural landscape of Ireland. Ostensibly rendering Ireland more comprehensible, these works can be read as "colonialist representations," which, according to Clare Carroll, work to "enact the colonizers' appropriation of the memory, language, and space of the colonized, at once recording and destroying what they describe."[46] Advertised at the same time and in the same section of the newspaper, *The Irish Hudibras*, however, suggested that the historical and cultural landscape of Ireland was difficult to chart. While offering multiple glosses and notes that appeared to offer knowledge about Derry, a place unfamiliar to English readers but which was beginning to attract considerable notice in the newspapers, *The Irish Hudibras* in fact reinforced a sense of the complexity of the Irish situation.

"The Subjects of Most Mens Discourse and Conversation": The Siege of Derry as Media Event

The site of the *Irish Hudibras*, Derry during the siege, would prove the focus of a number of further mediations that shaped the representation of the rest of the events that constituted the War of the Two Kings. The siege of Derry began shortly after James landed when he marched his troops to the gates on April 18, 1689, expecting to take the city. Finding it resistant, however, he left his commanders to lay siege to it. The May 6–9, 1689, issue of the *London Gazette* indicated optimistically: "There are letters from Londonderry, of the 19th past, which give an Account, that the Protestants there were furnished with Provisions for three or four Months, and resolved to defend the place to the last; Which is confirmed by several Persons lately come from thence."[47] More details were provided in the report in the *London Gazette* for May 9–13, 1689, including the information that "There were in the Town Eight or Nine Thousand Fighting Men, who had chosen Mr. *Walker*, a Minister, to be their Governor"; this report, too, confirmed that the inhabitants "were prepared to defend themselves to the last."[48] A report from Chester included in the

---

[46] Clare Carroll, "Barbarous Slaves and Civil Cannibals," in *Circe's Cup: Cultural Transformations in Early Modern Ireland* (Cork: Cork University Press, 2002), 12–13.
[47] *London Gazette*, May 6–9, 1689.   [48] *London Gazette*, May 9–13, 1689.

May 16–20, 1689 issue presented a similar positive account, asserting that "the Protestants in Londonderry continue to make a very vigorous Defence."[49]

The siege lasted 105 days until finally Major-General Kirk managed to break through the boom over the River Liffey at the end of July 1689. After months of concern about government plans for Ireland, the lifting of the siege constituted the first victory in the Irish conflict for the Williamite forces, and it was eagerly celebrated throughout the nation's capital. The news appeared first in the August 1–5, 1689, issue of the *London Gazette*. In addition, *A True Account from Colonel Kirke, of the Relieving of London-Derry, Brought by Mr. Beale the Messenger, in an Express to the Court* was "Licensed and Entred according to Order" and published on August 6, 1689.[50] In the weeks to come, a host of other narratives focusing on Derry went to press. While earlier newspaper reports and printed works had given English citizens a general understanding of the conflict in Ireland, the lifting of the siege provided a specific focus for public attention, constituting a media event, an event which, as Warner suggests, generates a discourse that "feeds upon itself, producing a sense that [it] has become an ambient, pervasive phenomenon."[51] The author of *An Exact Account of the Affairs in Ireland* confirms that sense when he indicates that "the state of *Ireland* in general, and the condition of *London-Derry* in particular is now become the subjects of most Mens Discourse and Conversation."[52] Representations of the siege in printed texts, in embodied performances and in commemorations helped render it a model for later victories as well as determining the narrative through which the Williamite wars in Ireland would be understood for the duration of William's reign. Chief among those shaping the new narrative regarding Irish events was the man previously mentioned in the *London Gazette*: George Walker, the Episcopalian minister who had served as joint Governor of Derry during the siege, first with Major Henry Baker, then, after Baker's death in June

---

[49] *London Gazette*, May 16–20, 1689.
[50] *A True Account from Colonel Kirke, of the Relieving of London-Derry, Brought by Mr. Beale the Messenger, in an Express to the Court* (Edinburgh, 1689).
[51] Warner, *Licensing Entertainment*, 178. See Leith Davis, "Cultural Memory and Cultural Amnesia: Ireland and the 'Glorious Revolution,'" in *Studies in Eighteenth-Century Culture* 47 (2017): 185–205. In their discussion of John Mitchelburne, Sharon Alker and Holly Nelson also briefly suggest the siege of Derry "could be called a media event" (*Besieged: Early Modern British Siege Literature, 1642–1722* [Montreal: McGill-Queen's University Press, 2021], 147), although they do not elaborate on this suggestion.
[52] *An Exact Account of the Affairs in Ireland, and the Present Condition of London-Derry* (London, 1689).

1689, with John Mitchelburne.⁵³ Walker helped turn the siege of Derry into a providential template for the rest of the events of the war.⁵⁴ As we will see, however, the popular focus on the siege of Derry during the course of the War of the Two Kings was to contrast startlingly with the forgetting of Derry and of Ireland in the later articulation of the cultural memory of the 1688 Revolution.

Walker travelled to London via Scotland soon after the lifting of the siege. On August, 22, 1689, he attended William and Mary at Hampton Court, where he was rewarded with £5,000 for his services and was invited to wait on William in the afternoon. While at Hampton Court, Walker delivered a public address to the King from the "Governors, Officers, Clergy, and other Gentlemen in the City and Garrison of Londonderry."⁵⁵ The address praised God and King William and thanked Major General Kirk for coming "at the very nick of time" and saving those citizens of Derry who "were just ready to be cut off, and perish by the hands of barbarous, cruel, and inhuman wretches." The address also vilified the Catholic forces, who, it was claimed, "no sooner saw the delivery and that could not compass their wicked designed against this Your Majesties City, and our Lives (for which they thirsted) immediately set all the Country round us on fire; after having plunder'd, robb'd and stripp'd all the Protestants therein, as well those Persons they themselves granted Protection to as others." In Walker's address, Kirk's arrival is attributed to "Divine Providence," the same providence which was responsible for William's ascension to the throne: "we do therefore most sincerely rejoyce with all our Souls, and bless GOD for all his singular and repeated mercies and Deliverances; and do forever adore the Divine Providence for Your Majesties Rightful and Peaceable Accession to the Imperial Crown of these Kingdomes." The address represents Derry as a site of testing for Irish Protestants, staging William and his forces as "Glorious Instruments" of divine providence.

Walker himself became a celebrity, an embodiment of the victory, as the September 2–5, 1689, edition of *London Gazette* indicates: "The applauses of the People as he passes, are very troublesome to him, for his Modesty is as great, and as deservedly admired, as his Courage and Conduct, and both render him … esteemed by all sorts of Persons, that wish well to their

---

⁵³ Also referred to as "Michelborne," "Michelburne" or "Mitchelbourne." I use the spelling found in the *Oxford Dictionary of National Biography* entry. See C. I. McGrath, "Mitchelburne [Michelborne], John (1648–1721), Army Officer and Military Governor," *Oxford Dictionary of National Biography*, September 23, 2004, https://doi.org/10.1093/ref:odnb/18652.
⁵⁴ *London Gazette*, September 5–9, 1689. ⁵⁵ *London Gazette*, September 2–5, 1689.

Figure 2.3 Engraving of Rev. George Walker (1618–90), Governor of Londonderry (1689). Courtesy of the National Gallery of Ireland. License: CC by 4.0

Majesties, and the Protestant Interests."[56] Walker's likeness was also painted by Godfrey Kneller, engraved by Peter Vanderbanc and, as the *Gazette* notes, available for sale (see Figure 2.3). Walker's physical presence in London – and his afterlife as a celebrity – amplified the message that he was representing.

Walker's address was printed in the *London Gazette*, and it was also included in his printed narrative, *A True Account of the Siege of London-Derry*, helping to disseminate his message to a wider audience. Like the printed works about Ireland advertised earlier in the *London Gazette*, Walker's *True Account* aims to provide an impression of a place foreign

[56] Ibid.

to most English readers. But Walker's subjective perspective allowed for a closer affective identification between English readers and Irish Protestant subjects, for it continued the work of the address in representing Derry as a providential site. Walker's account begins by focusing on the geographical location of the confrontation with a "Description of the City of London-Derry," including detailed measurements of the length and depth of the walls as well as the locations of prominent towers and buildings. Having given his readers a sense of the spatial parameters of the siege, he then provides a condensed overview of events dating back before the commencement of the siege to December 7, 1688, when the apprentices of Derry first refused entry to the troops of the Earl of Antrim. Walker gestures to the exceptionalism of Derry, noting how remarkable it was that the city "came to be out of the Hands of the *Irish* when all places of the Kingdom of any strength or consideration were possessed by them."[57] *A True Account* then proceeds with a detailed account of events from March 14 to the lifting of the siege on July 29, 1689. The affective impact of the account is generated throughout by alterations in the narrative perspective. Although it represents the unfolding of the siege in diary form, the narrative slips between different tenses. Utilizing the present tense, for example, the entry for May 5, 1689 notes, "This Night the Besiegers draw a Trench cross the *Wind-Mill Hill*, from the Bog to the River, and there begin a Battery," but it shifts mid-sentence to the past tense as it considers retrospectively the outcome of this attempt: "from that they endeavour'd to Annoy our Walls, but they were too strong for the Guns they us'd" (25). The narrative stance also alternates, at times adopting a first-person plural perspective ("At this time we took three pairs of Colours" [25]), but at other times referring in objective language to "the Besieged." Further complicating the narrative stance is the fact that when he recounts specific personal actions that he undertook, Walker refers to himself in the third person as "Mr. Walker" or "the Governor." Walker describes his rescue of Colonel Adam Murray in the third person, for example, noting that the officer was under such fierce attack that "Mr. *Walker* found it necessary to mount one of the Horses and make them rally, and to Relieve Col. *Murry*, whom he saw surrounded with the Enemy" (24). The ambiguous narration positions the reader with Walker as participating in the unfolding of the action and also as responding to the larger providential arc of the narrative.

---

[57] George Walker, *A True Account of the Siege of London-Derry* (London, 1689), 11.

A True Account is written in language that Walker refers to as reflecting "natural Simplicity, Sincerity and plain Truth" (8). He includes a precise statistical account of the weaponry employed as well as lists detailing the number of military companies in the garrison and the reduction of the population of the garrison from July 8 (5,520) to July 25 (4,892). In the midst of the calculations and lists which give readers a sense of the day-to-day losses and deprivations, however, Walker also provides his interpretation of the religious ontology behind the siege. In the entry for April 18, 1689, for example, the official beginning of the siege when the city refused to surrender to King James's troops, Walker pauses in his account to reflect on the circumstances in which the citizens of Derry found themselves:

> our Enemies all about us and our Friends running away from us; a Garrison we had compos'd of a number of poor people, frightned from their own homes, and seem'd more fit to hide themselves, than to face an Enemy; ... few Horse to Sally out with, and no Forage; no Engineers to Instruct us in our Works; no Fire-works, not as much as a Hand-Granado to annoy the Enemy; not a Gun well mounted in the whole Town; ... so many Mouths to feed, and not above ten days Provision for them. (22)

They face, moreover, an "Enemy ... so Numerous, so Powerful and Well appointed an Army, that in all human probability we could not think our selves in less danger, than the *Israelites* at the *Red Sea*" (22). Walker reads Derry as a scene of Old Testament testing, with its citizens characterized as Hebrew slaves escaping from bondage. Despite the great odds that Derry faces, however, Walker comments retrospectively at this moment that:

> the Resolution and Courage of our people, and the necessity we were under, and the great confidence and dependance [sic] among us on God Almighty, that he would take care of us, and preserve us, made us overlook all those difficulties. And God was pleased to make us the happy instruments of preserving this Place, and to him we give the Glory. (23)

Walker himself plays the role of Moses within his narrative, as he suggests in recounting the sermon he preached to keep up the spirits of his people:

> The Governour [Walker] being with good Reason apprehensive, that these Discouragements might at length overcome that Resolution the Garrison had so long continued, considers of all imaginable methods to support them, and finding in himself still that confidence, That God would not (after so long and miraculous a Preservation) suffer them to be a prey to their Enemies, Preaches in the Cathedral, and encourages their Constancy, and endeavours to establish them in it, by reminding them of several Instances of Providence given them since they first came into that place,

and of what consideration it was to the Protestant Religion at this time; and that they need not doubt, but that God would at last deliver them from the Difficulties they were under. (40)

The *True Account* concludes with a similar statement to the reader: "Thus after 105 days, being close besieged by near 20000 Men constantly supplied from *Dublin*, God Almighty was pleased in our Extremity to send Relief, to the Admiration and Joy of all good People, and to the great disappointment of so powerful and inveterate an Enemy" (33–34). Like his address, Walker's *True Account* represents the citizens of Derry as an elect group protected from savage Catholic hoards only through God's mercy.[58]

Walker's *True Account* sparked a lengthy and heated pamphlet war.[59] He was taken to task by John Mackenzie, a Presbyterian chaplain to one of the regiments during the siege, in his *A Narrative of the Siege of Londonderry*. Setting out *"To Rectify the Mistakes, and Supply the Omissions of Mr. Walker's Account,"* Mackenzie accused Walker of minimizing the role of Presbyterians in his *True Account*.[60] In turn, Walker was defended by Joseph Clark in *Mr. John Mackenzyes Narrative of the Siege of London-Derry a False Libel*, to which Mackenzie responded in *Dr. Walker's Invisible Champion Foyl'd*.[61] Other contributions to the debate included *An Apology for the Failures Charged on the Reverend Mr. George Walker's Account of the Late Siege of Derry* and *Reflexions on a Paper Pretending to Be an Apology for the Failures Charged on Mr. Walker's Account of the Siege of Londonderry*.[62] In *A Vindication of the True Account of the Siege of Derry*, Walker responded to some of the accusations levelled against him.[63]

These various accounts of the siege of Derry produced by printers in London contributed to a sense that the discourse on Derry was indeed "feed[ing] upon itself" and "becoming an ambient, pervasive phenomenon."[64] Although the accounts differed in their interpretation of the

---

[58] The work also advertises "*A new and exact map of* London-Derry, *and* Culmore Fort *by Captain* Macullach, *who was there during the Siege*" (Walker, *A True Account*, title page).

[59] For more on the differences between Walker's and Mackenzie's perspectives, see Karen Holland, "Disputed Heroes: Early Accounts of the Siege of Londonderry," *New Hibernia Review* 18, no. 2 (2014): 21–41.

[60] John MacKenzie, A *Narrative of the Siege of Londonderry* (London, 1690).

[61] *Mr. John Mackenzyes Narrative of the Siege of London-Derry a False Libel* (London, 1690); John MacKenzie, *Dr. Walker's Invisible Champion Foyl'd* (London, 1690).

[62] *An Apology for the Failures Charged on the Reverend Mr. George Walker's Account of the Late Siege of Derry* (London, 1689); *Reflections on a Paper Pretending to Be an Apology for the Failures Charged on Mr. Walker's Account of the Siege of Londonderry* (London, 1689).

[63] George Walker, *A Vindication of the True Account of the Siege of Derry* (London, 1689).

[64] Warner, *Licensing Entertainment*, 178.

specific details of events, as a whole they confirmed the story of trial and providential delivery that Walker had represented, a narrative that also resonated with William's promotion of himself as the saviour of the Protestant cause in Europe.[65] Moreover, in relaying their interpretations of the siege of Derry as a providential narrative, these accounts drew upon an earlier Irish *lieu de mémoire*: the 1641 Rebellion. While the representation of a superior and vulnerable English population surrounded by barbaric native Irish hoards had been common in colonial discourse from Giraldus Cambrensis onward, as Clare Carroll notes, it took on a particularly providential resonance in the wake of the traumatic events of the Irish Rebellion of 1641 during which the dispossessed and disenfranchised Catholic population had risen against the Protestant colonists.[66] Stories of Catholic atrocities and Protestant providential delivery at the time of the Rebellion were widely circulated in the form of a large number of popular, cheap pamphlets, printed in London but based on letters allegedly "sent over" from Protestants in Ireland.[67] These works professed to give the latest "newes" of the Rebellion and confirmed the notion that Catholic Ireland was the "Mother of all *treachery* and Nurse of Treason."[68] *More Newes from Ireland, or, the Bloody Practic[e]s and Proceedings of the Papists in That Kingdome at This Present*, for example, reads the violence as the Catholic population's desire for the complete extirpation of Protestants:

> There are thousands of *English* Familyes with other Protestants which are ruin'd in their estates, and many forced to flye form their Habitations, divers put to the Sword, some imprisoned, which puts the Kingdome into great feare, and unless some helpe and ayd be sent to relieve and rescue us, we shall utterly be destroyed and rooted out of the Kingdome, for they surpass us in strength and number.[69]

---

[65] See Claydon, *William III and the Godly Revolution* and Abigail Williams, *Poetry and the Creation of a Whig Literary Culture, 1681–1714* (Oxford: Oxford University Press, 2005). The parallel between the Irish Protestants and the Old Testament Israelites that was referenced in several accounts also resonated with the perspective put forward in Protestant discourse from the Exclusion Crisis onward.

[66] See Carroll, "Barbarous Slaves and Civil Cannibals," 11–27. For accounts of the 1641 Rebellion, see Nicholas Canny, *Making Ireland British, 1580–1650* (Oxford: Oxford University Press, 2003); Eamon Darcy, *The Irish Rebellion of 1641 and the Wars of the Three Kingdoms* (Woodbridge: Boydell Press, 2013); and Jane Ohlmeyer, *Ireland from Independence to Occupation, 1641–1660* (Cambridge: Cambridge University Press, 1995).

[67] In *The Irish Rebellion of 1641*, Darcy examines "how Irish politicians manipulated the news and intelligence that they sent to England" (14), comparing the representation of violence in Ireland with accounts of massacres in the North American colonies.

[68] *Joyfull Newes from Captain Marro in Ireland* (London, 1642).

[69] *More Newes from Ireland, or, the Bloody Practic[e]s and Proceedings of the Papists in That Kingdome at This Present* (London, 1641), 2.

The mediation of this narrative continued after the quelling of the rebellion as Irish government authorities at set up a "Commission for the Despoiled Subjects," which, as Eamon Darcy notes, "recorded 8,000 witness testimonies from Protestant settlers and a small number of Irish Catholics."[70] John Temple's influential history *The Irish Rebellion*, subtitled *An History of the Beginnings and First Progress of the Generall Rebellion Raised within the Kingdom of Ireland*,[71] published five years after the outbreak of the rebellion, further monumentalized "the horrid cruelties most unmercifully exercised by the Irish Rebels upon the British; and Protestants within this Kingdome of Ireland."[72] As James Kelly observes, "following the defeat of the Catholic Confederation and the restoration of the Protestant establishment in church and in state, the [Protestant Irish] were anxious to give thanks to God for their delivery from 'a conspiracy ... inhumane, barbarous and cruel.'"[73] Together, these works shaped Irish Protestants' view "that they had narrowly escaped total destruction in the 1640s."[74]

In addition to being shaped by textual sources, the cultural memory of the earlier rebellion was kept alive in Ireland by annual commemorations on October 23, marking the day in 1641 when the Catholic attempt on Dublin Castle was discovered and the rising began in Ulster. As Tony Barnard observes, the sermons preached in Church of Ireland services created a particular kind of cultural memory, "emphasiz[ing] what the Protestants of Ireland regarded as unique in their historical experience: the belief in being a chosen, if not *the* chosen people, who, like the Israelites of the Old Testament, had been refined in the fires of persecution and had survived to be owned with special marks of God's favour."[75] These annual commemorations combined with and reinforced the accounts found in textual materials, consolidating the identity of Irish Protestants around the cultural memory of the 1641 Irish Rebellion. Walker's *True Account* and

---

[70] Darcy, *The Irish Rebellion of 1641*, 12.
[71] Temple had been a Lord Justice and Master of the Rolls in Ireland during the time of the conflict. The Earl of Clarendon also produced a *History of the Rebellion and Civil Wars in Ireland* that circulated in manuscript but was not published until 1720. Portions of it were included, however, in Edmund Borlase's *The History of the Execrable Irish Rebellion Trac'd from Many Preceding Acts, to the Grand Eruption the 23 of October, 1641* (London, 1680).
[72] John Temple, *The Irish Rebellion: or, an History of the Beginnings and First Progresse of the Generall Rebellion Raised within the Kingdom of Ireland* (London, 1646), "The Preface to the Reader."
[73] James Kelly, "'The Glorious and Immortal Memory': Commemoration and Protestant Identity in Ireland 1660–1800," *Proceedings of the Royal Irish Academy* 94, no. 2 (1994): 26.
[74] Ibid.
[75] Tony Barnard, "The Uses of 23 October 1641 and Irish Protestant Celebrations," *The English Historical Review* 106, no. 421 (October 1991): 890.

the narratives that commented on it may have differed in their details, but they were in agreement about interpreting contemporary events within the context of the earlier site of cultural memory.

The connection between the Siege of Derry and the 1641 Rebellion was also encouraged by the fact that more works concerning the earlier rising began to be published in 1689. In her *A Full and True Account of the Inhumane and Bloudy Cruelties of the Papists to the Poor Protestants in Ireland in the Year 1641*, Lady Lettice Digby self-consciously indicates the use she is making of the memory of the past, suggesting that she is publishing her account now "to Encourage all Protestants to be Liberal in their Contribution for their Relief, and speedy Delivering them now out of the hands of the Bloudy-minded People."[76] *A Relation of the Bloody Massacre in Ireland Acted by the Instigation of the Jesuits, Priests, and Friars*, published in December 1689, similarly focused on "*those horrible murders, prodigious cruelties, barbarous villanies, and inhuman practices executed by the Irish papists upon the English Protestants.*"[77] The *State of the Papist and Protestant Proprieties in the Kingdom of Ireland in the Year 1641* drew attention to the issues of land-ownership during and after the Rebellion, concluding by focusing on "how the proprieties [*sic*] stand this present year 1689, with the survey, loss cost and charge of both parties by the aforesaid war."[78] The author implies that lands appropriated by Protestants would be in danger of reverting to Catholics should the current war in Ireland not be successful. Reinforcing the effect of these works of print culture, the annual October 23 commemoration was transplanted to a London location by Irish Protestant refugees. As the notice in the *London Gazette* of October 14–17, 1689, announced:

> the Protestants of Ireland, at present in and about the City of London, intend to meet ... upon Wednesday the 23th of this instant October, at ten of the Clock in the Morning, in pursuance of an Act of Parliament in that Kingdom to give Thanks to Almighty GOD for the Deliverance from the Bloody Massacre and Rebellion, begun by the Irish Papists the 23rd of October, 1641.[79]

---

[76] Lady Lettice Digby, *A Full and True Account of the Inhumane and Bloudy Cruelties of the Papists to the Poor Protestants in Ireland in the Year 1641* (London: Peter Richman, 1689), 1. Contemporary works circulating about atrocities committed in France against Huguenots also resonated with the anti-Catholic rhetoric of the accounts of the 1641 Rebellion in Ireland.

[77] *A Relation of the Bloody Massacre in Ireland Acted by the Instigation of the Jesuits, Priests, and Friars* (London, 1689), title page.

[78] *State of the Papist and Protestant Proprieties in the Kingdom of Ireland in the Year 1641* (London, 1689).

[79] *London Gazette*, October 14–17, 1689.

The sermon preached on the occasion was duly printed by Robert Clavel, the same printer who had published Walker's work, further circulating details of the embodied commemoration.

In "Travelling Memory," Astrid Erll suggests that "Travel, migration and transmigration, flight and expulsion, and various forms of diaspora lead to the diffusion of mnemonic media, contents, forms and practices across the globe."[80] She indicates that "media and carriers of memory appear to be key factors" determining how memories travel, both in our contemporary era and in what she suggests is the "deep history" of cultural memory which "goes back hundreds and thousands of years."[81] The presence of survivors of the siege of Derry and other Protestant refugees who had travelled to London reinforced the contemporary newspaper stories, advertisements, works of print culture and embodied commemorations produced in London and served as carriers of cultural memory during the War of the Two Kings. They translated the providential narrative generated by Protestants in response to the events in 1641 across time and space to the citizens of London in 1689. The year 1641, in other words, became a "travelling memory" which, when re-activated in the context of the events of the siege of Derry, produced a narrative template for the rest of the conflict in Ireland up to its conclusion in 1691. The subsequent victories for William's forces at the Boyne (July 1690), Aughrim (July 1691) and Limerick (October 1691) were interpreted in terms of and served to reinforce the sense of the Irish conflict as a providential narrative.

This re-activation of the earlier cultural memory of the rising by commentators also encouraged a peculiar representation of Irish temporality. In contemporary accounts after the Revolution, Ireland was identified as the site of an endlessly repeating cycle of colonization, violence and re-colonization. *The History of the Kingdom of Ireland*, published by R.B. in 1693, commences by remarking that "The Kingdom of *Ireland*, has for several Ages been an Aceldama, or Field of Slaughter, watered with the Blood of *English* Men; occasioned by their Repeated Rebellions, and inveterate aversion to the *English* Nation."[82] In previous eras, the account notes, rebellions were begun "under pretence of Recovering their Liberty," but "since the Reformation," the unruliness has been "upon account of Difference in Religion, which made them very Troublesom to the Renowned Queen *Elizabeth*, and as one Chief occasion of the Horrid

---

[80] Erll, "Travelling Memory," 12.   [81] Ibid., 16.
[82] R.B., *The History of the Kingdom of Ireland* (London: Nathaniel Crouch, 1693), 1.

and Bloody Massacre in *1641*."[83] As commentators drew parallels between past and present and warned either obliquely or directly of future possible atrocities, they reinforced a representation of time in Ireland as repetitive rather than progressive. "Once, at least," wrote the author of *A Short View of the Methods Made Use of in Ireland for the Subversion and Destruction of the Protestant Religion and Interest*, "in Forty years there breaks forth there some cruel and bloody Rebellion, to the Subversion of all Law and Government."[84] *The History of the Wars in Ireland* draws an even closer connection between the 1641 and the 1689 conflicts, noting that arms were taken from the Protestants and "put into the hands of the Off-spring of the Bloody Murtherers of *Forty One*; nay, not only the Off-spring, but many of the very hands that committed those Massacres, were Arm'd by Authority."[85] To employ Nora's terms, it is as if the same "moment of history" were being "plucked out of the flow of history" in an Irish context and "returned to it," not in an "altered" but in an identical state, almost fifty years later.

As Tim Harris comments, the 1688–91 War of the Two Kings "left a bitter legacy," leading to "a hardening of attitudes and an intensification of hatreds, while at the same time encouraging a tendency to see the Irish problem in most starkly polarized terms."[86] Fears that the Irish Catholics would continue to rise up in bloody rebellion if they were not kept severely in check led to the passing of a series of penal laws that contravened the Treaty of Limerick of October 3, 1691. The imposition of the administrative apparatus that was part of the Williamite land settlement represented, as David Hayton suggests, a "critical moment in the expansion of English control over the other parts of the British Isles, and thus a milestone in the development of empire."[87] In the wake of the war, the Irish Catholic population became the objects of printed discourse, their speech and their customs represented in print to new audiences as dangerous, foreign and, at the same time, a source of entertainment and satire.[88] *A Brief Character of Ireland with Some Observations of the*

---

[83] Ibid.
[84] *A Short View of the Methods Made Use of in Ireland for the Subversion and Destruction of the Protestant Religion and Interest* (London, 1689), 1.
[85] An Officer of the Royal Army, *The History of the Wars in Ireland, between Their Majesties Army, and the Forces of the Late King James* (London: Benjamin Johnson, 1690).
[86] Harris, *Revolution*, 462.
[87] David Hayton, *Ruling Ireland, 1685–1742: Politics, Politicians and Parties* (Woodbridge: Boydell Press, 2007), 9.
[88] Andrew Hadfield and John McVeagh note that "Travellers' accounts in the seventeenth century, reacting to war and the uncertain tenure of property, stress Ireland's savagery, poverty, disaffection

Customs &c. of the Meaner Sort of the Natural Inhabitants of that Kingdom, for example, offers debasing images of the Irish Catholic population, assuring its "Courteous Reader" that its representation of "*a Neighbouring* Nation *here presented to View, may to Strangers appear like a* Piece *of meer* Grotescoe, *an extravagant mixture of* Reality *and* Fiction, *or* Truth *and* Fable"; but it suggests that those who "*have resided amongst, and* conversed *with them, do allow it bears so near* resemblance *with the* Original, *that they have acknowledg'd it to be exact in all its* Features *and* Symmetry."[89] The author apologizes that "*I might, indeed, have bestowed my Pains on a much* Nobler *Subject, but the* Figures *and* Postures *of* Owls, *or* Apes *may sometimes be as diverting to the Eye, if Naturally represented, as the more stately* Objects."[90] While the image of the Irish as animalistic prefigures the simian imagery that would become so prevalent in nineteenth-century representations, the language of "Features *and* Symmetry" resonates with the priority given to measurement when the conclusion of the war led to the expropriation and reapportioning of land. The conclusion of the Williamite wars also saw the republication of earlier texts of imperial control: William Petty's *Political Economy of Ireland*, which reduced the complex situation in Ireland to a question of "political arithmetic" in anticipation of a "new Settlement,"[91] and Temple's *History of Ireland*, which, with its repetition of the atrocities committed by the Irish Catholics in 1641, further reinforced the idea of the Irish as capable of turning at any moment on their Protestant rulers.

The death of William in 1702 and the assumption of Queen Anne to the throne resulted in a rewriting of the narrative of the 1688 Revolution during which time Ireland's role shifted yet again. The representation of Ireland as a colony chronologically on repeat mode and the memories of the savagery of the Catholic Irish may have served to justify the implementation of Penal Laws in the wake of the Williamite wars, but they ill suited the new shaping of the role of the "Glorious" Revolution as a milestone in the development of a Britain based on individual liberty and enlightened government. Accordingly, in the re-creation of the

---

and foreignness, or, in a more purposeful mode, they merely measure out the acres. The major genres are the economic-analytical and the racialist-comic" (*Strangers to That Land: British Perceptions of Ireland from the Reformation* [Gerrards Cross: Colin Smythe, 1994], 17).

[89] *A Brief Character of Ireland with Some Observations of the Customs &c. of the Meaner Sort of the Natural Inhabitants of that Kingdom* (London, 1692), n.p.

[90] Ibid.

[91] See Ted McCormick, *William Petty and the Ambitions of the Political Arithmetic* (Oxford: Oxford University Press, 2009).

memory of the Revolution as a "bloodless" regime change, the Williamite wars in Ireland were necessarily decoupled from events on mainland Britain. Instead of being an important part of the theatre of war that enabled William's assumption of power, Ireland was pushed to the sidelines of official histories of the Revolution.

Forgetting to Remember: John Mitchelburne's *Ireland Preserv'd: or the Siege of London-Derry*

The erasure of Ireland from the story of the "Glorious" Revolution can be seen as early as 1705 in the history of the five-act "tragi-comedy" entitled *Ireland Preserv'd: or the Siege of London-Derry* by John Mitchelburne. Taking its title from Thomas Otway's earlier *Venice Preserv'd* (1682), *Ireland Preserv'd* depicts the unfolding of events in Ireland through the adventures of the main character, Granade, an English soldier serving at the opening of the play in the Lord Deputy of Ireland's forces in Ireland. Hearing of William's arrival in England, Granade heads to Derry just before the long siege, where, distinguishing himself by his military service and his commitment to William's cause, he is eventually made joint governor of the town and leads its inhabitants during the difficult weeks of the siege. In fact, Granade is a fictionalized representative of the author himself, as Mitchelburne had taken up a commission under William and served, with Walker, as joint Governor of Derry for part of the long siege of that city after the death of Henry Baker. Mitchelburne's reasons for writing and publishing *Ireland Preserv'd* were without doubt personal; he was owed back-pay for services rendered during the siege. A House of Commons committee considering his petition in 1698 had determined that he was owed £1,392 13 s., but, according to the pamphlet circulated by Mitchelburne, King William died before the sum could be paid. *Ireland Preserv'd* was written while Mitchelburne was in Fleet Prison for debt. Mitchelburne dedicates the 1705 edition of the play "TO THE SURVIVORS, Colonels, Officers and Soldiers, That Served in the late SIEGE of LONDON-DERRY," suggesting that he has not thought of "any Satisfaction or Reward, wherein you were not included."[92]

Critics have debated whether or not Mitchelburne's play was ever performed. Although, according to Desmond Slowey, *Ireland Preserv'd* was "never meant for production," but rather was intended to be

---

[92] John Mitchelburne, *Ireland Preserv'd: or the Siege of London-Derry* (London, 1705).

"circulated and discussed,"[93] the Irish dances and Irish songs included in the play suggest that Mitchelburne was not oblivious to the idea of performance.[94] Regardless of whether or not it did appear on stage, however, it is clear that Mitchelburne intended *Ireland Preserv'd* to reactivate the memory of the siege of Derry and of the Williamite wars at a time when they were vanishing from English cultural memory. The 1705 edition of *Ireland Preserv'd* includes a wealth of paratextual materials which complement the text and inform the audience about the subject of Derry: an elaborate preface, official documents, poems and maps as well as the prologue, some of which were published separately. While the text of the play re-creates the events of 1689 in an affective manner, "striking deeper Impressions in the Memory" than mere "historical method" could, the paratexts elaborate on and authenticate the historical circumstances. Eager to reinforce the importance of Derry as a *lieu de mémoire* in the history of the British Isles, Mitchelburne emphasizes the colonial connection between Ireland and England. Echoing Cox and the earlier histories written during and just after the Williamite wars, he notes the civilizing project of the English conquest of Ireland amid Irish resistance:

> That Kingdom has been upwards of these five hundred Years subject to *England*, yet could never be brought to understand its true Happiness; but they have bent their Endeavours ever since the first Conquest, to shake off (as they call it) the *English* Yoak; tho', if rightly consider'd, the *English* are no more than their Preservers, allowing the same Laws, Liberties, and Freedom, they themselves enjoy. (n.p.)[95]

The preface draws attention to the special connection between London and "London-Derry" when it recalls the plantation of Ulster and the establishment of the city undertaken by the London livery companies:

> this City and County of *Derry*, was by Grant given by King *James* the First to the *Londoners*: A Country that was always before accounted a Nest of Rebels, ... inhabited by the *O-Neiles, O-Ca'hans*, and the *Macdewls*; and not in subjection till an *English* Colony was Planted there; and to forward

---

[93] Desmond Slowey, *The Radicalization of Irish Drama 1600–1900* (Dublin: Irish Academic Press, 2008). See also chapter 10, "The Derry School of Drama," in Kerrigan, *Archipelagic English*.

[94] Alker and Nelson suggest that Mitchelburne chose his medium carefully in order to resonate with other siege dramas (Alker and Nelson, *Besieged*, 147).

[95] Mitchelburne is particularly interested in the economics of empire, commenting on "what the State of *England*, and the Crown Revenues" were "able to endure" in times past. Queen Elizabeth, he suggests, was "forc'd to keep in continual Pay" a strong fleet to prevent the collusion of Ireland and Spain. Although she "ever paid the Soldiers well," her rewards "consisted chiefly in land grants and "Places of Judicature," favours that were subject to her good will rather than being permanent (*Ireland Preserv'd*, n.p.).

that work, which was of so great Consequence, the *Londoners* spared no Cost, sent over Masons, Carpenters, Smiths, and other Artizans, to build that City, and gave it the name of *London-derry*; they likewise devided [*sic*] the County into twelve Proportions, and each of the twelve Companies had a Lot, which is their Estate to this day . . . . (n.p.)

The map of the besieged city that is in the published version of the play reinforces this association: it indicates the "Goldsmith's Proportion" and "Part of the Grocer's Proportion," for example, inscribing the London connection onto the topography of the conflict.

Mitchelburne also makes a direct connection between the London company's earlier expulsion of the Irish from the area and events in 1689: "those worthy Patrons of Industry, may be justly term'd *Ireland*'s Preservers; they soon expell'd the *Irish* from those Parts; which has ever since been an entire *English* Settlement." According to Mitchelburne, it was the English nature of the city that made Londonderry particularly able to resist the onslaughts of the Irish "when the other parts of *Ireland* afforded them very little help." The victory at Derry, he observes, should be commemorated not just for its own sake but for its historical connection with the London companies: "Providence has so ordered (as by this following Discourse makes appear) that the Memory of those famous Cittyzens of *London*, their Ancestors, and themselves, their Charitable Deeds, and their good Works, will for ever be had in Remembrance" (n. p.). Mitchelburne represents the London company's colonization of Derry as a kind of presaging of the later events, and, likewise, the siege of Derry as a providential recollection of the original plantation.

As well as recalling for readers the long history of colonial connections between Ireland and England, particularly London, the paratexts and text of *Ireland Preserv'd* also remind readers of the important role that Ireland had played in James II/VII's plans for the re-Catholicizing project of Britain. The map "A Prospect of King James's Forces in IRELAND as they ENCAMPED on the Plains of KILDARE August 10 1688" visually depicts the strength of James's troops in Ireland "the Sum[m]er before the Happy REVOLUTION." In addition, at the beginning of the play proper, the comments of two soldiers, Goodman and Servewell, indicate the dire situation for Irish Protestants at the time just before William's expedition: "How is the *Protestant Interest* swallowed up, and we made a Scorn to the *Irish*, that will Massacre and Ruin us all, and under colour of pretended Power, like Wolves let loose, devour our Goods and Substance?" (1–2).

Although the outcome of the siege was, of course, known to readers by 1705, Mitchelburne attempts nevertheless to re-create the atmosphere of apprehension and threat that Protestant subjects throughout the British Isles experienced a mere sixteen years earlier. The action of the play is peppered with servants bringing "expresses" that assert pieces of information or contradict the assertions from previous expresses, recalling for readers the sense of uncertainty at the time of the conflict. The maps encourage this sense of tension. The map of "LONDON-DERRY" indicates the sacrifices that the besieged were willing to make as it illustrates where they set fire to the suburbs surrounding the walls of the city. The "Survey of the CITY of LONDON-DERRY as it was Besieged by the Irish Army" further depicts the odds faced by the Protestants in Derry, showing the city surrounded by encampments (see Figure 2.4). The key, "A Description of the CITY, the OUTWORKS, and the Enemy's CAMP," lists the strengths of both sides as a kind of balance sheet. On the one hand, it provides details on the bastions of Londonderry's walls, and on the other, it describes the Jacobite fortifications, including trenches, batteries, and ditches that have been dug into the land. The tension between these two sides is graphically depicted here by the image of the tall ship straining against the boom that was erected by James's troops to prevent the relief of the siege by William. The entire last section of play encourages this sense of tension as its scenes alternate between "The Irish Camp" and inside the city walls.

Like the earlier representations of Derry, *Ireland Preserv'd* also suggests the role of Providence in tipping the balance of the siege toward the Protestant cause. Particularly telling here is Granade's series of four "Prophetick" dreams: a "Bloody Sword" hanging over his head, "pointing to the North"; an "Army on their Flight"; "a City in Flames" and "Hundreds starving for want of Food"; and, finally, a great feast and "Honour and Renown" attending him "at the Gate" (59–60). In his bleakest moments, Granade is also sustained by an imagined dialogue between Britania [*sic*] and Hibernia. Britania is "shaded over with a black Veil," suggesting her identification with and sympathy for the nation of Ireland, with Hibernia "Weeping at her Feet" and indicating that she has "nothing left but one poor Town, and that in Flames" (124). Mitchelburne imagines the nations familiarly here as Empress and Queen, mother and daughter, with Britania "melting with Compassion, between Joy and Grief" and assuring Hibernia that "*you shall have timely Succours*" in the form of "a *True Born Briton*" who "*shall your Town preserve, and dear* Hibernia *shall be as great as ever*" (124). Here, Mitchelburne's emphasis is not on sending over English troops to come to Ireland's aid, but on activating the Britishness of those who are already in Ireland.

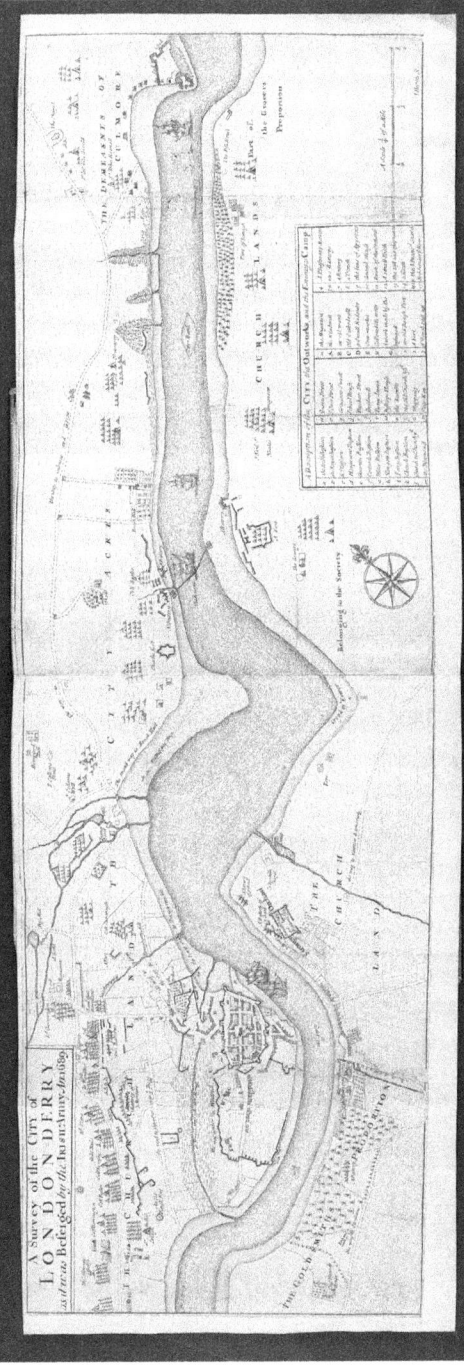

Figure 2.4 "A Survey of the CITY of LONDON-DERRY" from John Mitchelburne, *Ireland Preserv'd* (London, 1705). Courtesy of the British Library

As well as reinforcing the importance of Ireland within a British context, Mitchelburne is also eager to represent the conflict in Derry in a wider European perspective. In the preface he asserts that the port of Derry was "the last Stake" not only in resisting James II/VII's occupation of Ireland after the 1688 Revolution, but ultimately in preventing the French King Louis XIV from launching an invasion of England and eventually "Establish[ing] his Designs on *Europe*" (n.p.). Drawing again from Cox, he paints for his readers the series of dire circumstances that would have ensued had Derry fallen to the Jacobite forces: "The *Irish* Wool wou'd have cloath'd [Louis's] Armies, her Plenty wou'd have fed them, her Oak wou'd have built their Navies; and all these wou'd have endanger'd the Liberties of *Britan* [*sic*], and shook the Foundation of her State." The French King would have confiscated Protestant estates, which "together with the Publick Revenues, wou'd have maintain'd a Formidable Fleet and Army" for him. Mitchelburne emphasizes that the future of the entire British Isles and Protestant Europe in 1689 "hung by [the] slender Thred" of the fate of Derry (n.p.).

The poem "To the Honourable Colonel *John Michelburn*, late [G]overnour of *London-Derry*" by "N.T." included in the prefatory material reinforces the metaphor of Derry as the "last Stake," going so far as to attribute "Europe's Freedom" in the present to the earlier siege: "*This her last Stake, which if the Foe had won, / Lost* Europe *had for ever been undone*" (n.p.). The poem addresses "you brave Warriors" who have "preserv'd" Europe's "Rights" since Derry:

> *Forgive th' impartial Muse if she declare*
> *That* Derry's *Debtors for your Fame you are.*
> *Her loss your Fields of Action would forestall,*
> *For ever buried under* Derry's *Wall.*
> *Fam'd* Schellenberg *in silence wou'd remain,*
> *And* Blenheim's *self a poor inglorious Plain:*
> *To* Derry's *bold Defence those Wreaths you owe*
> *The Laurels that in* Hocksted's *Valleys grow:*
> *To* Derry's *Chief the Triumphs of that Day,*
> *And all the Blessings of our* ANNA's *Sway.* (n.p.)

The poem links current events of the War of the Spanish Succession to the victory at Derry. By re-animating the circumstances of Derry through the text and paratexts in *Ireland Preserv'd*, Mitchelburne attempted not only to gain his back-pay, but also to remind readers of the importance of Ireland to Britain and Europe both historically and in the present.

But the case of *Ireland Preserv'd* also speaks to larger systems at work in the establishment of cultural memory – and cultural amnesia – in the

British archipelago. In his prologue, Mitchelburne recalls how news of the lifting of the siege of Derry was fêted initially in London:

> Derry *Preserv'd! Oh, how it Rung at Court!*
> *What great Rewards promis'd for its Support:*
> *To those who for our Cause, so Nobly Fought* ... (n.p.)

Mitchelburne also suggests the way the event and its participants were unduly forgotten by 1705, however:

> *But how soon was it made a thing of Nought?*
> *Honour, Reward and Favour, quite forgot,*
> *Neglect and Disesteem'd their only Lot.* (n.p.)

In the end, Mitchelburne's attempt to revive interest in the defence of Derry as an important moment not just in Irish but in British and European history fell on deaf ears, for he himself struggled for years to obtain compensation for his services during the siege.

Although Mitchelburne's play and the siege of Derry vanished from British cultural memory, however they continued to play an active role in the construction of Irish cultural memory. *Ireland Preserv'd* was republished in Ireland throughout the eighteenth century – albeit without the paratexts to deliberately reinforce the relationship between Derry and the metropolitan centre. Without these paratexts, the play became more easily read as a conflict between Protestants and Catholics in Ireland. It continued to be published in popular form in the nineteenth century and to be performed by amateurs. In his *Autobiography*, the Irish writer William Carleton suggests that "The plays 'The Siege of Londonderry' and 'The Battle of Aughrim'" served as "school-books" when he was young, but he also notes that both plays "were acted in barns and waste houses night after night, and were attended by multitudes, both Catholic and Protestant."[96] While *Ireland Preserv'd* failed to embed Derry into *British* cultural memory, the continual republication of the play – together with its performance in popular contexts – reinforced an understanding the siege of Derry in Ireland as a contested *lieu de mémoire* of sectarian conflict rather than as a manifestation of a long complicated story of colonialism and settler colonialism in the British archipelago.[97]

As I have argued, the original printed mediations of the Williamite wars, particularly the representations of the siege of Derry, re-activated Protestant

---

[96] William Carleton, *The Life of William Carleton; Being His Autobiography and Letters* (London: Downey and Co., 1896), 26.
[97] See the Siege Museum in Londonderry and the accompanying online resource (thesiegemuseum.org) for contemporary representations of the siege.

memories of 1641, memories that had themselves been stored in a specific narrative form and made portable through earlier processes of print publication and performance. Ironically, however, the same images that made those memories so compelling for an English public during the course of the War of the Two Kings also enabled the subsequent "Neglect" of Ireland in a British imperial cultural memory constructed around a revolution of "compromise, agreement and toleration." Ultimately, in the reconstruction of 1688 as "Glorious," Ireland, as a place of repeated and violent uprisings, came to be perceived as an anomaly, a foil to British liberty and modernity.[98]

A polarization of Protestant and Catholic perspectives was reflected in and encouraged by issues of mediation throughout the rest of the eighteenth century in Ireland. There were few presses during this time period, and those that did exist were controlled by Protestants. As Mary Pollard observes, "the book trade was rooted in the English-speaking Protestant establishment."[99] In her examination of Irish historical writing during the eighteenth century, Bernadette Cunningham concurs: "The availability of partisan historical works facilitated by print helped reinforce Protestant dominance by shaping historical memory. It allowed Protestant perceptions of deliverance from Catholics in 1641 and 1691 to become established as part of the official calendar of history, and to be fed into sectarian tensions at times of political crisis."[100] Gaelic Catholic countermemories continued to circulate through oral and manuscript means. Vincent Morley describes the vibrant and enduring Irish Gaelic Jacobite poetic tradition responding to the Williamite conflict, suggesting that "Jacobite loyalties were sustained among the common people by political song and verse in the everyday speech of the countryside."[101] According to Morley, within this tradition, "the Stuart cause was identified with that of Catholicism, the Gaelic origins of the ousted dynasty were affirmed, and Ireland's constitutional status as a distinct kingdom was asserted."[102] As suggested in Chapter 1, as print came to play a greater role in the media ecology in the British Isles, Gaelic and Catholic perspectives expressed through oral and script forms were marginalized.[103]

---

[98] See David Lloyd, *Anomalous States: Irish Writing and the Post-colonial Moment* (Durham, NC: Duke University Press, 1993).

[99] Mary Pollard, *Dublin's Trade in Books, 1550–1800* (Oxford: Oxford University Press, 1989), 16.

[100] Bernadette Cunningham, "Historical Writing, 1660–1750," in *The Irish Book in English, 1550–1800*, ed. Raymond Gillespie and Andrew Hadfield (Oxford: Oxford University Press, 2006), 270.

[101] Morley, *The Popular Mind*, 56.   [102] Ibid., 53.

[103] Moyra Haslett observes that "Systematic discrimination against Catholics entailed that print culture in Ireland in the period was overwhelmingly in English rather than in the Irish which they spoke, recited, transcribed, and sung" ("Introduction," in *Irish Literature in Transition, 1700–1780*, ed. Moyra Haslett [Cambridge: Cambridge University Press, 2020], 10).

At the same time, however, there was also an active contact zone between the Gaelic Irish and Anglophone traditions in Ireland throughout the eighteenth century, particularly in the cases of popular song and music.[104] Writing in 1740 in his "A Dissertation on *Italian* and *Irish* Music, with Some Panegyrick on *Carralan* Our Late *Irish Orpheus*" (1740), the Dublin mathematics teacher and poet Lawrence Whyte comments on how Jonathan Swift engaged with the Gaelic song tradition in translating "Pléaráca na Ruarcach" by Aodh Mac Gabhráin (Hugh McGauran):

> A *Dean* the greatest Judge of Wit,
> That ever wrote amongst us yet,
> Gave us a Version of the Song,
> *Verbatim* from the *Irish* Tongue.[105]

As Moyra Haslett points out, through a humorous description of a lavish feast given by Brian na Múrtha Ó Ruairc, the original song represents a nostalgic celebration of sixteenth-century Ireland and of resistance to English rule; Ó Ruairc was executed in 1591 for treason.[106] Although Swift's translation does not reference Ó Ruairc's politics, it is likely that he was aware of the details of the historical figure. Whyte also suggests the way in which other songs from the Gaelic tradition that appeared in printed form in the eighteenth century such as "Drimin duh" and "Eveleen a Rune" are given a new lease on life in the Dublin social scene: they are "by the *Muses* kept in Tune," despite the current vogue for Italian songs. Whyte provides evidence for the way memories can migrate across linguistic and media borders, commenting that the Gaelic songs that already have "thriv'd" for "many Centuries" are subsequently "doom'd by fate to be long liv'd" along with other well-known tunes "Which do in harmony excel" (158). While the "Cloud in *Ireland*" that disturbed the narrative of the "Glorious" Revolution was "dispersed" in the course of creating a consolidated British cultural memory,[107] Whyte's comments suggest how the conditions that produced that cloud continued to play out in complex climactic cycles within the Irish nation itself.

---

[104] See Leith Davis, *Music, Postcolonialism, and Gender: The Construction of Irish National Identity, 1724–1874* (Notre Dame, IN: University of Notre Dame Press, 2005). Andrew Carpenter also comments on the multiplicity of linguistic and literary communities in Ireland: "Ireland was made up of many distinct but interdependent and interwoven social and cultural communities in which two main languages, English and Irish – or versions of them – were living side by side, and influencing each other at a local level" (*Verse in English*, 3).
[105] Lawrence Whyte, *Poems on Various Subjects, Serious and Diverting* (Dublin, 1740), 158–59.
[106] Haslett, "Introduction," 4.   [107] Story, *A True and Impartial History*, 2.

CHAPTER 3

National Correspondences
Print, Letters and the Company of Scotland's Darien Expedition

In 2010 the records of the Company of Scotland Trading to Africa and the Indies held in the National Library of Scotland and the archives of the Royal Bank of Scotland were selected for digital preservation as part of the UK Memory of the World Register. The records consist of material about the company's inception in 1695, the establishment of a Scottish colony at Darien in present-day Panama, the failure of the colony and the company's metamorphosis in 1727 into the Royal Bank of Scotland within a newly unified nation of Great Britain.[1] As a national subsection of UNESCO's Memory of the World project, the UK Memory of the World Register is designed to "to preserve, promote and protect" "documentary heritage of national and regional significance" in Great Britain.[2] The description of the Company of Scotland archives featured on the UK Memory of the World Register suggests that the material both tells "the story of how Scotland in the 1690s understood the world and its place in it" and documents "the economic circumstances underlying the foundation of modern Scotland and its political union with England."[3] The UK Memory of the World site further confirms that the manuscript collection is a virtual *lieu de mémoire* for the entire British nation, as it "is Britain's collective memory."[4]

In this chapter, I bring renewed attention to the role of Darien in the history of the British nation. As in my examination of the memory of the War of the Two Kings in Chapter 2, I am interested in the processes of

---

[1] "RBS Heritage Hub: Company of Scotland Trading to Africa and the Indies," www.rbs.com/heritage/companies/company-of-scotland-trading-to-africa-and-the-indies.html, accessed July 16, 2020.
[2] "UK Memory of the World," www.unesco.org.uk/portfolio/memory-of-the-world/. As the website indicates, the Memory of the World Programme was established in 1992 as "a global plan to safeguard the world's documentary heritage against collective amnesia, the ravages of war, decay and deterioration" (https.unesco.org.uk/portfolio/memory-of-the-world/).
[3] *Unesco in Scotland* (London: UK National Commission for Unesco, 2016), 27.
[4] "UK Memory of the World."

forgetting involved in the creation of British cultural memory, and I examine how Darien was effectively erased from "Britain's collective memory." But whereas the memory of the War of the Two Kings, while also erased from British cultural memory, still played an active part in Irish cultural memory, the story of the failure of the Company of Scotland was effectively sidelined even in Scotland for over a century until the rediscovery of the Darien papers in 1848. A crucial issue that I consider throughout this chapter is the mediation of the story of Darien as what Linda Colley calls a "parable" of empire.[5] In this case, it was a parable of a failed empire, however, one that erased the possibility of a separate Scottish colonial empire at the same time as it contributed to a different kind of identity for the Scottish nation, an identity that would exist uneasily inside a united Britain after 1707. The representation of Darien in cultural memory offers an important comment on how national and imperial struggles played out in Britain within the changing media landscape at the turn of the seventeenth century. Darien provides an example not, as in the War of the Two Kings and Ireland, of the geopolitical unevenness of cultural memory in a complex colonial situation, but rather of interruptions of memory within a consolidated English-oriented British empire in which Scots were also eventual beneficiaries.

The creation of the Company of Scotland Trading to Africa and the Indies took place not only at a significant moment in Britain's shifting position in the imperial global network, but also at an important juncture in the media shift that was occurring in Britain at the end of the seventeenth century. The year in which the company received royal approval, 1695, was the same year in which the English Parliament failed to renew the Licensing Act, opening the way to a proliferation of printed works.[6] While the process of authorizing printed works was different in Scotland, as Karin Bowie suggests, there was a parallel increase in print publication in Scotland at this time, a result of the growth of a parish education system and increased literacy, as well as expanding communication and

---

[5] Linda Colley, *Captives: Britain, Empire and the World, 1600–1850* (New York: Anchor Books, 2004), 1.
[6] Geoffrey Cranfield notes that the lapse of the pre-publication censorship came about as Whigs raised objections about the overzealousness of oversight of William III/II's "Tory licenser," who was trying to stifle criticisms of the government: "[There was] every intention of formulating more effective and less politically-objectionable measures. But the [parliamentary] session came to an end before a Select Committee had been able to come to any agreement, and the Printing Act quietly expired" (*The Development of the Provincial Newspaper, 1700–1760* [Oxford: Clarendon Press, 1962], 7).

transportation networks.[7] The Company of Scotland was the first joint-stock colonial venture to be "born" into this brave new world of print culture in the British Isles.[8]

But, as suggested earlier, the establishment of this world of print took place only over a significant period of transition. During that time, older media continued to play an important role. In 1695 the affordances of manuscript letters – including their symbolic communicative and connective functions in both informal and official situations – made them essential in the creation of the Company of Scotland. Moreover, letters in printed form also played a vital role in inscribing Darien, as they authorized the news of the Scottish global economic venture, circulated it to a wider public and, ultimately memorialized the failure of the company. The letters and papers of the company were lost in the course of the establishment of the new political and economic administrations and the increasing focus on print in the early eighteenth century, and, in the aftermath of the Union, the Darien venture itself lost its significance in Scotland. Despite the emphasis on the importance of Darien in the formation of Britain in the UK Memory of the World Register, the Darien letters themselves tell a story of lapses of memory in the consolidation of Britain.

"The Life of All Commerce Depends upon a Punctual Correspondence": Letters and the Creation of the Company of Scotland

The 1688 Revolution encouraged a split in the Scottish nation down ideological and religious as well as linguistic lines.[9] Those loyal to the Stuarts continued to voice support for James and the Jacobite cause, but the accession of William and Mary shifted power to Whig supporters as

---

[7] Karin Bowie, *Scottish Public Opinion and the Anglo-Scottish Union, 1699–1707* (Woodbridge: Boydell Press, 2007), 19. See also Bowie, *Public Opinion* and Alastair J. Mann, *The Scottish Book Trade, 1500–1720: Print Commerce and Print Control in Early Modern Scotland; An Historiographical Survey of the Early Modern Book in Scotland* (East Linton: Tuckwell Press, 2000).

[8] See Douglas Watt, *The Price of Scotland: Darien, Union and the Wealth of Nations* (Edinburgh: Luath Press, 2007), 26. Christopher Whatley notes that there were forty-seven joint-stock companies founded in Scotland by 1695 (*The Scots and the Union: Then and Now* [Edinburgh: Edinburgh University Press, 2014], 139).

[9] Jack MacQueen suggests that "After 1688, Latin poetry and Jacobitism became virtually synonymous" ("Scoto-Latin Tradition," 203). See also Clare Jackson, *Restoration Scotland, 1660–1690: Royalist Politics, Religion and Ideas* (Rochester, NY: Boydell, 2003), 49.

well as confirming Presbyterianism.[10] The regime shift also offered opportunities for Scottish investors of all political persuasions as William turned to the use of public credit in order to fund his military operations abroad.[11] The Act for Encouraging of Forraigne Trade was passed in 1693,[12] and in May 1695 a group of Anglo-Scottish merchants led by William Paterson published *Proposals for a Fond to Cary* [sic] *on a Plantation*. *Proposals* asserts that "Persons of all Ranks, yea the Body of the nation, are Longing to have a Plantation in *America*" and argues for the joining together of "A Body of the Treading [sic] Men of the Nation (not excluding either Nobility or Gentry)" into a company that would be supported by "such Grants, Priviledges, and Immunities" from the King and Parliament as would be necessary to encourage such an initial business venture.[13] Paterson, a Presbyterian clergyman, had travelled to South America and returned to Britain convinced that "on the Isthmus of Darien there was a tract of country running across from the Atlantic to the Pacific, which the Spaniards never possessed, and inhabited by a people continually at war with them"[14] Although Paterson first concentrated his efforts on another project, the establishment of the Bank of England, he kept his eye out for opportunities to advance the scheme he had developed of founding a colony at Darien. Paterson and his associates were successful in their efforts, and the Company of Scotland was granted a patent on June 26, 1695, which allowed it to trade as well as to make treaties and plant colonies "by consent of the Natives or Inhabitants thereof, and not possest by any European Sovereign, Potentate, Prince or State."[15] The Act also promised the company royal protection and a twenty-one-year exemption from paying taxes. Because William was in Holland at the time at which

---

[10] MacQueen, "Scoto-Latin Tradition," 203. See Reid and McOmish, *Neo-Latin Literature and Literary Culture*.

[11] See John Brewer, *The Sinews of Power: War, Money and the English State, 1688–1783* (Cambridge, MA: Harvard University Press, 1990). Whatley remarks that there was a "seven-fold increase in military expenditure" which was "backed by mechanisms for raising tax and public credit which if not as efficient as their equivalents in the Netherlands, were at least effective" (*Scots and the Union*, 141). See also Richard Dale, "Exchange Alley and the Evolution of London's Securities Markets," chapter 2 of *The First Crash: Lessons from the South Sea Bubble* (Princeton, NJ: Princeton University Press, 2004).

[12] David Armitage, "The Scottish Vision of Empire: The Intellectual Origins of the Darien Venture," in *A Union for Empire: Political Thought and the British Union of 1707*, ed. John Robert (Cambridge: Cambridge University Press, 1995), 99.

[13] *Proposals for a Fond to Cary* [sic] *on a Plantation* (Edinburgh, 1695).

[14] Edward Cullen, *The Isthmus of Darien Ship Canal*, 2nd ed. (London: Effingham Wilson, 1852), 148.

[15] Company of Scotland Trading to Africa and the Indies, *Act for a Company Trading to Affrica* [sic] *and the Indies* (Edinburgh, 1695), 5.

the Act was brought before the Scottish Parliament, royal approval was granted by his Lord High Commissioner in Scotland, John Hay, first Marquess of Tweeddale, who was later dismissed from his position because of this action. There were ten promoters from Scotland and ten from London named in the Act, and they were given until August 1, 1696, to find other investors who would constitute the company. Half of the funds were to be reserved for "*Scottish* men within this Kingdom."[16]

In the early history of the Company of Scotland, manuscript letters enabled the communication between projectors across the geographical distances between Edinburgh, London, Amsterdam and Hamburg, linking them together in a network of anticipated global commerce in the new economic climate, while printed letters served as a means to debate the economic and political future of the company. Letters also enabled Paterson's formation of the company, as the missives that he wrote on behalf of his fellow Company of Scotland merchants in London connected them with their counterparts in Scotland in the summer and fall of 1695.[17] The projectors' letters provide evidence of the embryonic company's plans in the early months, and they also indicate the projectors' canny understanding of how the affordances of different media suited different business activities. The letter of July 4, 1695, from Paterson to Robert Chiesley, a company director who was then Lord Provost of Edinburgh, indicates how crucial letters were to the company at that point in order to establish what was "necessary to be dispatched before the meeting of the Corporation."[18] Paterson wrote with some impatience to Chiesley on August 6, 1695, regarding the importance of prompt response to letters in this business enterprise: "The life of all Commerce depends upon a punctual

---

[16] *An Act of Parliament for Encourageing the Scots Affrican and Indian Company* (Edinburgh, 1695), 2. The individuals who were initially involved in the company were: "*John* Lord *Belhaven, Adam Cockburn of Ormistoun*, Lord Justice Clerk, Mr. *Francis Montgomery of Giffen*, Sir *John Maxwell of Pollock*, Sir *Robert Chiesley* present Provost of *Edinburgh, John Swinton* of that Ilk, *George Clerk* late Baillie of *Edinburgh*, Mr. *Robert Blackwood*, and *James Balfour* Merchants in *Edinburgh* and *John Cross* Merchant in *Glasgow; William Paterson* Esquire, *James Foulis, David Nairn* Esquires, *Thomas Deans* Esquire, *James Chiesley; John Smith, Thomas Coutes, Hugh Frazer, Joseph Cohaine, Daves Ovedo*, and *Walter Steuart* Merchants in *London*" (2). In the printing of the original Act, James Smith was mis-named "John Smith," and Joseph Cohen D'Azvedo was mistakenly printed as two men, "Joseph Cohaine" and "Daves Ovedo."

[17] Although the letters all conclude with Paterson's elaborate signature, the letters were only scripted by Paterson "by order of the Gentlemen." They are in fact collective documents, representing the perspectives of the rest of the directors as well. Most of the letters are directed to Sir Robert Chiesley.

[18] William Paterson to Robert Chiesley, July 4, 1695, National Library of Scotland (hereafter NLS), Adv. MSS 83.7.4, fol. 3.

Correspondence."[19] While he notes that many issues could be "dispatched" through letters, however, Paterson also affirms his fellow directors' sense that a meeting in London was needed "where most of the Persons named in the Act ought to be present" to take advantage of "the Advice and Assistance of some Gentlemen here."[20] In order for the company to act as "one intire body" rather than "several interfering Parts and Interests," the directors agreed that there had to be an in-person encounter of all the actual bodies involved.[21]

One of the additional affordances of the face-to-face meeting that suited the company's purpose was impermanence, the minimal trace left by meeting in person. This was particularly important at this point, as the company understood that it potentially constituted a threat to English trade and particularly to the East India Company, which had recently undergone a parliamentary investigation into bribery and was attempting to raise more capital in order to recover from reduced share prices.[22] As Paterson notes on October 15, 1695, certain issues are "neither fit nor safe for us to write."[23] Fearing the influence that East India Company directors might have on the English government, Paterson further indicates the importance of keeping "private and Close for some months that no occasion may be given for the Parliamt. of England directly or indirectly to take notice of [the company] in the ensueing Session, which might be of ill consequence."[24] Accordingly, the face-to-face meetings of the company began in London in November 1695, when the Scottish directors finally travelled south.

Despite all attempts to keep things quiet, however, the activities of the Company of Scotland did not escape the notice of the rest of the London merchant community. References in newspapers to the positive progress of the Company of Scotland served to generate anxiety about its impact on English trade. The *Post Boy* for November 14–16, 1695, for example, informed readers of the Company of Scotland's current success, indicating that, even though subscription books had opened only on November 6, 1695, "the Directors have closed up their Books ... there being 600000 l. subscribed for the carrying on of that Trade."[25] Significantly, in its description of this success, the *Post Boy* referred to the company as

---

[19] William Paterson to Robert Chiesley, August 6, 1695, NLS, Adv. MSS 83.7.4, fol. 5.
[20] William Paterson to Robert Chiesley, July 9, 1695, NLS, Adv. MSS 83.7.4, fol. 4.   [21] Ibid.
[22] Watt, *Price of Scotland*, 37.
[23] William Paterson to Robert Chiesley, October 15, 1695, NLS, Adv. MSS 83.7.4, fol. 8.
[24] William Paterson to Robert Chiesley, July 9, 1695.   [25] *The Post Boy*, November 14–16, 1695.

"The *East-India* Company of *Scotland.*" Accordingly, negative responses to the activities of the company began circulating.

In the swirl of communication focused on the potential impact of the Company of Scotland on the trade of the nation, letters continued to play an important role, but now they took the form of letter pamphlets, printed works referencing themselves as letters from "a gentleman" elaborating on his perspectives on the company to a "friend."[26] Rachael King notes that the letter served as an important "bridge genre" at the end of the seventeenth century, offering familiar "interpretative guideposts" when appearing within printed texts, signposts that "proved valuable to writers and readers" as they negotiated between the worlds of manuscript and print.[27] Letter pamphlets, in particular, which emerged as a genre from 1650 onward, put "political, as well as religious and scientific, opinions into the context of a missive between two correspondents."[28] The letter pamphlets written about the Company of Scotland assume the reader's proficiency in what Eve Tavor Bannet terms "letteracy," "the collection of different skills, values and kinds of knowledge beyond mere literacy that were involved in achieving competency in the writing, reading and interpreting of letters."[29] *Remarks upon the Scotch Act, in a Letter to Friend*, for example, a letter pamphlet arguing against the Company of Scotland, begins with a conventional epistolary greeting, "Sir." The author re-creates the sense of an ongoing conversation that characterizes an exchange of letters by noting that he anticipates the response of the addressee. He further reinforces the fiction of epistolarity on which his pamphlet depends by indicating that he is practicing the convention common in actual letters of including occasional printed material, writing to his supposed friend, "To satisfie you that there's such a thing as a *Scotch* Act . . . I send you the Printed Copy enclosed."[30]

As well as suggesting the use of a "Printed Copy" as a source of authenticity, *Remarks upon the Scotch Act* capitalizes upon the communicative affordances of print in employing a mixture of typographical

---

[26] Rachael Scarborough King, *Writing to the World: Letters and the Origins of Modern Print Genres* (Baltimore: Johns Hopkins University Press, 2018), 3, 26.
[27] Ibid., 26.
[28] King notes that they often had the conventional title "A Letter from a Gentleman in Town to His Friend in the Country" and that "The English Short Title Catalogue records more than 6,500 variations on the title, comprising book, newspaper, and pamphlet formats, between 1650 and 1800" (ibid., 8–9).
[29] Eve Tavor Bannet, *Empire of Letters: Letter Manuals and Transatlantic Correspondence* (Cambridge: Cambridge University Press, 2005), xvii.
[30] *Remarks upon the Scotch Act, in a Letter to a Friend* (London, 1695), 1.

features. "REMARKS" appears in italicized solid capitals, while "upon the Scotch Act, in a Letter to a Friend" is represented in both capitals and lower-case italics. The varied typography creates visual interest and serves to emphasize the word "REMARKS" with its triple valences of perception, oral commentary as well as written remediation (to "re"-mark). Although he relies on the affordances associated with the manuscript letter, then, the author of *Remarks* also makes use of the features of print in order to direct readers' focus in his work and disseminate his arguments about the Company of Scotland beyond the bounds of a small circle of correspondents.

Much of the evidence in *Remarks*, however, draws self-referential attention not to manuscript or print, but to hearsay. "If Reports be true, and we may believe what we hear," notes the author, the full sum of the subscriptions has already been raised, and half of the subscribers are "*English Merchants, and others*" (1). The author suggests that there are so many different "Opinions of Men about this Company," and that they "differ so much therein," that he is "at a loss to give you any Account of them," but despite these concerns, he presents a clear list of the "Opinions of Men," each beginning with the phrase "Some say" (1). The writer represents the letter as the first volley in a rational form of discourse and suggests, "Now, Sir, if these will be the Consequences of this *Scotch* Act, it appears very formidable, and should require a speedy Remedy; but some Men may be of another Mind, and I am always for submitting to better Judgements" (1). But all of the "Opinions" expressed in his pamphlet, despite the author's protestations that they differ, lead to the same conclusion that the "Scotch Company" will "destroy the whole Trade and Navigation of *England*, and carry it to *Scotland*" (1). At its conclusion, the document shifts back to epistolary conventions as the narrator indicates, "I … am, SIR." This particular "*Letter to a Friend*" leaves off without the expected name or profession of friendship, however. Instead of a conventional subscription, a solid line appears at the bottom of the page, followed by details about the publication: "*John Whitlock*, near *Stationer's Hall*, 1695" (1). *Remarks* presents the affairs of the Company of Scotland as a matter of gentlemanly concern between scribal correspondents, but it also relies on a mixture of oral, epistolary and print techniques within its fiction of "letteracy."

Some Considerations upon the Late Act of the Parliament of Scotland, for Constituting an Indian Company in a Letter to a Friend responds to the concerns of the *Remarks*, purporting to be an answer to the author: "Sir, Your last to me brought a Printed ACT of the Parliament of

Scotland, for Constituting an *Indian* Company in or for that Kingdom, together with your own Thoughts, and those of some others upon it."[31] In response to the concerns voiced in the *Remarks*, however, the author of *Some Considerations* indicates that "the *Scots* are in the right" if by being granted a "few Priviledges," "they can introduce a brave and vigorous Constitution of Foreign Trade into their Country," and, over the space of twenty-one years, "entice and allure any considerable part of the Rich, Warm, and Fertil [*sic*] *Indies* to the Poor, Cold and Barren *Scotland*" (1). The writer suggests that there is little cause for alarm from "those remote, cold and doubtful Designs of the *Scots*, of which even the Success can come to but little in the present Age" (2). Rather, he suggests, "should any thing relating to [the company] be restrained, or prohibited by the Government, it would be like a Fountain enclosed, break out with the greater Violence in other places" (30). In particular, he suggests, other nations, sensing that there were profits to be had, would rush in to take advantage of the situation. Like the *Remarks*, *Some Considerations* also concludes with representations of epistolary conventions at the bottom – a date of "Nov. 22, 1695" as well as the printed representation of a signature" "*I am, &c.*" – in addition to the publication information: "*LONDON:* Printed in the YEAR 1695" (4).

Other letter pamphlets took up the cause of defending the company. *A Letter from a Member of the Parliament of Scotland to His Friend in London*, written by the company secretary Roderick MacKenzie using the pseudonym "Philanax Verax," counteracted the author of the *Remarks* in order to argue on behalf of the company and to suggest that the majority of the "Sober and Tradeing People" of England, rather than being worried about the Company of Scotland, "generally express an Inclination to be concerned in it."[32] MacKenzie intimates that any negative perspectives on the enterprise are the products of irrational thinking spread through rumour. "Noisie Arguments" against the company, he suggests, are "daily with an Ayre of Magisterial Stiffness dictated at *Garraways* [a coffeehouse], and from thence diffus'd amongst the credulous Multitude" (2). Like the *Remarks*, MacKenzie's letter pamphlet also points to the authority that was beginning to be associated with print when the author suggests that if there had been anything questionable about the company's

---

[31] *Some Considerations upon the Late Act of the Parliament of Scotland, for Constituting an Indian Company in a Letter to a Friend* (London, 1695), 1.
[32] Philanax Verax (Roderick MacKenzie), *A Letter from a Member of the Parliament of Scotland to His Friend at London* (London, 1695), 2.

enterprise that could not stand up to "the Tryal of the Strictest Enquiry," it "had certainly been long e're ... printed in Capital Letters" (3). *A Letter from a Member of the Parliament of Scotland to His Friend in London* incorporates objections that are made to the company in the text as a dialogue:

> *Obj.* But (you say) the Out-cry is, That these are such unprecedented Concessions and Exceptions as never were, or ought to be granted by a Prince to any Society of Company of Traders in the World. (6)

While the objections are represented as short oral introjections associated with the "Out-cry," the rebuttals appear as regular text expounding eloquently against what "you say" by using carefully chosen examples. The author associates those who look negatively at the company with oral introjection, connecting any objections expressed with the "Hue and Cry" of unthinking crowds who believe lies that are "industriously preached in Coffee-houses"; in contrast, he suggests that "the Great, the Grave and Wise Men of the Nation, do never joyn in that Chorus" (7).

Notably, all three letter pamphlets are not addressed to the general public; rather, they are written as exchanges between gentlemanly friends, and as such, they place the reader in a dual perspective. On the one hand, the reader is literally put in the place of the fictional "friend" who is the recipient of the letter and who is receiving confidential information. On the other hand, the reader also occupies the position of a consumer of the pamphlet, one who is represented as an intelligent arbiter of the arguments presented. The letter pamphlet relies on this positional ambivalence to represent the intimacy of actual letters within a marketplace situation. As is clear in all three pamphlets, even though they present themselves as mediations of script, the writers are very aware of the multi-mediated manner in which the so-called letters will operate: their ideas are circulated and discussed not just in gentlemen's salons but in coffee-house conversations and hearsay.

Despite the best efforts of writers such as "Philanax Verax," the naysayers won the debate regarding the Company of Scotland, for, on December 14, 1695, members of the House of Lords and the House of Commons jointly presented an address to the King expressing their concerns regarding the impact of the Company of Scotland on "the Trade of the [English] Nation."[33] Largely repeating the points raised by

---

[33] *The Journals of the House of Commons*, vol. 11 (London: Printed for the House of Commons, 1803), 362.

the author of *Remarks upon the Scotch Act, in a Letter to a Friend*, the address also expresses concerns that, because the Company of Scotland is saved from paying taxes for twenty-one years, Scotland will become a "free port" for commodities from the East Indies, and England "will lose the Benefit of supplying foreign Parts with those Commodities [from the East Indies]."[34] The address also objects to the fact that the King had agreed to take responsibility for "Restitution, Reparation, and Satisfaction, made for any Damage that may be done to any of the ships, Goods, Merchandize, Persons, or other Effects whatsoever, belonging to the said Company."[35] The address itself was printed and circulated, further fuelling the popular antagonism against the Company of Scotland.[36] The company thus found itself blocked by the English Parliament and the King at every turn. With English merchants forbidden by law from investing and further negative propaganda about the company circulating in London, Paterson, along with his fellow projectors Daniel Lodge and James Smyth, removed to Scotland in February 1696, intent on promoting the company solely among Scottish investors.

Subscription books were set up in in Edinburgh on February 26, 1696, in Glasgow on March 4, 1699, and in Ayr on April 4, 1696, with a closing date of August 6, 1699.[37] Subscribers quickly signed up in astonishing numbers, including a number of women as well as individuals from the middling ranks.[38] Helen Julia Paul, drawing on Fischer Black's concept of "noise trading," explains the enthusiasm of Scottish subscribers for the company, noting that the Scots were "making decisions to buy or sell shares by trading on 'noise'" rather than expectations based on information and facts.[39] The "noise" about the Company of Scotland was generated in multiple ways. Oral communication played an important role. As Douglas Watt observes, "The promoters principally relied on word of mouth to sell shares in the Company, which was already the main subject of gossip in the coffee-houses of Edinburgh, indeed throughout the whole country, following the events in London."[40] But in addition, the directors also relied on the affordances of the expanding print market to publish material

---

[34] Ibid., 363.   [35] Ibid.   [36] Watt, *Price of Scotland*, 42.   [37] Ibid., 51–53.
[38] Whatley, *Scots and the Union*, 167. See also Armitage, "Scottish Vision."
[39] Attempting to analyze subscribers to the company within the context of the new post-1688 investment economy, Helen Julia Paul, "Risks and Overseas Trade: The Way in Which Risks Were Perceived and Managed in the Early Modern Period," Working Papers 7017, Economic History Society, 2007, 6. See Fischer Black, "Noise," *The Journal of Finance* 41, no. 3 (1986): 529–43.
[40] Watt, *Price of Scotland*, 49–50.

aimed at generating interest in the company. Lists of subscribers and the "Terms" of subscription were published, as well as a multitude of other broadsides and pamphlets, including an elaborate advertisement for the July 28, 1696, meeting of the Court of Directors that included an image of a ship being guided across the ocean by Neptune with his trident.[41] Several of the broadsheets published by the company at this time featured an engraving of the company's elaborate coat of arms that had been "illuminated by herald painter George Porteous" (see Figure 3.1).[42] The coat of arms features figures representing the New World and Africa flanking a saltire illustrated with forms of global mobility: a cargo ship, a camel, an elephant and a "Peruvian sheep."[43] The company's motto, "*Qua panditur orbis / Vis unita fortior*" ("Where the world stretches forth / Its joint strength is stronger"), sums up the imperial aspirations of the Scottish company as it gathered together its resources for the impending journey.

As before, letter pamphlets were also an important part of this printed propaganda campaign. The author of *A Letter from a Gentleman in the Country to His Friend at Edinburgh*, subtitled, *Wherein It Is Clearly Proved, That the Scottish African, and Indian Company, Is Exactly Calculated for the Interest of Scotland*, writing allegedly in response to having received in his friend's recent letter "an account of the Parliament of *England's* Address," asserts among his many points that Scotland is "as much as any of her Neighbours, and more than many of them, fitted to be the Seat of such a Company, and a Mother to Plantations, especially in *America*."[44] The company's efforts to generate "noise" clearly paid off, as when subscriptions closed in August, they had raised £400,000.

The creation of the Company of Scotland, then, took place through multiple mediations. Letters were the primary ways in which the projectors communicated with each other in the early stages of the company's existence. But in the new post-1695 world of no pre-publication censorship in England, print was also used to promote – or prevent – the early activities of the company. Letter pamphlets did indeed facilitate change "by providing writers and readers with paths across shifting media

---

[41] Company of Scotland, *A List of the Subscribers to the Company of Scotland Trading to Africa and the Indies: Taken in Edinburgh, &c. until the 21 of April Inclusive 1696* (Edinburgh, 1696).
[42] Watt, *Price of Scotland*, 8. See also Company of Scotland Trading to Africa and the Indies, *Advertisement. Edinburgh, the 9th of July 1696* (Edinburgh, 1696).
[43] Watt, *Price of Scotland*, 23.
[44] *A Letter from a Gentleman in the Country to His Friend at Edinburgh* (Edinburgh, 1696), 3.

Figure 3.1 "Arms of the Company of Scotland" (1698). By permission of University of Glasgow Library, Archives & Special Collections, Spencer fol. 51

landscapes" in this time of media transition as print was gaining currency and authority.[45] Letters in both manuscript and print between the company directors and the colonists and from the directors to English government officials and the King himself would come to play an even greater role as the joint-stock company became a truly national venture.

Official Letters and the "Honour and Independency of the Nation"

Having raised sufficient capital within Scotland, Paterson and several other directors went to Amsterdam and Hamburg to arrange ships and supplies and generate more "noise" about the enterprise among foreign investors through both word of mouth and printed pamphlets. On April 7, 1697, however, William's ministers sent instructions to his envoy at the court of Lüneburg as well as to Paul Rycaut, the English Resident at Hamburg. Rycaut subsequently delivered a memorial to the Senate of Hamburg to pressure merchants of that city not to "enter into Commerce" with the commissioners for the Company of Scotland, "nor Encourage them in any sort," or the King would "not fail to Resent it."[46]

---

[45] King, *Writing to the World*, 2.
[46] Company of Scotland Trading to Africa and the Indies, *A Full and Exact Collection of All the Considerable Addresses, Memorials, Petitions, Answers, Proclamations, Declarations, Letters and Other Publick Papers, Relating to the Company of Scotland Trading to Africa and the Indies, since the Passing of the Act* (Edinburgh, 1700), 4. See Julie Orr, *Scotland, Darien and the Atlantic World, 1698–1700* (Edinburgh: Edinburgh University Press, 2018), 56.

In response to information they received from their European deputies, the council general of the company sent an address to the King on June 28, 1697. Although the Secretary of State, James Ogilvy, Marquis of Tullibardine, responded that the King would instruct the Resident not to hinder the company's officials, nothing seems to have been done. Over the next months, a series of official letters went back and forth between the directors, the Secretaries of State and the King during which the directors requested a declaration from the King of his support for the company as well as reparations for the damages that had already been done to their finances and reputation as a result of the memorial.

The escalating level of concern in these documents is clear. Letters from the directors during this time period also take on a new role as they rhetorically link the fortunes of the company to that of the Scottish nation as a whole. In a letter sent on December 22, 1697, "To the Right Honourable, The Lord High Chancellor, and remanent Lords of His Majesty's most Honourable Privy Council," for example, the council general of the company indicate: "Your Lordships very well know of what Concern the Success of this Company is to the whole Kingdom, and that scarce a particular Society or Corporation within the same can justly boast of so unanimous a Suffrage or Sanction, as the Acts of Parliament, by which this Company is established" (18). They further suggest that the King's memorial was "an open and violent Infringement of, and Encroachment upon the Priviledges" of Scotland and could potentially serve as a precedent "for invading and overturning even the very Fundamental Right, Natural Liberties, & indisputable Independency of this Kingdom" (18). On July 22, 1698, the council general petitioned His Majesty's High Commissioner and the Right Honourable the Estates of Parliament. After giving a brief history of the issues that the company had faced, they emphasize the company as a national enterprise, asserting "most of the Nobility, Gentry, Merchants, and the whole Body of the Royal Boroughs have ... contributed as Adventurers, in raising a far more Considerable Joint-Stock, than any was ever before rais'd in this Kingdom for any Publick Undertaking or Project or Trade whatsoever" and that it is this fact "which makes [the fortunes of the company] now of so much the more universal a Concern to the Nation" (21). They add that, "though our Company is more immediately and sensibly touched in many Respects by such Proceedings than any other; yet we humbly conceiv[e] also, that the Honour and Independency of the Nation, as well as the Authority and Credit of the Parliament is struck at through our sides" (24). Accordingly,

Parliament's address to the King on August 5, 1698, indicated "the whole Nation's Concern in this Matter" in asking the king to "take such Measures as may effectually vindicate the undoubted Rights and Priviledges of the said Company, and support the Credit and Interest thereof" (26).

While the council general's comments clearly focus on the company as a reflection of the Scottish nation, Paterson's early correspondence, on the other hand, had stressed that neither national interest nor religion should be considerations of the company. As he writes on July 9, 1695,

> Above all it's needful for Us to make no Distinction of Party's in this great and Noble Undertaking, but that of whatever Nation or Religion a man be (if one of Us) he ought to be look'd upon to be of the same Interest and Inclination, ffor We must not Act apart in any thing but in a firm and united Body, and distinct from all other Interests whatsoever.[47]

In the formal letters and petitions complaining about English interference, however, the directors shifted the Company of Scotland from being a joint-stock venture to symbolizing the "Honour and Independency of the Nation."[48] It was a shift that, repeated in yet more manuscript and printed letters, would be further amplified over the following years as the colony sought to establish itself.

Writing Home: Letters between the Directors and the Colonists

When the five Company of Scotland ships left Leith harbor in July 1698, they carried with them 1,200 individuals who, it was later claimed, had no idea where they were going.[49] It was only when they reached the thirty-first degree of latitude that the colonists learned that they were "to proceed to the Bay of Darien, and make the Isle called the Golden Island . . . some

---

[47] William Paterson to Robert Chiesley, July 9, 1695.

[48] Company of Scotland Trading to Africa and the Indies, *A Full and Exact Collection*, 24. See also Alasdair Cameron MacFarlane, "'A Dream of Darien': Scottish Empire and the Evolution of Early Modern Travel Writing" (PhD diss., Durham University, 2018).

[49] Their only information at the time of departure was that they were to "settle and plant a Colony in some place or other not inhabited in America, or in or upon any other place, by consent of the inhabitants and natives thereof, and not possessed by any European Sovereign Potentate Prince or State" (John Hill Burton, ed., *The Darien Papers: Being a Selection of Original Letters and Official Documents Relating to the Establishment of a Colony at Darien* [Edinburgh: Thomas Constable, 1849], 49). According to the retrospective account of Captain Pinkerton, the specific orders of where to sail were "sealed with the Company's seal" and not to be opened until the ships had reached the thirty-first or thirty-second degree of latitude (Ibid., 105).

few leagues to the leeward of the mouth of the great River of Darien ... and there make a settlement on the mainland."[50] Even before they knew where they were heading, however, the colonists knew that they were required to write about it. The list of "Instructions to the Council of the Colony" from the directors specified as its third item that, following landing and taking possession, the colonial council "shall with all possible speed dispatch home to us an exact journal of your voyage, Landing, proceedings and condition of the place."[51] In addition, the tenth item of the Instructions required the council to send back to Scotland both true copies and duplicates of all "Proceedings, Books, and Registers."[52] The directors envisioned a stream of "punctual correspondence" that would keep the company connected with its new colony.

Letters were intended to provide a networked connection between the colonists and the company directors as well as friends and family back home. Over the course of the next year and a half, letters between the directors and the colonists did indeed criss-cross the Atlantic Ocean. Abiding by the instructions they themselves had sent to the colonists, the directors kept both a signed copy and an unsigned copy of each letter sent, and the colonists also dutifully wrote back home giving details of their experiences. But, although both sides kept up their share of writing, the actual process of communication between Scotland and its new colony differed drastically from the flow of "punctual correspondence" that the company directors had imagined.

One of the biggest problems impacting communication was the time that it took for letters to travel back and forth between Scotland and the Scottish expedition, time that was also a function of unorganized space as, unlike letters that travelled within the postal systems within Britain and Europe, the letters between the colonists and the directors were not conveyed at regular intervals using pre-existing routes. Once the colonists had sailed out of Leith, successful correspondence depended not on the punctuality of the writers but on the fate of ships that they encountered and used to relay their letters. The company directors received word that the colonists had arrived at Madeira at the end of summer, 1698 through several different means. As they noted on April 22, 1699: "Yours of the August 29 last from ye Maderas by the way of Portugal and your other of

---

[50] George Pratt Insh, *Papers Relating to the Ships and Voyages of the Company of Scotland Trading to Africa and the Indies, 1696–1707* (Edinburgh: Edinburgh University Press by T. and A. Constable for the Scottish History Society, 1924), 64.
[51] Burton, *Darien Papers*, 54. [52] Ibid., 55–56.

ye same day and date by the way of Holland came safe to hand which gave us abundance of satisfaction for the time."[53] After this initial positive communication, however, the directors received no further word for a number of months, although the company later indicated that they attempted to send out "dispatches" to the colonists "at a venture, even before we had any direct acco[unt] from yourselves."[54] Finally, on March 25, 1699, Captain Hamilton arrived in Edinburgh, bearing the welcome news that the colonists had reached Darien and delivering as well a "sealed packet containing a journal of events on the voyage and at the isthmus."[55] Two days later, Major Cunningham arrived with another packet. Although Hamilton and Cunningham had set out on the same ship, they had taken different routes back to Scotland.

The letter from the directors written back to the colonists on April 22, 1699, acknowledges the receipt of the news of the colonists' safe arrival: "We have lykeways yours of ye 28. December last by Mr. Hamiltoun who arrived here by way of Bristol the 25 ultimo. As also your other of the same date by Major Cunningham who arrived here yesterday thereafter."[56] The response of the directors suggests that they, like the colonists, made a practice of sending out copies of the same letter via different routes: "We send Copies ... by the way of Jamaica, Antegoa & Barbadoes under covers to severall other Friends in those Respective parts."[57] As these comments make clear, letter-writing between the company and the colony involved an elaborate process of writing and rewriting to create not just copies and true copies, but also multiple "original" versions to send.

Examining letters from the early modern period, James Daybell and Andrew Gordon suggest that "much correspondence incorporated a phatic element – in a climate of uncertain delivery, confirming receipt of previous letters, advising of letters to be received, and detailing the networks of transmission through which a letter ought to pass, were important features, often vital to the effective tracing of correspondence."[58] The letters sent back and forth across the Atlantic by the company directors and the

---

[53] Court of Directors of the Company of Scotland to the Council of Caledonia, April 22, 1699, NLS, Adv. MSS 83.7.4, fol. 114.
[54] Court of Directors of the Company of Scotland to the Council of Caledonia, April 15, 1699, NLS, Adv. MSS 83.7.4, fol. 111.
[55] Watt, *Price of Scotland*, 14.
[56] Court of Directors of the Company of Scotland to the Council of Caledonia, April 22, 1699.
[57] Ibid.
[58] James Daybell and Andrew Gordon, "Introduction: The Early Modern Letter Opener," in *Cultures of Correspondence in Early Modern Britain*, ed. James Daybell and Andrew Gordon (Philadelphia: University of Pennsylvania Press, 2016), 3.

colonists represent not just the regular degree of "self-reflection" which Daybell and Gordon note, but a hyper-awareness, as a large percentage of the contents of the letters describes the processes through which they will be sent or establishes the correspondence received to date. In the letter of April 22, 1699, for example, the directors elaborate, "We send this by the way of New England under cover to our and your trusty friend Mr. Robt Maxwell Mcnt. in Bridge Town being well satisfied of his fidelity and good Inclinations to our Country, Company & Collony by the Testimony of Mr Willm Hamiltoun his intimate acquaintance."[59] The reference to "fidelity" in this letter also points to another problem which the company faced in its correspondence with its colony: maintaining secrecy. Details of the enterprise had to be kept hidden from ill-wishers, and therefore letters needed to be sent only through trusted agents.

If secrecy in transit of letters was of paramount importance to the success of the Darien venture, however, the dissemination of the successful news that those letters conveyed was also crucial, as the company directors used the information in the letters sent from the colonists to advance their cause with the King and the English Parliament. Crucially, the letters from the colonists were used as evidence to prove that the area surrounding Darien belonged to the Indigenous peoples and was not part of the Spanish settlements of Carthagena, Panama and Portobello, and that it had been freely given up by the Indigenous owners to the Scottish colonizers.[60] Finding the news presented by Hamilton satisfactory on both these counts, the directors expressed their optimism to the colonists: "we have reason to hope and doe believe that his Maj'ty will give us and you his generous Countenance and Royal protection. And that the Government of England will now find it in their Interest also to be friendly to us in the Maintenance of your Sd. Settlement against the attempts of any foreign Enemies."[61]

The directors also sent letters including details of how negotiations with the government were progressing. On April 22, 1699, they noted, "we send you here enclosed some Copies of our Acts and Resolutions which

---

[59] Court of Directors of the Company of Scotland to the Council of Caledonia, April 22, 1699.
[60] A pamphlet published on behalf of the company, *Scotland's Right to Caledonia (Formerly Called Darien)* (Edinburgh, 1700), emphasizes the importance of this point: "the Natives were undoubtedly the Possessors or Proprietors" and the "Colonies coming to Settle amongst them, must derive Right from them, and that either by Consent, Surrender, or Conquest" (5). See also Ignacio Gallup-Diaz, *The Door of the Seas and Key to the Universe: Indian Politics and Imperial Rivalry in the Darien, 1640–1750* (New York: Columbia University Press, 2004) and Orr, *Scotland, Darien and the Atlantic World*.
[61] Court of Directors of the Company of Scotland to the Council of Caledonia, April 22, 1699.

were ordered to be printed and published."[62] A missive sent from the company directors on August 17, 1699, included a package of material regarding the ongoing negotiations in addition to the letter itself and the copy of the letter that was being responded to: "We send you inclosed an exact copy of some proposals given in to our Court from the Commission of the late General Assembly, to which we desire you may have a just and due regard; and for a further explanation of the five articles therein contained, we refer you to the printed copy of a letter sent to you directly from the said Commission."[63] Made up of manuscript letters, handwritten copies of printed documents and printed copies of manuscript letters, and presenting the ongoing struggles of the company through documents grouped together in one package, the letters epitomize the way in which the company saw correspondence as a crucial part of creating a sense that "the honour and Interest of this Kingdome" was "firmly and inseparably linked" with that of the colony.[64]

An "Abundance of Letters Spread over the Countrey": Letter Pamphlets from Darien

At the same time as they were reinforcing the connection between the nation and its colony in their official correspondence, the directors were also working to confirm that same sense within Scotland, and they took pains to ensure that positive information about the colony was disseminated "to the whole Nation in general."[65] The initial excitement about the colony was conveyed to the general population through visual and aural means. As the April 22 letter from the directors notes: "the severall Corporations throughout the Kingdom did testify yr satisfaction by publick rejoycings, by Bonefires, Illuminations, Ringing of bells, and all the other ordinary demonstrations of joy."[66] Print technologies were also employed to disseminate the good news to the literate or those who could listen to others read. James Watson printed the information in his newspaper, the *Edinburgh Gazette*.[67] A news sheet entitled *An Express from the African and Indian Scots Company's Fleet, Landed in New-EDINBURGH IN CALEDONIA* also announced the receipt of the long-awaited letter confirming the colonists' arrival: "On *Saturday* last, the 25 [March]

---

[62] Ibid.
[63] Court of Directors of the Company of Scotland to the Council of Caledonia, August 17, 1699, NLS, Adv. MSS 87.7.3.
[64] Court of Directors of the Company of Scotland to the Council of Caledonia, April 22, 1699.
[65] Ibid.   [66] Ibid.   [67] Watt, *Price of Scotland*, 13.

instant, 1699, here Arrived an Express to the *Court of Directors* of the *Indian* and *African* Company, from the Council of their Collony in *America*, bearing date at *New Edinburgh* in *Caledonia*, the 28. Of *December* last, which brings the Welcome News of their being Arrived save [sic] at *Darien* the 2 of *November*."[68] With an eye on the negotiations taking place between the company directors and the English government, the news item also emphasized the details of the colonists' "Kind and Welcome Reception" by the Indigenous peoples: "the Natives came immediatly on Board of them, with all Imaginable Demonstrations of Joy at their Arrival."

The news of the arrival of the colonists at their destination prompted a flurry of other printed publications celebrating the occasion and anticipating forthcoming riches for Scotland, as Kirsten Sandrock discusses.[69] In addition to including the news in the *Edinburgh Gazette*, Watson also printed *An Ode Made on the Welcome News of the Safe Arrival and Kind Reception of the Scottish Collony at Darien in America*. The *Ode* calls upon all "SCOTS" to give thanks to "*Heaven's Protecting Pow'r*" for the safe arrival of the colonists, depicting the colonization of the people and land of Darien by Scots as part of God's plan. Although the Indigenous peoples are represented as joining with the Scots "as *Brethren*" in their "*Jovial Feasts*," they indicate their subservience by offering up their possessions and their labour to their colonizers:

> Their *Land* they freely did Resign,
> and all the *Treasures* of their Soil,
> and frankly bear a share i' th' Toil.

The *Ode* also suggests the national economic benefits of imperial exploits when it boasts: "*Indian Gold* shall soon release / The Nation from its *Tempral Grand Disease*," with the "*Grand Disease*" being glossed in a footnote as "Poverty."[70]

Another poem printed at the time, *Caledonia Triumphans: A Panegyrick to the King* by Alexander Pennecuik, also interconnects a sense of Scottish nationality with a larger imperial identity. It begins by praising William and presenting to him the benefits of the Darien project for the larger

---

[68] Company of Scotland Trading to Africa and the Indies, *An Express from the African and Indian Scots Company's Fleet* (Edinburgh, 1699), n.p.
[69] Kirsten Sandrock, *Scottish Colonial Literature: Writing the Atlantic, 1603–1707* (Edinburgh: University of Edinburgh Press, 2021).
[70] *An Ode Made on the Welcome News of the Safe Arrival and Kind Reception of the Scottish Collony at Darien in America* (Edinburgh, 1699).

nation of Britain and the Protestant cause, but it moves to asserting the way in which Scotland has resisted attempted invasion by other European nations throughout history when it suggests that

> ... as our Valour flew all Europe round,
> So now our Trade scarce both the Poles shall bound.[71]

Ultimately, like the *Ode Made on the Welcome News, Caledonia Triumphans* asserts a Scottish imperial vision: "Our ships through all the World shall go and come, / Even from the Rising to the Setting Sun." *A Letter from the Commission, of the General Assembly, of the Church of Scotland; to the Honourable Council and Inhabitants of the Scots Colony of Caledonia in America* also confirmed the providential nature of the safe landing of the colony and celebrated the way the expedition was impacting the world's sense of Scotland's capabilities: "The Eyes of God, of Angels and of Men are upon you; The World begins to take Notice of you, as an almost hopeful *Colony*, to the Envy of your Enemies, and the Joy of your own Country and Friends."[72]

In addition to these printed works, letter pamphlets from, or at least purporting to be from, the colonists themselves were a vital component of the dissemination and shaping of information about the colony during this time. In connection with the poems and broadsides, these letter pamphlets helped amplify and advertise the points that the directors were trying to make through diplomatic channels. They also offered a positive perspective on the viability of future colonial prospects at Darien. For the most part, these printed letters were at best amalgams of actual accounts sent by the colonists to the company, combined with paraphrases or plagiarized passages from other works that had recently been published describing the geography and ethnography of the West Indies and Central America. As purportedly eyewitness accounts, however, they claimed to offer first-person testimonials about life in the new colony. They relied on what Gary Schneider calls a "rhetoric of epistolarity," designed to "verify reliability, authenticity, and intimacy."[73]

Like the letter pamphlets written during the time of the creation of the company, these letter pamphlets addressed readers familiarly, encouraging them to take a personal interest in the subject and relying on the

---

[71] *Caledonia Triumphans: A Panegyrick to the King* (Edinburgh, 1699).
[72] *A Letter from the Commission, of the General Assembly, of the Church of Scotland; to the Honourable Council and Inhabitants of the Scots Colony of Caledonia in America* (Glasgow, 1699), 9.
[73] Gary Schneider, *The Culture of Epistolarity: Vernacular Letters and Letter Writing in Early Modern England, 1500–1700* (Newark: University of Delaware Press, 2005), 55.

"perceived ability of the letter to bear witness to the truth."[74] *A Letter, Giving a Description of the Isthmus of Darian*, subtitled *(Where the Scot's Colonie Is Settled)*, for example, represents itself as sent *"from a Gentleman who lives there at present."*[75] In accordance with the frequent custom of letter pamphlets, it styles itself as a response to a request to provide news: "Conform to your Desire, and mine own Promise: I have sent You the following Description of *Darian* (3). Responding to the imagined correspondent's instructions, the writer offers an encyclopedic overview of "the *Nature* of the *Ground, Animals, Fruits,* and *Trees*; and what *Minerals* they have, with a Draught of the Place, the *Habits* of their *Kings* and *Queens*; The *Form* of their *Houses,* The *Way* of their *Fighting* with the Spaniards and other Enemies" (3). The writer also anticipates criticism of the pamphlet's authenticity because of its publication well after the arrival of the package of information taken back to Scotland by Hamilton and Cunningham, as he explains: "I was up the Country when the two Gentlemen went for *Scotland* who brought the News of our arrival: but having now an Occasion I have sent you the following Account" (3).

Leaving out the entire journey across the Atlantic, the account begins from the time when the colonists made landfall, the author indicating that the Scots have taken possession of the area through survey, fortification and an act of naming: "We have named it CALEDONIA and there is a Fort very conveniently built which We call *New-EDINBURGH*" (3). The account moves to pinpoint the location of the colony through latitude and longitude, using a brief geographical description of the area to comment on the convenient "Situation of our *Fort*" (4). From this general description, however, the writer moves unexpectedly to focus on the specifics of the flora, indicating the Latin names and medicinal uses for several of the plants. The "*Lignum sanctum,* or *Guiacum,*" he notes, possesses "Virtues" which "are very well known, more especially to those who observe not well the VII. Commandment, and are giv'n to impure Copulations" (4). At the same time, the writer offers a gruesome description of the uses that the Indigenous people make of the "*Prickle palm*" in order to "torment their prisoners" (4). In order to authenticate the macabre description of torture, the author draws on purportedly oral testimony of the Indigenous people themselves, writing that "This Custom was told me by an Indian, who said He had used his Enemy thus, oftentimes" (5).

---

[74] King, *Writing to the World,* 72.
[75] *A Letter, Giving a Description of the Isthmus of Darian* (Edinburgh, 1699).

In fact, these descriptions, along with most of the first fifteen pages of the *Letter*, which discuss "the *Nature* of the *Ground, Animals, Fruits,* and *Trees*; and ... *Minerals*" as well the customs of the Indigenous peoples, are extracted from *The History of the Bucaniers in America* by Alexandre Olivier Exquemelin, which had been published in an English translation in 1684, then republished in 1695 and 1699.[76] Whereas the sections selected from *The History of the Bucaniers* concerned other locations such as Jamaica and Hispaniola, the writer of *A Letter, Giving a Description of the Isthmus of Darian* alters them to suggest that the events have actually happened to the colonists at Darien. Where the *History of the Bucaniers* includes a description of the "Manner of Planting Tobacco" on Hispaniola, for example (190), the author of *A Letter, Giving a Description of the Isthmus of Darian* includes the same information virtually verbatim, commenting that "We begin now to plant *Tobacco* for Trade" (8). *A Letter, Giving a Description of the Isthmus of Darian* also includes a number of sections taken from *The History of the Bucaniers*, which it prefaces with a series of first-person statements such as "I shall proceed now to give you an Account of the Men, Women, and their Habits" and "I shall further give You an Account of our going up the country to their King or chief Captain" (15).

The final section of *A Letter, Giving a Description of the Isthmus of Darian*, however, largely repeats information from a different source: an actual journal that was sent back to the directors from the Council of Caledonia.[77] The journal includes a daily record of the weather and the activities of the colonists on board the *Unicorn* under the command of Captain Pennycuik from the point at which they left Madeira to the point at which Hamilton and Cunningham were leaving to carry the news of the colonists' arrival back to Scotland. *A Letter, Giving a Description of the Isthmus of Darian* dispenses with the diary form which the journal employs, however, in favour of presenting a continuous narrative describing the system of land ownership and the government of the isthmus as well as describing the Indigenous leaders and their relations with each other and with the Spanish. The author of *A Letter, Giving a Description of the Isthmus of Darian* also rewrites the specific details concerning the Indigenous inhabitants. Both the journal and *A Letter, Giving a Description of the Isthmus*

---

[76] Alexandre Exquemelin, *The History of the Bucaniers of America* (London, 1699).
[77] "Mr. Hugh Rose's Journal in going to Caledonia, and after his arrival there," NLS, Adv. MSS 83.7.4.61. See Burton, *Darien Papers*, 60–78. This journal is similar to "Captain Pennycook's Journall from the Madera Islands to New Caledonia in Darien" in Insh (*Papers Relating to the Ships and Voyages*, 78–97), with the exception that Rose's journal contains more details about the weather.

of Darian, for example, describe Captain Andreas, one of the Indigenous leaders, being offered a commission and protection from the Spanish in return for giving up "all his right to this part of the Country."[78] In an entry dated November 30, 1698, the journal indicates that Andreas "went away and promised to return in 2 or 3 dayes."[79] Then, it notes, in an entry for December 4, 1698, that he returned on board the *Unicorn*, having the commission read to him in Spanish and being presented with the commission "written on parcement [sic], with the Colonyes Seal and very broad gold stript and flour'd ribben appended."[80] In *A Letter*, in contrast, the transaction is represented as happening immediately:

> A *Commession* was ordered for Capt. *Andraeas*, and being read and approven of, it was delivered to Him ... The *Commission* being read, and rendered *Verbatim* to Him in *Spanish*, He agreed to every *Article*: then before 7 or 8 of his own People, and severall of ours, it was delivered unto Him with a broad basked-hilted *Sword*, and a Pair of *Pistolls*, with which He solemly promised to defend Us to the last *Dropp* of His Blood, against all our Enemys. (24)

By situating the curiosities of Darien within the context of the colonial appropriation described in the journal, *A Letter, Giving a Description of the Isthmus of Darian* reinforces the messages that the Company of Scotland was anxious to convey: that Darien was a colony worth having, that the land was being skillfully used by the Scots and that the Scots were also managing the Indigenous peoples.

Another pamphlet published at the time, *The History of Caledonia: or, the Scots Colony in Darien in the West Indies*, also makes use of the "rhetoric of epistolarity," shifting its narrative stance part of the way through so as to approximate that found in the letter pamphlet form. Claiming also to be written by "a Gentleman Lately Arriv'd," *The History of Caledonia*, like *A Letter, Giving a Description of the Isthmus of Darian*, promises "*an Account of the Manners of the Inhabitants, and Riches of the Countrey.*"[81] *The History of Caledonia* commences in the third person, describing not the history of Caledonia, but the history of the Company of Scotland itself, and suggesting that the success of the Darien venture affirms the capabilities of the Scots as colonizers:

> to shew to the World that they were not so Chymerical as some gave out, they set themselves more warmly to carry the Project on, and accordingly

---

[78] Burton, *Darien Papers*, 73.   [79] Ibid.   [80] Ibid.
[81] A Gentleman Lately Arriv'd, *The History of Caledonia: or, the Scots Colony in Darien in the West Indies* (London, 1699).

subscrib'd 400000 *l.* most of the Nobility and Gentry, and all the Cities and Royal Boroughs unanimously concurring, giving the World a sufficient Proof that *Scotland* was neither so Poor, nor so Dis-jointed, as some people would have it believed. (10)

Like *A Letter, Giving a Description of the Isthmus of Darian*, *The History of Caledonia* jumps quickly from Edinburgh to New Edinburgh, omitting the transatlantic journey: "Three Stout Ships and Two Tenders . . . sayl'd from the *Frith* with a prosperous Gale, and went round by the *Orcades,* and having a prosperous Voyage, about the middle of *November,* the last Year, 1698 arrived safe in the Bay of *Darien,* having lost few or none of their men" (11). Similarly, *The History of Caledonia* also appeals to the interests of Scottish readers as it recounts the geography and rich natural resources that lie untouched in Darien, paying particular attention to the "Mines of Gold" about which the Indigenous people inform the deputies of the colonists. As with *A Letter, Giving a Description of the Isthmus of Darian*, most of the text of *The History of Caledonia* is actually drawn from another contemporary source, although in this case, the author relies heavily on Lionel Wafer's *A New Voyage and Description of the Isthmus of America*, which did include some information about Darien.[82]

Notably, the inclusion of sections from Wafer's first-person account is accompanied by a stylistic shift in *The History of Caledonia*, with the narrator beginning to include self-conscious remarks that also call attention to the act of reading. Introducing a passage drawn verbatim from Wafer, he writes: "here it may not be unpleasant to the Reader, to give him an Account of the manner of getting the Gold dust, which is as follows" (19). The subsequent inclusion of a long passage from Wafer also offers the author an opportunity to include his own subjective observation that promotes the general project of the company: "It's easy to guess from this what vast Mines may in time be discovered, when Art and Industry are joyned together, and of what importance it will be to *Great Brittain,* to take all possible measures to preserve this Colony" (19).

By the end of the narrative, however, the author has himself become a character in the account, for he writes about events as if he himself experienced them: "As soon as we were come within sight of *St. Andrews*

---

[82] Lionel Wafer, *A New Voyage and Description of the Isthmus of America* (London, 1699). Wafer had, in fact, been interviewed by the directors of the company and also had been asked to delay the publication of his account to conform to the timeline of the company's venture.

Fort, we all fell down on our Knees to give God most hearty thanks for our Success, and happy Return, and were presently met by a great part of the Garrison" (51). He concludes by suggesting that not only Scotland but also England will benefit from the colonial enterprise at Darien, as it will be "one of the most thriving Colonies in the world" once it is able to prosper: "As we grow stronger, we shall endeavour to procure a part in the *South Sea*, from whence it's not above 6 weeks Sail to *Japan*, and some parts of *China*," notes the author, indicating that the prosperity of the colony at Darien should be the "wish of all the Inhabitants of *Great Britain*" (53). The "Gentleman Lately Arriv'd" arrives late as a narrator in his own *History*, but when he does appear, he takes advantage of the affordances of the letter pamphlet and the "rhetoric of epistolarity" to address his readers in a familiar way.

A Letter, Giving a Description of the Isthmus of Darian and *The History of Caledonia* were only two of a host of works published at the time in Edinburgh and London (and reprinted in Dublin) which claimed to offer first-hand accounts of Darien to those curious about the economic viability of the company as well as about the details of settling and living in this area of the "torrid zone."[83] The author of *A Short Account from, and Description of the Isthmus of Darien, Where the Scots Collony Are Settled* suggests the existence of many such accounts, referring to the "Abundance of Letters [from Darien colonists] spread over the Countrey."[84] Printed letters from the colony containing information about the "Success" of the colony as well as "where they Design to Settle, and what is the Climate, Air, Soil, People, &c. of that place," suggests the author of *A Short Account from, and Description of the Isthmus of Darien*, appeal to all "True *Scots* Men" (1). Echoing the company's emphasis on the colony as a national enterprise, he notes that he himself has included "the Contents of some Letters writ from the Place where they are Settled" because "the Honour and Happiness of the Nation, does in a great Measure depend" on the "Success" of the colony at Darien (n.p.). Through

---

[83] "Part of a Journal kept from Scotland to New Caledonia in Darien, with a short account of that Country, communicated by Dr. Wallace, F.R.S." was published in volume 20 (1700–01) of the *Philosophical Transactions of the Royal Society*, while "the Substance of several Journals that were sent from our Colony in *Darien* upon their first Settlement there" was included in Philo-Caledon, *A Defence of the Scots Settlement at Darien with an Answer to the Spanish Memorial against It* (1699), 5.

[84] *A Short Account from, and Description of the Isthmus of Darien, Where the Scots Collony Are Settled* (Edinburgh, 1699), n.p. The author of this pamphlet includes material from Dampier and Wafer, but in contrast to other authors who borrow from these accounts, he acknowledges these sources.

their employment of a "rhetoric of epistolarity," the letters purporting to be from the Darien colonists did not just satisfy curiosity; they also forged an affective connection between readers in Scotland and the colonists. In their printed form, then, letter pamphlets encouraged the imagination of a new kind of Scottish identity, one that was both national and imperial.

Letter Trouble: "We Have Never Heard So Much as One Silible"

Letters from the colony, however much demanded and desired, could also threaten the "Honour and Happiness" of the Scottish nation. As Julie Orr suggests, from the beginning, the colony experienced treachery and desertion.[85] The directors wrote with displeasure to the colonists, for example, on June 24, 1699: "We think fitt to acquaint you, that we have dayly advices of many by-accounts sent from your Colony to people at London, and likewise to some here, who have not made such use thereof as we could have wish'd."[86] The directors suggested to the colonists that "The safest course both for your and our interests, is to have all your material advices wholy confin'd at first to such as are or shall be immediately concern'd in the administration of the company's affairs ... and who will no doubt always communicate or publish so much thereof as they will think proper or requisite for the common interest of the Company and Colony."[87] An important part of administering "the company's affairs" included managing communication leaks.

Adding to the difficulties of the colony were further actions taken by the Spanish, by the French and by William and his government. On May 3, 1699, the Spanish ambassador presented a memorial to the King objecting to the Scots settling in territory that the Spanish considered their own. In response, William sent instructions to Richard, Earl of Bellomont, Captain General and Governor in Chief of Massachusetts Bay, New York and the West Indian colonies, to cut off communication with the Scots colony. *A Proclamation* was published in each of those locations demanding that "all His Majesties Subjects" or those residing in the territories "forbear holding any Correspondence with, or giving any assistance to such Person

---

[85] Orr, *Scotland, Darien and the Atlantic World*.
[86] Court of Directors of the Company of Scotland to the Council of Caledonia, June 24, 1699, NLS, Adv. MSS 87.7.4.
[87] Ibid.

or Persons, who have ... settled in a certain place, which they have called *Caledonia*."[88] Through the course of their later correspondence with the colonists, the directors indicate their uncertainty about whether any of the copies of their letters will arrive at all. In a letter dated August 18, 1699, for example, the directors warned the colonists about the possibility of a Spanish invasion: "We have this minute got account of great preparations making against you. Mr. Mackenzie sends a copy of it to one of your number."[89] Even in the course of issuing the warning, however, they acknowledge that the warning might never arrive: "we know not whether Proclamations which we now understand are issued out in those parts against yr settlement, might not have hindred our said letters from coming to your hands."[90]

Unbeknownst to the directors when they penned this letter, the Scots had already abandoned the colony on June 21, 1699. The two relief ships that arrived in August, the *Olive Branch* and the *Speedy Return*, found no one at New Edinburgh. Denied supplies by English proclamation and suffering from diseases that had spread during the onslaught of the rainy season, many colonists had died. Those who had managed to survive had made their way to Jamaica or, in the case of Paterson and some others, to New York.[91] On August 18, 1699, Captain Colin Campbell wrote to the Court of Directors from Port Royal, informing them of the fate of the colony: "I thought it proper to acquaint you, yt ane inevitable necessity, occasioned by want of provisions, and a great mortality, oblidged us, upon the twenty first of June last, to leave our new Settlement in Caledonia."[92]

The letter of Robert Drummond, captain of the *Caledonia*, written from New York on August 11, 1699, gives an even bleaker account of the situation of the colonists after leaving Darien (see Figure 3.2): "I arrived heire the 3d of August. And in our passage from Caledonia heither our sickness being so universall aboard, And Mortality so great, that I have hove over board 105 Corps. The sickness and Mortallity continues still aboard, I have buried 11 Since I came heire already."[93] The act of

---

[88] Richard Coote, Earl of Bellomont, *A Proclamation* (New York, 1699). See also Orr, *Scotland, Darien and the Atlantic World*, 72–73.
[89] Court of Directors of the Company of Scotland to the Council of Caledonia, August 18, 1699, NLS, Adv. MSS 87.7.4, fol. 154.
[90] Ibid.   [91] Watt, *Price of Scotland*, 174.
[92] Captain Colin Campbell to the Court of Directors of the Company of Scotland, August 18, 1699, NLS, Adv. MSS 83.7.4, fol. 112.
[93] Robert Drummond to Mr. Hugh Montgomerie, August 11, 1699, NLS, Adv. MSS 83.7.4, fol. 22.

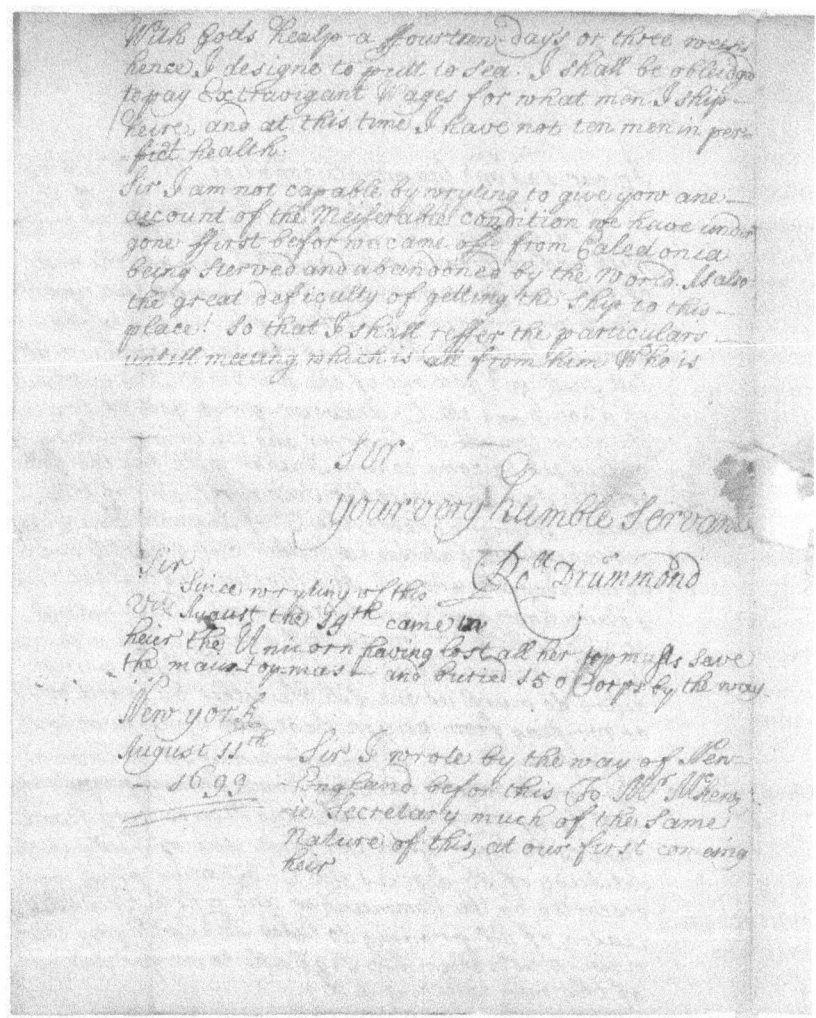

Figure 3.2 Robert Drummond to Mr. Hugh Montgomerie, August 11, 1699 (Adv. MSS 83.7.4, fol. 22). Courtesy of the National Library of Scotland

describing the situation in his letter leaves Drummond literally at a loss for words as he notes, "Sir I am not capable by wryting to give you an account of the Meiserable condition we have undergone ffirst befor we came offe from Caledonia being sterved and abandoned by the World. As also the great deficulty of getting the ship to this – place!"⁹⁴ Instead, he indicates that "I shall reffer the particulars until meeting."⁹⁵ In the midst of detailing the horrendous loss of life, Drummond also confirms the directors' fears about the embargo on their letters: "We have never heard so much as one silible either by word – or wryting from any in Scotland since ever wee came from thence."⁹⁶ As Drummond's letter suggests, none of the letters that the directors sent with the intended purpose of connecting the nation and its colony ever arrived. Despite the obvious travails he had experienced as a result of the attempt to colonize Darien, however, Drummond concludes his letter with an elaborately scripted signature, and with a farewell greeting indicating that he remains still the "very humble servant" of the company.

Drummond's letter was not read by the directors until November 28, 1699. By that time, indications of the loss of the colony were already in circulation. The *London Post* for October 4–6, 1699, noted, "Letters yesterday from Scotland say, they had a general Report there, that the Scots Colony at Darien, had abandoned their new Settlement of Caledonia, having been forced thereto for want of Provisions."⁹⁷ This "general Report" was initially viewed with suspicion by the directors as false news by ill-wishers. In the midst of the increasing concern, however, they gave orders to a second "Convoy" expedition to proceed to Darien and "ordered a Reinforcement of 300 able Men on Board, there being 1500 on board before."⁹⁸ Upon arriving in Darien in November 1699, this second expedition, consisting of four ships led by the *Rising Sun*, also found that the original settlement was deserted. Lacking sufficient resources, refused aid by the governors of the West Indian settlements and attacked by the Spanish, the second colony surrendered to the Spanish on March 31, 1700, ending the Scottish colonial venture at Darien in less than two years.⁹⁹

What is notable in the letters that bear witness to the venture is that, despite the company's expectations for productive connection between the "Mother" country and its new plantation, uncertainty, secrecy, desertion

---

[94] Ibid.   [95] Ibid.
[96] Ibid. The letter itself is written with a steady hand and indicates the use of a straight-edge for writing straight lines. A comment at the bottom right of the page, also written in steady straight lines, suggests that this is only one of several letters sent: "Sir I wrote by the way of New-England before this To Mr. McKenzie Secretary much of the same Nature of this, at our first coming heir." A hastily scribbled postscript between the signature and this note appears to have been added afterwards: "Sir Since wryting of this viz August the 14 came in heir the Unicorn having lost all her topmasts save the main topmast – and buried 150 Corps by the way."
[97] *London Post*, October 4–6, 1699.   [98] Ibid.   [99] Whatley, *Scots and the Union*, 173.

and betrayal were a significant part of the enterprise. The situation of the Darien letters encourages us to see the transatlantic communications of the eighteenth century as a network consisting not just of known agents but also of multiple modes of mediation, alternate routes, secret actors, dead ends and disconnections. In his *Mobility Studies: A Manifesto*, Stephen Greenblatt asserts that examining mobility "in a highly literal sense" is a necessary step in "understanding the fate of cultures."[100] According to Greenblatt, "the physical, infrastructural, and institutional conditions of movement ... are all serious objects of analysis. Only when conditions directly related to literal movement are firmly grasped will it be possible fully to understand the metaphorical movements."[101] In the case of the Company of Scotland, the letters were expressions and physical manifestations of the hopes of the directors for a positive outcome. Letters claiming to be from the colonists were used by the company directors to forge an imagined affective connection between Scotland and Caledonia. As printed traces of writing ostensibly done by hand, they symbolized a joining of the hands of a nation and its colony across the wide ocean. Because of their lack of mobility, however, the actual manuscript letters also literally and metaphorically represented the disconnection between the aims of the company, the fortunes of colonists and the fears of the King and his English government.

Inscribing Darien in the Aftermath of the Disaster

Watt suggests that "two parallel views" emerged from the "voluminous" pamphlet war that accompanied the Darien expedition: "one in which a well managed Company was undermined by English opposition and another in which the directors squandered the Company's capital."[102] He comments on the unprecedented support that the company enjoyed as a result of the "relentless and vigorous" propaganda campaign on the part of the directors

---

[100] Stephen Greenblatt, *Cultural Mobility: A Manifesto* (Cambridge: Cambridge University Press, 2010), 250. On the networked aspect of oceanic communication, see also Bruno Latour, *Reassembling the Social: An Introduction to Actor-Network Theory* (New York: Oxford University Press, 2005).

[101] Greenblatt, *Cultural Mobility*, 250.

[102] Watt, *Price of Scotland*, 168. Bowie suggests that the Country party "encouraged grass-roots engagement in all its addresses with the distribution of pamphlets and news" (Bowie, *Scottish Public Opinion*, 31). On May 1, 1700, the Scottish Parliament opened, only to be adjourned by the Duke of Queensbury nine days later after eight petitions from shires and burghs were presented, and it became clear that the opposition had seized political control. When Parliament re-opened on October 29, 1700, eighteen more grievances from shires and burghs were presented.

who embarked on a strategic campaign to exonerate themselves, helped by the emerging Country party, which was also intent on generating opposition to the government-supported Court party.[103] Ultimately, it was the narrative that blamed the disaster on English hostility that was more widely recirculated in the aftermath of the disaster and that was carefully selected by those sympathetic to the company as it sought to curate the cultural memory of Darien.

As in previous episodes in the company's history, printed letters figured importantly at this stage of events. One of the earliest interventions maligning the capabilities of the directors of the Company of Scotland, circulated before the loss of the colony, was written by Walter Herries, who had been a surgeon on the first expedition and who also appears to have been a spy for the English Secretary of State. Herries left the colony soon after arriving at Darien, and upon his return to Britain he penned a pamphlet, *A Defence of the Scots Abdicating Darien*, that was prefaced by a letter addressed to "the Right Worshipful, THE COURT of DIRECTORS OF THE Scots *Affrican* and *Indian* Company."[104] In this letter, Herries, a Scot by birth himself, reflects negatively not just on the directors but on the entire nation of Scotland. *A Defence of the Scots Abdicating Darien* excoriates the directors for their mismanagement of the colony, but also suggests that by complaining about the restrictions on their trade, they were demonstrating ingratitude for the benefits that Scotland had enjoyed since the Union of Crowns:

> by being Subjects of the King of *Great Britain*, you are not only shaded from the Insults of all Nations, but by the Authority of your *British* Sovereign, you are freed from the daily Feuds, and bloody little Wars, which, before the Union [of Crowns], for a Tract of Time, not less than *1900* Years, were continually raging amongst your selves … These Barbarities have been quite turn'd out of Doors since the Union, and they are now, either almost or altogether forgot. (n.p.)

Herries drew material from the worst of ethnographic prejudices against the Scots in order to castigate the Scottish directors: "Your People now enjoy the Blessings of Heaven, and Products of the Earth, and Ocean without any interruption; and whereas formerly they liv'd on the Mountains, and under the Shelter of some strong Rocks or Castles, they

---

[103] Watt suggests that by 1699, the council general of the Company of Scotland "had become a forum in which political battles were being fought between the Court and Country" (*Price of Scotland*, 166).

[104] Walter Herries, "Epistle Dedicatory," in *A Defence of the Scots Abdicating Darien Including an Answer to the Defence of the Scots Settlement There* (Edinburgh, 1700).

are now come down to the Plains, and can sleep sound in Beds, without the least Apprehension of Blood and Rapine" (n.p.).

Unsurprisingly, Herries's comments generated a flood of outraged responses, many of which either incorporated letters into their texts or adopted the form of the letter pamphlet in order to counteract Herries's accusations. George Ridpath, the editor of the newspaper *The Flying Post*, took up the cause, writing a series of works designed to restore Scotland's reputation and to disparage Herries's claims. In *An Enquiry into the Causes of the Miscarriage of the Scots Colony at Darien*, Ridpath weaves letters from the colonists into his narrative to provide documentary evidence to refute Herries, relating the story of the Company of Scotland from its beginning to the abandonment of Darien. He remediates the entire contents of "Abstract of a Letter sent from a Person of Eminence and Wealth at *Caledonia* to a Friend at *Boston* in *New-England*," for example, as well as including references from "Capt. *Pennicook*'s Journal sent to the Company" to prove his point regarding the Darien colonists' gestures of goodwill toward the nearby Spanish settlements.[105]

Ridpath also musters evidence from "Journals and Letters sent from our Colony" to counteract the "Falshoods and Inconsistencies" of Herries's description of the unsuitability of the location at Darien: "To put this Matter out of all doubt," indicates Ridpath, "we shall here subjoin the first Letter sent from Caledonia by the Council of the Colony to the Company" (101). Not only does the council's letter bear witness to the "Fruitfulness" of the land, argues Ridpath, but it also bears witness to the "incomparable" situation "for the Trade of the Coast" (103–04). Writing before the full extent of the colony's failure was understood, Ridpath uses the letter to further affirm that this "hopeful Design" not only promises "Profit and Glory" for the Company of Scotland, but also offers "the likeliest means that ever yet presented towards the inabling our Countrymen to revive, recover, transmit to Posterity, the Virtue, Lustre, and wonted Glory of their Renown'd Ancestors: And to lay a Foundation of Wealth, Security, and Greatness to our Mother Kingdom for the present and succeeding Ages" (105). Although he was not an eyewitness to the events in Darien, Ridpath employs letters in order to provide authority and authenticity for his assertions.

---

[105] George Ridpath, *An Enquiry into the Causes of the Miscarriage of the Scots Colony at Darien* (Glasgow, 1700), 74–75.

Once the news of the disaster became better known, letters and letter pamphlets also served to rally the nation around grief and indignation on behalf of the Company of Scotland and to memorialize the nation's colonial venture. In *A Short and Impartial View of the Manner and Occasion of the Scots Colony's Coming Away from Darien*, for example, Andrew Fletcher adopted the form of a letter pamphlet addressed to "A Person of Quality" to relate the history of Darien.[106] Fletcher's pamphlet reinforces the idea that the fate of the Scots colony was a matter of national pride, writing: "*My Lord*, I need not tell you the Ferment that the Body of the Nation seems to be in, upon Account of the Disasters and Misfortunes, that have attended the Undertakings of this Company; and really ... the Affections, as well as the Interests of many People seem to be wrapt up in its Fate" (38). Letters also serve as one of the main subjects in the body of the pamphlet: Fletcher blames the colony's abandonment on the fact that the colonists had received "no Word from Scotland all the time" as a result of the strict enforcement of the proclamations that prevented correspondence from being sent between the American colonies and any persons travelling to or from the Scots colony (17).

Edited collections of letters and documents also worked, in Aleida Assmann's term, to store the cultural memory of Darien in printed form in the aftermath of the disaster. *The Original Papers and Letters, Relating to the Scots Company Trading to Africa and the Indies*, for example, presents itself as an impartial collection of primary sources published "without any Reflection" so that they "cannot justly be taken ill by any Person or Party whatever."[107] Like the collections of official documents regarding the Revolution examined in Chapter 1, *The Original Papers and Letters* reprints the official public documents that formed part of the complex history of an important event, including addresses and petitions, but, unlike the earlier collections of documents, *The Original Papers and Letters* also features letters sent to individuals that are presented typographically in such a way as to suggest their earlier material existence in manuscript copies. The remediated version of a letter sent on September 28, 1697, to Tullibardine, for example, by the "several Subscribing Directors ... who are now in Town," includes a list of seven printed names (including Paterson's) arranged to look like signatures on a page,

---

[106] Andrew Fletcher, *A Short and Impartial View of the Manner and Occasion of the Scots Colony's Coming Away from Darien in a Letter to a Person of Quality* (Edinburgh, 1699).

[107] Company of Scotland Trading to Africa and the Indies, *The Original Papers and Letters, Relating to the Scots Company Trading to Africa and the Indies* (Edinburgh, 1700), 3.

followed by a "Memorandum" stating that "The Duplicate hereof was likewise sent at the same time to the Right Honourable Sir James Oglivie, Knight, &c. [the other Secretary of State at the time]" (12). The editor of *The Original Papers and Letters* further gestures toward the material practices associated with the original letters by drawing attention to the fact that a particular letter "was under Cover which containeth what followeth" (29). The printed versions of the letters are represented as if they have been extracted from the company's papers and captured in print, encouraging readers' sense of their immediacy and authority.

A Full and Exact Collection of All the Considerable Addresses, Memorials, Petitions, Answers, Proclamations, Declarations, Letters and Other Publick Papers, Relating to the Company of Scotland Trading to Africa and the Indies, published later in 1700, offers an even more complete and up-to-date version of events, covering the period from "*the passing of the Act of Parliament*" to "*November 1700*" and including the company's letters sent to the King to persuade him to negotiate the release of Darien colonists captured by the Spanish. Like the editor of *The Original Papers and Letters*, the editor of the *Full and Exact Collection* represents his work as bipartisan, commenting that he has chosen to gather together the "*publick Papers*" in order to provide those readers who are up to this point "*indifferent*" with "*positive Matters of Fact*," free of "*any artificial Embellishments or Reflections thereupon*" (i). What becomes clear in the course of reading through *The Original Papers and Letters* and the *Full and Exact Collection*, however, is the way in which the letters and printed documents make a positive case for the Company of Scotland without the need for any editorial intervention. Material justifying the company's stance makes up the bulk of the texts that are in the collection, largely because, as Bowie points out, aside from several "published speeches of the royal commissioner and chancellor and letters from William to his privy council" and several pamphlets by Herries, "William's government … did not provide a compelling justification for the crown's stance on the African Company."[108] Moreover, as each of the items included in the collections also incorporates a brief summary of events up to the point when the document was written, the contents of the collections present and re-present an overwhelming number of histories that are sympathetic to the company. The letters and documents work as a whole to create a cultural memory of events that emphasizes the ill treatment of the colony by the English government and that confirms the connection between the company and the Scottish

[108] Bowie, *Scottish Public Opinion*, 47.

nation. As the second memorial presented to the King in May 1699, reprinted in both works, suggests, "there was never any Enterprize of a more National Concern, than the foresaid Plantation is to the Kingdom of Scotland."[109]

The losses at Darien indeed turned out to be a disaster on a national scale. Only three of the fourteen vessels bound for Darien ever returned.[110] Of the roughly 2,800 souls who set out across the Atlantic, only thirty made it back to Scotland. Roughly 1,500 colonists died, while the others deserted, were taken prisoner or were dispersed among other colonies in America. The amount of money lost was staggering, contributing to the perception on the part of many Scots that they needed to unite politically with England in order gain access to English markets and to eliminate the Navigation Acts that hampered their trading activity.[111] At the same time as Scots were reassessing their political position, circumstances altered in 1702 with the accession of the now childless Queen Anne and the concern by the English Parliament to settle the succession on the Protestant Sophia of Hanover.[112] The year 1702 saw the start of a new round of negotiations on union. The pamphlet debate addressing the pros and cons of a union over the next five years was voluminous, as Bowie notes.[113] Bruce Levack suggests that "The volume of recorded opinion on the union, in the form of speeches, letters, proclamations, and pamphlets, is truly astonishing. Between 1603 and 1707 there was no other issue in the history [of] either nation, with the one exception of the English civil war, which attracted more attention and created more controversy than the union."[114] The sheer number of pamphlets flying from the presses meant that the popular awareness of national identity in Scotland that the discourse on the Darien venture had raised would continue to live on in the context of new debates.

Darien and the Union of 1707

Scholars have commented on the connections between the discourse circulating in the pamphlet war on Darien and the later pamphlet debates on the Union. As Bowie observes, although "historians of the union have tended to focus on the pamphlet exchanges of 1706–7, these tracts

---

[109] Company of Scotland Trading to Africa and the Indies, *Scotland's Right to Caledonia*, 12.
[110] Whatley, *Scots and the Union*, 166.   [111] Watt, *Price of Scotland*, 192–93.
[112] Anne's last surviving child, the Duke of Gloucester, had died in 1700.
[113] See Bowie, *Public Opinion*, chapter 6.
[114] Bruce Levack, *The Formation of the British State: England, Scotland, and the Union, 1603–1707* (Oxford: Clarendon Press, 1987), 14.

represented the final stage of a question that had been under public discussion since the late 1690s."[115] Whatley concurs that "The scale of the so-called pamphlet war" about the Union "has been acknowledged, but its precursors had been the flood of polemical writing that had been published on Darien, the succession and the infamous *Worcester* incident."[116] The conceptual connections between Darien and the Union need to be further stressed, however. In particular, it is important to recognize that the same authors who had jumped into the fray regarding Darien – in particular, George Ridpath, Andrew Fletcher and another journalist writing from London, James Hodges – also penned responses to the Union. Significantly, they drew on many of their earlier points in order to support their position against an incorporating union.

For Ridpath and Hodges, the discussions on Union were intimately connected to the historical power imbalance between England and Scotland that dated from the time of the Union of Crowns, an imbalance that they argued had contributed most recently to the disaster at Darien. Hodges concluded that Scots "hath had so much sensible Experience of very great and almost innumerable Disadvantages in their National Rights and Interests, and of the unavoidable influence of *England* upon their Government Civil and Ecclesiastical, their Trade, and all other public Affairs" that they have "great reason to be very cautious in putting themselves further in the Power of *England*."[117] Andrew Fletcher published his parliamentary speeches as well as pamphlets on the Union controversy. Echoing the sentiments of Ridpath and Hodges, and opposing Herries's perspective that the Union of Crowns had been beneficial for Scots, Fletcher maintained that Scotland's political hands had been tied since 1603:

> All our Affairs since the Union of Crowns, have been manag'd by the Advice of English Ministers, and the principal Offices of the Kingdom fill'd with such Men as the Court of England knew wou'd be subservient to their Designs: By which means they have had so visible an influence upon our whole Administration, that we have from that time appear'd to the rest of the World, more like a conquer'd Province, than a free and independent People.[118]

---

[115] Bowie, *Scottish Public Opinion*, 67.
[116] Whatley, *Scots and the Union*, 6–7. See Armitage, "Scottish Vision," too, for a discussion of the influence of Darien on the Union.
[117] James Hodges, *The Rights and Interests of the Two British Monarchies* (London, 1703), 8.
[118] Andrew Fletcher, *Speeches by a Member of the Parliament, Which Began at Edinburgh the 6th of May 1703* (Edinburgh, 1703), 6–7.

All three writers sought a federal union that would re-assert Scotland's rights vis-à-vis England, rather than an incorporating union which they felt would further erode Scottish "Liberties, Privileges, and Independency" (7). They used the example of Darien to argue for a fairer situation for Scotland.

John Hamilton, second Lord Belhaven, also drew attention to the Darien episode in arguing against an incorporating union. Belhaven was one of the signatories listed on the 1695 Act to establish the Company of Scotland and had himself invested heavily in the company. In his passionate *Speech in Parliament, the Second Day of November 1706*, Belhaven represents the Scottish nation as a homogeneous group, the sons of an "Ancient Mother CALEDONIA" who is being threatened with violence.[119] While critics have focused rightly on the rhetorical power of Belhaven's imagery, including his reference to a female Scotland who, "like *Caesar* sitting in the midst of our Senate" (6) is betrayed by those she most trusts, the less colourful sections of the speech also merit consideration for the light they shed on "the Motives which have engaged the two Nations to enter upon a Treaty of Union at this time" (15–16). Indicating the way in which the English have historically "never thought it worth their Pains of Treating with us," Belhaven suggests that the "first Notice they seem'd to take of us, was in our Affair of *Caledonia*, when they had most effectually broke off that Design" (16). He does not go into specific details, as he notes that the unfolding of the Darien affair happened "in a Manner very well known to the World, and unnecessary to be Repeated here." But despite suggesting that details of Darien are so "well known to the World" as not to need repeating, he flags the venture as a turning-point in English–Scottish relations and indicates its continuing relevance both in the present debate and in the future: he asks his fellow Members of Parliament to reflect on how events will be seen retrospectively if and when "our Posterity, after we are all dead and gone, shall find themselves under an ill-made Bargain, and shall have a Recourse unto our Records, and see who have been the Managers of that Treaty, by which they have suffered so much" (18). Belhaven makes a clear connection here between "Records" and cultural memory, anticipating that the Scottish people of the future will want to have access to information about the current

---

[119] John Hamilton, second Lord Belhaven, *Lord Beilhaven's Speech in Parliament the Second Day of November 1706* (Edinburgh, 1706), 6. See chapter 1 of Leith Davis, *Acts of Union: Scotland and the Literary Negotiation of the British Nation, 1707–1830* (Stanford, CA: Stanford University Press, 1998) for an analysis of Belhaven's speech.

controversy and assuming that in their time, too, Darien will be "well known to the World."

Ultimately, after several false starts and much debate, and despite the vocal opposition from figures such as Ridpath, Hodges, Fletcher and Belhaven, the parliaments of Scotland and England accepted the terms of the Treaty of Union that had been negotiated by commissioners from both nations, and each parliament passed its own Act of Union. On May 1, 1707, the united nation of Great Britain officially came into existence. The fate of the Company of Scotland was written into the Articles of Union. The fifteenth article, addressing an "equality of Trade throughout the united Kingdom," stipulated the payment of £398,085 10s. to Scotland, a sum "Equivalent" to the "Debts of *England*" for which the Scottish nation would assume responsibility;[120] it also arranged for future payments to Scotland based on a percentage share of the tax revenues for Great Britain. The Equivalent was to be used first to pay for "any Losses which privat persons may sustain" (14) because of the regulation of the coinage between the two nations and, second, to reimburse the "Capital Stock or fund of the African and Indian Company of Scotland advanced together with the interest for the said Capital Stock after the Rate of Five Pounds *Per cent. per annum*" (13). The article also made provision for the elimination of the "African and Indian Company of Scotland," which would "be Dissolv'd and Cease" just as soon as payment of the Equivalent was completed (13). In essence, the Equivalent was designed to cancel out financial debts incurred by Scottish investors in the Darien episode and, metaphorically, to negate accusations of Scottish ill treatment by the English government in the Darien episode.

The political impact of the Union was immense. Although Scotland maintained control over its legal and educational systems, and a separate act recognized Presbyterianism as the state religion, Scotland's political representation in the combined Parliament at Westminster was limited to 45 members out of 558 in the House of Commons and 16 members out of a total of 168 in the House of Lords. The cultural impact of the Union was also drastic. Whatley suggests that the Union encouraged a sense of Scottish "cultural nationalism." This newly invigorated sense of cultural nationalism, he suggests, "emerged as an important form of creative consolation to which many Scots were drawn as a result of the sense of loss of Scottish political nationhood caused by the union."[121] As this chapter has suggested, that "cultural nationalism" had been partially

---

[120] *Articles of Union* (Edinburgh, 1706), 9.   [121] Whatley, *Scots and the Union*, 13.

created earlier in the context of the Darien venture. Ironically, however, the cultural memory of Darien itself became occluded after 1707.[122]

Scots after the Union were, on the whole, more concerned with creating a positive representation of their nation than with recollecting memories that reflected badly on it. The career of the Edinburgh printer James Watson suggests this shift. In 1700 Watson had been prosecuted for printing a pamphlet by George Ridpath criticizing William III/II for his actions regarding Darien, *The People of Scotland's Groans and Lamentable Complaints* (1700). Watson was rescued from the Tolbooth and moved to Glasgow; then six years later, in the midst of the debates about the Union, he took up the cause of his nation again, this time focusing on its literary output by publishing the first volume of his *Choice Collection of Comic and Serious Scots Poems Both Ancient and Modern*. The *Choice Collection*, as Watson notes in the preface "From the Publisher to the Reader," is the first collection "of its Nature which has been publish'd in our own Native Scots Dialect."[123] It represents Scottish poems from historical as well as more recent periods, beginning with "Christ's Kirk on the Green," a poem in Scots that was, as Watson asserts, "Composed ... by King James the Fifth," and including older works like Alexander Montgomerie's "The Cherry and the Slae" and William Drummond's "Polemo-Middinia" as well as works that were being republished in contemporary broadsides such as Robert Sempill's "The Life and Death of the Piper of Kilbarchan." As a Jacobite himself, Watson features a significant number of Jacobite poems such as "The Banishment of Poverty," a celebration of the beneficence of the Duke of Albany (who became James II/VII), and "King Charles's Lament," but he also includes the occasional Whig work such as "Lintoun Address, to His Highness the Prince of Orange," which praises William for being the "Moses" who can "guard our Martial Thistle with the Roses" (1: 11). The *Choice Collection*, the second and third parts of which appeared in 1709 and 1711, was designed as a heterogeneous miscellany in which the literary output of the past intermingles with works from the present to suggest the continuing cultural dynamism of the nation despite its changed political circumstances.[124]

---

[122] See Ibid., 16, and Colin Kidd, "North Britishness and the Nature of Eighteenth-Century British Patriotisms," *History Journal* 39, no. 2 (1996): 361–82.

[123] James Watson, *A Choice Collection of Comic and Serious Scots Poems Both Ancient and Modern* (Edinburgh, 1706), 1: n.p.

[124] For further details on Watson's *Choice Collection*, see Leith Davis, "Imagining the Miscellaneous Nation: James Watson's *Choice Collection of Comic and Serious Scots Poems*," *Eighteenth-Century Life* 35, no. 3 (2011), 60–80.

Two years after the first volume of the *Choice Collection* appeared, Watson printed the first volume of another national project, a biographical treatment of the *Lives and Characters of the Most Eminent Writers of the Scots Nation* by George Mackenzie, a physician and a fellow of the Royal College of Physicians in Edinburgh. Like Watson, Mackenzie demonstrates his concerns with cultural nationalism, noting in his preface that although "our Nation has produc'd as Great Men as any other Nation in the World, yet we have been so unjust to their Memories and to our Posterity, that hitherto there has not been made a Collection of their Lives."[125] Also like Watson, Mackenzie suggests that Scotland needs a specific genre of printed work in order to bring it up to the level of other nations. He proposes that his *Lives and Characters of the Most Eminent Writers of the Scots Nation* will constitute a "Paper-Monument" to Scotland's "mighty Heroes in Learning" that will bring Scotland into par with "All the Wise Nations in the World" (1). The *Lives and Characters* targets a more affluent readership than Watson's miscellany. At a price of twenty shillings, a volume of the *Lives and Characters* sold at twenty times the price of a volume of the *Choice Collection*. Moreover, where Watson presents his material ahistorically, paying little attention to chronology, Mackenzie is concerned to establish an accurate chronological account of those of Scotland's "Illustrious Predecessors, as have been Eminent, either for Piety, Valour, or Learning" (1: n.p.). What is apparent, however, is that Mackenzie is as much concerned with establishing the character of the nation as he is with chronicling the nation's characters. Each author represented in the *Lives and Characters* stands as a palimpsest not only for the writers who have come before him, but for the nation's citizens in general. Where Watson's *Choice Collection* served to imagine Scotland as an ahistorical collection of readers, Mackenzie is concerned to delineate a specific character for the nation that is consistent through historical time.[126]

Watson's *Choice Collection* and Mackenzie's *Lives and Characters* were succeeded by a number of other post-Union publications concerned with collecting and commenting on a canon of Scottish cultural works in the wake of the loss of Scotland's Parliament, including Allan Ramsay's *The*

---

[125] George Mackenzie, *Lives and Characters of the Most Eminent Writers of the Scots Nation*, vol. 1 (Edinburgh, 1708), 1.
[126] For a fuller exploration of Mackenzie's *Lives and Characters of the Most Eminent Writers of the Scots Nation*, see Leith Davis, "The Aftermath of Union," in *The Cambridge Companion to Scottish Literature*, ed. Gerard Carruthers and Liam McIlvanney (Cambridge: Cambridge University Press, 2012), 56–70.

Tea-Table Miscellany and *The Ever Green, Being a Collection of Scots Poems, Wrote by the Ingenious before 1600*, both of which were published in 1724.[127] What is significant in this flourishing of Scottish literary activity, however, is that none of these works include any reference to Darien, either to Scottish hopes or to Scottish anger in the aftermath. While, as is made abundantly clear in these publications, Jacobite counter-memories continued to circulate in Scotland after the Union in opposition to the cultural narrative of British consolidation, Darien, as an enterprise that had been officially supported by the Presbyterian Church and conceived of as a colony representing Presbyterian values, was overlooked in the establishment of the cultural memory of Scotland. This dismissal was made easier by the fact that the directors and the major shareholders of the company had been compensated for their losses under the terms of the Acts of Union and were continuing to reap the financial benefits of the shifting ways in which the original Equivalent and the subsequent compensation to Scotland were disbursed.[128] They therefore had little incentive to keep the negative memory of Darien alive. As Watt notes, "the Scots would now develop their empire within a British context."[129]

For their part, English writers were also eager to gloss over the memory of Darien. Daniel Defoe, who had been sent to Scotland by Robert Harley in order to refute "By writing or Discourse" any "Objections, Libells or Reflections on the Union, the English or the Court, Relateing to the Union," took pains to direct the Scots away from dwelling on the past.[130] In the barrage of periodical writing, poetry and pamphlets that he produced in support of the Union, Defoe urged Scots to dispense with "the Rubbish of [Scottish] Ancient Fame" and embrace "THAT BLEST HOUR" of Union when a "WHOLE BRITTAIN" will awaken to her

---

[127] Allan Ramsay, *The Tea-Table Miscellany* (Edinburgh, 1724); Allan Ramsay, *The Ever Green, Being a Collection of Scots Poems, Wrote by the Ingenious before 1600* (Edinburgh, 1724).

[128] Watt points out that the funds from the Equivalent reached Edinburgh on August 1, 1707, and were dispersed originally by twenty-five commissioners appointed for the task. He notes that "The vast majority of shareholders and creditors were paid by the end of the year, but there was not enough to honour the military and civil lists" (*Price of Scotland*, 240–41). The commissioners also issued debentures for those who could not be paid with an interest rate of 5 percent, and two subsequent Acts of Parliament (in 1708 and 1718) addressed the unfinished business. Meanwhile in order to help them collect payments, investors in Scotland organized into the Society of the Subscribed Equivalent Debt, which became the Equivalent Company in 1724 and the Royal Bank of Scotland in 1727. See "The Royal Bank of Scotland Group Plc," in *International Directory of Company Histories*, ed. Jay P. Pederson, vol. 38 (Farmington Hills, MI: St. James Press, 2001), 392–99, Gale eBooks.

[129] Watt, *Price of Scotland*, 241.

[130] Daniel Defoe, *Letters of Daniel Defoe*, ed. George Harris Healey (Oxford: Clarendon Press, 1955), 126.

"former Glory."[131] Ironically, in *Caledonia, &c: A Poem in Honour of Scotland*, published in Edinburgh in 1706 and then in London the following year, Defoe suggests that it is only through accepting the "*Blest Conjunction*" of the Union rather than remaining separate that Scotland can restore its "Ancient dear bought Name" (18–19). In his *History of the Union of Great Britain* (1709), a retrospective rewriting of the cultural history of the Union, Defoe does include a brief account of the Company of Scotland, noting how the directors "put the *English* Nation under a Necessity of opposing" the company and how the scheme for a colony at Darien "had not one Branch belonging to its Contrivance, but what was big with necessary Abortions."[132] In justifying the government's decision to forbid "Trade or Correspondence" with the Darien colony because of the treaty with the Spanish, Defoe suggests that the managers of the company should have anticipated the situation and that, had the colonists been supplied with "Money or Letters of Credit," they would not have lacked provisions regardless of any "Proclamations of the *English* against Correspondence" (35). The tenor of *The History of the Union*, however, is to celebrate the Union as a providential act, a "Threed of History" that would sew the two nations fortuitously together; all events up to this point, suggests Defoe, have in fact led to the moment of Union: the "various Turns the Island of Britain has had in the Compass of a few past Years" have "had their direct Tendency to this great Event" (1). A pamphlet entitled *The Union-Proverb* published in 1708 and attributed to Defoe mentions Darien by name, but only to urge both Scots and English to forget the event, suggesting that "'tis to be hoped that the unfortunate Business of DARIEN will be *forgotten* ... and that all exasperating *Reflexions*, or ignominious *Provocations*, will be wholly *forborn* on *both sides* for the future."[133]

Over the course of the eighteenth century, the Company of Scotland's Darien expedition was referenced occasionally in the stored memory of printed books. Watt suggests that "Darien became a topic of concern for historians and writers," but it was represented only tangentially and then largely as an unfortunate episode that was remedied by the Union.[134] In his influential *The British Empire in America*, written the year after the

---

[131] Daniel Defoe, *Caledonia, &c: A Poem in Honour of Scotland, and the Scots Nation* (Edinburgh, 1706), 4.
[132] Daniel Defoe, *The History of the Union of Great Britain* (Edinburgh, 1709), 34.
[133] *The Union-Proverb* (London, 1708), 13.   [134] Watt, *Price of Scotland*, 248.

Union and republished in 1741, for example, John Oldmixon observes that the "Settlement of the Scots" at Darien was an "open Breach" of the "strict Alliance with the King of *Spain* at that time" so that King William "could not suffer his *English* Subjects to be assisting to the new Colony."[135] He notes, however, that "Satisfaction has been since made them, upon the Conclusion of the late happy Union between the two Nations" (1: 305). Similar sentiments were voiced by the historian John Campbell in his highly successful *The Lives of the Admirals, and Other Eminent British Seamen* (1742–44). The fourth volume of the work begins by announcing Campbell's intention to make the "Union of the two Kingdoms, the great Event from whence ... I shall deduce our Naval History to the present Times."[136] Accordingly, in relating the story of the Union, he suggests the numerous "Advantages on the side of Scotland," including the fact that "Those who had engaged far into the Design of Darien, and were great Losers by it, saw now an honourable way to be reimbursed" (13). While the history of Darien and the brief possibility of a Scottish empire were displaced throughout the eighteenth century by the story of the providential inevitability of Union, the papers and letters that had been so important in establishing the colony were also displaced, being removed to the Advocates Library after the post-1707 disbanding of the company. With the rediscovery of the letters in the mid-nineteenth century, however, the interrupted memory of Darien was revived, but this time under very different circumstances.

"Mute and Methodical Memorials": The Nineteenth-Century Rediscovery of the Darien Papers

In 1848, while conducting research for "a History of Scotland," John Hill Burton discovered a "curious collection" of documents "in an old oak press in one of the under rooms of the Advocates Library": the papers "connected with the Proceedings of the Company of Scotland trading to Africa and the Indies, commonly known as THE DARIEN COMPANY."[137] The exact details of how the papers ended up in this neglected site for safe-keeping are uncertain, although Burton speculated that when "the affairs of the Company were wound up after the Union,

---

[135] John Oldmixon, *The British Empire in America*, 2 vols. (London, 1708), 1: 305.
[136] John Campbell, *Lives of the Admirals, and Other Eminent British Seamen*, vol. 4 (London, 1744), 1.
[137] Burton, *Darien Papers*, xv.

and its miscellaneous property was dispersed, the oak press, containing the business books of the establishment, was carried from Bristo Port, across the Cowgate, and deposited in the Advocates Library, as an Institution where it might not unappropriately be preserved, and which was conveniently near" (xvi). Although Burton's attention was focused at the time on writing a more comprehensive history of Scotland, this unexpected discovery suggested to him that the papers concerning Darien might "present a separate and independent value to those curious in the history and manners of the times, or interested in the episode of our national history to which they refer (xvi). The "Council of the BANNATYNE CLUB" supported Burton in his project to "preserve ... the more valuable part of the documents ... in a printed form" (xvi). Accordingly, in 1849 the *The Darien Papers: Being a Selection of Original Letters and Official Documents Relating to the Establishment of a Colony at Darien by the Company of Scotland Trading to Africa and the Indies* was published, providing typographical remediations of the manuscripts that Burton considered most important.

What surprised Burton most in 1848 was the contemporaneity of the manuscript papers, in particular their "fresh, business appearance" and "their perfect similarity to those volumes which in the present day are methodically removed from the office safe, laid on the mahogany desk, and turned over by individuals throned on three-legged stools" (xxii). He notes, for example, that the "journals and ledger books" of the Company of Scotland, "many of them of gigantic size – would excite no passing remark on their obsolete appearance if they were seen lying open, with the ink wet, on a bank counter" (xvii). Employing the double-entry method of book-keeping, the cash journal book "resembles pretty minutely in its details a Journal" of the present, he notes (xvii).

Although the papers suggest to Burton the affinity between the late seventeenth century and his own time, however, he suggests that they also bear witness to the progress that has been made in the development of business practices. Drawing the reader's attention to "Sederunts of the Committee appointed by the Directors for Equipping their Ships," for example, Burton suggests that they contain "curious information on the mercantile practices of the day," the most remarkable of which for him is the "very miscellaneous and apparently totally indefinite character of the duties of the Committee, for their proceedings appear to have ranged from the founding of Colonies, and the establishment of their constitution, to the humble arrangements for supplying the wants of the people employed by them" (xvii). For Burton, these unfocused activities are also indicative of the fundamental ignorance and inexperience of the directors of the company: "Colonising and trading, like all other efforts of human skill or labour, are not, it would appear from these documents, to be lightly undertaken by those who are new to a practical acquaintance of their details" (xx). He expands on this theme: "In every thing they did, the Company at home and the colonists abroad went from one blunder to another. The central and supreme authority, so absolutely necessary for a body of men pursuing a purpose at a distance from their parent state, appears to have been totally wanting" (xx–xxi). Burton later points out that English neglect was also partially responsible for the disaster, but he still maintains that Scots were not good colonial administrators in the seventeenth century (although they would go on to play a dominant role as colonial servants to Britain's empire in his own era).

Burton did acknowledge, however, that seventeenth-century Scots were good writers, and he remarks on the unique attractiveness of the handwriting on the business papers: "The writing is singularly beautiful and distinct and at the present day would be called the perfection of bank clerk cal[l]igraphy" (xxii). In Burton's account, however, it is not just the aesthetics of the writing that is important. He suggests that the writing in fact reflects the essence of the writer. Paterson's writing, suggests Burton, "is very characteristic of his ardent, restless mind" (xxi). Eager to offer readers the opportunity to evaluate for themselves the singularity that he observes from first-hand access to the papers, Burton turns to a new technology: anastatic printing. Invented in Germany seven years earlier, anastatic printing was a technique for reproducing handwriting on the printed page.[138] Burton selects particular documents from the vast numbers of manuscripts that constitute the "Darien papers" to render into anastatic printing (see Figure 3.3), indicating his hope that "the accompanying fac-simile of some entries" will give "a general idea of the appearance of the subscription books; and the list of subscriber's names and titles, with their respective sums" and so "will render a more minute examination of the books unnecessary" (xxiv).

Burton intends that these mechanical reproductions of the manuscripts will save readers the time and energy of examining the originals themselves, but they also alter the status of the original papers so that they become

---

[138] Charles Jacob Jordan, *A Treatise on Anastatic Printing, or the Art of Reprinting from Prints on Paper* (London, 1853).

ENTRIES IN THE SUBSCRIPTION BOOK.

We Anne Dutches of Hamilton and Chastlerault, &c. Doe Subscrive for Three Thousand Pounds Sterling. *Hamilton* 3000

I Lo: Basil Hamilton Doe Subscribe for One Thousand Pounds Sterling — *Basil Hamilton* 1000

I Andrew Fletcher of Saltoun subscrive for a thousand pounds sterling *Fletcher* 1000

John Haldane of Gleneagles doe subscrive for six hundreth pounds *Haldane* 600

Mr. Andrew Wotherspoon minister of the gospell at the Burrough Rottoun for ane hundreth pound sterling *Wotherspoon* 0100

We, Dame Jean [...] Robert Chieslie for ourself of £500 for ye [...] *R. Chieslie* 3000

Figure 3.3 "Entries in the Subscription Book." from John Hill Burton, *The Darien Papers: Being a Selection of Original Letters and Official Documents Relating to the Establishment of a Colony at Darien*. Courtesy of the National Library of Scotland. License: CC by 4.0

"double-authored," in Ina Ferris's terms. As Ferris explains in her examination of the antiquarian editing of the Bannatyne Club, "when texts of the past turn into documents, they no longer inhabit either the past or the present but the space of their intersection."[139] A "double-authored" text, she argues, is "fully coincident neither with its original author nor with its later editor. Importantly, it is the product of both" (155–56). Burton's anastatic representations of the writing from Darien are similarly between worlds. In Burton's *Papers*, the letters and other manuscript materials become re-inscribed as artifacts of cultural memory. Plucked from the world of ink on paper, much like Nora's shells on the beach of living history, they collectively offer readers a glimpse into both an earlier era of Scottish cultural memory and also into a pre-mechanized era of manuscript culture. Burton's claims suggest that his text constitutes a printed version of "mute and methodical memorials" of Darien, conveying the "excitement and suffering" of the lost colonists, the "hopes and disappointments" of company men, as well as "the exultations and humiliations of a whole people" (xxi). Burton's edition of the Darien papers represents not only a Scottish national identity lost after the Acts of Union, but also an earlier medium – manuscript culture – that had been lost in the media shift of the eighteenth century. In Burton's resurrection of the Darien papers, the old technology of handwriting helps to foster a nostalgic cultural memory of a never-to-be-realized imperial possibility while, conversely, reflections on the memory of the nation are employed to create a nostalgic memory of a media landscape in which handwriting as a non-industrial form of technology played a key part.

As this chapter has argued, the original inscription of the cultural memory of Darien took place through a combination of letters and print, illustrating what David McKitterick has identified as the intimate and mutually determining relationship between the two media at the time.[140] Moreover, as I have suggested, the joint-stock company established in 1695 by Scottish and English businessmen in fact set the terms for the cultural nationalism of early eighteenth-century Scotland as the fortunes of the company became synonymous with the historic "Honour" and economic and political "Independency" of the nation. In the wake of the colony's failure, printed letters also served to inscribe

---

[139] Ina Ferris, "Printing the Past: Walter Scott's Bannatyne Club and the Antiquarian Document," *Romanticism* 11, no. 2 (2005): 155.
[140] David McKitterick, *Print, Manuscript and the Search for Order, 1450–1830* (Cambridge: Cambridge University Press, 2005).

Darien as part of Scottish cultural memory as the nation formed a new layer of identity around its loss. This memory was shaped as a footnote on the way to a consolidation of the nation under the 1707 Union, but it resurfaced in a new guise with Burton's rediscovery and publication of the Darien papers and was given a new lease on life within a re-activated cultural memory.

CHAPTER 4

Writing the 1715 Jacobite Rising
Periodical Networks and the Inscription of News

The death of Queen Anne, the last remaining Stuart monarch, on August 1, 1714, shifted control of the British state to the Protestant hands of Anne's distant cousin George of the House of Hanover. It also precipitated a new set of armed conflicts within Britain that would collectively become known as "the '15." Daniel Szechi has examined the way in which the 1715 Rising has been perceived as a "damp squib," an "irrelevance" in contrast to the other "major attempts by the Jacobites to resist or overthrow the 'Glorious Revolution.'"[1] The 1745 Rising, in particular, he maintains, with its stories of Bonnie Prince Charlie and the defeat at Culloden, continues to overshadow other attempts made to reinstate the Stuarts. Szechi's comments raise questions about how and when the minimizing of the 1715 Rising took place. In this chapter, I trace the representation of the 1715 Rising as it was unfolding and as it was shaped into a site of cultural memory in the immediate aftermath of the conflict.[2] I focus in particular on the role of the newly expanding networks of printed newspapers and periodicals in the initial inscription and storage of the events. I begin by comparing how news of the events in the summer of 1715 was initially inscribed both in manuscript newsletter form and in the newly expanding genre of the printed newspaper. Manuscript newsletters conveyed the domestic crisis as a series of connected events occurring sporadically around the mainland of Britain. The affordances of the newspaper, however, including the material presentation of news on the page, amplified the impression of events as a domestic crisis, sharing that sense of crisis with a larger percentage of the population. I move next to consider how the new form of the periodical essay as practiced by Joseph Addison and Richard Steele worked to counteract the alarming

---

[1] Daniel Szechi, *1715: The Great Jacobite Rebellion* (New Haven, CT: Yale University Press, 2006), 2 and 6.
[2] Rigney, "Plenitude," 17.

representation of events in the newspapers. *The Town-Talk* and *The Free-Holder*, published during the winter and spring of 1715–16, referenced the newspaper accounts, but attempted in different ways to minimize the threat posed by the Rising. I conclude by reflecting on how popular histories of the 1715 Rising written after its suppression continued the project of minimizing the '15, and, additionally, how the republication of those histories in the context of the 1745 Rising inscribed the 1715 conflict as a site of what Erll calls "pre-mediation" for the later crisis, reinforcing its relative unimportance. Like Chapters 2 and 3, then, this chapter focuses on the forgetting that is a crucial aspect of cultural memory by considering the mediated processes through which the substantial anti-Hanoverian sentiment that existed in the early part of the century was initially expressed and then occluded. At the same time, as I suggest, traces of counter-memories are also visible in the printed discourse of the '15, evidence of the complex ways in which knots of memory are created and circulated.

Networking the News in 1715

The 1715 Rising was the most extensive conflict to occur within the British Isles since the time of the 1688 Revolution, directly involving the citizens of all three nations in actual and potential violence and raising the possibility of the reinstatement of a Catholic Stuart monarch. Historians have analyzed the diverse causes of the unrest that led so many subjects to take up arms against the newly established Hanoverian government in 1715. Szechi, for example, notes that "Jacobitism in the British Isles was . . . a very complex phenomenon, involving national and confessional divisions in every one of the three kingdoms."[3] English Jacobites, and Tories in general, were disgruntled about the diminishment of their power under the new Hanoverian regime. Scottish Jacobites were unhappy with the consequences of the union with England, and many were concerned for the future of the Episcopalian Church. Although Ireland was not involved to the same degree as Scotland and England in the military action of 1715, Irish Catholics, too, supported a change back to the Stuart regime.[4] While they had different, sometimes conflicting national and

---

[3] Szechi, *1715*, 61. See also Bruce Lenman, *The Jacobite Risings in Britain: 1689–1746* (London: Eyre Methuen, 1980) and Frank McLynn, *The Jacobites* (London: Routledge & Kegan Paul, 1988).
[4] See Éamonn Ó Ciardha, *Ireland and the Jacobite Cause, 1685–1766: A Fatal Attachment* (Dublin: Four Courts Press, 2002).

religious reasons for wanting to see a Stuart king on the throne again, Jacobites in all three nations were united in their desires to reverse the regime change that had occurred in 1688. Unlike the 1688 conflict, however, which was initiated by a foreign leader landing his troops on English soil and gaining support while marching to London, the actions that subsequently became known as the 1715 Rising were organized by diverse local leaders and took place at different times and in different locations within the whole of mainland Britain. As Szechi indicates, "northern, central and western Scotland; Lowlands and Borders Scotland; and northern England" were all sites of conflict.[5]

If the temporal and spatial parameters of the crisis in 1715 were more complex than in 1688, so, similarly, were the media parameters as there were more opportunities for more people to read about events in print. The lapse of the Licensing Laws in 1695, discussed in Chapter 3, prompted an exponential growth in printed periodical news. Within a year of the lapse, three thrice-weekly newspapers went into circulation: the *Post-Boy* on May 14, 1695; the *Post-Man* on October 24, 1695; and the *Flying-Post* on February 25, 1696. All of these works were published on Tuesdays, Thursdays and Saturdays, the days on which the posts left London for the provinces, to maximize the spread of news to the population outside London.[6] While the 1712 Stamp Act caused some specific publications to cease production or to modify their price, form or frequency, newspapers in general continued to grow in the early years of the eighteenth century.[7] During the eventful months of summer, 1715, the newspapers in publication included one daily and seven tri-weekly newspapers in London, at least fifteen newspapers in the provinces, two newspapers in Scotland and one in Ireland. In fact, a number of new newspapers were begun in the course of the crisis.[8] The nation was hungry for information about the conflict which surrounded them.

---

[5] Szechi, *1715*, 5.
[6] See Fries, "Newspapers from 1665–1765," 57–58 for a list of papers that began publication after the lapse of the Licensing Act.
[7] Michael Harris, "London Newspapers," in *The Cambridge History of the Book in Britain*, vol. 5, *1695–1830*, ed. Michael Suarez and Michael Turner (Cambridge: Cambridge University Press, 2010), 421. For histories of the early eighteenth-century newspaper, see Hannah Barker, *Newspapers, Politics, and Public Opinion in Late Eighteenth-Century England* (Oxford: Oxford University Press, 1998) and Jeremy Black, *The English Press in the Eighteenth Century* (London and Sydney: Croom Helm, 1987).
[8] James Sutherland, *The Restoration Newspaper and Its Development* (Cambridge: Cambridge University Press, 1986), 250–53. Cranfield notes that "with the excitement of the Jacobite Fifteen with its aftermath of great trials and plots, new papers sprang up all over the country" (*Development of the Provincial Newspaper*, 19).

In order to understand the impact of what has been seen as an unprecedented increase in printed news, however, it is crucial to situate the genre of the newspaper within the context of the existing media ecology.[9] In 1715 oral news continued to play an important role in news transmission, and manuscript newsletters which had pre-dated printed news were still an active part of the media landscape.[10] In fact, Ian Atherton suggests that "Manuscript was the more important form of written news" right up until the early eighteenth century: "it was more plentiful than printed news; it was more accurate, less censored, and regarded as more authoritative."[11] During the tense period from summer, 1715 to spring, 1716, both manuscript newsletters and newspapers conveyed news about the events that would become known as the 1715 Rising. But their representation of that news took different material forms with different implications for how events would be shaped in cultural memory.

In the following two sections, I compare the news as represented in a series of manuscript newsletters with that published in issues of printed newspapers from the same time period. The newsletters that I examine are drawn from one of a small number of archives that contain a long-term run of manuscript newsletters beginning in the seventeenth and continuing into the early eighteenth century: the Newdigate Family Collection of Newsletters, currently held at the Folger Shakespeare Library in Washington, DC.[12] The period I consider is from June 1, 1715, to September 29, 1715, the date at which the collection ends.

For purposes of comparison, I examine a range of newspapers. *The Daily Courant*, the only daily paper at the time, was Whig-leaning, as was the *St. James's Evening Post*, begun by Abel Boyer in June 1715. *The Post-Man*, edited by John Fonvive, was, according to Snyder, a "non-partisan" journal, while *The Post-Boy* and *The Evening Post* were the "chief Tory organs."[13] I am interested less in the specific political differences between the newspapers, however, which have already been analyzed by other

---

[9] Rachael Scarborough King describes the multi-media manner through which news circulated during the time: "written and printed media worked in tandem and in addition to the traditional oral circulation of news, offering users a range of communicative options" (*Writing to the World*, 25).

[10] Adam Fox and Daniel Woolf, eds., *The Spoken Word: Oral Culture in Britain, 1500–1850* (Manchester: Manchester University Press, 2003).

[11] Ian Atherton, "The Itch Grown a Disease: Manuscript Transmission of News in the Seventeenth Century," *Prose Studies* 21, no. 2 (1998): 40.

[12] Folger Library, MS L.c.1–3950 and also available in digital form, the archive includes close to 4,000 manuscript newsletters sent to three generations of the Newdigate family between January 1674 and September 1715.

[13] See Henry L. Snyder, "The Circulation of Newspapers in the Reign of Queen Anne," *The Library*, 5th ser., 23, no. 3 (1968): 210–11. Snyder estimates that the *Daily Courant* had a circulation of

scholars, than in the implications of the newspapers' material differences from manuscript newsletters. I suggest that by comparing and contrasting the treatment of political news in manuscript newsletters and printed newspapers during this specific and limited time period, we can see in relief the different affordances of each medium and gain further information about what role scribal news played in conveying political information and why it eventually lost traction. It was during the 1715 Rising, I suggest, that the genre of the newspaper began to overtake the manuscript newsletter as an authoritative vehicle of news and also began to take on a more prominent – albeit complex – role in the inscription of what would become cultural memory.

"Some Advices Say": Mediations of the 1715 Rising in Manuscript Newsletters

The Newdigate family manuscript newsletters constitute what I refer to elsewhere as official manuscript newsletters, those compiled and written behind closed doors by a cadre of clerks at Whitehall and sent out from the Secretaries of States' offices to a limited number of individuals with whom the government wished to maintain connections.[14] Official manuscript newsletters differ from commercial newsletters, such as those that were produced by John Dyer and William Wye for profit. The first letters in the Newdigate archive were sent in January 1674 to Richard Newdigate of Arbury Hall, Warwickshire, a judge and serjeant-at-arms who became a Member of Parliament briefly in 1660.[15] The newsletters written during the summer of 1715 were sent to Sir Richard Newdigate, third Baronet (1668–1727), who had taken over the estate in 1710, the same year he was elected to Parliament for Newark upon Trent, Nottinghamshire.[16]

Like the earlier Newdigate newsletters, those sent during the summer of 1715 maintain the sense of a formal exchange of letters that was typical for

---

about 800 in 1704, possibly 600 in 1712. The *Post-Man*, he suggests, had a circulation of 3,800 in 1704. The semi-weekly *Evening Post* sold about 3,500 to 4,000 copies per number.

[14] See Davis, "Official Manuscript Newsletters and the Glorious Revolution," 148–74.

[15] Elisabeth Chaghafi, "The Newsy Baronet: How Richard Newdigate (Per)Uused His Newsletters," The Collation: Research and Exploration at the Folger, September 19, 2019, https://collation.folger.edu/2019/09/newsy-baronet/.

[16] He was granted a baronetcy in 1677. His son, Sir Richard Newdigate, second Baronet (1644–1710), an investor in innovative coal-mining technology, continued the practice of receiving the newsletters, as well as becoming an avid consumer of printed news. See Richard Newdigate, *The Case of an Old Gentleman, Persecuted by His Own Son* (London, 1707) and *An Alphabetical List of the Knights and Commissioners of Shires, Citizens and Burgesses* (London, 1711).

the genre of manuscript news, beginning invariably with a stylized "Sir" in the top left corner. They frequently commence by acknowledging which foreign mails have arrived and what information has been gleaned from them. The newsletter for July 19, 1715, begins, for example: "Last Night Arrived ye Maile due from H[o]ll[a]nd with ye foll[owing] News . . . ."[17] Several letters, however, such as that sent on September 20, 1715, begin with news of Parliament, then announce the arrival of the foreign mails in the middle of the letter, an indication that by 1715 the genre of manuscript news was changing.[18] Like other manuscript newsletters, the Newdigate manuscript newsletters employ expressions which signal the oral and scribal origins of the news being passed on. The July 21, 1715, newsletter relays information by indicating that "There are Advices from [F]rance which *say*," while other newsletters include phrases such as "We *hear*" or "It is *said*."[19] Derived from a number of sources, the newsletters that travelled to the Newdigate family in 1715 thus served as vectors for other media, including other manuscript materials as well as printed works, as is suggested by occasional references to an enclosed "gazette" and ink marks from a printed newspaper on the newsletters themselves.

In terms of content, the manuscript newsletters in the Newdigate collection written in the summer of 1715 pay particular attention to identifying subversive activities. They pass on information obtained from domestic reports about "ryots" and tumults in Manchester,[20] Kidderminster[21] and Wolverhampton,[22] together with an account from Glasgow of the seizure of "three Chests Laden w[i]th Musquets, Bayonets, Swords and pistols said to belong to a Laird of Highland Clan[s]."[23] A number of the newsletter writers' comments focus on cases of transgressions by and punishment of particular individuals. On June 16, 1715, for example, the writer indicates, "We have an Accnt. From Cambridge yt one Mr. Watson has been lately Expelled yt University for drinking ye Pretenders Health."[24] As well as selecting accounts of events from provincial locations, the writers offer information on items of concern within

---

[17] Newdigate Family Collection of Newsletters, July 19, 1715, Folger Library, MS L.c.3921.
[18] Newdigate Newsletters, to Richard Newdigate, September 20, 1715, MS L.c.3947.
[19] Newdigate Newsletters, July 21, 1715, MS L.c.3922. My italics.
[20] Newdigate Newsletters, June 21, 1715, MS L.c.3909.
[21] Newdigate Newsletters, July 23, 1715, MS L.c.3923.
[22] Newdigate Newsletters, July 5, 1715, MS L.c.3915.
[23] Newdigate Newsletters, June 7, 1715, MS L.c.3903.
[24] Newdigate Newsletters, June 16, 1715, MS L.c.3907.

London. On June 9, 1715, "a written paper" purporting to offer "a declaration in favour of ye Pretender" was "taken down & delivered by one of ye beedles to ye Justices of Peace for Westm[inste]r."[25] On June 16, 1715, a "ffrench Schoolmaster was whipt from Stocksmarket [sic] to Aldgate" for making disparaging remarks on the King, although the newswriter also indicates that "as soon as he was taken from ye Car abundance of people gave him money & others treated him wth. Wine."[26] Other individuals were apprehended by the King's messengers for spreading seditious pamphlets during this time. The manuscript newsletters represent a nation that is unsettled in its urban centres as well as its remote regions, in its university towns as well as in the nation's capital.

While the clerks writing the newsletters provided details about the variety of questionable activities taking place within the nation, they also situated those activities within a narrative comprising other information, including details from the foreign mails about the Great Northern War and the Ottoman–Venetian War. In addition, writers note the activities at the court of James Stuart, son of James II/VII, at Bar-le-Duc, including the comings and goings of visitors to the court. On July 21, 1715, the writer notes, "There are Advices from ffrance which say that the Lord Bolingbrook is come to Paris and that the Pretender was there and had frequent Conferrences with that Lord and that an Attempt would shortly be made on Great Brittain – It is further said that the Pretender has given that Lord a sham Garter –."[27] Nine days later, however, the writer indicates the contradictory information that has been received: "Some advices say yt ye Pretender is still at Paris and frequently sees ye L[or]d. Bolingbrook & others will have it yt he is gone back discontented to Bar Le Duc."[28] Also contradictory is the news regarding the ill health of the French King that began to circulate at the end of August. News of Louis XIV's eventual death is at first denied in "letters from France" and then obtained in a circular manner, first carried by means of "advice" from merchants,[29] then given in an express from France on August 23 and eventually confirmed by an express from the English ambassador to France, the Earl of Stair, who sent "an Acco[un]tt. yt ye ffrench King did not dye till Sunday last at 10 a Clock in ye Morning."[30] Rather than expressing relief about the King's death dashing the hopes of the Jacobites

---

[25] Newdigate Newsletters, June 9, 1715, MS L.c.3904.
[26] Newdigate Newsletters, June 16, 1715. [27] Newdigate Newsletters, July 21, 1715.
[28] Newdigate Newsletters, July 30, 1715, MS L.c.3926.
[29] Newdigate Newsletters, August 20, 1715, MS L.c.3935.
[30] Newdigate Newsletters, August 25, 1715, MS L.c.3937.

for French aid, the writer, in a rare speculative comment, suggests that there "is like to be great Disturbances in yt Kingdom" and indicates continuing suspicion of the new Regent of France and his power.[31]

Considerable space in the Newdigate Newsletters is also taken up with details about the bills being read and voted on in the House of Commons and House of Lords, a number of which are directly related to the disturbances conveyed by the newsletters. On July 2, 1715, for example, four days after an indication about "Rioters at Manchester,"[32] the writer indicates that a "Bill ... to suppress all Ryots & Tumults" is brought before the House of Commons.[33] Three weeks later, a "bill to impower the king to set aside ye Habeas Corpus Act" is approved to "be in force to ye 24th of Jan. next."[34] One particular narrative thread running throughout the newsletters' parliamentary accounts during the summer of 1715 concerns the charges against the Earl of Oxford and Viscount Bolingbroke for "High Treason & other High Crimes & Misdemeanors."[35] The writer of this newsletter suggests the contentiousness of this issue when he includes information regarding the vote on whether to adjourn and postpone consideration of the report. Another ongoing activity of the House of Commons is the work of settling the elections, which, frequently postponed by other pressing issues, is usually conveyed in the last line of the newsletters.

By the end of August, however, the focus of the newsletters sent to Richard Newdigate changed. Instead of devoting attention to detailing the crimes of specific disaffected individuals, the newsletters switch to providing information about the government's response to the Jacobite threats, including the mustering of troops in the camp at Hyde Park. In the midst of reporting on events in London, the newsletter writers do attempt to find out about and transfer information about the activities of the Jacobites. But the reports that arrive are sporadic, making it difficult to pass them on in a chronologically accurate fashion. On August 25, 1715, for example, the writer indicates that "Letters from Scotland bring advice that the Earl of Marr [sic] is in that Kingdom and that 3 Scotch Lords and one Commoner (viz) Mr. Lockhart Author of the Memoires of Scotland are confined in the Castle of Edinburgh on suspition of being in the Interest of

---

[31] Newdigate Newsletters, August 27, 1715, MS L.c.3938.
[32] Newdigate Newsletters, June 28, 1715, MS L.c.3912.
[33] Newdigate Newsletters, July 2, 1715, MS L.c.3914.   [34] Newdigate Newsletters, July 23, 1715.
[35] Newdigate Newsletters, June 11, 1715, MS L.c.3905.

the Pretender."³⁶ More letters apparently arrived between the initial writing and the posting of the newsletter, and consequently the writer adds the more recent news further down the page: "this day came in Letters from Scotland wth an Acc[oun]tt. yt ye Highlanders attempted to take possession of ye Castle of Drummond, but were obliged to retire –."³⁷ In addition to arriving irregularly, the reports are often contradictory, as is suggested by the newsletter writer's remarks on August 30, 1715, correcting information he had provided previously: "Last Tuesday it was Reported yt a Camp was forming in ye Highlands of Scotland in favour of ye Pretender, but ye Letters which came in yesterday from thence bring no acctt. of it."³⁸

As the crisis deepened and concerns mounted, the newsletters came to rely more frequently on "express" letters, those that were not sent by regular post but instead were sent by special messenger. On September 22, 1715, for example, the newsletter writer indicates that "yesterday arrived an Express from Scotland that the Highlanders have received reinforcements and have taken the town of Perth … and afterwards Entred the Town and Imprisoned the Magistrates and Appointed others in the Name of the Pretender."³⁹ Information provided about this incident, however, is minimal, and no further details about the taking of Perth are forthcoming in later newsletters. Instead of trying provide such information, the writer focuses instead on Parliament's actions in regard to the alleged rebel leaders in England, noting that "A motion was made in the House of Lords to secure Severall Lords and Commons."⁴⁰ He confirms that "the Lords Landsdown and Duplin" were "taken into Custody Yesterday" and that "Warrants" are out for several other lords."⁴¹ Notably, however, the specific names of the other lords concerned are blacked out. The writer does list the names of others arrested, however, as well as the ridings that they represent: "S[i]r. W[illia]m Windham Knight of the Shire for Somerset, S[i]r John Packington, Knight of the Shire for Worcester, Edward Harvey of Combe Esqr. Member for Clithero[e] in Lancashire, Corbet Kynaston Esq[ui]r[e], Member for the Town of Shrewsbury, John Anstis Esq[ui]r[e] Member for Launceston in Cornwall and Thomas [F]orster Esq[ui]r[e] Junn[ior]. Member for Northumberland –."⁴² The information contained in the newsletter makes it clear just how diffuse the English Jacobite resistance was, but it also

---

³⁶ Newdigate Newsletters, August 25, 1715.   ³⁷ Ibid.
³⁸ Newdigate Newsletters, August 30, 1715, MS L.c.3939.
³⁹ Newdigate Newsletters, September 22, 1715, MS L.c.3948.   ⁴⁰ Ibid.   ⁴¹ Ibid.
⁴² Ibid.

provides minimal details about specific events in the actual locations of conflict.

Official manuscript newsletters, like their commercial counterparts, were "confidential" documents, in Donald Reiman's classification, not "intended for the eyes of a wide and diverse readership," but rather "addressed to a specific group of individuals all of whom either [were] personally known to the writer or belong[ed] to some predefined group that the writer has reason to believe share communal values with him or her."[43] The official manuscript newsletters sent out during the early stages of the 1715 Rising served to create a specific limited elite community, connecting its members personally to government officials.

Moreover, through their regular appearances on specific days of the week, manuscript newsletters served to unite that elite community through a common sense of temporality. Daniel Woolf argues that the circulation of periodical news from the time of the Civil War onward produced a new understanding of the present. Before the mid-seventeenth century, he suggests, "from the point of view of a person receiving news of a great event, and recording it or passing it on to an acquaintance, there was an unbridgeable temporal gap between the event itself and his or her perception of it."[44] In contrast, according to Woolf, the practice of providing regular updates about events through the periodical circulation of news led to a new expectation among the population that they would hear about an event in due course, even if that event took place at a distance. The present, he argues, changed from being a moment distinguishing past from future to being a common perception of the "duration" of time.[45] In a similar fashion, the regular manuscript newsletters circulating in 1715 encouraged their readers to think about the events of the Rising as a narrative that they were experiencing in a common present. The newsletters also implicitly affirmed their addressees' networked connections with each other as privileged readers of the national narrative provided by the government.

At the same time, however, the manuscript newsletters also generated a sense of uncertainty about that shared sense of a present. Szechi observes

---

[43] Donald Reiman, *The Study of Modern Manuscripts: Public, Confidential and Private* (Baltimore: Johns Hopkins University Press, 1993), 39.

[44] Daniel Woolf, "News, History and the Construction of the Present in Early Modern England," in *The Politics of Information in Early Modern Europe*, ed. Brendan Dooley and Sabrina Baron (London and New York: Routledge, 2001), 83.

[45] Ibid., 82. See also Brendan Dooley, "Preface," in *The Dissemination of News and the Emergence of Contemporaneity in Early Modern Europe*, ed. Brendan Dooley (Farnham: Ashgate, 2010), xiii.

that "in many respects there was not a single Jacobite rebellion [in 1715], but rather a very loosely coordinated set of rebellions."[46] By concentrating primarily on events in London, the official newsletters made their readers very aware that they were receiving only part of the story, and not the most active part at that. Consumers of official newsletters, like those of newspapers at this time, were used to a certain level of disorder in the communication of information and were arguably used to correcting for what Tony Claydon calls the gaps and numerous "updates and expansions of stories" in the reception of information.[47] But as the events that would later be collectively viewed as the Jacobite Rising of 1715 unfolded in the remote parts of the nation, both the temporal and spatial gaps in the manuscript newsletters' conveyance of news took on more serious implications than ever before. Newspaper compilers, however, as we will see, were willing and eager to try to fill in some of those gaps.

Expanding Coverage: Newspaper Accounts of the 1715 Rising

Like manuscript newsletters, newspapers were multi-modal vectors of communication, conveying information derived from oral sources, letters and other newspapers. Like their manuscript counterparts, the newspapers published in the summer of 1715 frequently signal the oral origin of the news they carry with phrases such as "we hear," and they identify material gleaned from letters by employing such phrases as "Letters from Edinburgh," "They write from Newcastle" or "From Edinburgh ... it is advised."[48] Information is relayed under headings that indicate not only the location from which it is derived but also the specific date when it was sent. In conveying this information, newspapers frequently employed the same kind of temporally relational language as that found in the newsletters, referring to "last night" or "instant." At times, the provision of information about the origin of the reports results in a dizzying layering of remediations, however. Under the heading "*London*, September 1," the September 1, 1715, edition of the *Daily Courant* passes on news that was

---

[46] Szechi, *1715*, 251.
[47] Tony Claydon, "Daily News and the Construction of Time in Late Stuart England, 1695–1714," *Journal of British Studies* 52, no. 1 (2013), 63. According to Claydon, "There could not be one present narrative, but rather there was a shattered series of events, inevitably reported out of their true order" (66).
[48] As King suggests, newspapers at this early stage adopted many conventions of manuscript newsletters in order to represent themselves as authoritative sources of news for a population more likely to credit the written than the printed word ("Manuscript Newsletter").

originally conveyed in "letters" from "*Venice*, August 23," then printed in the *Amsterdam Courant*, then reprinted in the *Courant*. Like the manuscript newsletters, the newspapers in 1715 represented themselves as part of the world of traditionally conveyed information.⁴⁹

Importantly, however, newspapers, being considerably less expensive, were designed for a wider readership than the manuscript newsletters. Even though, as Alex Barber points out, elite readers also consumed newspapers, newspapers were largely designed for those in the "middling ranks" of society who were concerned with business and trade.⁵⁰ In addition, because there were so many varieties of newspapers readily available in public places such as coffee-houses, newspapers were also consumed by a significant number in the lower ranks.⁵¹ Whereas the manuscript newsletters circulated among an exclusive readership who knew and communicated with one another by other means, newspapers were one-way systems of communication designed for a wider body of readers who were unknown to each other.⁵²

Like the manuscript newsletters, the newspapers published in the summer and early autumn of 1715 provided readers with details about the escalating crisis, starting with increasing acts of opposition during the early summer months. While describing in great detail the celebrations of George I's birthday on May 28, the *Flying-Post* of June 11–14, 1715, for example, also includes a letter from London describing the actions of the Jacobite faction: "witness their making a Bonfire; and ringing the Bells in White-Chappel [*sic*], and the strolling about of several Scoundrels, with Cockades in their Hats, on what they call the Pretender's Birth-day."⁵³ The newspapers also note occasions of drinking of toasts. The *St. James's Evening Post* for August 15–17, 1715, gives notice that "On Wednesday last, one William Way was committed to Newgate, for speaking certain Words reflecting on the King and Government; as was the next Day James

---

⁴⁹ *Daily Courant*, September 1, 1715.
⁵⁰ Alex Barber, "'It Is Not Easy What to Say of Our Condition, Much Less to Write It': The Continued Importance of Scribal News in the Early 18th Century," *Parliamentary History* 32, no. 2 (2013): 293–316. See also Michael Harris, *London Newspapers in the Age of Walpole: A Study of the Origins of the Modern English Press* (Rutherford, NJ: Fairleigh Dickinson University Press, 1987), 41.
⁵¹ Harris, in *London Newspapers in the Age of Walpole*, notes that "in London in particular the range of potential newspaper purchasers was increasing" (192).
⁵² Harris suggests that there were approximately "a quarter of a million" readers and users of newspapers around this time period ("London Newspapers," 423). As King indicates, however, certain newspapers also encouraged contributions on the part of their readers ("Manuscript Newsletter," 430–31).
⁵³ *Flying-Post*, June 11–14, 1715.

Osborn, on the Oath of two Persons, for drinking the Pretender's Health, by the Name of *James the Third*."⁵⁴

The official manuscript newsletters, as productions of the Secretary of State's offices, had official government support. Newspapers, however, needed to be wary of incurring government disapproval. While the changing censorship laws had opened up the option of printing news without obtaining government approval, authors and printers could still be prosecuted for conveying opposition to the government. The newspapers give an indication of the frequency of prosecutions of editors and publishers at the time. In early August, for example, Edward Berrington and John Morphew, the printer and publisher respectively of the *Evening Post*, were "taken into Custody ... for printing a pamphlet" which "reflect[ed] on King & Parliament."⁵⁵ While the manuscript newsletters were at liberty to list anti-government behaviour without comment, newspapers attempted to contain or qualify any information regarding the growing crisis that such information might convey. The *Daily Courant* for July 5, 1715, for example, includes a letter dated July 2, 1715, from Manchester that refers to the recent riots: "Several Justices of the Peace having received particular Orders from his Majesty to inquire into the late Riots in and about this Town, came hither on the 29th past, and Sit frequently to take Examinations."⁵⁶ The writer is reassuring, however, concluding that "From the time that Major Wivill [Wyvill] with two Troops of Dragoons arrived here, we have not had the least Disturbance, and still continue in perfect Quiet."⁵⁷ On June 15, 1715, the *Daily Courant* published a statement from the Vice-Chancellor of Oxford University condemning a recent riot in its midst. The statement describes how a "Multitude of Persons, who assembled together" wandered "from one Part of the City to the other, breaking of Windows, rifling of Meeting-Houses, and committing other Outrages."⁵⁸ The vice-chancellor is quick to note that the rioters were "to Us unknown."⁵⁹ The fact that this declaration is the first item appearing in the paper indicates its importance in the eyes of the editor as an indication of loyalty.

Although newspapers needed to be cautious of focusing too much on dissent, readers could infer growing cause for concern in other ways. Information that was included in the newspapers about the steps the

---

⁵⁴ *St. James's Evening Post*, August 15–17, 1715.
⁵⁵ Newdigate Newsletters, July 2, 1715. See also Alexander Andrews, *The History of British Journalism: From the Foundation of the Newspaper Press in England to the Repeal of the Stamp Act in 1855* (London: R. Bentley, 1859).
⁵⁶ *Daily Courant*, July 5, 1715.   ⁵⁷ Ibid.   ⁵⁸ *Daily Courant*, June 15, 1715.   ⁵⁹ Ibid.

government was taking in order to contain unrest, for example, offered insight into situations otherwise not discussed. On July 28, 1715, the *Daily Courant* indicated the publication the day earlier of "his Majesty's Royal Proclamation for suppressing Riots and Rebellious Tumults."[60] The language of the proclamation itself describes the subversive activities that had been taking place:

> some of the meanest of the People have of late been Stirred up to Riots and Tumults to the disturbance of the Publick Peace, and are now carried into open Rebellion and levying War against the King and his Authority; they having with an armed Force in many distant Places, proceeded to pull down, burn, and destroy, the Houses and Buildings of peaceable Subjects, declared for the Pretender, and actually resisted with force of Arms such as by lawful Authority were endeavouring to disperse them.[61]

The reference to "open Rebellion and levying War against the King" offers readers a brief glimpse into the escalating national threat.

Indications of the seriousness of the crisis that was brewing were also provided by the addresses of loyalty that began appearing in the newspapers at the end of July. These addresses assert the loyalty of specific towns, cities and organizations and portray confidence in the government's ability to quell any conflict. The King's replies to these addresses, which were also printed in the newspapers, further asserted the bond between monarch and subjects. Nevertheless, the addresses also raised the fears they sought to quell. The "humble Address" of "*the Lord-Lieutenant and ... the Deputy-Lieutenants and Justices of the Peace of the County of* Middlesex," printed in the July 26–30, 1715, edition of the *London Gazette*, for example, asserts "our firm and unshaken Adherence to your Majesty and your Royal Family," but also draws attention to "Seditious and Rebellious Tumults, raised and fomented in several Parts of this Kingdom by the Enemies to your Majesty's Person and Government, encouraged by the Hopes of an Invasion from Abroad in favour of a Popish Pretender."[62] As addresses assuring the King of the loyalty of his subjects continued to pour in, it became apparent just how much the nation was under threat.

With the deepening crisis, the newspapers, too, had difficulty obtaining accurate news about the conflict. Like the manuscript newsletters, the newspapers also represented "numerous updates and expansions of stories," in Claydon's phrase, reporting initially on preliminary information and then reporting about it again with more details or corrections. In

---

[60] *Daily Courant*, July 28, 1715.   [61] Ibid.   [62] *London Gazette*, July 26–30, 1715.

the September 15, 1715, edition of the *Daily Courant*, for example, the arrival is noted of an express from Edinburgh that carried the "News that a Party of about 80 Rebels had attempted to Surprize the Castle in the Night time by Scaling-Ladders, and that three of them were entred before the thing was discovered."[63] Four days later, the event is reported again with further information, including details of the "Design" of the attackers, which was "to mount the Wall on the West Side of the Castle by Rope-Ladders provided for that purpose, which were to be pulled up by Lines let down from within by some Soldiers belonging to the Garrison who had been corrupted."[64] The account indicates that "the Government having had some Intimation of this Design, had ordered part of the Town-Guards and some Gentlemen Volunteers to Patroll on the West Side of the Castle: and the Officers within to double their Guards and to make diligent Rounds."[65] This same edition of the *Daily Courant* also contains information that had just arrived from Dundee and Perth about the raising of the Pretender's standard there on September 6, 1715, eight days before the attempt on Edinburgh Castle.

Although they represented the same kinds of temporal lapses that the manuscript newsletters did, the newspapers were able to give readers more information about events occurring in the sites of action and provide more extensive coverage than the manuscript newsletters. In reporting on the Jacobites' seizure of Perth and the decision made in London to arrest a number of Jacobite leaders in England, for example, the newspapers offered a more expanded perspective on events north of the border. The manuscript newsletter sent to Richard Newdigate on September 22, 1715, had provided details about the arrests, including the names and constituencies of the non-nobility who were arrested, but had included little information about the capture of Perth. In contrast, newspapers offered a condensed version of the arrests, but considerably more information about events at Perth. The *Daily Courant* for September 22, 1715, for example, noted that "We hear, that Yesterday two Lords were taken into Custody and a Warrant out against a third: And that by Order of the House of Commons, Sir W. W[y]ndham, and five more Members of that House, will be also taken into Custody."[66] In addition, the newspaper provides a full account regarding the events in the north:

---

[63] *Daily Courant*, September 15, 1715. [64] *Daily Courant*, September 19, 1715. [65] Ibid.
[66] *Daily Courant*, September 22, 1715.

> By Express from Scotland there is Advice, that the Rebels having received their Reinforcements, passed the River Tay and had seized the Town of Perth, before the Lord Rothes with his Vassals to whom the Duke of Argyle (who arrived at Edinburgh the 15th) had given Arms, could arrive there. Some Highlanders, as ordinary Passengers, came by one or two at a time, and loitering at the Gate, found an Opportunity to seize the Guard of Townsmen whom the Magistrates had placed there, and immediately a Body of 100 Horse appeared and enter'd the Town, where they imprisoned the Magistrates and created others in the Name of the Pretender. The Lord Marr has taken the Title of Lieutenant-General of the Troops of the Pretended King James.[67]

As this example suggests, although the official newsletters trumped newspapers in their ability to provide confidential details about court, city and foreign news, newspapers were able to convey to their readers more information regarding the conflict that was unfolding in far-flung locations around the country. Indeed, as the crisis deepened, newspapers began to expand their coverage of the Jacobite fronts, sometimes reprinting entire letters from supposed eyewitnesses. Newspapers thus offered more "timely, accurate and authoritative news" about the national crisis than their manuscript counterparts at this historical juncture.[68] It was the newspapers, then, that more readily satisfied readers' desires to find out the details of the rapidly changing situations in the centres of conflict throughout Britain in 1715. But as a consequence of their material form, the newspapers also shaped that news in distinct ways, amplifying the discontinuities in the communication of news.

Fitting to Print: Newspapers and the Discontinuities of Form

As domestic news, reports on the Jacobite Rising were presented on the back pages of newspapers alongside advertisements for goods and services designed for a nation that was experiencing a consumer revolution. Although the papers might feature addresses to the King on the first page, or occasionally news about the conflict itself when an important battle had taken place, for the most part, readers got their information about the ongoing crisis in their nation on the same pages to which they turned in order to find out about the latest opportunities for commerce or entertainment. As advertisements were taking up proportionately more space on those back pages of newspapers in relation to news, the space for domestic

---

[67] Ibid. [68] King, "Manuscript Newsletter," 412.

news varied considerably. In the case of the *Daily Courant*, the advertisements often occupied the entire last page; the November 19 and 21, 1715, editions of the *Daily Courant*, for example, include only advertisements on the last page, despite the recent battle at Sheriffmuir on November 13.

Chapter 2 examined how advertisements in the *London Gazette* at the time of the War of the Two Kings responded to and encouraged readers' interest in the conflict by featuring works of Irish history and maps of Ireland. The same dialogic process was in operation in 1715 as printers capitalized on news events to advertise items of interest. Maps were popular items in the newspaper advertisements of 1715, as they had been in 1689. The November 9, 1715, issue of the *Daily Courant* indicates that the following item had been "Lately Published": "Mr. Moll's Map of Scotland, in two Sheets, with considerable Improvements, and many Remarks not Extant in any Map, according to the Newest and Exact Observations. D. Midwinter at the 3 Crowns in St. Paul's Church-Yard."[69] Other advertisements worked in a closer dynamic relationship with the news items. The *Post-Man* for September 22–24, 1715, for example, features news from London about the "Rebel" leaders taken into custody and news from Edinburgh about the "necessary Precautions" the government is undertaking "for defeating the designs of the Rebels" who have now "proclaim'd the Pretender at Dundee and Inverness."[70] Included in the "Advertisements" sections on the same page is a notice about a work that promises to put events into context for readers: "This Day is published, The Political State of Great Britain, &c. For the Month of August 1715" which was available from "J. Baker at the Black Boy in Paternoster Row. Price 1 s."[71] Similarly, on October 1, 1715, in the midst of reporting on the Duke of Argyll's preparations to march against Lord Mar's camp, the *Daily Courant* included in its advertisements a note drawing readers' attention to the fact that "This Day is Published A Letter from the Earl of Mar to the King, before His Majesty's Arrival in England. With some Remarks on my Lord's Subsequent Conduct. By Sir Richard Steele. Jacob Tonson, and sold by R. Burleigh in Amen Corner."[72] The publication of Mar's earlier expression of loyalty to George I and Hanoverian rule served to further blacken his character by pointing out his hypocrisy.

But in the case of newspapers in 1715, the vast majority of advertisements had no thematic connection with the news stories that preceded

[69] *Daily Courant*, November 9, 1715.   [70] *Post-Man*, September 22–24, 1715.   [71] Ibid.
[72] *Daily Courant*, October 1, 1715.

them, and because there were so many advertisements, the net impact was to increase the general sense of disorientation. In the November 17, 1715, edition of the *Daily Courant*, information about the capture of Jacobites at Preston subsequent to the inconclusive battle at Sheriffmuir is squeezed into the upper left corner of the last page. The items on the rest of the page invite readers to engage with issues other than news. Theatrical advertisements encourage them to attend either the tragedy of *Timon of Athens* at Drury Lane or the comedy of *The Devil of a Wife* at Lincoln's Inn Fields. Notices regarding the leasing of a "large House and Garden ... furnished or unfurnished" and a "Dye house ... with or without all the Utensils" and the purchase of a "Convenient Tavern, with good Vaults" offer readers opportunities for mobility. Lost items are also brought to readers' attention, including a "Kerry-stone seal fix'd in gold" and a "Pocket-Book with Green Vellum Cover." Items for sale featured in this issue include "Fifty Hogsheads of Tobacco, Sweet-scented," "Peter's Famous Bill and Cordial Tincture" and several books such as *Clerk's Writing Improv'd* and *An Essay on the Theory of Painting* by Jonathan Richardson.

Joad Raymond comments in general on the way in which newspapers' juxtaposition of "unrelated items ... required the reader to recognize and synthesize diversity."[73] Looking at newspapers in the later eighteenth century, Daniel O'Quinn also notes the lack of "logical links between items," suggesting that readers are "rarely placed in a consistent relation to narrated events."[74] According to O'Quinn, each reader consequently has to make that arrangement in a different way: "Reading the paper becomes all about complex acts of dispersion and collection that vary from reader to reader and from reading event to reading event" (9). In the case of the newspapers during the 1715 Rising, the juxtaposition of news regarding the Rising with the large number of goods and services, advertised in the papers amplified the sense of discontinuity surrounding the events taking place. While readers might vary in the particulars of their individual acts of "dispersion and collection," they were nevertheless united in their experience of being distracted by the diversity of material that they were reading. The newspapers thus amplified the lack of a "continuous narrative" in the

---

[73] Joad Raymond, "The Newspaper, Public Opinion, and the Public Sphere in the Seventeenth Century," *Prose Studies* 21, no. 2 (1998): 132.
[74] Daniel O'Quinn, *Entertaining Crisis in the Atlantic Imperium, 1770–1790* (Philadelphia: University of Pennsylvania Press, 2011), 9.

events of the Jacobite Rising even as they increased the population who were experiencing a sense of that discontinuity.

Making things even more complex for readers was the sheer number of printed newspapers circulating at the time, often operating in competition with each other. Within the pages of the daily, tri-weekly and weekly papers, news items were reprinted and circulated, often using the same language. The notice about the details of the Jacobite attempt on Edinburgh Castle published in the *Daily Courant* on September 15, 1715, for example, was also repeated virtually verbatim in the *London Courant* of September 13–17, 1715, the *London Gazette* of September 13–17, 1745, the *Post-Man* of September 17–20, 1715, and the *Weekly Packet* for September 17–24, 1715.[75] By replicating those items of news in multiple periodical locations, newspapers fostered a sense of the news as a constant circulation of disconnected units of information.

For readers of both manuscript newsletters and newspapers trying to keep up to date with the national conflict, the events of the 1715 Rising unfolded in a disturbing manner. Manuscript newsletters transmitted a sense of uncertainty to their readers through their inability to provide accurate and timely coverage of events in the north. Newspapers, for their part, conveyed the news of the Rising as a series of consumable, portable items circulating between print venues. Rather than helping to contain the crisis by giving information "a precise location in space and in time" and providing "a bogus closure in a developing reality," as, according to Sommerville, early printed periodicals had done, newspapers in 1715 presented events as more dispersed and discontinuous.[76] In its initial inscription on the pages of the manuscript newsletters and the newspapers, then, the 1715 Jacobite Rising was spread out before the reading citizens of Britain either as missing data or as endlessly circulating units of information. Although the newsletters and the majority of newspapers generally conveyed messages of loyalty, the forms in which those messages were represented suggested that the Rising was neither contained nor easily containable. Subsequently, in the aftermath of the Rising, it was the containment of the newspaper coverage of the events of the Rising that became of particular consequence.

---

[75] The *Flying-Post* for September 17–20, 1745, also published an account which employs similar language, although the editor made some adjustments. "Care and Vigilance" becomes just "Care"; names of the individual officers who thwarted the plan are supplied.
[76] Sommerville, *News Revolution*, 11.

"One Continued Absurdity": Periodical Essays and the Information Management of the 1715 Rising

How exactly did this initial depiction of the events of the Rising as incomplete and discontinuous information turn into the site of cultural memory known as "the '15"? While the newspaper accounts communicated events to citizens at the time in a disjointed manner, it was the management of this information within another new print genre that helped shape how the 1715 Rising would ultimately be stored in cultural memory. That genre was the periodical essay. The origins of the periodical essay can be traced back to the British Civil Wars, but in 1715 readers would have been more familiar with more recent examples of the form such as John Dunton's *The Athenian Gazette* (1691), Daniel Defoe's *Review of the British Nation* (1704–13) and Richard Steele and Joseph Addison's *Tatler* (1709) and *Spectator* (1711–12). Robert DeMaria, Jr. points out the close connection between the development of the newspaper and the development of the periodical essay.[77] Indeed, Steele had been the editor of a newspaper, the *London Gazette*, while *The Spectator* was published by the printer of the *Daily Courant*, Samuel Buckley. But the form of the periodical essay was very different from that of the newspaper, as it offered sustained commentary and featured the editorial perspective of specific narrative personae or avatars. While there were a number of periodical essays in circulation during the 1715 Rising, I focus here on Richard Steele's *The Town-Talk* and Joseph Addison's *The Free-Holder*, both of which began publication at the height of the Rising and finished shortly after its suppression. Now largely forgotten by literary critics, *The Town-Talk* and *The Free-Holder* were modelled on the two authors' extremely popular earlier periodical essay projects.[78] In *The Town-Talk* and *The Free-Holder*, Steele and Addison combine their earlier concerns with shaping taste and manners with an attempt to ameliorate the way the national crisis was being represented.

Steele makes it clear that he intends both his and Addison's publications to serve as antidotes to the presentation of events in the newspapers. In no. 7 (January 2, 1716) of *The Town-Talk*, for example, he refers to "all the prepense impertinencies" which are "premeditate[d]" by "authors of

---

[77] Robert DeMaria, Jr., "The Eighteenth-Century Periodical Essay," in *The Cambridge History of English Literature, 1660–1780*, ed. John Richetti (Cambridge: Cambridge University Press, 2005), 527–48.
[78] But for a discussion of the politics of the periodical essays, see Nick Harding, *Hanover and the British Empire, 1700–1837* (Woodbridge: Boydell Press, 2007), 54–56.

daily or weekly papers, who do not only gravely sit down, and take pen, ink, and paper, to communicate our crudities to our private friends, but also make the press labour to spread our errors among the rest of the people."[79] His narrator offers colourful descriptions of several of the newspapers in circulation:

> You are to look upon the Daily Courant, in general, as a man in his every day cloaths; but when he has any thing that is new, he wears it without giving himself airs; and you may receive him in it, as one that comes to visit you out of kindness to you, much more than for his own sake, or to set himself off. (79)

Utilizing a metaphor from the transportation technologies that were so important to the development of early eighteenth-century news networks, Steele suggests that the *Post-Man*, in contrast, is like "an admirable Stage-coach, and goes whether he has passengers or not. One cannot forbear looking in upon him; but you are sure to see every thing in his vehicle in its homeliest garb; all is dressed for a journey, and muffled up" (80). Steele's comments indicate the way in which news was constantly changing and was as likely to be "muffled up" and inaccessible as to be understandable. Importantly, he also suggests a solution to the problems associated with reading news in newspapers: the reading of a different kind of "paper," which, "if attended to, cannot but, at the same time that it is an entertainment, be very serviceable to the public" (80). That paper, he indicates, is *The Free-Holder*, which "comes out in the midst of the confusion and animosity, which are fomented by pamphlets and other loose papers, like a man of sense in a multitude, whose appearance among them suppresses their noise, and gains him an authority to be heard with attention for their common service" (79–80). Steele is not only praising his friend Addison's work here; he is also articulating the goal of both their projects, as *The Town-Talk* and *The Free-Holder* were designed by their authors as sources of authority to contrast with the "noise" of pamphlets and other "loose papers" and the discontinuities of newspapers.

Steele's *Town-Talk*, published weekly from December 17, 1715, to February 13, 1716, is written as a series of letters from a gentleman in town to a "Lady" living "at a distance from the town" who has requested information and opinions on "every thing which passes in town" (79). Steele builds a gendered sense of duty and obligation into the relationship,

---

[79] Richard Steele, *The Town Talk, the Fish Pool, the Plebian, the Old Whig, the Spinster, &c.* (London, 1790), 79.

suggesting that he is "without those commands, naturally averse" to such an enterprise as gathering and sending news and demurring that "to write you constantly once a week the news and occurrences of the preceding seven days" is "a task I must be forgiven if I should sometimes omit" (1–2). He resolves, however, to provide his addressee with whatever "happens to be in discourse or agitation among the pleasurable and reasonable people" of the town (13). But unlike the manuscript newsletter form, which was also written as a letter to specific addressees, Steele's *Town-Talk* was designed with print in mind. The narrator indicates that he will publish his missives both to raise funds for postage of the actual letters and also to seek a wider audience for the opinions expressed.

The Town-Talk is, from its first to its last issue, concerned with the events of the Rising. Despite the fact that the Rising was recognized as a serious threat to the entire nation, however, the narrator of *The Town-Talk* represents political events as peripheral to the main task he has been assigned, and by extension, peripheral to the concerns of those living in the nation's capital. In no. 1 (December 17, 1715), after relating a story that he indicates is "the newest adventure in the Town," the narrator indicates that he has grudgingly fulfilled an obligation which the "Lady" has imposed on him: to see the Jacobite prisoners brought from Preston (12). He offers a brief description of the process through which two hundred of them were brought to town on December 9, 1715, and paraded through the streets of London, commenting on the mixed emotions that the spectacle aroused:

> to see a number of deluded zealots sacrificed to the pride and ambition of those who will venture nothing but their interest in another world for any cause or party, was matter of sorrow and pity to me; though at the same time I could not but rejoice in seeing the open enemies of my country disarmed and at mercy. (15)

In no. 2 (December 23, 1715), he intimates that he has been asked by the "Lady" to provide a follow-up explanation for why it is that "the most popular cause, and a prince at the head of it with the most humane qualities that ever blessed a throne [George I], should not be more popular, and the principles and persons of men who have so many years meditated the general ruin not yet the scorn and abomination of mankind" (13). Although he indicates that he will "confine [him]self to the rehearsal of Town Talk" and eschew discussing "the science of Politics," the narrator has already drawn the question to his reader's attention (12).

In no. 5 (January 13, 1715), the narrator indicates that the "Lady" has again requested political news and suggested that such news is in fact within the parameters of the orders that she sent to him in the first place. By the time at which this issue was printed, news had reached London about James Stuart's landing in Scotland on December 22, 1715, and the narrator reluctantly admits that "it has so happened just now, that the town is too busy for pleasure or speculation, and all the chat is of the Pretender" (47). He minimizes the threat posed to the nation, however, suggesting, "I should never have heard of it, if all this had not been brought to town, and made the whole talk of it" (47). He represents his "chief intelligence" on the matter as coming from an unlikely source, the conversation of "two courtesans" sitting in the gallery in the theatre "who were warm in politics" (57). One, a Whig, asserted that the "Pretender was ruined" because General Mar "had left Perth" (57). In response, the other triumphantly threw at her a document which turned out to be "the Pretender's declaration" that had been given her by her "gallant," the exiled Bolingbroke (64). This document was then "conveyed from one hand to the other" until it finally was taken up by "a hand which I will not take upon me to name to you," who wrote a "long answer" to the "*Manifesto*" (58). No. 5 reprints James's declaration as well as the "long answer" that, the narrator suggests, will serve as an "antidote to the poison of it" (58); Steele himself also published the refutation of the "*Manifesto*" as a separate pamphlet.[80] Although Steele directly addresses the "science of politics" in this issue of *The Town-Talk*, he downplays the threat to the nation by putting the discussion of the actions of the Jacobites into the mouths of women of questionable social reputation who are engaged in a dispute. Unlike the Prince of Orange's *Declaration*, which was printed and widely distributed to generate a media buzz in 1688, James Stuart's document is represented by Steele as *billet doux* to a courtesan that is subsequently transferred "from one hand to the other" with minimal impact (58).

In no. 8 (February 3, 1715), Steele sets the Jacobite Rising in historical context. This time, after having read all the "public papers and pamphlets" about events in the current crisis (82), the "Lady" has requested a summary of the historical circumstances leading up to the present moment, including "the late peace, the successful war before it, and the imminent danger we are in after it" (90). The narrator's account counteracts any sense of alarm circulating in the news by providing a sense of reassurance regarding the Hanoverian succession and also vilifying the character of James Stuart. In response to what appears to be the addressee's "curiosity to know

[80] Richard Steele, *The British Subject's Answer, to the Pretender's Declaration* (London, 1716).

something of [James Stuart's] private character," the narrator asserts, "you are to understand, that he has never in his whole life, or upon any incident of it, been known to have said or done what might intimate him to have the least genius for the arts of war or peace, business or conversation" (115). Although addressed to his female correspondent, the narrator's reassurance is designed to reach all readers: "I hope therefore, you will lay aside all fears for a great and glorious people, fighting in defence of all that is dear to them, against an undisciplined multitude, and an *Indolent Invader*... Till stupidity can form, or giddiness execute great designs, you are safe from the Pretender and his followers" (100).

No. 9 (February 13, 1716) continues with the political discussion of the previous issue, with the narrator providing details of "advices" that confirm "new incidents," in particular the fact that the man to whom the narrator again refers as an "*indolent* invader," James Stuart, has "actually made his escape from that body of men who took up arms in his cause" (119). The narrator emphasizes James's craven behaviour upon departing, indicating how, even at the point at which he could have distinguished himself for his leadership by thanking his followers for their efforts and "exhorting them to future undertakings," he wasted his time "in poor lamentation of himself, and his unhappy circumstances" (101). Steele's account reduces James to being merely an "unhappy man deluded into an opinion of a title," while the "rebellion" itself becomes but "one continued absurdity" which was "entered into without provocation from injuries" and "undertaken without any expectation, or reasonable hope of popular favour towards him who was to be exalted by it" (119). Through such comments which minimize the threat of the 1715 Rising, Steele sowed the seeds for later interpretations of the 1715 as a "damp squib."

Unlike the newspapers, which represented the day-to-day events as a series of constantly changing disjointed moments of conflict, *The Town-Talk* clusters the events of the Rising together in a narrative that draws to a definite conclusion. The narrator notes that he "deferred writing" the February 13 issue of *The Town-Talk* "till I could, according to your request, give you a further account of [James and his followers], by telling you what passed with relation to those noblemen who were taken at Preston" (102–03). Accordingly, after reflecting on James's character flaws and the futility of the Rising, the ninth issue of *The Town-Talk* moves to a detailed discussion of the sentencing of the six peers captured at Preston and accused of high treason: Robert Dalzell, fifth Earl of Carnwath; William Gordon, sixth Viscount of Kenmure; William Maxwell, Earl of Nithsdale; James Radclyffe, third Earl of Derwentwater; William Murray, second Lord Nairne; and William Widdrington, fourth Baron Widdrington.[81] Although the narrator suggests that "it is not for me to give you an account of the transactions in that High Court of Parliament" that day, he nevertheless offers, in accordance with his correspondent's desire, a description "in the most lively manner I can" of the scene that took place (120). He notes that all the lords "said what they could to excite pity," but commends Lord Chancellor Cowper, the High Steward, for urging spectators to reject any "compassion" that they might feel for the men and to acknowledge instead the appropriateness of their "fatal sentence" (120). Directing his attention to the "Lady" and any readers who also might feel sympathy for the peers, the narrator of *The Town-Talk* moves from politics back to concerns of "Pleasure or Speculation" (57). Indeed, with the discussion of the meting out of justice, *The Town-Talk* came to an end.

Addison's counterpart to Steele's *Town-Talk*, *The Free-Holder*, was launched on December 23, 1715, and ran for fifty-five issues, appearing every Monday and Friday until June 29, 1716. It was created to fulfill a political obligation, as, soon after he ended work on *The Spectator*, Addison had been granted a place on a trade commission and a salary of £1,000 per year, in return for which he was responsible for presenting a positive perspective on the new king and his government.[82] Although the country was eager for news about the Jacobites during this time, Addison deliberately refrains from providing specific details of events being reported in his publication, choosing rather to use the particulars of "the present Situation of Affairs in *Great-Britain*" to reflect generally "upon Government."[83] Addison's narrative persona in *The Free-Holder* represents him as an owner of property worth forty shillings a year, enough to secure his voting privileges. He contrasts himself with the "Grub-Street Patriot" who writes to "get something of his own," suggesting that, as a voter, he has a vested interest in the welfare of the nation and so is writing in its service. Moreover, he argues that those like himself who enjoy the franchise possess a "remote Voice" in the nation by virtue of the fact that they

---

[81] Derwentwater and Kenmure were executed on Tower Hill on February 24, 1716, Nithsdale escaped, and the other three lords were granted stays of execution.

[82] Lillian Bloom, "Joseph Addison (1 May 1672–17 June 1719)," in *Dictionary of Literary Biography*, vol. 101, *British Prose Writers, 1660–1800*, 1st ser., ed. Donald T. Siebert (Detroit, MI, and London: Gale Research, 1991), 24.

[83] See Charles Knight, "The Spectator's Generalizing Discourse," in *Telling People What to Think: Early Eighteenth Century Periodicals from* The Review *to* The Rambler, ed. J. A. Downie and Thomas N. Corns (London: Routledge, 1993), 44–57.

help elect Members of Parliament who make the laws: "Such is the Nature of our happy Constitution," he suggests, "that the Bulk of the People virtually give their approbation to every thing they are bound to obey, and prescribe to themselves those Rules by which they are to walk."[84] In the pages of the *Free-Holder*, Addison's persona employs what Charles Knight refers to as "generalizing discourse," indicating he will "endeavour to open the Eyes of my countrymen to their own Interest, to shew them the Privileges of an *English* Free-holder, which they enjoy in common with myself, and to make them sensible how these Blessings are secured to us by his Majesty's Title, his Administration, and his Personal Character" (5). Addison's narrator maintains that strengthening people's appreciation for the uniqueness of the British Constitution is as important as achieving military success in the field. As he asserts, "While many of my gallant Countrymen are employed in pursuing Rebels … I shall labour to improve those Victories to the Good of my Fellow-Subjects; by carrying on our successes over the Minds of Men" (5). Recognizing that providing specific details about news would only encourage a sense of discontinuity, Addison focuses instead on uniting the nation through a common belief in British exceptionalism.

In the issues that follow, Addison employs what he calls "common Sense" to try to bring readers of different political persuasions together to defend the king and his government (38). Critically, in no. 2 (December 26, 1715), Addison makes a direct connection between the maintenance of the Constitution and the Hanoverian succession, comparing James II/VII's and George I's attitudes to the Constitution and arguing that while James set himself above the Constitution, dispensing with the laws of the land, George I regards "those which are our Civil Liberties, as the natural Rights of Mankind" (9). If a Stuart monarch such as the "Pretender" or his son were to gain the throne, argues the narrator, the rights and responsibilities that English freeholders enjoy would be exchanged for vassalage such as is found in Catholic France.

In no. 5 (January 6, 1716), Addison leads his readers through a series of precepts in order to convince them of the benefits of the Hanoverian succession. Beginning with the statement that "There is no greater Sign of general Decay in a Nation, than want of Zeal in its Inhabitants for the Good of their Country," he alludes to the present conflict, suggesting that the sense of patriotism in the nation has languished recently because a party of men has been able to "destroy in the Minds of the People the

---

[84] Joseph Addison, *The Free-Holder: Or, Political Essays* (London, 1716), 2.

Sense of national Glory, and to turn to Ridicule our natural and ancient Allies" (22). "*The Love of one's Countrey,*" he suggests, is, like "Self-love," an "Instinct planted in us," but whereas "Self-love" focuses on individual happiness and preservation, "the Love of our Countrey is impress'd on our Minds for the Happiness and Preservation of the Community" (23). Not only is patriotism "natural," he indicates, but it is also "reasonable" because it helps us secure a supportive community around us. Having established the general importance of "*The Love of one's Countrey,*" the narrator moves his attention "to our present Case," arguing that "A Man must be destitute of common Sense, who is capable of imagining that the Protestant Religion could flourish under the Government of a Bigotted *Roman-Catholick*, or that our Civil Rights could be Protected by One who has been trained up in the Politics of the most Arbitrary Prince in Europe" (29). Whereas newsletters addressed elite readers and newspapers catered to the desire for up-to-date information, Addison appeals to his readers' common assumptions on the basis of nature and reason, discouraging them from focusing on political differences. As he indicates: "I shall only desire the honest, well-meaning Reader, when he turns his Thoughts towards the Public, rather to consider what Opportunities he has of doing Good to his Native Countrey, than to throw away his Time in deciding the Rights of Princes, or the like Speculations, which are so far beyond his Reach" (29). The tools for action, suggests Addison, lie within each reader's common capabilities, while "Speculations" around such issues as "the Rights of Princes" are niceties best handled by legal experts (29). *The Free-Holder* worked to counteract the discontinuity and uncertainty associated with the newspapers by focusing readers' attention on the "common Sense" principles behind the political events.

Conscious that the readership of periodical essays also included a significant percentage of women, Addison's narrator devotes a number of the issues of *The Free-Holder* to considering how women could also contribute to promoting the good of the nation. Addison's narrator positions himself in the role of advisor to the women who wish to form a "FEMALE ASSOCIATION," providing them with a "rough Draft" of a manifesto which includes an oath: "we do hereby engage our selves to raise and arm our Vassals for the Service of His Majesty King *George*, and Him to Defend with our Tongues and Hearts, our Eyes, Eye-Lashes, Favourites, Lips, Dimples, and every other Feature, whether natural or acquired" (47). Although the narrator's remarks are designed to amuse readers by representing political factionalism as a matter of fashion, they also suggest a deeper interest in appealing to the entire population, both men and women, to do whatever they can to support the government of George I in the midst of the current political crisis. Despite belittling women for their focus on their appearance, the narrator also frequently appeals to their "common Sense," too. In no. 4 (January 2), for example, he draws a connection between the political affiliation and the character of a woman, suggesting that "the Women of our Island, who are the most eminent for Virtue and good Sense" are those who support "the present Government" (17). He reminds women who "amuse themselves in the reading of travels" that in nations which do not have the same numbers of freeholders or that do not place the same value on individual liberty (such as China, India and Persia), women are merely "Slaves to Slaves" (17).

In *The Town-Talk* and *The Free-Holder*, Steele and Addison presented their ideas as "disinterested" at the same time as they counteracted the sense of disconnection and confusion that accompanied the news about the Rising found in the newspapers. The two periodical essays worked in tandem during the crisis. While Steele submerged the political news within a discussion of entertainment and gossip sent from London, Addison encouraged readers to consider the wider issues behind the information circulating in the news. The authors also cross-referenced each other's work, encouraging readers to consult both sources. In no. 9 (January 26, 1716) of *The Free-Holder*, for example, Addison drew attention to Steele's concurrent publication with his narrator's comments that he has seen "an Excellent Answer to [James Stuart's] Declaration" in the form of "a Letter from a Celebrated *English*-Man" published in *The Town-Talk* (48). Steele returned the favour, quoting from *The Free-Holder* in no. 7 (January 27, 1716) to affirm his agreement with Addison's observation that "One may venture to affirm, that all honest and disinterested Britons, of what party soever, if they understand one another, are of the same opinion in points of government" (80). Presenting themselves as complementary centres of authority, Steele and Addison minimized the actual threat of the Rising as they sought to manage how citizens of the nation reacted to the news about the events in the north. By reading Addison's and Steele's publications on Monday, Wednesday or Friday, for example, readers could learn how to respond to the news they read in the thrice-weekly newspapers on Tuesday, Thursday and Saturday.

The Free-Holder and *The Town-Talk* continued to shape public perceptions of the cultural memory of the 1715 Rising throughout the rest of the eighteenth century: unlike the newspapers whose perspectives they sought to correct, these periodicals were reprinted in complete sets after they ceased initial publication. A collected edition of all the issues of *The Free-Holder* went through ten editions by 1761 and appeared in a "new edition" in 1779, while *The Town-Talk* was republished in 1789 by John Nichols in London and in 1790 by Zachariah Jackson in Dublin. Steele's and Addison's representations of a "happy" constitution based on the Protestant succession, individual freedom and property rights would prove instrumental in establishing a sense of a distinctive British modernity and exceptionalism.

Un-mediating the Rising: "Authentick Accounts" and "Lasting Monuments"

While periodical essays such as *The Town-Talk* and *The Free-Holder* focused readers' attention during the Rising away from discrete and accumulating chronological details to general concepts – and to entertainment instead of politics, in the case of *The Town-Talk* – other works published after the suppression of the Rising helped to shape its early history. In *Jacobite Prisoners of the 1715 Rebellion: Preventing and Punishing Insurrection in Early Hanoverian Britain*, Margaret Sankey argues that the government of George I implemented "subtle and calculated" policies in the aftermath of the Rising, punishing a representative number of Jacobite prisoners, including the two peers Derwentwater and Kenmure, and confiscating Catholic lands, but also pardoning many leaders whose families petitioned for them. Sankey suggests that the government's clemency toward the Jacobites "created the basis of the modern nation" by cultivating the loyalty of those who had sought to undermine the government instead of punishing them.[85] Popular histories published in the wake of the 1715 Rising performed a similar task, justifying the punishments meted out by the government, but also establishing the narrative template and affective conditions for the re-integration into the fabric of the nation of those who had risen against the government. Significantly, many histories simply reworked the mobile and shifting units of information found in the newspapers into longer and focused narratives.

In the year following the suppression of the Rising, the Sun Fire-Office drew attention to its efforts to provide a long view on recent events, announcing that it was changing from printing the weekly *British Mercury* to producing a quarterly publication, *The Historical Register: Containing an Impartial Relation of All Transactions, Foreign and*

---

[85] Margaret Sankey, *Jacobite Prisoners of the 1715 Rebellion: Preventing and Punishing Insurrection in Early Hanoverian Britain* (Burlington, VT: Ashgate, 2005), 156.

Domestick.[86] The "chief Inducement" for the change, the editors noted, was "the Request of many of their Subscribers" who pointed out "that the great and still increasing Number of News-Papers that are publish'd every Day had spoil'd the Design of Weekly Intelligences, and render'd them of little or no Use or Value" (i). In the present day, the editors note, "News-Papers and Lies are become almost synonymous Terms" (ii–iii). In contrast, they suggest that they will not relate any news that "wants Confirmation," but only that which "all Hands is agreed to have happen'd" (i). Instead of the "Falshoods" that the newspapers spread as a result of their constant correcting of earlier reports, the editors indicate that they will wait to see what has been proven to be accurate over a longer period. As they announce, 'Time alone it is that in this Age of Fiction, can teach us to discover Truth from Falshood" (i). In order to provide "an authentick Account of Affairs" and to avoid "unsaying" what has already been printed, the editors indicate that they consider it necessary not only to publish less frequently, but also to dispense with the customary phrases used by the newspapers (iii). Phrases such as "*'Tis reported, 'Tis believ'd, 'Tis not doubted, We hear,* and the like," they suggest, only serve to introduce a "Train of groundless Conjectures, and airy Speculations" (i). Notably, these are exactly the expressions which newspapers, following the lead of manuscript newsletters, had used to assert their own authority. By omitting these expressions from their publication, the editors suggest a shift in the authority of news away from oral and manuscript sources and toward the medium of print.

The editors note that their newly fashioned and less frequent publication will also be more permanent. Unlike "common News-Papers" which are subject to many other "Accidents," they suggest, the *Historical Register* will be printed as a "Book" and will be printed "on a much better Paper than any other the like Sort that has hitherto been publish'd" (iii). The editors of the *Historical Register* align printedness within the covers of a "Book" not only with durability but also with authenticity, and in creating a version of recent events that will last into the future in book form, they also advertise their interest in shaping a cultural memory of the past that will endure beyond the ephemerality of newspaper reports.

The goal of providing an "authentick Account of Affairs" connected with the events of 1715 also inspired the publication of four self-styled histories that appeared in print immediately after the suppression of the

---

[86] Sun-Fire Office, *The Historical Register: Containing an Impartial Relation of All Transactions, Foreign and Domestick* (London, 1717), i.

Rising: *A Compleat History of the Late Rebellion* (1716), *The Faithful Register of the Late Rebellion* (1718), *The History of the Late Rebellion* by Robert Patten (1717) and *The History of the Late Rebellion* by Peter Rae (1718). Like the *Historical Register*, all four of these histories incorporated newspaper reports into their historical record of recent events. While the newsletters and newspapers represented the conflicts with Jacobites that occurred in various locations at different times as separate events, the histories attempted to knit the separate threads of Jacobite activity at each site into a narrative of a single rising. As attempts by their authors to curate and shape the information from the newspapers, however, the histories also exemplify how printed works served in complicated ways to represent knots of cultural memory at this time of the expansion of print.

The text of *A Compleat History of the Late Rebellion* consists of reprinted accounts from the newspaper reports woven together virtually verbatim, although, as with the *Historical Register*, the traces that link the information to the oral and manuscript media through which it was originally conveyed have been removed. The newspaper account of the attack on Edinburgh Castle published in the *Daily Courant* for September 19, 1715, for example, indicates that "Letters from Edinburgh of Sept 10 bring an Account of a Conspiracy being formed to surprise the Castle on the 8th between 11 and 12 at Night; which was happily prevented by the Care and Vigilance of the Government there."[87] *A Compleat History* includes the same account, but it removes the references to the letters that were the source of the information: "Besides the Measures concerted among the Chiefs of the *Highland-Clans*, a Conspiracy was form'd at *Edinburgh*, to surprize the Castle there, on the 8th of September between 11 and 12 at Night; which by the Care and Vigilance of the Lord Justice *Clerk*, who had early Notice of it, was happily prevented."[88] The rest of the long account is identical in the two texts. *A Compleat History*, in other words, extracts the news that the newspapers derived from letters and repositions it as objective information rather than data conveyed within a communication event. In such a manner, *A Compleat History* works to "un-mediate" the newspaper reports from their networked origins.

Moreover, whereas the newspapers presented information as it was received, creating a discontinuous series of individual daily news items that appeared even more disjointed in competition with advertisements on the last pages of the newspapers, *A Compleat History* provides connections

---

[87] *Daily Courant*, September 19, 1715.
[88] *A Compleat History of the Late Rebellion* (London, 1716), 22.

between the disparate pieces of information, linking them in time and space. Commenting on the bill that the government introduced for encouraging loyalty among vassals in Scotland, the author of *A Compleat History* notes, "We shall see presently the Necessity of this wise Act, when we shall find that the Rebellion was first publickly avow'd and declar'd in Scotland" (7). Similarly, after relating the account of the attempt on Edinburgh Castle, the author writes, "Having seen this horrid Design, by the Grace of God, thus happily frustrated, let us return for a while into *England*, where the watchful Guardians of the State are taking such Measures, at this hazardous Crisis, as well deserve the Notice of my attentive Reader" (24). As the actions of the Jacobites occurred in various locations at different times between September 1715 and January 1716, the author follows the thread of each rising in each location separately. He suggests that the arrests that happened at Bath and Oxford put an end to the Jacobite plans in those areas, then turns his attention to the "The Conspirators in the *North*" before switching focus again: "Here then let us leave the *English* Rebels, while we attend to the Progress of their Brethren in Iniquity in *Scotland*" (35). After relaying the details of the Battle of Preston and the capture of the Jacobite prisoners, the author notes, "Upon the self same Day that the Rebels agreed to surrender at *Preston*, it pleas'd God to bless his Majesty's Arms with a Victory of great Importance in Scotland; of which we will here give an Account, as also of some other Affairs in that Kingdom, and then take up the Thread of our History where we left it" (77). The author attempts to unite the various conflicts that took place around the nation within a wider perspective. By doing so, he generates a narrative arc that depicts the events not just as a "Thread of our History" but also as a "Plot of *Providence*" (2) leading inexorably to the defeat of the Jacobites.

Most importantly, *A Compleat History* attempts to unite its readers by placing the events that have been collectively experienced into an affective site of national memory. The author indicates how he sees himself performing a service to the nation in gathering the facts of the Rising together in one volume, suggesting that "it cannot ... but be very acceptable to every true-hearted *Briton*, to receive, in one View, an Historical Relation of the Disappointment of all the repeated Efforts of impious Men to enslave us" (1). He indicates in his dedication to the Duke of Argyll that his efforts, imperfect as they are, serve an immediate purpose. He reflects with pleasure "on the happy Effects the Perusal of this History I have collected, must have upon the Minds of my Readers," but he indicates that of all "Effects," the one he most wants to encourage is gratitude toward the

Duke (vi–vii). The author sees himself as a vehicle channelling the gratitude of "honest" citizens toward the Duke.

The conclusion of *A Compleat History* also works to generate readerly affect in the service of the nation. After providing a summary of what he has just narrated, the author suggests that "when we reflect on these Things, we cannot but perceive the Finger of *God*; who not only refused to bless the Arms of *perjured* Traytors, but also *infatuated* their Understandings and bereaved them of Wisdom and Council" (170). Further reinforcing the sense of divine support for the government, he draws an analogy between the Jacobite retreat from Perth and the Old Testament defeat of King Benhadad of Syria's army who, when they attacked the Israelites in Samaria, were convinced by God that they heard the noise of a great army and subsequently ran away (175). By representing the government troops as God's chosen people and the Jacobites as their ancient enemies, *A Compleat History* aims to reinforce national and spiritual bonds between the people of Britain and their monarch. The work concludes by emphasizing the sense expressed in the beginning that "the very Arm of the *Almighty* manifestly engag'd to assert the Cause of his Church, in the Defeat and Infatuation of her Enemies" and that George I is "the only *Defender* of our holy Faith" (1–2).

But, while it provides the narrative tools for the imagining of national and confessional consolidation, *A Compleat History* also helps to circulate traces of Jacobite counter-memory. As well as including items that supported the government such as the "Circular Letter read in the Churches, for animating the People to take Arms in Defence of his Majesty and the Constitution," *A Compleat History* reprints Jacobite documents such as Mar's declaration in which he asserted that "Our rightful and natural King, *James* the 8th" is "now coming to relieve us from our Oppressions" (15). Mar had anticipated that his declaration would strike a chord in the "ancient Kingdom of *Scotland*" in particular, as it asserted that the Union had not served to lessen the differences between the countries and that the only way to "restore our ancient and independent Constitution" was to take up arms (15). Although *A Compleat History* attempts to dismiss Mar by also featuring his infamous "letter professing his loyalty to the House of Hanover" and thus denigrating his character, the reprinting of his declaration, as well as the "Manifesto by the Noblemen, Gentlemen, and others," in fact serves to promote the Jacobite perspective, as it accuses the British Parliament of having "impower'd a Foreign Prince … to make an absolute Conquest (if not timely prevented) of the Three Kingdoms, by investing himself with an unlimited

Power, not only of raising unnecessary Forces at Home, but also of calling in Foreign Troops" (19–20). Although it is tempered within an all-encompassing narrative of loyalty to the state, the manifesto as it appears within *A Compleat History* expresses what was not an uncommon view among Scots in these early years after the Union.

Even more problematic than the reprinting of Mar's declaration and the manifesto was *A Compleat History*'s representation of the fate of the peers who were accused of treason. In *The Town-Talk*, Steele had studiously avoided presenting verbatim accounts of the legal proceedings against the lords, suggesting that "it is not for me to give you an account of the transactions in that High Court of Parliament" (120). Instead, his narrator offers a "lively" description of events, at the same time managing his readers' responses by urging them to avoid any compassion for the prisoners. *A Compleat History*, however, tells all. It includes lists of the prisoners taken at Preston and replicates accounts of the trials.[89] It reprints the newspaper accounts of the ignominious procession of the Jacobite prisoners into London on November 26, 1715, noting how, from Highgate onward, they all had their arms pinioned behind their backs and were led "through innumerable Spectators of all Ages, Sexes, and Conditions" with "Drums beating all the Way a Triumphant March" (85). But *A Compleat History* also extends the newspaper's descriptions with reflections on the state of the prisoners' minds, especially those of the peers: "What Pains can equal the Distress of noble Souls expos'd to the Insults of the Populace? And how must it cut them to the Heart, first, to pass through the Rude Reproach and Contempt of the Vulgar, before they fall Victims to the violated Laws of their Country?" (85). In addition, *A Compleat History* provides complete coverage of the proceedings against the peers, including the Member of Parliament Nicholas Lechmere's speech in the House of Commons advocating their impeachment, the articles of impeachment against them, their trials and their sentencing by the Lord Chancellor Cowper, as well as their pleas for mercy.

While the bulk of the material reprinted in *A Compleat History* clearly weighs against the Jacobite leaders, the narrative also includes items that weave threads from Jacobite memory into the otherwise government-oriented account. Such is the case with the inclusion of the scaffold speech

---

[89] Trial and execution pamphlets were not a new genre. Pamphlets capitalizing on the sensationalism of trials and public executions, often publishing the (alleged) dying words of criminals, had been popular from the mid-seventeenth century onward. See Andrea McKenzie, "Martyrs in Low Life? Dying 'Game' in Augustan England," *Journal of British Studies* 42, no. 2 (2003): 167–205.

of Lord Derwentwater. In his last words, delivered at Tower Hill on February 24, 1716, Derwentwater asserted his continuing adherence to King James and indicated his hopes that the Jacobite cause would live on after him: "I only wish now, that the laying down my Life, might contribute to the Service of my King and Country, and the Re-establishment of the Ancient and Fundamental Constitution of these Kingdoms, without which no lasting Peace, or true Happiness, can attend them" (127). Moreover, he cast aspersions on George and his government, noting that in his death, "I hope to find Mercy, which I have not found from Men now in Power" (126). Szechi argues that Derwentwater's speech follows a common template in Jacobite rhetoric where the final words from the scaffold were crafted to have maximum theatrical effect, representing their speaker as a martyr as well as providing additional moral support for those carrying on the cause.[90] A contemporary pamphlet comments on this strategy of disseminating the speeches through publication: "Tis easy to perceive, that those who compose the Speeches of our Rebels which suffer, lay hold of the Opportunity of their Executions to do all the Service possible to a wretched, expiring CAUSE."[91] Derwentwater's speech was a particularly effective example of a posthumous promotion of the Jacobite ideology, for it was reprinted in numerous forms after his death. One such popular reprinting employs woodcuts of cavalier figures at a scene of execution linking Derwentwater's execution with the earlier figure of a Stuart who was depicted as a martyr, Charles I (see Figure 4.1).[92]

A Compleat History includes the entirety of Derwentwater's speech, although it does acknowledge the problem of readers' potential sympathetic responses, suggesting in the conclusion that certain "well-meaning tender Hearts" may have been offended at the execution of Derwentwater and Kenmure "after the appearing Frankness of their Confession, and the *seeming* Penitence which they solemnly profess'd" (171). In response, the author focuses on the way in which the two men renounced their earlier repentance and used the opportunity of their punishment to further their aims, "making a Merit of Suffering for the Cause of *Popery* and *Tyranny*" (171). He also

[90] Daniel Szechi, "The Jacobite Theatre of Death," in *The Jacobite Challenge*, ed. Eveline Cruickshanks and Jeremy Black (Edinburgh: John Donald, 1988), 57–74.
[91] *Some Matters of Fact, in Vindication of the King's Evidence from the Falsities, Calumnies, Equivocations, and Misrepresentations Set Forth in Mr. Gascoigne's Paper* (London: J. Baker, 1716), 3.
[92] *The Speeches of the Six Condemn'd L[ords] at Their Tryals in Westminster-Hall* (London, 1716?). The site of Derwentwater's tomb also became associated with miraculous cures, suggesting that he, too, was seen as a martyr. Evelyn Lord, *The Stuarts' Secret Army: The Hidden History of the English Jacobites* (Abingdon and New York: Routledge, 2014).

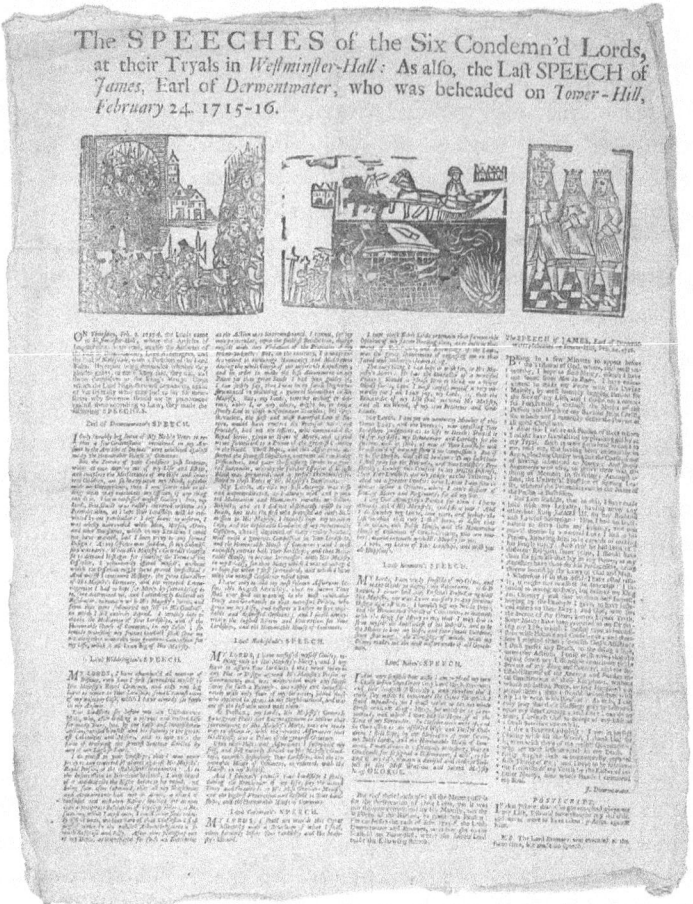

Figure 4.1 *The Speeches of the Six Condemn'd Lords at Their Tryals in Westminster-Hall* (London, 1716?). Courtesy of the National Library of Scotland

appeals to the sensibility of any "well-meaning tender Hearts" by painting a gruesome picture of the carnage at Preston and Dumblain:

> consider how many of our gasping Countrymen breathed out their Souls there in the glorious Defence of our holy Religion, and our Civil Liberties, and then tell me, is it not pity that *British* Ground should be thus fatten'd with the generous Streams of *British* Blood? Does not such a Sight as this demand our Sighs, our Sorrow and Compassion?" (171)

The negative affect conjured up by the imagined battle scene is designed to cancel out any compassion for the Jacobite sufferers.

The histories that followed *A Compleat History* represent similar complicated knots of memory. *A Faithful Register of the Late Rebellion*, for example, like *A Compleat History*, includes newspaper accounts as well as the "*Impeachments, Trials, Attainders, Executions, Speeches, Papers, &c. of All Who Have Suffered for the Cause of the Pretender in Great Britain*" in an attempt to construct what the author suggests will be "a lasting Monument" to the Rising.[93] Noting that he has "avoided all Partiality and Reflections, so that it might the better prove acceptable to all Parties," the author reproduces not only pro-government papers, but also papers that include the statements of individuals who were involved in the Rising, including the dying words of Derwentwater and others who refused to confess to the crime of rebellion or who critiqued the present government in their final moments. *A Faithful Register* includes the words of John Gordon, for example, who was executed at Tyburn on December 7, 1715, for his part in the Jacobite conspiracy at Oxford, and who spoke back to those who had condemned him: "I am not vers'd in the Laws of England; but if it is become a Fashion to take away Mens Lives upon Suspicion, it's a Severity not often practiced in other Nations" (14). *A Faithful Register* also reprints a "Copy of the Paper delivered to the Sheriff of London, by Richard Gascoigne." In his posthumous paper, Gascoigne not only asserts his continuing "Duty and Loyalty" for "King *James*," but also declares against the "false Accusations and Calumnies, that have been designedly spread by People, who I am afraid, took pains to procure unhappy Wretches to confirm them" (297); in particular, he targets those who turned king's evidence against him. The fact that printed pamphlets were produced "*in Vindication of The King's Evidence From the Falsities, Calumnies, Equivocations, and Misrepresentations Set Forth in Mr. Gascoigne's Paper*" suggest that his final words were in fact reaching a sympathetic audience.[94]

Patten's *The History of the Late Rebellion* entered public discourse in order to counteract claims such as those of Gascoigne against those who turned king's evidence. Patten himself had been engaged with the Jacobite cause, serving as chaplain to Thomas Forster, the leader of the English Jacobite troops. As he suggests, he was "One among the rest deluded to take an unhappy Share" in the "Progress and Consequences" of the Rising.[95] Taken prisoner at Preston, he subsequently turned king's

---

[93] *A Faithful Register of the Late Rebellion* (London, 1718), iv.
[94] See, for example, *Some Matters of Fact*, 3.
[95] Robert Patten, *The History of the Late Rebellion* (London: Printed for J. Baker and T. Warner, 1717), 3.

evidence, serving as a key witness in trials against a number of his fellow prisoners, including Derwentwater. Patten's *History* is a mixture of previously printed material combined with what he presents as his own eyewitness observations. For his account of the progress of the Rising until he joined it at Preston, he offers an abridged form of the same newspaper accounts that appeared in *A Compleat History*, only adding occasional details of local colour. Once he arrives in his account at the Jacobites' march to Wooler in Northumberland on October 19, 1715, he shifts to a more personal narrative, as he indicates: "Here they rested all *Friday*, where I, with some Men which I had Inlisted, joyned them, and was kindly entertained by the Chiefs" (38). Having been convinced of the error of his ways, Patten observes that he considers the writing of his *History* to be "A Duty incumbent upon me to make all the Reparation I could for the Injury I have done the Government" (preface). Although he indicates that he has no regrets about turning against his fellow Jacobites, Patten also presents a much more overtly positive perspective on the Jacobites than is evident in *A Compleat History* or the *Faithful Register*. He is complimentary toward both the Highland chiefs and the common Highlanders, noting of the latter that "It was very agreeable to see how decently and reverently the very common Highlanders behav'd, and answer'd Responses according to the Rubrick, to the Shame of many that pretend to more polite Breeding" (40). He also offers a favourable depiction of Lord Derwentwater, whom he knew personally, indicating that his "sweetness of his Temper and Disposition" had earned him the "Affection of all his Tenants, Neighbours and Dependents" and that "The Truth is, he was a Man form'd by Nature to be generally beloved" (59–60). Patten's final reflection on Derwentwater encourages rather than discourages the compassion that the author of *A Compleat History* suggests arises in tender hearts: "His Fate will be sensibly felt by a great many who had no Kindness for the Cause he died in, and who heartily wish he had not forwarded his ruin, and their Loss, by his Indiscretion in joining in this Mad as well as Wicked Undertaking" (60).

Patten's description of his own conversion also constitutes a potentially positive perspective on the Jacobites, suggesting that those in opposition to the government can be re-educated under the right circumstances. He notes that "whilst I continued among those unfortunate Gentlemen [the Jacobites] ... I look'd no farther than esteeming what I had done the least part of my Guilt" (preface). But, he suggests, once he was "removed into the Custody of a Messenger" and confined, he had "Leisure to reflect upon my past Life" and was therefore able to see the error of his ways. He praises members of the clergy in particular who "by their Example, Pen, and Preaching" support "the Establish'd Government in Church and State," suggesting that it was the "*Learning and solid Reasoning*" of the clergyman Dr. Cannon, rather than being "*Brib'd and* Brow-beaten," that convinced him to renounce his former principles. Patten's *History* was designed to exonerate him from blame. It also served to refute what had been "Printed and Reported by the Enemies of the Government." But as a Jacobite who had been converted, Patten also offered a potential model for the rehabilitation of Jacobites in general. Such an example resonated with a government for which punishment of all Jacobites was both impractical and dangerous, as it risked alienating those who were only nominally willing to support the Hanoverian government. Moreover, while he condemned the Rising, Patten offered positive commentary on the Jacobites, putting forth the suggestion that, rather than being evidence of a character flaw, the adherence to Jacobite ideology could be seen as a question of enculturation. This was a perspective that would be expanded upon by commentators after the 1745 Rising.

Patten's *History* represents a brief window into Jacobite perspectives on the Rising, perspectives that were later largely erased from the historical record. Peter Rae's *The History of the Late Rebellion; Rais'd against His Majesty King George, by the Friends of the Popish Pretender* also counters what he considers historical erasures perpetrated at the time by attempting to write the role of Scots loyal to the Crown into the memory of the Rising. A minister in Kirkbride, Rae indicates that he was inspired to write his own history after reading other accounts of the "late Rebellion" and finding that the "Good Services of his Majesty's Friends in some places" are "wholly pass'd over in Silence," while others, "especially in the North of Scotland," are "mis-represented."[96] The long list of subscribers in the *History* indicates that he had the support of a broad cross-section of the local population, including ministers, merchants and booksellers, as well as the occasional tanner and mason. Rae makes a point of inserting local knowledge and perspectives into his account, noting, for example, that the town of Kilmarnock stood out in the group of the Western-Shires in giving early "Proof of their Zeal and Forwardness" for King George's service, owing to the encouragement of the Earl of Kilmarnock (182). He also includes the names of the officers of the company of volunteers that was formed in Dumfries, all of whom were in fact subscribers to his *History*,

---

[96] Peter Rae, *The History of the Late Rebellion; Rais'd against His Majesty King George, by the Friends of the Popish Pretender* (Dumfries, 1718), vii.

excusing himself in a footnote: "That I have said so much for *Galloway* and *Nithsdale*, may admitt of an easy Apology; Since none that has heretofore written on the *late Rebellion*, has so much as Noticed them" (205). Rae makes a conscious effort to weave the efforts of individuals in his locality as well as the "establish'd Ministry" of the Church of Scotland into what he also refers to as the "Threed" of this *History* (32). He demonstrates his awareness of the importance of the way the inscription of a site of memory can have lasting impact.

As a printer himself who had brought the first printing press to Kirkbride and overseen the first printed work there, Rae also offers further insight in his *History* into the specific ways in which the initial inscription of events through print affected the way those events would be later re-inscribed.[97] In his prefatory comments "To the Candid Reader," he indicates his self-consciousness about publishing in the wake of the earlier histories when he explains why his own *History* was late appearing. He notes that he had attempted to gather information from people living in the locations connected to the Rising, but the responses he received were slow to arrive. Rae's *History*, like the other historical accounts of the 1715 Rising, includes a variety of documents: "Acts and Votes of Parliament, Proclamations of Council, private Letters, approven Authors, and good Informations from such as were Witnesses of the Matters inform'd of" interspersed with "authentick Doubles of *Letters, Maifesto's, Declarations, Proclamations, Speeches, Addresses, Associations*, and other Original papers, worthy to be preserv'd" (vii). Aware of the fact that his history contains passages similar to some in Patten's *History*, he remarks generally that both accounts derived their information from the same source, including "many Things, which we had all collected from the publick Papers" (preface). But, perhaps because of his own awareness of the particularities of print culture, Rae draws attention not just to general similarities but to the specific passages that parallel those of Patten, providing notes in the margins that draw readers' attention to the specific pages under question. The description of the attack on Edinburgh Castle, for example, is flanked by a marginal note indicating "*Paten's* His. Of the *late Rebellion*, pag. 159,160" (198). Rae's marginal notes do not just draw attention to passages from Patten's *History*, however; they offer a behind-the-scenes perspective on his own process of compiling historical narratives from a

---

[97] Anette Hagan, "The Spread of Printing," in *The Edinburgh History of the Book in Scotland*, vol. 2, *Enlightenment and Expansion, 1707–1800*, ed. Stephen Brown and Warren MacDougall (Edinburgh: Edinburgh University Press, 2012), 114.

variety of sources: he includes marginal notes referring to passages in *A Compleat History of the Rebellion* and the *Annals of King George I* as well as to the *London Gazette* and Scottish newspapers, which Rae refers to as the "Scottish Prints." In discussing the request for Dutch troops, Rae even refers to the sources of information on which the newspapers relied as references: "Letters from the *Hague* 10th *Sept*. N.S. in the Prints" (198). Although Rae himself is exceptional in the way in which he carefully records the texts he uses, his *History* serves as an example of the work of compilation involved in the writing of popular histories and suggests how, once stored in printed form, information became easily imported into and replicated in other printed works.

In re-creating the events that unfolded between autumn, 1715 and spring, 1716 as a *lieu de mémoire*, popular histories written in the aftermath of the Rising such as Patten's, Rae's and the two anonymous works examined here attempted to reinforce a providential history of the nation and to encourage an affective relationship between subjects of Britain and their new monarch. Picking up on the idea that the 1688 Revolution was God's plan, Rae notes in the dedication to King George I in his *History*, "The late happy Revolution [of 1688]" would have been in danger from the Jacobite threat, "had not Almighty God so signally interpos'd for the Prevention of it" to reaffirm "Your Majesty's happy Accession to the Throne of Your Royal Ancestors" (vi). Information once represented as disparate units in the newspapers was integrated into longer narratives focused on managing the crisis, convincing readers that the dangers to Crown and church had been contained, justifying the punishment of those who rose against the government and, occasionally, demonstrating the mercy of the government in pardoning their enemies. By emphasizing this containment, these early histories also served to retrospectively minimize the actual threat of the 1715 Rising and to further reinforce the identification of the British nation as exceptional in its possession of a "happy Constitution" based on modern notions of "common Sense" and "natural rights."

The 1715 Rising was also retrospectively re-inscribed "with a difference," to invoke Catherine Belsey's phrase, during the 1745 Rising in such a way as to further minimize its threat to the nation.[98] A number of histories of the earlier Rising were reprinted in 1745 and 1746, including two more editions of Patten's *History of the Late Rebellion* along with a second edition of Rae's account, published this time with the title

---

[98] Belsey, "Remembering as Re-inscription."

The History of the Rebellion, Rais'd against His Majesty King George I to signify its earlier occurrence.[99] Although none of the reprintings included new prefatory material, the republications nevertheless encouraged readers to view the earlier Rising in a causal relationship to the later one, as a less threatening lead-up to the 1745 engagement. A number of histories published after the defeat at Culloden also reflected on the 1715 Rising, reconfiguring the earlier event as what Astrid Erll calls a site of "premediation."[100]

At the same time as they shaped the events of the '45 Rising, these accounts also represented the '15 Rising as much less narratively compelling – and politically dangerous – in comparison. *A Review of the Two Late Rebellions, Historical, Political and Moral*, published in 1747, for example, writes the two "Rebellions" as different chapters in the same story; the focus of the narrative, however, is on part 2, the 1745 conflict, which is represented as the more serious threat to the nation.[101] In *Poetry and Jacobite Politics in Eighteenth-Century Britain and Ireland*, Murray Pittock suggests that the "essential premiss" of what he calls "incremental history" is "a commitment to prioritize certain aspects of British political and intellectual life, to minimize opposition and to exclude marginal or different interests."[102] Histories of the 1745 Rising that presented the 1715 as a site of "premediation" served to further minimize the opposition that had been so formidable in 1715, reinforcing the sense that the 1715 was a "damp squib."

In keeping with Erll's observation that "the medium is the memory," this chapter has examined the way in which the 1715 Rising was initially inscribed within both manuscript and print news genres and then "reiterated" and "adapted to new circumstances" – and to new genres – in the years following the Rising.[103] As I have suggested, the 1715 Rising presented an opportunity for newspapers to compete with manuscript's established authority, as they conveyed news that was occurring in the locations of conflict in a more timely and thorough manner. But while the affordances of the newspaper made it better able to convey information

---

[99] Robert Patten, *The History of the Rebellion in the Year 1715*, 3rd and 4th eds. (London, 1745) and Peter Rae, *The History of the Rebellion, Rais'd against His Majesty King George I* (London, 1746).

[100] According to Erll, "existent media which circulate in a given society provide schemata for new experience and its representation" ("Literature, Film, and the Mediality of Cultural Memory," 392).

[101] *A Review of the Two Late Rebellions, Historical, Political and Moral* (London, 1747).

[102] Murray Pittock, *Poetry and Jacobite Politics in Eighteenth-Century Britain and Ireland* (Cambridge: Cambridge University Press, 1994), 1.

[103] Rigney, *Afterlives of Walter Scott*, 19.

about the conflicts that were occurring, the form of the newspaper also amplified the sense of the Rising as a disjointed and uncontrollable series of events. Newspapers also made information more widely available to more people, storing it for use in the later construction of the cultural memory of the '15. Steele's and Addison's periodical essays offered a form of immediate containment, training readers to read beyond the representation of discrete units of information and to use their comprehensive rational powers, but it was the histories that were produced in the aftermath of the 1715 Jacobite conflict that wove the units of the newspaper reports together into providential accounts that ultimately minimized the danger that the events of 1715 had actually posed. An examination of the representation of the 1715 Rising at the time at which events occurred has suggested the important role that Jacobite politics and ideology played in early eighteenth-century Britain, despite the fact that the Jacobite cause was subsequently dismissed as "an irrelevance." Such an examination has also allowed us to see the impact of media networks, particularly the growing periodical press, on the formation of cultural memory at this time and to understand how ambivalences portrayed through printed works helped produce complex knots of national memory as they evolved over time and between media.

CHAPTER 5

Reading the 1745 Jacobite Rising
"Transitory News-papers," "Fleeting Pamphlets" and Knots of Cultural Memory

On July 23, 1745, Charles Edward Stuart landed on the remote Hebridean island of Eriskay with seven of his followers. Over the course of the next eight months, he amassed a sizeable army, seized Edinburgh, embarrassed the government troops at Prestonpans and marched his troops to Derby before retreating to Scotland and finally being defeated at Culloden Moor on April 16, 1746. The story of Culloden would subsequently become one of the most pervasive of national cultural memories, helping to constitute a Scottish identity based on loss and nostalgia. Scholars have analyzed how later eighteenth-century and nineteenth-century works of historiography and literature helped to create the cultural memory of the Jacobites as doomed to failure.[1] In this chapter, I trace the memory of the 1745 Rising back to its initial inscription in popular printed works produced during and immediately after the conflict. Following from the examination of news networks in Chapter 4, I begin by examining the manner in which news of the events of the 1745 Rising circulated within a media environment which was more saturated with printed news than ever before, but also, as a consequence, more self-reflective about mediation. As I argue, the proliferation of printed information about the conflict in 1745 generated increased concern not only about possible "Falshoods" being conveyed in the newspapers (a perennial issue), but also about how the news was being consumed by the nation's subjects. The Jacobite Rising of 1745 was perceived not just as a crisis of state; it was also perceived as a crisis of reading.

---

[1] See Murray Pittock, *The Myth of the Jacobite Clans: The Jacobite Army in 1745*, 2nd ed. (Edinburgh: Edinburgh University Press, 2009) and *Culloden (Cùil Lodair)* and Rigney, *Afterlives of Walter Scott*. Jaqueline Riding attempts to debunk some of the myths of the Rising and to present an objective account in *Jacobites: A New History of the '45 Rebellion* (London: Bloomsbury, 2016). See Viccy Coltman's *Art and Identity in Scotland: A Cultural History from the Jacobite Rising of 1745 to Walter Scott* (Cambridge: Cambridge University Press, 2019) for an excellent discussion of the incorporation of Jacobite culture into Scottish identity.

I move from a consideration of printed news to an examination of how the Rising was represented within the flood of popular narratives published after April 16, 1746, narratives that, like those examined in Chapter 4, drew their material from but also consciously distinguished themselves from newspapers. As the marketplace had expanded, there were substantially more popular works published about the events of the 1745 Rising than there had been about the 1715 Rising. These narratives about 1745 kept the conflict alive in the public consciousness in the days, months and years just after Culloden, serving to "immediately invest" the Rising "with symbolic significance" and treating it as if it were "being commemorated in advance," in Nora's terms.[2] By analyzing the construction of the 1745 Rising in such narratives, we can see the geopolitical and sociological contours of a new British nation being sculpted, one that marginalized the Highlands in the course of asserting its own modernity. At the same time, as popular printed works that borrowed from each other and from a number of other print and non-print sources, the narratives of 1745 also inscribed within the new cultural memory of the nation traces of the counter-memories that were in the process of being transformed or expunged. Such printed works constitute knots of memory that, in Rothberg's terms, "exceed attempts at territorialization":[3] in other words, they challenge the homogeneity of of the British nation they were being used to create.

"Fleeting Pamphlets" and "Transitory News-papers" in 1745

The anonymous author of the pro-Jacobite *Aeneas, and His Two Sons. A True Portrait* (1746) provides a picture of the contemporary mediascape at the time of the 1745 Rising, commenting on the intensity with which the inhabitants of Britain involved themselves in thinking, speaking and writing about the ongoing conflict in public venues. Exclaiming about the proliferation of news concerning the events of "these crazy Times," the author remarks that "every Man who has the Capacity or Opportunity of exhibiting his Thoughts to the Publick (whether as a Speaker or Writer, whether in the Senate, the Pulpit, or Coffee house, whether in the fleeting Pamphlet or yet more transitory News-paper) is ever representing Persons and Things not as they are, but as he would have them to be."[4] While the

---

[2] Nora and Kritzman, *Realms*, 18.
[3] Rothberg, "Introduction: Between Memory and Memory," 7.
[4] *Aeneas, and His Two Sons. A True Portrait* (London, 1746), i.

author of *Aeneas, and His Two Sons* acknowledges the continuing use of oral and manuscript media, by specifically drawing attention to the role of the "fleeting Pamphlet" and the "yet more transitory News-paper," he also intimates the way in which print was coming to dominate the media landscape in mid-eighteenth-century Britain.

News networks – and the media landscape in general – had changed considerably since 1715. While manuscript newsletters had dwindled, printed newspapers had flourished. According to Bob Harris, eighteen papers were produced within the nation's capital in 1745, including "eight weeklies, four thrice-weekly evening papers, and six dailies," and "nearly forty" papers in the English provincial towns as well as four Scottish papers.[5] Harris suggests that during the 1745 Rising, the newspaper "assumed a very substantial importance," particularly "between late September and early December 1745," when "the demand, the anxiety for news and for information reached an intensity that was probably unparalleled for the whole of the century."[6] As the contemporary Hudibrastic poem, *The Strolling Hero, or Rome's Knight-Errant*, asserted, "The *Affair*" of the Rising "fill[ed] the News."[7] In addition to generating an increased desire for domestic news, Harris argues, the 1745 Rising also changed the networks of newspaper communications throughout Britain, resulting in more authority for provincial papers. Scottish newspapers, especially the *Edinburgh Evening Courant* and the *Caledonian Mercury*, were important sources of information particularly until the time when the Jacobites crossed into England. Once the conflict escalated and the Jacobites starting moving south, however, it was the English provincial newspapers of the north and midlands that had the most current information.[8] The Rising, then, disrupted established patterns of geopolitical spatial authority because the provincial papers were able to supply more current and accurate information than those based in the metropolitan centre of London.

---

[5] Bob Harris, "'A Great Palladium of Our Liberties': The British Press and the 'Forty-Five,'" *Historical Research* 68, no. 165 (1995): 68.

[6] Ibid., 67. Harris also notes that "So great was the increase in demand [for news of the conflict] that at least three new provincial papers actually came into existence during the crisis" ("England's Provincial Newspapers and the Jacobite Rebellion of 1745–1746," *History* 80, no. 258 [1995], 7).

[7] Jemmy Butler, *The Strolling Hero, or Rome's Knight-Errant* (London, 1744), 23.

[8] As Cranfield suggests, "newspapers printed in such towns as Newcastle, Manchester and Derby had a personal knowledge of the rebel army, for which reason they were in great demand throughout the rest of the country" (*Development of the Provincial Newspaper*, 75). Bob Harris notes that "Large numbers of official and unofficial networks of communication appear to have been established during the crisis, and much of the information that these produced found its way into the provincial press" ("England's Provincial Newspapers," 8).

Harris further suggests that the "British press" had "an arguably crucial role to play" in ensuring that "the image of the rebellion" and responses to it created at the time were "remarkably uniform."[9] As indicated in Chapter 4, however, it is important to consider the material manner in which that information was conveyed. Like the newspapers produced during the 1715 Rising, the newspapers of 1745 created a discontinuous impression of events as they were occurring, as they represented those events as uncertain and endlessly circulating units of information intermingled with advertisements. As in earlier newspapers, foreign news still came first despite the Rising's paramount importance to the nation. While there were "Extraordinary" issues of newspapers devoted to particular crisis points in the Rising such as the Jacobites' march to Derby, national events were still discussed only after a thorough consideration of the European events. Like their predecessors, newspapers in 1745 and 1746 challenged readers "to construe a view of the world from the page[s] before them."[10]

But in 1745, more news was being printed and circulated in more publications than ever before, and, partly as a result of this increase in production and consumption, news was also viewed with an increased sense of anxiety. Scholars have identified the mid-eighteenth century in Britain as a tipping point in the establishment of the dominance of print culture, noting that the growth in the amount of printed material available was also accompanied by an increasing consciousness of the processes of mediation.[11] Christina Lupton's observations regarding the "self-reflexivity" of mid-eighteenth-century literary culture in Britain can be usefully applied here. Lupton suggests that "The culture of self-consciousness about literary production and consumption ... must be understood as a culture in which critical awareness becomes compatible with the production and consumption of fairly predictable and widely berated literature."[12] Newspapers, like other periodical forms, had always registered a high degree of self-reflexivity and "critical awareness" in attempting to assert their authenticity as editors revealed their objectives to their readers,

---

[9] Harris, "'A Great Palladium of Our Liberties,'" 76.
[10] Raymond, "The Newspaper, Public Opinion, and the Public Sphere," 132.
[11] See, in particular, McDowell, *The Invention of the Oral*. Other scholars who discuss the development of media consciousness over the course of the eighteenth century include Christopher Flint, *The Appearance of Print in Eighteenth-Century Fiction* (Cambridge: Cambridge University Press, 2011); Thomas Keymer and Peter Sabor, Pamela *in the Marketplace: Literary Controversy and Print Culture in Eighteenth-Century Britain and Ireland* (Cambridge: Cambridge University Press, 2015); and Carey McIntosh, *The Evolution of English Prose, 1700–1800* (Cambridge: Cambridge University Press, 2009).
[12] Lupton, *Knowing Books*, 3.

wrote disparagingly of rivals' claims and promised to offer unique sources of information.[13] But in 1745, as rumours of yet another challenge to the Hanoverian regime began to trouble the nation, and because the number of newspapers and periodicals was so much greater, media self-consciousness acquired a new sense of political urgency. The process of reading news about the Rising could have profound implications for the future of the nation. Reading – and the response to that reading – became politicized in a new way in 1745.

Like their earlier counterparts, newspapers in 1745 were able to provide only uncertain information about the activities of Jacobites, although, unlike the action in the earlier Rising, the sites of conflict in 1745 were limited to Scotland, at least in the beginning. A pamphlet entitled *A Compleat and Authentick History of the Rise, Progress and Extinction of the Late Rebellion* retrospectively comments on how the *London Gazette* inadvertently reprinted false information about Charles Edward Stuart's location that was supplied by the Jacobites themselves: "The Manner of his Departure ... and his Journey to *Genoa*, where he took up some Bills of Exchange which were very *duly paid*, made a fine Piece in *Italian*, which was presented to all the Friends of the family at *Rome*, and an Extract sent from thence was printed in our *Gazette*, by Authority."[14] While the *Gazette* was reporting on this fictional visit to Genoa, Charles was in fact making his way toward the coast of Scotland. The *London Evening Post* for July 27–30, 1745, indicates a slightly more informed sense of the activities of the man they referred to as "the Pretender's Son," quoting a dispatch from the *Hague Gazette* for July 30, 1745, that observed that "Considerable Wagers are laid here, that the Pretender's Son is actually arriv'd in Scotland, where he keeps *incog.*, and that there is a strong Party ready to start up in his Favour; It is certain at least that he set out the 8th Instant for Nantz [sic], in order to embark there."[15] As with the news in 1715, news reports about the events leading up to the 1745 conflict were printed and subsequently corrected by other reports. The larger number of newspapers in circulation during the 1745 Rising, however, meant that there was an even greater sense of uncertainty discussed by an even great number of readers. As John Home recalled in his *History of the Rebellion*, a

---

[13] As Manushag Powell suggests, "Periodicals have a tendency towards self-reflexivity that seems to surpass that of other genres" ("Afterword: We Other Periodicalists, or, Why Periodical Studies?," *Tulsa Studies in Women's Literature* 30, no. 2 [2011]: 447).
[14] *A Compleat and Authentic History of the Rise, Progress and Extinction of the Late Rebellion* (London, 1747), 6–7. This pamphlet is sometimes attributed to Henry Fielding.
[15] *London Evening Post*, July 27–30, 1745.

work which was begun in 1746 but not published until 1802, "every body spoke of nothing but the young Pretender," even though "very few people knew what to believe."[16]

Confirmed reports began to trickle in at the beginning of August 1745. Accordingly, the Lords Justices used the *London Gazette* to advertise a reward of £30,000 to "any person or persons that should seize and secure the Pretender's eldest son."[17] While some commentators expressed deep concern about events in the north, however, others dismissed such reports as alarmist. Given the fact that information about the events was presented as a confusion of vague facts and deliberate fictions, it is not surprising that several commentators referred to the reported landing of Charles Edward Stuart as a "Chimera."[18] In his *History of the Present Rebellion*, for example, John Marchant comments on the state of events at that time, indicating: "Scarce any Notice was taken of him; and it was some Time before any Credit was given to the News of [Charles Edward Stuart's] being landed in one of the Islands of *Scotland*."[19] As Geoffrey Cranfield affirms, "the country as a whole knew very little about what was happening in the north," and as a result, neither specific newspapers nor "the local civil authorities took the rebellion seriously – until perhaps, the very last moment."[20] W. B. Coley has discussed the lack of response to the Jacobite threat in the context of the complexities of parliamentary rivalries during the summer of 1745.[21] But I suggest that the political discourse concerning how to react to the news of the early events of the Rising both informed and was informed by a more general discourse at this historical juncture about the process of reading news.

Although news of the invasion was originally dismissed as "chimerical," the subsequent growth of the Jacobite army and their ensuing victories made the existence of a Rising impossible to dismiss. The subsequent confirmation of the existence of a Jacobite Rising was also accompanied by a corresponding discussion about the proper consumption of news. *The True Patriot*, a weekly periodical which Fielding started on November 5, 1745, for example, satirizes the uncertainty of newspaper reporting.

---

[16] John Home, *History of the Rebellion in the Year 1745* (London: A. Strahan, 1802), 54.
[17] Ibid., 53.
[18] Andrew Henderson, *The History of the Rebellion, 1745 and 1746. Containing, a Full Account of Its Rise, Progress and Extinction* (London: Reprinted from the Edinburgh Edition and sold by Ralph Griffiths, 1748), 7.
[19] John Marchant, *The History of the Present Rebellion* (London, 1746), v.
[20] Cranfield, *Development of the Provincial Newspaper*, 78–79.
[21] Henry Fielding, *The True Patriot and Related Writings*, ed. W. B. Coley (Middleton, CT: Wesleyan University Press, 1987), xxx–xxxii.

The "Apocrypha" section that was included in the first seventeen issues of *The True Patriot* ridiculed newspapers' practice of providing continuous updates and corrections.[22] Comments on news reading also became a common subject in the "fleeting Pamphlets" of the day. Some writers, following Marchant's line of argument, worried that if news accounts were too dismissive of the threat, people would not take the invasion seriously enough. *The History of the Present Rebellion in Scotland. From the Departure of the Pretender's Son From Rome, Down to the Present Time* suggests the perils of not attending closely enough to the accounts given by the papers. The author recalls the initial confusion about the origins of the invasion caused by conflicting newspaper accounts: "whoever recollects the Accounts which the News Papers gave us of the first Landing of the Pretender, must remember with what Incertainty they spoke of a few Men being landed in the West of *Scotland*, who were sometimes Gentlemen from *Ireland* hunting, and sometimes were quite vanished, every subsequent Account actually contradicting the former."[23] The result of this continual contradiction was that no one, "except the most credulous," gave "any Belief" to reports about a Jacobite landing (9). Instead, they imagined it was "a Story devised by some Persons for particular Purposes which need not be mentioned" (9). This uncertainty, claimed the author, threatened to train readers in disbelief so that they became accustomed to "treat[ing] this Rebellion as imaginary" (10). Such a perspective could become so entrenched that "even when it was impossible to doubt longer of its Reality," news readers would make it "still the Subject of Contempt and Ridicule; saying, it was only a Company of wild Highlanders got together, whom the very Sight of a Body of Troops, however small, would infallibly disperse" (9–10). With so many conflicting reports circulating, it could become "customary" to dismiss them all, the author warns, which could in turn have deleterious effects on the nation. Politically irresponsible reading, in other words, could become a habit, and the truth could be mistaken for a hoax.

Other commentators worried that representations of the rebels as a major threat could instil too much fear in readers, which could also have adverse effects. The author of *Seasonable Considerations on the Present War in Scotland*, writing ostensibly "*In a Letter to a Person of Distinction*,"

---

[22] See Davis, *Acts of Union*, 52–53.
[23] *The History of the Present Rebellion in Scotland. From the Departure of the Pretender's Son from Rome, Down to the Present Time* (London, 1745), 9.

suggests how impressions of the news could change from one extreme to the other:

> At first it was looked at as a Thing below Notice, and for several Weeks People were in doubt here, whether there was any Rising in that Country at all ... but the marching of a Body of 4000 Men down to *Edinburgh*, and what follow'd soon after the Defeat of General *Cope*, rais'd the Credit of the *Highlanders* so much, that from being a low and despicable Rabble, they swell'd of a sudden into daring and intrepid Troops, which Character they chiefly derived from the Reports of those whom they had defeated.[24]

A Review of the Two Late Rebellions confirmed that it was "those dreadful Accounts they had heard" of the Highlanders that, together with the "horrors of the Night" and the "unexpected" method of battling, "made an Impression in the Breast of the boldest" of the government troops at Prestonpans and ultimately caused their defeat.[25] By "cultivat[ing] discursively the impression of understanding their own mediation" – as well as the mediation of other texts like themselves – these texts conveyed the sense that consuming news did not just represent events: it could also alter them.[26]

In response to such concerns, works like the *Journal of the Pretender's Expedition to North Britain* attempted to walk a middle ground, demystifying fearful representations of the Jacobites while still presenting them as enough of a threat to require a decisive military response. The author suggests that he will use reason to defuse fears: "This Journal will unveil to the speculative Reader some of [the Jacobites'] hidden Springs of Motion, which will be apparently found no other than an obstinate inflexibility, and daring Rashness."[27] This reasonable approach also includes, however, a realistic assessment of the threat so that "Those who have suffered themselves to be deceived by an obstinate, invincible Prepossession, of the Smallness of [Charles Edward Stuart's] Numbers, and the Unskilfulness of his Officers, cannot fail of being cured of those Prejudices" (vii). Similarly, *The History of the Present Rebellion in Scotland*, published after the Battle of Prestonpans, offers what it calls "the best Intelligence" and provides what it claims is an eyewitness account from a former Jacobite solider, James Macpherson, along with a "list of the Slain." The purpose of providing this information, notes the author, is that

---

[24] *Seasonable Considerations on the Present War in Scotland* (London, 1746), 3.
[25] *A Review of the Two Late Rebellions*, 39.   [26] Lupton, *Knowing Books*, 10.
[27] *Journal of the Pretender's Expedition to North Britain* (London, 1745), v–vi.

the reader "may safely rely on the Truth of the Facts related."[28] After presenting an account of events "Down to the Present Time," the writer attempts to rally the "brave Nation" so that the "Religion, Laws, Liberties, and Lives" of Britain will not be "exposed to the Mercy and Disposition of a licentious Rabble and cruel Banditti" (45). The pamphlet concludes with a strongly affective tone as the author makes an appeal to readers: "THE WHOLE is in Danger, and for God's Sake! Loose not a Moment in ARMING YOURSELVES" (47).

Implicitly and explicitly, works such as *Seasonable Considerations on the Present War in Scotland*, the *Journal of the Pretender's Expedition to North Britain* and *The History of the Present Rebellion in Scotland* suggest that the problem lies less with incomplete or faulty reporting of information in the papers than with faulty reading of the news by the nation's citizens. Readers, they imply, must learn to read discerningly so as to be alert to but not overwhelmed by any potential dangers within the nation. In providing a view of the entire year's events, the editors of *The Scots Magazine, Containing, a General View of the Religion, Politicks, Entertainment, &c. in Great Britain* for the year 1745 speculate that the problem of determining how to respond correctly to information is endemic to a situation of civil war because, in the course of a national conflict, most people are caught up in their own perspective. It is difficult, they suggest, even for "the most steady heads and closest thinkers to keep free of all bias in such a situation of things," and it is therefore "scarcely to be expected but the many must lean so much to some one side, as not to be capable of seeing distinctly what is the other."[29] When their "interests, passions or prejudices, happen to be affected by an argument, or even by a matter of fact," the editors note, readers are not able to judge candidly what they see in front of them, "especially on a first reading, while their minds are in agitation" (iii). That people will believe what they "wish to be true," the editors suggest, was "never more plainly verified in any age or country than now in ours" (iii). The editors of the *Scots Magazine* accordingly suggest that it is the responsibility of "writer[s] and collector[s]" of news to present both sides of a conflict with the "strictest impartiality" and, in the process, to train readers to follow suit: "If a reader is impartial, studying only to find and follow truth, he will be so far from flying into a violent passion, that he will not take the least offence at those who publish

---

[28] *History of the Present Rebellion in Scotland*, 2.
[29] *The Scots Magazine, Containing, a General View of the Religion, Politicks, Entertainment, &c. in Great Britain* (1745), iii.

the strongest arguments that can be framed against his own opinions" (v). But at the same time, they imply, readers must learn to read so as to recognize some "truth" as more correct than others.

Determining the correct version of "truth" in the time of conflict – indeed, even attempting to determine what specific "interests, passions or prejudices" inform a particular argument – was complicated in 1745, and particularly so because Jacobites were adept at ambiguity. As Pittock and Guthrie suggest, Jacobite culture, because of its politically treasonous nature, relied for its continued existence on codedness and secrecy.[30] The author of the pamphlet *Aeneas, and His Two Sons. A True Portrait* confirms the way in which "interests, passions or prejudices" can be misinterpreted. In the preface, the author of *Aeneas, and His Two Sons* describes his visit to "a Coffee-house near *Ludgate*" just after the Jacobites had crossed into England, where he beheld "a moderate, well-meaning Citizen," who in "turning over the Papers," happened to praise what he read about Charles Edward Stuart's "indefatigable Vigilance" and to suggest that he was "no despicable enemy."[31] Overhearing his words, an enraged British officer condemns "News-Writers, or Printers" for representing anything positive about the Jacobites and then accuses the reader of the newspaper himself of being a Jacobite (x). Meanwhile, a non-Juror, someone who might have actually been a *bona fide* Jacobite, takes the opportunity of the officer's attention being otherwise engaged to slip away unmolested. The author of *Aeneas, and His Two Sons* thus draws attention not just to the implications of misreading "News-Papers," but to the dangers of misreading the reactions of citizens who read those "News-Papers." He implies that the perceived "truth" of any situation exists more in the mind of the reader than in a text itself. This example also serves on a meta-critical level to deflect accusations of Jacobite sympathies from the author himself, for the main text of *Aeneas* presents a positive perspective on the Stuart family. *Aeneas, and His Two Sons* both comments on and embodies the fact that printed news of the events of the Rising could reveal different truths, depending on who was reading them.

The 1745 Rising thus unfolded within a mediascape in which print genres, particularly the "fleeting Pamphlet" and "transitory News-Paper," provided citizens with a massive amount of material to sift through and

---

[30] See Murray Pittock, *Material Culture and Sedition, 1688–1760: Treacherous Objects, Secret Places* (Houndmills: Palgrave Macmillan, 2013) and Neil Guthrie, *The Material Culture of the Jacobites* (Cambridge: Cambridge University Press, 2013).
[31] *Aeneas, and His Two Sons. A True Portrait* (London: J. Oldcastle, 1746), ix–x.

assess. The same issues of uncertainty and disconnection held true in 1745 as in 1715, with newspapers representing the crisis as discontinuous and ever-changing. But in a world more saturated with works of print, readers in 1745 were even more self-aware about the implications of consuming media than their predecessors had been. This is strikingly symbolized by the case of Charles Edward Stuart, who, according to John Burton, when he was fleeing after the Battle of Culloden, read "in the Newspapers" about the direction which the troops pursuing him expected him to take and accordingly decided to alter his plans.[32] The same self-awareness and the same worries about the implications of consuming information through print continued to pervade the discourse on the Rising as the cultural memory of the conflict began to be constructed in the aftermath of Culloden.

Commemorating in Advance: Recollecting the Rising

As suggested in the Introduction, the Battle of Culloden was constructed as a site of a cultural memory almost instantaneously. The *Particulars* of the battle of Culloden delivered by Lord Bury circulated extensively in newspaper and broadside form, and citizens were also made familiar with the details through other forms of mediation. The British government and the general population continued to focus intensely on the subject of the Jacobites in the aftermath of the battle at Culloden. As Pittock observes, "both the 'Forty-five and the Prince's subsequent career were a source of immediate fascination."[33] "Transitory News-papers" kept citizens abreast of government efforts to restore order and to punish those responsible for the Rising. In addition, "fleeting Pamphlets" and more substantial works that drew their material from newspaper accounts also took stock of the recent events of the Rising.

At the same time, memories of the events from a Jacobite perspective were also circulating, albeit in mediations designed for more confidential audiences. One important pro-Jacobite site that set out to "immediately invest" the Rising "with symbolic significance" and to treat it as if it were "being commemorated in advance" was the manuscript "The Lyon in Mourning" compiled by Robert Forbes.[34] An ordained Episcopalian

---

[32] John Burton, *A Genuine and True Journal of the Most Miraculous Escape of the Young Chevalier* (London, 1749), 58.
[33] Murray Pittock, "Charles Edward Stuart," *Études écossaises*, no. 10 (2005), 60.
[34] The NLS possesses the original manuscript volumes of "The Lyon in Mourning." Scanned images of the manuscript are available as a Digitized Collection at Simon Fraser University's library,

minister at the outset of the Rising, Forbes had attempted to join Charles Edward Stuart's forces but, along with a number of other men travelling with him, was arrested at St. Ninian's on September 7, 1745.[35] He was imprisoned at Stirling Castle until February 4, 1746, then at Edinburgh Castle until May 29, 1746, and it was probably during this period that he conceived of the idea of recording the experiences of the Jacobite followers. Upon his release, Forbes took up residence in Leith, where he interviewed those who had been involved in the Rising, acquired copies of letters and other materials sent to him and kept up a correspondence with fellow Jacobites, urging them to provide him with further information. Within the first five years after Culloden, Forbes had filled eight volumes with handwritten accounts.[36] The manuscript volumes include editorial apparatuses that associate them with printed works, including title pages with volume numbers, epigraphs and dates. But they also serve as material relics of Jacobite memory. The cover of volume 3, for example, has several items pasted to it, including "a piece of that identical Gown, which the Prince wore for four or five Days, when he was obliged to disguise himself in Female-Dress, under the Name of Bettie Burk" and a "piece of the Apron" that he also wore on that occasion.[37]

Anticipating the way in which official cultural memory would erase the experiences of the Jacobites, Forbes set out to write out by hand "A Collection (as exactly made as the Iniquity of the Times would permit) of Speeches, Letters, Journals, &c. relative to the Affairs, but more particularly, the Dangers and Distresses" of those who had been involved in the Rising.[38] As he indicated, "I have a great Anxiety to make the Collection as compleat & exact as possible for the Instruction of future Ages in a piece of History the most remarkable & interesting that ever happened in any Age or Country."[39] Attempting to provide further proof that his work was a genuine transcription of the experiences of those who were represented within, he also included in his massive collection copious notes and editorial remarks about the sources of his information. According to his

---

https://digital.lib.sfu.ca/lyon-mourning. See also Leith Davis, "The Lyon in Mourning Project," May 2021, https://author.sfu.ca/.

[35] Robert Forbes, *The Lyon in Mourning*, ed. Henry Paton, 3 vols. (Edinburgh: Edinburgh University Press by T. and A. Constable for the Scottish History Society, 1895–96) and William Donaldson, "Forbes, Robert (bap. 1708, d. 1775)," xii. Jacobite Annalist and Scottish Episcopal Bishop of Ross and Caithness," *Oxford Dictionary of National Biography*, September 20, 2019, www.oxforddnb.com/view/10.1093/ref:odnb/9780198614128.001.0001/odnb-9780198614128-e-9845.

[36] He was working on the tenth volume at the time of his death.

[37] Robert Forbes, "The Lyon in Mourning," NLS, Adv. MS 32.6.18, boards.

[38] Ibid., Adv. MS 32.6.16, cover.   [39] Ibid., Adv. MS 32.6.19, fol. 83 recto.

notes, he often confirmed the accuracy of what he collected orally by allowing interviewees to read and correct their accounts. Forbes managed to the keep his work hidden, moving the papers when necessary to the home of a friend in order to evade the searches of the authorities. Although he refused to publish his collection in print during his lifetime, the verbal and manuscript accounts that he collected provide insight into the network of Jacobite memories in circulation at the time and offer a counter-memory to the official Hanoverian construction of the Rising as a rebellion doomed to failure.

In the next sections, I examine three genres of printed textual works that inscribed the government-oriented memory of the Rising in the early years following Culloden: narratives of the trials of the Jacobite prisoners; and popular histories accounts of the escape of Charles Edward Stuart. All three of these textual genres drew information provided in the newspapers into narrative forms, attempting to replace what the editors of the *Scots Magazine* identified as the "agitation" accompanying the "first reading" of news about the Rising with a more "lasting" memory. Narratives describing the trials and executions of Jacobite leaders trained readers to see the punishments meted out not just as pain inflicted on individual bodies but as the purging of the body politic; narratives about the escape of Charles Edward Stuart after the Battle of Culloden entertained readers and served to mythologize and minimize the Rising; and popular histories of the Rising foregrounded their own mediation of memory while commenting on the issue of reading for future cultural memory. All three genres encouraged readers to imagine a unified British state by vilifying and rejecting undesirable elements within it. However, as popular works that remediated material from many other sources, including, at times, Jacobite accounts similar to those collected by Forbes, these narratives also suggest the ways in which this politically marginalized group continued to "live on" – indeed, live within – British cultural memory. It is important to note that there also existed at this point a growing industry of anti-Jacobite visual representations as printed engravings were becoming cheaper and more easily accessible to more people.[40] These visual representations, as I will demonstrate, appeared in and interacted with the textual accounts to

---

[40] See Stana Nenadic, "Print Collecting and Popular Culture in Eighteenth-Century Scotland," *History* 82, no. 266 (1997), 203–22; Diana Donald, *The Age of Caricature: Satirical Prints in the Reign of George III* (New Haven, CT: Yale University Press, 1996); and Eirwen E. C. Nicholson, "Consumers and Spectators: The Public of the Political Print in Eighteenth-Century England," *History* 81, no. 261 (1996): 5–21.

amplify negative public perceptions of the Jacobites, but they often served as further marks of Jacobite counter-memory.

Trials of a Nation: Narratives of Jacobite Prisoners

On May 5, 1746 the *London Evening Post* affirmed that the Jacobite Rising had been crushed, exulting, "Three Posts have arriv'd from the North since Thursday, all the Advices which they bring agree, that the Rebellion is in a Manner entirely suppress'd."[41] While the military action that constituted the "Rebellion" itself might have been "entirely suppress'd," the process of rounding up and punishing those involved in it was just beginning. This process was much more extensive than it had been in 1716. According to the official List of Prisoners, 3,471 Jacobite men, women and children were kept in prisons and on transport ships in the wake of the 1745 Rising.[42] Over the next year, newspapers reported on the details of the imprisonments, trials and executions of these Jacobite prisoners. The newspaper reports were subsequently re-inscribed, often word for word, in a number of popular narratives that themselves became re-inscribed in official histories.

In the months after Culloden, newspapers conveyed information about the huge number of prisoners being captured and transported to locations in Scotland and England. Citing "Letters from Inverness," the *London Gazette* for May 3–6, 1746, for example, reports that a growing number of prisoners were being rounded up, indicating that "The Prisons at Aberdeen, Montrose, and Stirling are filled, and Prisoners are continually brought into Perth, Dumferling, Dundee, Irwine, and Dumfreis."[43] According to the *General Advertiser* of June 17, 1746, vessels had arrived on the Thames carrying "1000 Rebel Prisoners from Scotland."[44] The sheer number of prisoners made it impossible to bring everyone to trial, and by the end of August, readers were informed that a lottery system had been set up for prisoners in England and that only "every 20th Man of the common men" would be selected to stand trial, with the rest "to be transported," although "Chiefs and officers" and those who had committed extreme acts of treason would also be tried.[45]

---

[41] *London Evening Post*, May 5, 1746.
[42] See Bruce Gordon Seton and Jean Gordon Arnot, *The Prisoners of the '45*, 3 vols. (Edinburgh: Printed by T. and A. Constable for the Scottish History Society, 1928), 1: 152. See also Pittock, *Culloden (Cùil Lodair)*, chapter 4, "Aftermath and Occupation."
[43] *London Gazette*, May 3–6, 1746. [44] *General Advertiser*, June 17, 1746.
[45] Seton and Arnot, *Prisoners of the '45*, 8.

Information about the arrests and trials of Jacobites was regularly shared in the newspapers throughout the summer and autumn of 1746 and into the spring of 1747. The *London Evening Post* for June 26–28, 1746, for example, listed the names of and details about the first thirty-six prisoners who were arraigned on June 23, 1746, at St. Margaret's-Hill, Southwark.[46] The newspapers also provided details about the subsequent punishments of the prisoners, starting with the executions of nine prisoners who were hanged, drawn and quartered at Kennington Common on July 30, 1746. The account printed in the *Penny London Post or the Morning Advertiser* on the day of the execution provides gruesome details about the victims' "Bodies being ripped up" and their "Bowels ... taken out and flung into the Fire," further condemning the villainy of those executed by noting that the heads of three of the executed men were displayed in Temple-Bar in London, at the Market Cross at Manchester and at the castle at Carlisle.[47] Michel Foucault's analysis in *Discipline and Punish* of torture as a process designed to "mark the victim" either "by the scar it leaves on the body, or by the spectacle that accompanies it" provides a useful perspective on the executions that took place during the suppression of the Rising. As Foucault suggests, the "liturgy of torture" must "be seen by all almost as its triumph."[48] But although crowds for the executions were reportedly immense, including, according to the *Penny London Post*, "the greatest Number of Spectators as ever were seen together in the Memory of Man,"[49] those who were able to see the marking and spectacle of the executions constituted only a fraction of the nation's subjects. It was newspaper accounts that disseminated the prisoners' executions to the British population who could not be present, ensuring that they were "seen by all," or at least by as many as possible, albeit in a mediated manner. The accounts include details such as the fact that the prisoners' "Stockings ... were all white" and that six of them had hats "which were laced with Gold" in order to convey a sense of authenticity and to help readers further visualize the event.

At the same time as they were providing accounts of the prisoners who were being tried and executed, newspapers were also following the stories of the four Jacobite lords who were brought to London, the first peers of

---

[46] *London Evening Post*, June 26–28, 1746. The first prisoners to be tried were English Jacobites who had been arrested at Carlisle.
[47] *Penny London Post or the Morning Advertiser*, July 30, 1746.
[48] Michel Foucault, *Discipline and Punish: The Birth of the Prison*, trans. Alan Sheridan, 2nd ed. (New York: Vintage, 1995), 35. See also Szechi, "Jacobite Theatre of Death."
[49] *Penny London Post or the Morning Advertiser*, July 30, 1746.

the realm to be tried for high treason since the trials following the 1715 Rising. George Mackenzie, third Earl of Cromartie, William Boyd, fourth Earl of Kilmarnock, and Arthur Elphinstone, sixth Lord Balmerino, were imprisoned in the Tower of London in May 1746. Simon Fraser, Lord Lovat, evaded capture until June 7, 1746, after which he, too, was brought to the Tower. Although Cromartie's life was spared, Kilmarnock and Balmerino were executed on Tower Hill on August 18, 1746, and Lovat on April 9, 1747. The lords' executions were represented in the newspapers in a notably more subdued and dignified fashion than those of the prisoners of lower rank. As Foucault remarks, there is a "legal code of pain" that correlates "the quality, intensity, duration" of pain "with the gravity of the crime, the person of the criminal, the rank of his victims."[50] The circumstances of the lords' deaths, like the circumstances of their lives, served to distinguish them from other men.

While newspaper accounts of the trials and executions were important in conveying the government's immediate response to the Rising, it was the pamphlets and popular books published in the wake of the executions that served to impress the longer-term implications of the conflict on the nation's readers. As seen in Chapter 4, trial and execution pamphlets had circulated in the wake of the 1715 Rising. But the number of Jacobite prisoners who were tried and executed and the extensive circulation and recirculation of their stories in all varieties of printed works produced an unprecedented print market phenomenon in 1746 and 1747. Even before sentencing was passed on the first rebels at Southwark, newspapers were advertising a pamphlet that would provide "A Genuine Account of these unhappy Persons ... as taken from their own Mouths, containing every Circumstance relating to the Rebellion, their Behaviour, &c. and every Thing material that happen'd on their Trials, &c."[51] Accordingly, *A Genuine Account of the Behaviour, Confession, and Dying Words, of Francis Townly [sic], (Nominal) Colonel of the Manchester Regiment, Thomas Deacon, James Dawson, John Barwick, George Fletcher and Andrew Blood, Captains in the Manchester Regiment* appeared around July 30, 1746, followed by *An Authentick Narrative of the Whole Proceedings of Court at St. Margaret's Hill, Southwark, in the Months of June, July and August, 1746*. The latter went quickly through three editions by the end of summer, 1746.

---

[50] Foucault, *Discipline and Punish*, 34.
[51] *Penny London Post or the Morning Advertiser*, July 21–23, 1746.

As works sold by "News-sellers" which were available "at all the Pamphlet-shops in *London* and *Westminster*,"[52] these pamphlets drew their material largely from the newspapers which were sold by the same individuals and at the same locations. The chief selling point of the pamphlets, however, as in 1716, was their promise to provide more extensive details than were available in newspapers. *An Authentic Narrative*, for example, boasts on its title page that it also includes material provided by one "who took the Whole down in Court in Short Hand." One contemporary commentator ventured to explain the appeal of these works, suggesting that the information in the pamphlets satisfied a readerly desire for closure. When the "Rebellion" was still in process, he suggests, "that alone drew the Attention of the whole Body of the People"; but when it was "happily extinguished," people wanted to know why it happened in the first place. Readers are "naturally desirous to know who were the first Movers, Contrivers and principal Actors in an Affair, which from the first might be justly suppos'd to be attended with the most fatal Consequences to all the Ringleaders of it."[53] The trial and execution narratives were designed to provide a government-sanctioned backstory to the trauma of the Rising.

The pamphlets devote considerable attention to the personal circumstances that led those found guilty to espouse the cause of the Stuarts. In the pamphlets, readers are encouraged to peruse short biographies which relate the circumstances of each "unfortunate Man." In addition, these works reproduce questions posed to the witnesses that had been designed to ascertain not just the crimes committed but also the "characters" of the accused: "Pray what Character does the Prisoner bear at *Manchester*?" the counsel for George Fletcher asks in *A Genuine Account*.[54] For some of the prisoners, the influence of family and friends is depicted as playing a significant part. *A Genuine Account* includes the information that Francis Towneley was born into "a Family remarkable for being ready for Rebellion at all Times" (30). His uncle was "out" in the 1715 Rising, and Towneley further imbibed Jacobite principles by serving in the army in France. Thomas Deacon, too, notes the account, was "unhappily prejudiced in Favour of the Pretender against the present Royal Family by the company he frequently convers'd with"; he, in turn, persuaded his brother Charles to join the Jacobite cause (52). The pamphlets describing

---

[52] Ibid.
[53] *An Account of the Behaviour, and Conduct, of Simon Lord Fraser, of Lovat* (London, 1747), 1.
[54] *A Genuine Account of the Behaviour, Confession, and Dying Words, of Francis Townly* [sic], *(Nominal) Colonel of the Manchester Regiment, Thomas Deacon, James Dawson, John Barwick, George Fletcher and Andrew Blood, Captains in the Manchester Regiment* (London, 1746), 37.

the prisoners suggest that their disloyalty was a result of either bad company or personal moral failings.

The process of putting those involved in the Rising on trial was itself intended to lend an institutional authenticity to the actions of the Hanoverian regime. As Geoffrey Plank notes, in order to distract from the questionable actions of British troops after Culloden, Cumberland's officers were "anxious to justify their decisions by reference to specific constitutional and legal principles, accepted military traditions, and the dictates of enlightened social policy."[55] The popular narratives giving details of the trials reinforced the legitimacy of the government's actions by weaving the stories of the individual prisoners into more inclusive chronologies of the Rising, reinforcing a Hanoverian government commitment to Britain's "constitutional and legal principles." *A Genuine Account*, for example, sets the trials of the first Jacobite prisoners within the context of "an Account of the taking of *Carlisle*" on December 30, 1745, at the same time as it defends what might be seen as the harsh punishments of the prisoners after they had surrendered themselves. Noting that a number of those on trial claimed "that his Royal Highness the Duke promised them Mercy" upon their surrender, the pamphlet includes a copy of the actual terms offered by the government troops at Carlisle, emphasizing the fact that the Jacobites were not promised clemency, but rather were told they would not immediately be "put to the Sword," but would "be reserved for the King's Pleasure" (5). The pamphlet suggests that the Jacobite prisoners misinterpreted the "King's Pleasure" for the "King's Mercy," misreading the circumstances of their fate entirely.

In addition to providing content sympathetic to the government, the pamphlets that reproduce the details of the trials also employ a format which places the reader in the role of judge. Pamphlets like *An Authentick Narrative of the Whole Proceedings of Court at St. Margaret's Hill* include the texts of the indictments, the approval of the jury by the accused and the questioning of witnesses, often in the form of an oral dialogue between those present. The author of *An Authentick Narrative* notes that he has "spared not Pains or Expence in making" the accounts "as complete, and as conformable to Truth as possible."[56] The accounts claimed to be objective, including "Evidence both for and against the Prisoners" (4). Through the

---

[55] Geoffrey Plank, *Rebellion and Savagery: The Jacobite Rising of 1745 and the British Empire* (Philadelphia: University of Pennsylvania Press, 2006), 23.
[56] *An Authentick Narrative of the Whole Proceedings of Court at St. Margaret's Hill, Southwark* (London, 1746), 4.

process of reading the details of the court cases, including the prisoners' and witnesses' own words, readers were invited to weigh the evidence objectively for themselves. But any evidence that might be seen as running counter to the verdict is summarily dismissed in these accounts. Anne Acton's speech in defence of George Fletcher, for example, in *An Authentick Narrative* is presented in her own words, but, rather than representing her cross-examination in full, the narrative sums up her claims with the observation that she "prevaricated so much in the Answers" to the questions put to her that "no Credit was given to her Evidence" (39). Readers may have been formally encouraged to come to their own conclusions, but the conclusions they were permitted to draw were always already predetermined within the narratives themselves.

These pamphlets served the additional function of cautioning readers against exercising sympathy for the prisoners. Sympathy for the accused was, as seen in Chapter 4, a concern in the aftermath of the 1715 Rising. It was perhaps even more of a practical concern following the 1745 Rising because of reports circulating about the brutality of the government troops. To this effect, the remarks of the council for the Crown, Sir John Strange, are reprinted in full in *An Authentick Narrative*, reinforcing the fact that the Jacobites constituted a threat to "one of the most Glorious and free Constitutions that was ever framed" (14). Strange's remarks also help temper any sympathy that the narrative generates for the prisoners: he is quoted cautioning that

> If an Attempt to subvert the Government, to destroy the King and set up a *Popish* Pretender, if in marching in a hostile Manner, carrying on a bloody War in this Nation, can move Compassion or be extenuated, any Rebellion may be palliated over and excused, since scarce any Circumstances can be added in Aggravation of that which hath lately been raised and carried on in this Kingdom. (15)

The pamphlets circulating the details about the trials of the Jacobite prisoners served to disseminate the government's justifications of its actions more widely and to prevent readerly "Compassion." They trained citizens to read and interpret the trials properly, viewing the punishments and executions of the Jacobites in terms of the larger good of the nation. Proper reading would, in turn, help readers to see that their nation possessed "one of the most Glorious and free Constitutions that was ever framed."

While the trials and executions of the Jacobite officers and men generated much popular interest, the fate of the four Jacobite lords caused an even greater media stir. Numerous pamphlets appeared from 1746 onward offering details of the lords' trials (and executions in the cases of Kilmarnock, Balmerino and Lovat) as well as their biographies. On August 19, 1746, the day after the executions of Kilmarnock and Balmerino, the *General Advertiser* gave notice of the publication of two accounts of the events. The advertisement for *The Trials of William Earl of Kilmarnock, George Earl of Cromartie, and Arthur Lord Balmerino, for High-Treason, before the House of Peers, at Westminster Hall, on the 28th and 30th of July, and the 1st of August, 1746* included the actual hour of its planned publication ("This Morning at Ten o'Clock") together with promises about the work's ability to offer material that had not been made available in the newspapers, including "the whole Judicial Proceedings against the above mentioned three Lords; and a faithful Relation of the Behaviour of the two Lords who suffered, while confined in the Tower," as well as their "Deportment" in the private house to which they were carried just before they went to the scaffold.[57] The other work advertised that day, *An Account of the Behaviour of the Late Earl of Kilmarnock, since his Sentence, and on the Day of his Execution; Together with a Genuine Attest Copy of his Speech at the Bar of the House of Lords*, was listed as becoming available "in a few Days." The advertisement for this latter work includes a note by the printer asserting the authenticity and uniqueness of the narrative: "To prevent the Public from being imposed upon by false Accounts, I declare, at Lord Kilmarnock's particular Desire, that no Narrative of this Kind can be depended upon as authentic, but what is either published by me, or with my Knowledge and Approbation." Both of these works went through four editions in 1746. Prints such as the "Whole Length Print of SIMON Lord Lovat," which was advertised as being "drawn from the Life, and etch'd in Aqua Fortis, by William Hogarth," also provided visual images of the condemned traitors (see Figure 5.1).[58] Hogarth's image represents Lovat counting inexplicably on his fingers, emphasizing his calculating nature. With his inscrutable smirk, the subject of Hogarth's portrait seems to acknowledge and feed the public's insatiable curiosity about the Jacobite peers.

Numerous accounts of the life of each lord circulated in print as separate pamphlets, as a series of works by the same printer, and also, bound together, as book-length works. Each life follows a similar template, beginning with a family history of the peer, usually extracted verbatim from other works like George Crawford's *The Peerage of Scotland*,[59] and then outlining the circumstances under which the man joined the Jacobite

---

[57] *General Advertiser*, August 19, 1746.   [58] *London Evening Post*, August 28–30, 1746.
[59] George Crawford, *The Peerage of Scotland* (Edinburgh, 1716).

Figure 5.1 Engraving of Simon Fraser, Lord Lovat (c. 1667–1747). Courtesy of the National Library of Scotland. License: CC by 4.0

cause and the details of his capture. A crucial point made by the prefatory material in many of these works is that the peers joined the Stuart cause for personal rather than political reasons. Kilmarnock, for example, is represented as confessing that "his rebellion was a kind of *desperate* scheme, proceeding originally from his vices, to extricate himself from the distress of his circumstances."[60] Balmerino, "being a younger son" who had not expected to inherit the family title and estate, is depicted as having nothing to lose and everything to gain by following Charles Edward Stuart's banner,[61] and Lovat's "deliberate and malignant purpose to ruin and subvert our present government" is presented as being due to the fact that the government had "not thought fit to gratify his ambitious and avaritious passions and desires."[62] By attempting to empty out the Jacobite cause of any political context, these pamphlets worked to disarm the movement ideologically at the same time as its adherents were being physically disarmed and, in many cases, transported or executed.

But, although there are similarities between the cases of all three lords, they are treated very differently, as the specific circumstances of each lord's trial and punishment are used to comment on different aspects of the justice of the Hanoverian regime. Accounts concerning Cromartie are the briefest. In addition to providing details about his life and his involvement in the Jacobite cause, they focus attention on the mercy of the King, who pardoned the peer "in consideration of his numerous family"; he was the father of nine children with a tenth on the way.[63] Cromartie says very little on his own account. Narratives about Kilmarnock, however, include extensive accounts of his penitence and his acceptance of his fate which serve to justify the government's punishment of those who took arms against it. In a pamphlet entitled *An Account of the Behaviour of the Late Earl of Kilmarnock, since his Sentence*, James Foster, who served as pastor to Kilmarnock when he was in the Tower, provides details of the dialogues he held with Kilmarnock in efforts to convince the lord to recognize his error in joining the Rising. Such details also serve as a form of catechism for the reader, providing lessons in the destructive nature of Jacobitism as not only an attack on "the *personal rights* of the King and his illustrious house," but also a threat to "the *national* happiness ... diffusing consternation and

---

[60] James Foster, *An Account of the Behaviour of the Late Earl of Kilmarnock* (London, 1746), 11.
[61] *The Life of Arthur Lord Balmerino, from the Time of His Birth to That of His Execution on Tower-Hill* (London, 1746), 3.
[62] *Memoirs of the Life of Lord Lovat* (London, 1746), 122–23.
[63] W. Wilkinson, *A Compleat History of the Trials of the Rebel Lords in Westminster-Hall* (London, 1746), 15.

terror through the land, obstructing commerce, giving a shock to the public credit, in the depredation and ruin of his country" (6–7). Foucault discusses the importance of repentance in justifying punishment, suggesting that "the only way that [torture] might use all its unequivocal authority, and become a real victory over the accused, the only way in which the truth might exert all its power, was for the criminal to accept responsibility for his own crime."[64] Foster's description of Kilmarnock's death affirms the authenticity of his penitence, for Kilmarnock is represented as "humble and relenting" on the scaffold, praying for the King and asking for forgiveness (37). Although Foster's account generated controversy among Calvinist clergy for focusing on penitence and absolution rather than Christ's mercy,[65] it was precisely the focus on penitence that made the story ideologically valuable from an official perspective. Foster's description helped turn Kilmarnock into an ideal example of a repentant criminal, one who recognized the importance of erasing his own treasonous soul and body from the nation. Once stored in pamphlet form, Foster's account was subsequently reproduced in virtually all other accounts of the trial and execution of Kilmarnock, along with a printed copy of the "professions and acknowledgements" that the peer had made to Foster (37). Such frequent reprinting helped to memorialize Kilmarnock as, in Foster's terms, a "sacrifice to the justice of his country" (37).

Accounts providing details about Balmerino, on the other hand, who was the only one of the first three lords charged to plead "not guilty," present him not only as treasonous but as unrepentant and therefore irredeemable. In *The Trials of William Earl of Kilmarnock, George Earl of Cromartie, and Arthur Lord Balmerino*, for example, Balmerino's arguments for his innocence are presented as based on mere technicalities, each one of which is given due consideration by the other lords before it is dismissed, and Balmerino is eventually forced to submit to his sentence of death. Balmerino's deportment on the scaffold accords with the arrogance he exhibits in his trials. The account notes that Balmerino appeared wearing the "very *same Regimentals* he wore at the *Battle of Culloden*, which was blue turn'd up with red, Brass Buttons, and a Tye Wig."[66] Whereas Kilmarnock was depicted as penitent, Balmerino is represented as behaving with great "intrepidity," strolling up to his coffin to see the

---

[64] Foucault, *Discipline and Punish*, 38.
[65] See Samuel Wilson, *Christ the Great Propitiation. A Sermon Preached at the Evening Lecture in Silver-Street, September 14, 1746* (London, 1746).
[66] *The Tryals of William, Earl of Kilmarnock, George, Earl of Cromertie [sic], and Arthur Lord Balmerino, for High Treason* (London, 1746), 28–29.

inscription and reading aloud a last speech asserting his continuing adherence to Jacobite principles. In these popular printed works, Balmerino's execution becomes a representation of the ultimate triumph of the Hanoverian government over Jacobite disloyalty, for he had previously been active in the 1715 Rebellion and had been pardoned afterward on condition of swearing to uphold the Hanoverian regime. The fact that he was depicted in the trial and execution narratives as professing his loyalty to the Stuart family until the very last moment of his life provides further justification for his execution.

Although Balmerino was depicted as misguided, he was nevertheless represented as an admirable opponent, someone who was indeed a noble foe. Simon Fraser, Lord Lovat, in contrast, was subjected to a very different kind of treatment in the trial and execution narratives. One of the earliest accounts about Lovat, *Memoirs of the Life of Lord Lovat*, which appeared in August 1746, just after the execution of Kilmarnock and Balmerino, presents an account of Lovat's intrigues and political dissembling in both 1715 and 1745. The author of the *Memoirs* further vilifies Lovat by borrowing from the conventions of anti-Catholic prose narratives, incorporating voyeuristic passages about Lovat's rape of an heiress and his "lascivious pranks" as a "pretended Jesuit," for example (54). The *Memoirs* concludes with an *ad hominem* invective against Lovat, representing him as both physically and morally grotesque. The author warns that Lovat is "crafty and subtle," so that, although he is "ambitious and proud," he is also able, when it serves his turn, to be "cringing, mean and fawning" (119). Other works on Lovat expanded on the material from the *Memoirs*. *The Life, Adventures, and Many and Great Vicissitudes of Fortune of SIMON, Lord LOVAT*, for example, went through three different editions, each one successively more interlarded with material unrelated to Lovat's present circumstances but designed to gratify the readers' appetite for salacious details about illicit encounters. Taking advantage of the brief reference to Lovat's "long confinement in the Bastil[l]e" mentioned in the *Memoirs* (118), for example, the writer of *The Life, Adventures, and Many and Great Vicissitudes* includes a long section detailing other prisoners' sexual adventures.[67] Such works memorialized Lovat not only as a traitor but also as a libertine anti-hero.

The extreme negative views of Lovat were not just a reflection of his constantly shifting loyalties, however; they must also be seen in the context

---

[67] *The Life, Adventures, and Many and Great Vicissitudes of Fortune of SIMON, Lord LOVAT* (London, 1746).

of the circumstances of his imprisonment and trial. Convicted in part through the testimony of John Murray of Broughton, who, like Robert Patten in the earlier Rising, had turned king's evidence to save himself, Lovat was the last of the Jacobite peers to be tried. He underwent a lengthy confinement in the Tower and was old and reputedly ill when finally executed almost a year after Culloden. By that time, with controversial accounts circulating about the behaviour of British troops after Culloden and the harsh treatments of Jacobite prisoners, public opinion had somewhat altered to become more sympathetic toward those who had risen against the government.[68] Works like the *Memoirs* tried to counteract the representation of Lovat as aged and sick. The writer comments, for example, that, although Lovat is physically grotesque, he has "taken such care of himself, that he still preserves a degree of health and vigour very uncommon at so advanced an age" (118). *A Genuine Narrative of the Life, Behaviour, and Conduct of Simon, Lord Fraser, of Lovat* addresses those who sympathize with Lovat by suggesting that "Enemies" of the government are at work "at Coffee-houses and Places of public Report, as well as in private Conversation," bent on challenging the "Justice or Policy of the Legislature, for making an Example of such a feeble old Man as Lord Lovat."[69] Such enemies, suggests the author, are intent on spreading the view that Lovat was utterly "incapable ... of influencing or propagating a Rebellion" because of his age and infirmities.[70] Like earlier narratives cautioning about proper reading, the author of the pamphlet warns the reader against being too credulous.

The poem "On the Lord Lovat's Execution," published in the *London Evening Post* of April 7–9, 1747, comments self-reflexively on the different uses made of the narratives of the Jacobite peers' trials and punishments, suggesting how the stories of the executions of Kilmarnock, Balmerino and Lovat appealed to different kinds of readers:

> PITY'D by *gentle Minds* KILMARNOCK dy'd;
> The *Brave*, BALMERINO, were on thy Side ...
> But LOVAT's End *indiff'rently* we view,

---

[68] See Pittock, *Culloden (Cùil Lodair)*, 104 and W. A. Speck, *The Butcher: The Duke of Cumberland and the Suppression of the '45* (Oxford: Basil Blackwell, 1981).

[69] It was not only the circumstances of Lovat's life that were the subject of controversy, but also those of his death. See *A Candid and Impartial Account of the Behaviour of Simon Lord LOVAT* (London, 1747) and *An Answer to a Dangerous Pamphlet Entitled A Candid and Impartial Account of the Behaviour of Simon Lord LOVAT* (London, 1747).

[70] *A Genuine Narrative of the Life, Behaviour, and Conduct of Simon, Lord Fraser, of Lovat* (London, 1747), 2–3.

> To no *King*, to no *Religion* true:
> No *Fair* forgets the *Ruin* he has done;
> No *Child* laments the *Tyrant* of his *Son*;
> No *Tory* pities, thinking what he *was*;
> No *Whig* compassions, for he *left the Cause*;
> The *Brave* regret not, for he *was not* brave;
> The *Honest* mourn not, knowing him a *Knave*.[71]

In representing the differences between the peers, the poem suggests that the narratives about the individual lords represent a collective attempt to appeal to all readers. Poignant accounts of the deaths of Kilmarnock and Balmerino are provided for the "gentle"-minded and the "brave," respectively, while all readers, both Whigs and Tories, can be united in their disgust at Lovat.

Taken together, the pamphlets and books detailing the trials and executions of the Jacobite prisoners represent an attempt to knit the nation together both rationally and affectively after a bloody civil war by justifying the actions and promoting the perspective of the Hanoverian government. But these printed works were not the only mediations using material from the accounts of the trials and executions to create the cultural memory of the Rising. Robert Forbes's "The Lyon in Mourning" also includes a number of transcriptions of speeches of Jacobite prisoners who maintained their faith in the Stuart cause even as they faced public execution. Forbes includes the entirety of 'The Speech of Mr. James Bradeshaw," for example, including his personal history, his account of the "Barbarity" of the English troops after Culloden and his celebration of Charles Edward Stuart as a prince who is "every Thing, that I could imagine great & excellent, fully deserving what He was born for – to rule over a free People."[72] Forbes also included "The Speech of the R[ight] H[onourable] Arthur, Lord Balmerino," in his "The Lyon in Mourning" manuscript, which, he indicates, is "faithfully transcribed from his Lordship's own Hand-writ."[73] At the same time as he includes Balmerino's gallows speech, Forbes also provides a "List of those, who were Evidences a[gainst] my Lord Balmerino" at his trial, again taken from Balmerino's "own Hand-writ."[74] The references to embodiment (Balmerino's own "Hand-writ") connect both Forbes and those reading or listening to his account more closely to the memory of the executed peer. In his final speech, as represented by

---

[71] *London Evening Post*, April 7–9, 1747.
[72] Forbes, "The Lyon in Mourning," Adv. MS 32.6.16, fol. 60 recto, fol. 61 recto.
[73] Ibid., fol. 66 verso.   [74] Ibid., fol. 68 verso.

Forbes, Balmerino takes aim at what he calls a "most wicked Report spread, & mentioned in several of the Newspapers; that His Royal Highness, the Prince, before the Battle of Culloden, had given out in Orders that no Quarters should be given to the enemy."[75] Balmerino also adopts the same strategies that Derwentwater had used earlier: he repeats his continuing adherence to the Stuart cause and commends all "the faithful Adherents to the Cause, for which I am now about to suffer," adding, "God reward them, make them happy here & in the World to come."[76] Forbes's manuscript collection works to preserve individual accounts of loyalty to the Stuarts and to call into question government representations of Culloden. Set within the context of other pro-Jacobite material in the "The Lyon in Mourning," Balmerino's speech helps to present him as another martyr to the Jacobite cause.

As with the popular printed works of the 1715 Rising, the inclusion of these pro-Jacobite items in pro-Hanoverian texts complicates their otherwise pro-government perspective. Although it does not include the entirety of Bradshaw's final speech, for example, *A Compleat History of the Trials of the Rebel Lords in Westminster-Hall; and the Rebel Officers and Others Concerned in the Rebellion in the Year 1745* notes that James Bradshaw "deliver'd a Paper, full of treasonable Expressions," while he and some of the other convicted traitors "in their last Moments ... pray'd for the Pretender and his Cause."[77] The publications representing Balmerino's trial also refer to the "treasonous" paper that he left behind him. But although the "treasonous" statement that Balmerino uttered on the scaffold was omitted from the first publications detailing his trial, the intrigue surrounding the unknown comments proved too much for printers to resist. Eventually, the inclusion of the speech would serve as a selling point for compilations of materials about the Rising, and the *True Copies of the Papers Wrote by Arthur Lord Balmerino* also circulated separately. By its third edition, for example, *The Trials of William Earl of Kilmarnock, George Earl of Cromartie, and Arthur Lord Balmerino* included not only Balmerino's last words in regular type, but also in engraved cursive script that serves as a mediation of his original hand, an extension of his physical presence into the present.[78]

---

[75] Ibid., fol. 67 verso.   [76] Ibid., fol. 68 recto–verso.
[77] Wilkinson, *A Compleat History of the Trials of the Rebel Lords*, 265.
[78] *The Trials of William Earl of Kilmarnock, George Earl of Cromartie, and Arthur Lord Balmerino, for High Treason, before the House of Peers, at Westminster Hall, on the 28th and 30th of July, and the First of August, 1746*, 3rd ed. (London, 1746), back matter.

A number of the editions of the trial and execution narratives also included visual images in the shape of engraved or woodblock portraits. While these images were designed to appeal to consumers who were developing a taste for visual culture, they also could potentially serve as commemorations of the Jacobite cause. The printed image of "The Earl of Kilmarnock and Lord Balmerino," for example, depicts a gruesome scene of an excecution on Tower Hill, but it also represents framed portraits of the two lords (with their heads back on their shoulders) rising above the scene (see Figure 5.2). By addressing readerly demand for more and more information about the fate of the Jacobite prisoners, particularly the Jacobite lords, the trial and execution narratives turned them into celebrity figures, inscribing ambivalent pro-Jacobite traces into the way contemporary and later readers would experience the story of the suppression of the "unnatural Rebellion."

"Chevalier" Narratives of the 1745 Rising

At the same time as the newspapers were communicating the re-assertion of British governmental authority through the punishment of the Jacobite rebels in the months following Culloden, they were also reporting on the continuing evasion of that authority by the leader of the Jacobite forces, Charles Edward Stuart. After the decisive fight that ended his chances to regain the throne (or even to negotiate with the British government from a position of power), Charles Edward Stuart had fled from the battleground. For the next five months, he concealed himself in the Highlands and Islands before finally boarding a ship bound for France in September 1746. The newspapers provided whatever details they could about Charles Edward Stuart's whereabouts for an eager public. The *London Gazette* for May 3–6, 1746, for example, noted that, in the aftermath of Culloden, "The Pretender's Son, Lord Perth, and the Person calling himself Lord John Drummond, are moving about in the Cameron's Country, with young Lochiel who was wounded again in the last Battle, and have not above 20 or 30 Men with them."[79] Although the *London Gazette* of June 8–10, 1746, claimed that Charles had fled to France,[80] the *London Evening Post* for June 21, 1746, contradicted that assertion, suggesting instead that "it is thought the Pretender's Son is still in the Country, since there are several small Parties of the Rebels yet in Arms."[81] Charles Edward Stuart's eventual escape was officially confirmed by the beginning of October. As

---

[79] *London Gazette*, May 3–6, 1746.   [80] *London Gazette*, June 8–10, 1746.
[81] *London Evening Post*, June 21, 1746.

Figure 5.2 Effigies of the late Earl of Kilmarnock and the late Lord Balmerino (London, 1746). Courtesy of the National Library of Scotland. License: CC by 4.0

the *Penny London Post or the Morning Advertiser* for October 1–3, 1746, asserted, "Tis now confidently assured, that the two Men of War mention'd in our last, hovered some considerable Time upon the Coast of Mull and Ardnamurchan ... but that having come upon the Coast of Ariseg ... they shot their Long-Boat with twelve Men in it."[82] The colourful language of this account as it continues suggests the affective appeal of the story of Charles Edward Stuart's escape:

> an old Man understanding who they were, informed them that the Pretender was lurking in a Cave at a small Distance, upon which they detained the old Man as an Hostage, till they found, as he said, the Chevalier, almost famish'd with Hunger and spent with Fatigue; they immediately carried him off, conducted him on board, hoisted Sail, and bid a long Farewel[l] to the beloved Country of Keppoch and Lochiel.[83]

In addition to providing intriguing content for readers of newspapers from April until September 1746, the story of Charles Edward Stuart's prolonged evasion of government forces also gave rise to a substantial number of separately published pamphlets and longer printed works. As one of these volumes acknowledged, there were "almost, daily accounts of the *young adventurer's* travels and hardships after the battle of *Culloden*."[84] Scholars, when they have considered them at all, have tended to discuss such works generically. In *The Historical Novel in Europe*, for example, Richard Maxwell considers them in relation to "an identifiable kind of 'pretender' novel" that took shape in Europe between 1680 and 1740,[85] while Pam Perkins suggests that these ephemeral documents demonstrate the speed with which Jacobitism was transformed, in the popular imagination, from political threat to sentimental romance.[86] In *Jacobitism and the English People*, Monod observes that "After the '45, Charles Edward Stuart's exploits in Scotland quickly became the stuff of myth, and were popularized in works like *Alexis; or, The Young Adventurer*, *Ascanius* and *Young Juba*."[87] Monod suggests that these fictionalized accounts of Charles Edward Stuart's exploits after 1745 demonstrate a "new politics" of

---

[82] *Penny London Post or the Morning Advertiser*, October 1–3, 1746. [83] Ibid.
[84] *The Wanderer, or Surprizing Escape* (London, 1747), 1.
[85] Richard Maxwell, *The Historical Novel in Europe, 1650–1950* (Cambridge: Cambridge University Press, 2009), 121.
[86] Pam Perkins, "'The 'Candour, Which Can Feel for a Foe': Romanticizing the Jacobites in the Mid-Eighteenth Century," *Lumen: Selected Proceedings from the Canadian Society for Eighteenth-Century Studies* 31 (2012): 131.
[87] Paul Monod, *Jacobitism and the English People: 1688–1788* (Cambridge: Cambridge University Press, 1989), 37. Monod also includes Eliza Haywood's *A Letter from H[enry] G[oring], Esq, One of the Gentlemen of the Bed-Chamber to the Young Chevalier* with these fictionalized accounts.

Jacobitism: "Party conflict and the commercial press had buried the reasoned absolutism of divine right under waves of populism and emotionalism; the god-like sovereign had been replaced by the fairy-tale Prince."[88] A closer examination of these texts with attention to their publication history, however, allows us to see a more nuanced picture of the work they performed in inscribing the cultural memory of the 1745 Rising.[89] The works that Monod lists are in fact significantly different from each other. *Alexis; or, the Young Adventurer. A Novel* is a printed version of a narrative included in Forbes's "The Lyon in Mourning." The other works combine different political perspectives, reflecting a number of other sources from which they borrow material. As intertextual works that re-inscribe reports from newspapers as well as pro-Jacobite accounts, these popular narratives of Charles Edward Stuart's escape offer representations of the official Hanoverian memory of the Rising that, like the trial and punishment narratives, also build traces of Jacobite counter-memory into their textual fabric.

In the course of compiling "The Lyon in Mourning," Forbes went to great lengths to obtain by word of mouth or by written account any and all information that he could find about the movements of Charles Edward Stuart after the Battle of Culloden, attempting to corroborate accounts wherever possible by presenting multiple individuals' perspectives. One item he includes in his manuscript is a "genuine & full account of the Battle of Culloden … together with the young Prince's miraculous Escape at, from & after the Battle, fought on April 16th, 1746. to his Return to the Continent of Scotland from the Western Islands on the 6th of the succeeding July."[90] This account, he notes, is "taken from the Mouths of the old Laird of MacKinnon, Mr. Malcolm MacLeod, &c. and of Lady Clanranald and Miss Flora MacDonald" and written down by John Walkinshaw or Dr. John Burton.[91] Directly after this account, Forbes inserts details of a conversation that he had with Alexander MacDonald of Kingsburgh during that gentleman's visit on July 11, 1747, to the house of Lady Bruce at the Citadel in Leith, where Forbes stayed after his release from prison. During the visit, Forbes notes, "it was proposed to read" the above account "in the hearing of Kingsburgh, that so he might give his

---

[88] Monod, *Jacobitism*, 38.
[89] I have adopted the term "Chevalier" rather than "Pretender" because it was used frequently within the texts themselves and suggests a more ambiguous ideological perspective instead of the Hanoverian perspective.
[90] Forbes, "The Lyon in Mourning, Adv. MS 32.6.16, fol. 75 recto–verso.   [91] Ibid., fol. 75 verso.

Observations or rather Corrections, upon it."[92] Forbes indicates that Kingsburgh made some corrections and additions to the account. In the course of detailing the conversation, Forbes also notes that "particular Questions were put to him w[ith] Respect to yt pamphlet, called Alexis, Part 1st," a copy of which he also included in the eighth volume of his manuscript.[93] Forbes also quotes Kingsburgh as suggesting during their encounter in Leith that he "knew no Body who could be the Author of that pamphlet but e[ithe]r Neil MacKechan or myself."[94] "The Lyon in Mourning" does not offer solid proof regarding Kingsburgh's authorship of *Alexis*, but it does suggest a way of understanding the pamphlet as a social text that was produced through a complex process of telling and retelling, like the other accounts about Charles Edward Stuart inscribed by Forbes in his collection. According to Forbes, Kingsburgh had actually had practice telling the story of Charles Edward Stuart, as he had relayed it to his fellow prisoners when he was imprisoned at Edinburgh Castle in "the same Room of the Castle with Major MacDonnell, George Moir, the Laird of Leekie, Mr. Thomas Ogilvie, &c."[95] Unlike the oral accounts, however, *Alexis* went beyond the bounds of the confidential group, entering into the print marketplace. This was a marketplace consisting not only of secret Jacobite readers but also other readers who had been primed by earlier intriguing newspaper reports to be interested in a longer narrative about Charles Edward Stuart's escape.

Advertising itself as *"A Novel,"* *Alexis* tells the story of the hero, "a shepherd of the first rank upon the continent of Robustia [Scotland]," who, perceiving the "degeneracy and miseries of the lower shepherds," seeks to reform their manners and lead them "back to that happy simplicity and innocence, for which their *hardy ancestors* are so famed in glory" and to extend the restoration of simplicity to "Felicia" (England), where the shepherds are "quite nummed [sic] with lethargy."[96] Alexis rallies the swains of Robustia and marches into Felicia but is unable to make any headway there, as its inhabitants are so "fatally drowned in luxury and thoughtless indolence" that they cannot "rouze themselves to one *manly* thought" (1). When Alexis and his "adventurers" retreat to their native Robustia, the evil Sanguinius orders his "numerous pack of Blood-hounds to execute the shocking scheme that was formed against the gentle Alexis and his followers, and upon the unlucky plain of Lachrymania" (4). The

---

[92] Ibid., fol. 83 verso. [93] Ibid., fol. 85 recto. [94] Ibid., fol. 87 recto.
[95] Ibid., Adv. MS 32.6.17, fol. 12 recto.
[96] *Alexis; or, the Young Adventurer. A Novel* (London, 1746), 1.

narrative elaborates on the brutality of Sanguinius's followers, who mercilessly slaughter the adventurers and innocent citizens. The narrator seeks to encourage a sense of outrage on the part of the reader, noting, for example, that "The pregnant shepherdesses are ripped up, and infants drop out with their intrails!" (4).

Alexis includes details that connect its story with the facts of the Rising and Charles Edward Stuart's subsequent ordeal. A connection to Culloden is suggested, for example, by the comment that the battle at Lachrymania was lost because Alexis's troops needed "rest and provisions" and the "very morning of that day had made a long march to attack the enemy, but by some fatal neglect, or something worse, in some of [the] officers, miscarried, and were obliged, without halting to return to the fatal plain" (9). The London edition even includes a "key" at the end, identifying specific characters. While it resonates with the secret history genre, however, *Alexis* also reverses the politics of the secret history. According to Rebecca Bullard, secret histories "attacked ... 'arbitrary government' – that is, absolute rule, or, in England, the rule of a monarch without reference to Parliament," providing an intimate glance of the intrigues of court and suggesting how the individual foibles of powerful figures have political implications.[97] Secret history, she suggests, "focuses attention on the body of the monarch, thereby compromising regal dignity and undermining the reverential distance between monarch and people." Like other "secret histories," *Alexis* "focuses attention on the body of the monarch," but instead of "compromising royal dignity," the focus on the regal body becomes a way of uniting readers in affective concern for the King.[98] Instead of revealing the fallibility of the monarch, *Alexis* elicits sympathy for the Stuart promotion of absolute rule.

Like many of the other narratives collected by Forbes, *Alexis* is primarily concerned with presenting a positive image of Charles Edward Stuart, drawing on the Jacobite ideology of the divine right of kings to depict Alexis as the "peculiar care of heaven" (5). Alexis is heroic, selfless and devoted to his cause. Reflecting on the battle at Lachrymania, he laments, "There my *faithful shepherds* were dispersed, and forced to roam through the bleak hills, wild deserts, dusky hollows and gloomy dens, exposed to all the nipping torments of hunger, thirst and cold – I share in their sorrows –

---

[97] Rebecca Bullard, "Secret History, Politics and the Early Novel," in J. A. Downie, ed. *The Oxford Handbook of the Eighteenth-Century Novel* (Oxford: Oxford University Press, 2016), 138.
[98] Rebecca Bullard, *The Politics of Disclosure, 1674–1725: Secret History Narratives* (London: Pickering and Chatto, 2009), 7.

I feel their pains, my heart bleeds for them" (7). At the same time, he remains optimistic, announcing that "there is something within me that tells me that I shall one day recompense them all, maugre all opposition of my enemies, and the infatuation of the deluded shepherds [of Felicia]" (7). Alexis indicates an unwavering belief in Providence: "How happy it is for us, that a good and unerring superintendency watches over us and directs all events, to the final perfection and felicity of mankind? All is will and will *yet* be better" (9–10). With this optimistic attitude, he is able to rally the spirits of Heroica and the men who are rowing him between the Western Islands in the midst of a terrible storm, for example, by singing "several pretty pastorals" (10). Despite its resonance with the specific circumstances of the Rising, then, *Alexis* consciously works to create a sense of the universality of its story as a celebration of divine monarchy. The characters and events to which it refers are only temporary and local manifestations of that more universal ideology.

By depicting a network of sympathetic connection between Alexis and his followers – one which involves, by extension, the reader – and by situating itself within a universal time-space rather than the specific historical event of the 1745 Rising, *Alexis* also represents a branch from an alternative development of the novel. According to Rachel Carnell, histories of the novel from Ian Watt onward have focused on works that represent the ideology of "Protestant Whig capitalist selfhood" derived from the works of John Locke.[99] In contrast, Carnell suggests, different political ideologies informed a variety of early British novels, such that fiction in the early eighteenth century took on different forms as it "responded to the competing Whig, Tory, and Jacobite versions of political selfhood" (10). The "version of political selfhood" represented in *Alexis* corresponds with a Jacobite ideology which promotes the establishment of affective bonds within a clearly defined hierarchy under a Stuart monarch chosen by God.

Murray Pittock suggests that *Alexis* provided the model for another work of fiction published in 1746 that narrativized the life of Charles Edward Stuart, *Ascanius; or the Young Adventurer*.[100] *Ascanius* appeared in two very different forms. The shorter version, consisting of sixty-three pages, represents the story of Charles Edward Stuart's escape after Culloden and, like *Alexis*, features Charles Edward Stuart as a heroic

---

[99] Rachel Carnell, *Realism, Partisan Politics, and the Rise of the British Novel* (New York and Houndmills: Palgrave Macmillan, 2006), 10.
[100] Pittock, "Charles Edward Stuart," 59.

character, an "illustrious Wanderer" who is attentive to the needs of others and worthy of being a leader.[101] A number of incidents in the short version of *Ascanius* are identical to those found in *Alexis*. In the midst of the tempest that threatens the crew of his boat "with a dreadful Voyage to the Regions of Death, for example," Ascanius "made light of the Danger they were in" and, like Alexis before him, "sung them several Songs, one in particular in [the boatmen's] own Language" (22). Like *Alexis*, *Ascanius* presents an affective connection between the leader and his followers. One of Ascanius's men "wept plentifully at parting" with Ascanius, while Ascanius, too "shed Tears by Sympathy, and a moving Scene it was to see the Regard paid to each other by two Persons so different in the Rank they bore in the World, the one being of the highest, the other of the lowest Class of Mortals" (40). As in *Alexis*, the mutual shedding of sympathetic tears suggests a symbiotic relationship between the subjects and the monarch.

The narrative of *Ascanius*, like that of *Alexis*, involves the reader in this affective economy, the author claiming that he is relating the story in order to gain sympathy for Charles Edward Stuart: "Enough already has the World heard of this Story to excite Compassion in the generous Breast" (3). Where *Alexis* identified itself as a "Novel," however, *Ascanius* uses another common eighteenth-century name for fictional prose, "A True History," with its title page suggesting that it was "Translated from a manuscript privately handed about at the Court of Versailles." Furthermore, while *Alexis* represents a mythic national time-space, *Ascanius* indicates a concern with providing a historically accurate account of Charles Edward Stuart's travels. Like the newspaper accounts tracking Charles Edward Stuart's movements, *Ascanius* provides an aura of "facticity," paying careful attention to include specific dates and locations and noting, for example, that on "The 24th," Charles and his followers "sailed for *Lochbusdale*" and that "on this dreary Waste they were forced to remain eight Days" (44).

An expanded version of *Ascanius* also appeared in 1746, its authorship being claimed by Ralph Griffiths. This version reprints the entirety of the shorter version of *Ascanius* as book 2, after a book 1 that presents a "more critical and candid History of the Rise, Progress, and Extinction of the late Rebellion, than any yet publish'd."[102] This "critical and candid History" that Griffiths claimed he wrote largely paraphrases one of the earliest

---

[101] *Ascanius; or the Young Adventurer, a True History* (London: Printed for G. Smith, 1746), 27.
[102] *Ascanius: or, the Young Adventurer; a True History* (London: Printed for T. Johnstone, 1746).

accounts of the Rising, Andrew Henderson's *The History of the Rebellion, 1745 and 1746, Containing, a Full Account of Its Rise, Progress and Extinction*, published originally serially in Edinburgh and then reprinted in book form in both Edinburgh and London in 1748.[103] By appearing with the two parts together, the expanded edition of *Ascanius* frames the pro-Jacobite story of Charles Edward Stuart's escape within a pro-Hanoverian history.

This combination of official memory and counter-memory is also represented within the expanded *Ascanius*. In the "Translator's Introduction," the narrator adopts a pro-Hanoverian perspective in blaming the Rising on a combination of French desire to "Increase their Dominions" and men who still maintain "unintelligible Notions of a natural Right" of Succession.[104] It asserts that King George is "tried and approved" and that, as the "British Nation hath no objection to the present King, nor the least Prospect of any of his Heirs," it was sheer "Madness" to attempt "the Subversion of the present Government."[105] Throughout the account, the narrator includes commendatory remarks on the government troops, celebrating the "brave, though very old General *Guest*" who refused to relinquish Edinburgh Castle to the Jacobites, and lamenting the death of the "brave Colonel *Gardiner*" at Prestonpans.[106] At the same time, footnotes reminding readers of the punishment of those who rose against the government pepper the bottom margins of the account. The author reminds his readers, for example, that "Counsellor Morgan" was executed on "*Kennington-Common* near *London, July* 30, 1746" along with "Col *Townley* and seven others."[107]

But the text also includes materials that are ideologically ambiguous. Like *Alexis*, *Ascanius*, too, adopts the language of secret history, regularly referring to the Jacobites as the "Adventurers" and the government troops as either the "English" or the "Georgians," while Charles Edward Stuart is represented frequently as "the P_____," indicating his princely rank. Along with the history of the "Rebellion" and the adventure of Charles Edward Stuart's escape, this edition of *Ascanius* also includes "Remarks" on "the celebrated Miss Cameron, Miss Mac Donald, the Duke of Perth, the Earl of Kilmarnock, Messieurs Sherridan and Sullivan." It does not just offer "Facts" about the Battle of Falkirk "admitted by the *English*" and "published by Authority," but also indicates that it consults "the Accounts given us by the other Party," including Thomas Sheridan's account of the government soldiers who were "seized with such a Panick on our Approach," that they fled to Edinburgh.[108]

---

[103] Henderson, *History of the Rebellion* (London, 1748), vi. [104] *Ascanius* (Johnstone), vi.
[105] Ibid., vi. [106] Ibid., 10. [107] Ibid., 21. [108] Ibid., 56.

The frontispiece engraving of Charles Edward Stuart combines aspects of both ideological perspectives (see Figure 5.3), too. It can be read on the one hand as what Pittock refers to as a "comic grotesque" Harlequin figure.[109] On the other hand, it also represents a positive image of a military leader in the foreground of the Jacobite camp. *Ascanius*, like the trial and execution narratives, provided material that appealed to readers of different political persuasions.

As a work that connected both Hanoverian and Jacobite interests, *Ascanius* was extremely popular. The popularity of the work, however, also brought it to the attention of government officials, resulting in charges of seditious libel for the author, printer and bookseller. In the petition that he submitted in his defence to the Secretary of State, the man claiming "authorship" of the work, Ralph Griffiths, admitted that he was capitalizing on the wide appeal of the story of the escape of Charles Edward Stuart in order to make a profit.[110] Griffiths suggested that he was first "induced" to "set about writing Ascanius" after he read the "Pamphlett" entitled *Alexis*.[111] But, in his defence, he also claimed that his own work was designed more to correct than to emulate the earlier book, asserting that he "saw, with indignation, a virulent Jacobite Tract called *Alexis*, in every body's hands" and that, "Liking the plan, but abhorring the manner in which it was executed," he determined to write "an Impartial thing of the same kind."[112] Griffiths argued that his motivation for attempting *Ascanius* had been to "serve the Government the more effectually, by exhibiting the Pretender's Character in another light" than the way it had been presented in *Alexis*.[113] Although he was aware that his work was suspected of portraying sympathy for the Jacobite cause, Griffiths asserted that "Ascanius met with a Favourable Reception from the world upon account of its Impartiality," and he claimed that loyal British subjects would be able to discern the work's intended pro-Hanoverian message.[114] Unlike the authors of pamphlets printed earlier in the Rising, Griffiths voiced his confidence in British readers' ability to discern the "truth" in the midst of an ambiguous text.

The popularity of *Ascanius* also spawned several other works that recounted the escape of Charles Edward Stuart. *The Wanderer, or Surprizing Escape*, published in 1747, was advertised as "A Narrative

---

[109] Pittock, *Culloden (Cùil Lodair)*, 124.
[110] Lewis M. Knapp, "Ralph Griffiths, Author and Publisher, 1746–1750," *The Library*, 4th ser., 20, no. 2 (1939): 197–213.
[111] Ibid., 202.   [112] Ibid., 204.   [113] Ibid., 205.   [114] Ibid., 202.

Figure 5.3 Frontispiece from *Ascanius; or the Young Adventurer* (London: G. Smith, 1746). Courtesy of the National Library of Scotland. License: CC by 4.0

founded on true Facts; containing a Series of remarkable Events during a late very extraordinary Adventure, from its first Projection to its Appearance in the North and total Defeat."[115] The author of *The Wanderer* promised to include "several curious and authentick Particulars, the Publick has hitherto been unacquainted with" in order to write his account "without Prejudice or Partiality."[116] The occasion of the second anniversary of the Battle of Culloden also prompted yet another account of Charles Edward Stuart's flight: *Young Juba: or, the History of the Young Chevalier, from His Birth to His Escape from Scotland at the Battle of Culloden*. *Young Juba* also appeared in serial form "in 12 Numbers, at 3d. each ... printed on new Letter and fine Paper, and adorn'd with all the original Copper Plates."[117] Like *Ascanius*, *Young Juba* paraphrases Henderson's account in order to present what its author also claims is an impartial account of the events of the Rising. Like *Ascanius*, *Young Juba* includes an engraving of Charles Edward Stuart, this time in a portrait form (see Figure 5.4). He is dressed in rich garments and confronts the reader directly. An image of his great-grandfather Charles I is visible at the left edge of the engraving, an appeal to all who considered his execution an affront to both human and divine law. The epigraph engraved below the image includes a riddle purporting to be spoken by the image of Charles Edward Stuart. Announcing that "Few men know my face, tho' all Men know my Fame," the image of the "Pretender" challenges the reader to "look strictly" in order to "guess my Name," while outlining the challenges he has faced: "Through Deserts, Snow & Rain I made my Way, / My Life was daily risqu'd to gain the Day." While it represents on one level the cryptic language of Jacobitism, the image also comments on the way in which the daily risks of Charles Edward Stuart have now turned into narratives which themselves seek to "gain the Day" by providing a variety of material for potential consumers.

In the course of jostling for readers' attention, the writers of these narratives about Charles Edward Stuart each comment on the different materials they have drawn on to construct the story. Griffiths, for example, staked his claim to authenticity by drawing his material from newspaper accounts, asserting that "he did not receive any written Memoirs from any person whatever in order to assist him in the composition" of *Ascanius*, but, rather, "composed the whole from Gazettes & other news Papers."[118]

---

[115] The *General Advertiser*, April 27, 1747.   [116] Ibid.
[117] *The Penny London Post or the Morning Advertiser*, April 18–20, 1748.
[118] Knapp, "Ralph Griffiths," 202.

Figure 5.4 Frontispiece from *Young Juba: or, the History of the Young Chevalier, from His Birth, to His Escape from Scotland, after the Battle of Culloden* (London, 1748). Courtesy of the National Library of Scotland. License: CC by 4.0

The author of *The Wanderer*, however, took *Ascanius* to task for embroidering the newspaper accounts with discussions of the motivations and thoughts of the characters. In contrast, *The Wanderer* advertises that it provides "the most genuine account of the Late Rebellion extant" by drawing "Facts" from "the Journal of two Persons principally concerned in the whole Transaction."[119] *Young Juba*, too, claims to be a more authentic account than the earlier works by representing the character of the "Adventurer" who led the Jacobite forces and by revealing aspects of the story to its readers from an eyewitness account; as the title page claims, the work was purportedly written by "M. Michell, formerly Secretary to the Old Chevalier, some Time Tutor to the Young One, and who attended him in the late Expedition" and subsequently translated from the Italian.[120] In the process of criticizing their rivals and promoting their own perspectives, these narratives further fuelled the self-consciousness about the mediation of the Rising, raising questions about the proper mode of "truth-telling." As Pittock and others have attested, after Culloden and the subsequent prosecutions of Jacobites, Jacobitism went even further underground.[121] While publications promoting the Stuarts were suspect, "Chevalier" narratives like *Alexis*, *Ascanius*, *The Wanderer* and *Young Juba* that drew on a variety of materials, ranging from the hagiographic narratives such as those collected by Forbes to government-biased histories, couched a sympathetic perspective on the Stuarts within accounts that were still acceptable to the government authorities. By mixing positive accounts of the "Exploits" of the "daring Youth" who gave "so terrible an Alarm to these Kingdoms" (*Young Juba*, v) with professions of loyalty to "his present Majesty King *George*" (viii), these "Chevalier" narratives were able to represent the 1745 Rising as composed of multiple "Threeds" of memory.

"Fit for the Perusal of the Present Age, and of Posterity": Popular Histories of the 1745 Rising

In addition to pamphlets outlining the trials and punishments of the Jacobites and "Chevalier" adventures, popular histories like Henderson's *The History of the Rebellion* (paraphrased in Griffiths's edition of *Ascanius*)

---

[119] *General Advertiser*, April 27, 1747.
[120] *Young Juba: or, the History of the Young Chevalier, from His Birth, to His Escape from Scotland, after the Battle of Culloden* (London, 1748).
[121] See Pittock, *Material Culture and Sedition* and Guthrie, *Material Culture*.

that offered retrospective accounts of the events of the 1745 also appeared in the aftermath of Culloden. While there had been only a handful of histories produced immediately after the 1715 Rising, by 1745, the marketplace had grown to accommodate many more printed works which vied for readers' attention. Some of those popular narratives published after 1745, as we saw in Chapter 4, folded the earlier Rising into the history of the later conflict, reshaping the former to emphasize the greater importance of the latter. Others focused exclusively on the history of the 1745 Rising.

Like the popular histories produced after the 1715 Rising, those published in the wake of the '45 shaped the "unnatural Rebellion" into a comprehensive narrative arc with a beginning, a middle and an end.[122] Using the imagery of a fire which is spread and then stamped out, *The History of the Rebellion Raised against His MAJESTY KING GEORGE II. From Its Rise in August 1745, to Its Happy Extinction by the Glorious Victory at Culloden, on the 16th of April, 1746* articulates what was the common plot of the popular histories of the 1745 Rising: "The Flame of Rebellion, which after being smothered for a Time in *Scotland*, broke out with such Force, as to spread itself into *England,* and not without Reason alarmed the Inhabitants of this Metropolis, was in a short Space totally extinguished by him who gave the first Check to its Force."[123] But the histories of the 1745 Rising express more self-consciousness about their readers – both in the present and in the future – than those of the 1715 Rising. They register a greater self-awareness of how they will be read in the future as works of cultural memory. They consider, in Belsey's terms, "the past not simply as it was," but "as it will turn out to have been, in consequence of [their] remembering it."[124]

Writers of the popular histories of 1745 registered a keen awareness of the issues of mediation that had been raised in the controversy over reading news of the Rising. The author of *A Complete and Authentick History of the Rise, Progress and Extinction of the Late Rebellion*, for example, comments on the different kinds of histories that were being printed after Culloden and hints at the different meanings: "The Event of which I am to speak, though so recent, and so remarkable," the author suggests, "is already

---

[122] See Rupert C. Jarvis, *Collected Papers on the Jacobite Rising*, 2 vols. (Manchester: Manchester University Press, 1972), 2: 4.
[123] *The History of the Rebellion Raised against His MAJESTY KING GEORGE II*, 16.
[124] Belsey, "Remembering as Re-inscription," 4.

differently represented by different sorts of People."¹²⁵ While some writers "still retain the Terror impres'd by the March of the Rebels to *Derby*, and consider the late Rebellion as an Engine of our Enemies, that brought us to the very Brink of Destruction," the writer notes, others "affect to treat it as a mere Bugbear, as a Raw-head and Bloody-bones, which only frighted weak Minds, and from which no well-grounded Apprehensions could arise" (2). The author of *A Complete and Authentick History* indicates the way his own history will help to temper these extreme versions: "strictly speaking, neither of these Representations deserve entire Credit; the Rebellion was certainly alarming, though not terrible, and a Mischief so great, that no Care ought to be spared to prevent anything of the like Kind in Times to come; and to this End nothing in my Judgment can more contribute than a History of the Past, fairly written" (2). Writers of the history of the present, suggests this work, have a national responsibility to interpret the Rising properly, steering a course between being too "frighted" and too complacent in such a way so as to encourage readers to do the same.

A Full and Authentic History of the Rebellion MDCCXLV and MDCCXLVI also comments on the benefits of reading the nation's recent history: "If we are delighted with perusing the Histories of former Ages, and distant Nations," the author reasons, "how much more does it behove us to be well acquainted with our own, which furnishes us with continual Reflections, improves our Judgment, and whets the Edge of that Enquiry, which is a Duty incumbent on the Legislative Power, to make on particular Occasions."¹²⁶ Reading about recent national history can serve as an antidote to wasting energy in travelling abroad:

> Many, too many young Gentlem[e]n, set out on their Travels, with hope of finding Instruction in foreign Nations, when they know no more of the Nature of the Government, or People, in their own Country, than if they had been born in the remotest Part of AMERICA. But will any Man say, that the Knowledge they thus acquire, tends to the Benefit of their native Country? (n.p.)

It is better for these "young Gentlem[e]n," asserts the writer, to read the history of their own nation at home rather than travelling abroad to learn about others. For the author of *A Full and Authentic History*, the reading of

---

¹²⁵ *A Complete and Authentick History of the Rise, Progress and Extinction of the Late Rebellion* (London, 1746), 2. This is sometimes claimed as the work of Henry Fielding.
¹²⁶ *A Full and Authentic History of the Rebellion MDCCXLV and MDCCXLVI* (London, n.d.), preface, n.p.

national history is itself a national activity which will encourage subjects to stay within the bounds of the nation.

As they considered their own relevance to situations that would arise in "times to come," however, writers of popular histories also expressed concern about how future readers would view their work. Lupton argues that eighteenth-century books that comment on their own mediation "invite readers to think about the long journey that brings a published text to hand, imagining impressions made by the printer on the page; the way pages are bound, or unbound; and the way books and papers are advertised, consumed, and, in possible futures, surfeited and recycled."[127] The authors of the popular narrative histories of the Rising, however, imagine not how their work will be recycled into different forms, but how it will be re-activated by different readers. The author of *A Complete and Authentick History* imagines the work's impact on future consumers, reflecting, "I thought a *succinct History of the Rebellion* equally fit for the Perusal of the present Age, and of Posterity" (2). In fact, much of the prefatory material to the histories focuses readers' attention on the question of how the works will be read by "Posterity." *The History of the Rebellion Raised against His MAJESTY KING GEORGE II*, for example, imagines the future deployment of his *History* as a resource for yet more histories that will be written in the future: "There is nothing that can contribute more to the furnishing proper Materials for the History of any Period of Time, than the setting down in a clear Chronological Order, a plain Narration of Facts, while they are yet recent, and it is in a manner impossible that any material Mistakes should be made about them."[128] This writer sees his job as supplying rough material for later shaping.

In his *The History of the Present Rebellion: Collected from Authentick Memoirs, Letters and Intelligences*, on the other hand, John Marchant sees his work as a corrective to future generations' misreading of the Rising: "It might, perhaps, be for the Honour of the British Nation, if this Part of its History should never find a Place in our Annals," he writes, for, although "Posterity" will "read with Pleasure the Heroic Actions of their Forefathers" in regard to earlier victories,

> when they shall come to this Period and read the Transactions recorded in the Year 1745, how will they be surpriz'd to find, that a small Company of Desperadoes ... with a young Italian, a Bigot of the Church of Rome at their Head should, in a few Months, be able to march unmolested into the

[127] Lupton, *Knowing Books*, 10.
[128] *The History of the Rebellion Raised against His MAJESTY KING GEORGE II*, 2.

Heart of England ... and threaten the Capital itself with a Visit, before the Career of their Progress could be stopp'd?"[129]

As a remedy, Marchant offers what he calls an "*impartial*" account that reveals any "Errors, which have been follow'd by mischievous Consequences" on the part of individuals on the government side (vii). His account shifts the focus of future readers away from admiring the fact that the Jacobites could achieve such successes to perceiving that their victory was due to human error on the side of the government forces.

But these popular histories, like the trial and execution pamphlets, also included content that was linked to Jacobite memory. Despite its pro-Hanoverian perspective, for example, *A Complete and Authentick History* also includes material that presents a positive perspective on the Jacobites. In describing Charles's attempts to reach Stornoway in the midst of a terrible storm, for example, *A Complete and Authentick History* relates the same story as that included in *Alexis* and *Ascanius*, noting Charles Edward Stuart's bravery and his connection with Gaelic song. Although the boatmen "all begged of him to go back," Charles refuses to comply, and, instead, to "keep up the Spirits of the People he sung them a Highland Song" (111). Other moments in the text also suggest a derivation from pro-Jacobite accounts. When the boat is driven onto the island of Benbecula after the storm, for example, "the Pretender helped to make a Fire to warm the Crew, who were almost starved to Death with Cold" (111). The author of *A Complete and Authentick History* self-consciously remarks on the fundamental difference between his own perspective and that of works like *Ascanius* which, he suggests, are "cooked up only to feast the present Cravings of Novelty" and are "more proper for *Romance* than an *History*" (165–66). But by replicating anecdotes that also appear in accounts such as *Alexis* and *Ascanius*, *A Complete and Authentick History* suggests its uncanny similarity to the works it disparages.

The publication history of Henderson's *The History of the Rebellion, 1745 and 1746. Containing, a Full Account of Its Rise, Progress and Extinction* also demonstrates the ideological knots represented in printed popular narratives that borrowed from and were borrowed by other works. Henderson notes that this account was originally published "at *Edinburgh* in Numbers" for fourpence each and, being written from the perspective of "*an Impartial Hand, who was an Eye-Witness to Most of the Facts* the

---

[129] John Marchant, *The History of the Present Rebellion: Collected from Authentick Memoirs, Letters and Intelligences* (London, 1746), v–vi.

History," was intent on relating the actions of both the Jacobites and the British forces.[130] Henderson's later comments provide insight into the way in which printed information migrated into different venues when he blames the "the Giddiness of the Times after Recovery from the general Consternation occasioned by the Rebellion" for the "great Freedom" that "some People" used "with my Performance and Name" (vi). The separate editions of Henderson's *History* were subsequently collected and republished in London by none other than Ralph Griffiths, the self-proclaimed author of the longer version of *Ascanius*. The prefatory comments in the London edition of Henderson's *History* in fact cross-reference Griffiths's version of *Ascanius*, indicating that, as the present volume "does not much enter into what befell the Chevalier after the Battle of *Culloden*," the reader should take note that "a full Account thereof has been lately published, and which may serve as a Second Part to this Work" (vii–viii). The comment advises the reader, in other words, to move seamlessly between the pro-Hanoverian perspective of Henderson's *History* and a text which offers a positive representation of the figure who has just challenged, albeit unsuccessfully, the Hanoverian regime. Henderson himself offers at times a sympathetic perspective on the Jacobites, noting the bravery of the Highlanders as well as remarking that the conduct of the Hanoverian soldiers "is not to be defended according to the strict Rules of War" (117). The frequent utilization of the term "Chevalier" instead of "Pretender" in Henderson's *History* also reinforces the slippage between perspectives, as it appears that pro-Jacobite ideology has leaked into his own language. *The History of the Rebellion, 1745 and 1746* ends by commending again the "Pamphlet lately publish'd, entitl'd The Young Chevalier" and commenting in sentimental terms on Charles Edward Stuart's escape: Henderson notes that the "unfortunate Adventurer, after wandering about the Isles and Highlands of *Scotland* for the Space of Five Months, had the good Fortune to escape on Board a French Ship" (126). Henderson's *History* suggests the fluid relationship between different genres and different political perspectives that occurs as a result of the mobility of printed information.

As the market for popular histories of the Rising became more and more saturated with the appearance of new publications, those writers entering the market for the first time and those issuing new editions of already published works attempted to outcompete each other in providing as complete an account of the events of the Rising as possible. Like the

---

[130] Henderson, *History of the Rebellion* (London, 1748), vi.

authors of earlier histories examined in previous chapters, they incorporated all varieties of extraneous materials into their works: official government documents, maps of battles, lists of the wounded and royal proclamations as well as manifestos and proclamations of the Jacobites. But in the process of making claims about their work, popular histories of the Rising also register a unique self-consciousness as they debate the nature of the media on which they draw. Like *The Wanderer* and *Young Juba*, and like Henderson's *History of the Rebellion*, James Ray's *A Compleat History of the Rebellion, from Its first Rise in 1745, to Its Total Suppression, at the Glorious Battle of Culloden, in April, 1746*, comments on the process of mediation when it promotes the value of "Eye-Witness" testimony over that of "Strangers, who must write only on Hearsay."[131] Drawing on his experiences as a volunteer under the Duke of Cumberland, the author promises his readers a "genuine Account of the late Rebellion, as it occur'd to me from ocular Demonstrations" (v). In contrast to the promotion of "ocular Demonstrations," however, Marchant announces, in *The History of the Present Rebellion*, a preference for a different medium, suggesting that he draws not from the relation of personal experience but from the process of poring over public documents: "*Truth has been my Aim, which I have not only sifted from Heaps of Rubbish in the publick Papers, but what I have likewise gleaned from Letters of Correspondents whose Veracity I have no Reason to doubt*" (viii). Accordingly, Marchant's *History* presents summaries of letters, affidavits given to magistrates, and other documents over which he has "por[ed]." The two works debate the question of where to find the most accurate historical "Truth": from embodied witnessing or from sifted-through official papers. What is key here, however, is that they are engaging in a debate on mediation, a debate that had been made all the more relevant by the issues of reading that had arisen during the events of the Rising itself.

In his *History of the Rebellion in the Year 1745*, Home claimed that "no history ha[d] yet been published" of the 1745 Rising until his own in 1802 (2). In fact, as this section has demonstrated, popular histories of the recent conflict filled the presses from the termination of the Rebellion steadily up to Home's time. Far from being a unique examination of "a war in which the inhabitants of Britain were so much interested" (2), Home's *History* was only the latest in a flood of printed works that contributed to establishing the cultural memory of the 1745 Rising. Indeed, Home's *History* itself

---

[131] James Ray, *A Compleat History of the Rebellion, from Its First Rise in 1745, to Its Total Suppression, at the Glorious Battle of Culloden, in April, 1746* (Manchester, 1747), 187.

incorporates some of the same material as the earlier popular works, such as letters from Jacobite leaders as well as "Resolutions by the Rebel Chiefs, after the Battle of Culloden" (384–87). Rather than creating a space of homogeneous British cultural memory derived from the "extinction" of the Jacobite forces, the popular histories that emerged after Culloden, like the trial and execution narratives and the "Chevalier" narratives of Charles Edward Stuart's escape, helped shape the Jacobite Rising of 1745 as a complex knot involving both memory and counter-memory.

Knots of Cultural Memory and the 1745 Rising

This chapter began with an examination of the events of the Rising in contemporary newspapers, suggesting that the '45 represented a time of increased self-awareness about the mediation of the news. By directing readers in how to consume information about the rebellion, commenting on the basis of their own "authenticity" and critiquing the perspectives of their rivals, newspapers encouraged an intense self-consciousness around the project of mediating the Jacobite Rising. They seem to suggest at times that what was represented through language was inconsequential, as readers would come to texts with their own biases due to their "interests, passions or prejudices," as the editors of the *Scots Magazine* suggested (iii). The discourse on how to read news in 1745, then, shifted the problem of political dissent away from the content of texts themselves and onto the ways in which they were read and interpreted.

As this chapter has also suggested, popular works published after Culloden contributed to the cultural memory of the 1745 Rising by encouraging a consciousness of mediation. As works produced quickly within an expanding consumer market for print, the three genres examined here – trial and execution narratives, "Chevalier" narratives and histories of the Rising – drew their materials from reports that had circulated in newspapers. They repurposed this material into a form that depicted the events of the 1745 as a rise, progress and extinction of the Rising, and they also self-consciously reflected on the process of their own creation as they guided readers in interpretation. Moreover, in seeking to explain the Rising by suggesting that the cultural backwardness of the Highlanders (and the Irish) led them to rebel, these popular works mapped ethnography onto the geography of Britain, representing the spatial margins – Scotland and Ireland – as existing at a more primitive state than the rest of Britain. Such observations arguably both reflected and contributed to the conceptualization of the stadial history that would be theorized by thinkers such as David Hume, Adam Smith and Adam Ferguson. But at the same time, by borrowing material from each other as well as from non-printed accounts such as materials included in Forbes's "The Lyon in Mourning," these printed works offered a complicated perspective on the Rising, inscribing traces of the counter-memories of the marginalized peripheries into the stored pro-government printed memories.[132]

---

[132] Many of the popular works I have examined here continued to be reprinted throughout the eighteenth century as the British public sought images of its own earlier consolidation and success in the midst of the American rebellion, the French Revolution and, in the case of Home's *History*, the Napoleonic wars. Such works also provided a continuing platform for the faint memory of Jacobitism, which, as Vincent Morley notes, was still politically "pervasive in the 1770s" in Ireland and would, on a residual level, "provide a fertile substrate for the Catholic republicanism of the Defenders" (*The Popular Mind*, 59).

Conclusion
"Living On" after 1745: From Cultural Memory to the Memory of Culture

The chapters in *Mediating Cultural Memory* have followed the consolidation of the idea of the nation of Britain from the 1688 Revolution to the aftermath of the 1745 Rising, paying attention to how the developing medium of print worked in conjunction with other media to shape and store national memories. In 1688 William set out to use his printed *Declaration* to persuade the English, Scottish and Irish peoples that he had arrived in England in order to restore the rights and liberties of their nations and the Protestant faith. After William and Mary assumed the throne, the 1688 Revolution was represented as a "Glorious" event that had provided the nation with a new model of governance based on a limited monarchy and individual liberty. Britons were encouraged to see their Constitution as something that distinguished them from their European rivals and to view their government and their nation as exceptional in that regard. The representation of Britain after 1688 as a nation unique in its government and value-system was affirmed at crucial junctures over the course of the next fifty years, gaining currency as it was reactivated in reprinted as well as newly created texts. The victory over Ireland during the War of the Two Kings was seen as a providential moment which confirmed God's plan for a new Britain. The challenge posed by Scottish imperial ambitions was swept away by the Union, and the ensuing discourse promoted the incorporation of divergent elements into a unified British political body governed from London. Commentaries on the state of the nation after the 1715 Rising further celebrated the superiority of a Constitution based on the Protestant values of "common Sense," "Civil Liberties" and "the natural Rights of Mankind."[1] Finally, in the wake of the battle at Culloden, popular narratives refashioned British exceptionalism for a new era by articulating a stadial model of history that positioned the Scottish Highlands and

---

[1] Addison, *Free-Holder*, 9.

Ireland at an earlier stage of civilization than the rest of a modern and commercial Britain.

As I have also suggested in the preceding chapters, this cultural memory of Britain developed as an English-oriented model. Within a Britain in which print was coming to play a larger role and in which the means of cultural reproduction were largely under the control of the government or those sympathetic to it, groups on the geopolitical edges of the British archipelago, in particular in Ireland, Scotland and Wales, were marginalized, appearing as tangential to the nation. As well as tracing the consolidation of British cultural memory, the previous chapters have examined the role of specific kinds of forgetting of Irish and Scottish matters in the establishment of that memory. In the dominant discourse following the War of the Two Kings, for example, the Irish were represented as a violent people who, despite the efforts of their civilizers, continued to rise up in murderous revenge at every possible moment. Ireland was de-linked in British cultural memory from the "Glorious" 1688 Revolution and from the benefits of constitutional freedoms for most of the rest of the eighteenth century, even though the traumatic events of the War of the Two Kings continued to circulate in Irish cultural memory. In the subsequent two decades, Scottish colonial efforts at Darien as well as the independent Scottish Parliament were represented as misguided and detrimental to the interests of the British nation. In practical terms, the Union of 1707 incorporated Scottish political voices into a larger English whole, while the memory of Darien was largely displaced until the nineteenth-century rediscovery of the Darien papers. The extent and threat of Jacobite insurgence were minimized in the wake of the 1715 Rising and further occluded by the Jacobite conflict that took place thirty years later, while, after 1746, the rising against the Hanoverian government was blamed on the primitive culture of the Highlanders combined with the efforts of the intractable Irish as well as foreign powers.

Taken together, the chapters of this book have demonstrated how the dominant cultural memory of the nation became more and more consciously entrenched as Britain reached a point of print saturation. As I have argued, the consolidation of British cultural memory was encouraged and enabled by the growth of print culture. At the same time, however, the increasing availability of print caused considerable anxiety, and existing counter-memories continued to challenge that national narrative. While many of these memories from the geopolitical peripheries were stored through oral and manuscript means, and so were re-activated in limited circumstances, many also made their way into print, albeit sometimes in coded forms. Even in the midst of crises such as the 1745 Rising, these counter-memories were also incorporated into pro-government materials as printed works were rushed off the press in order to meet readerly demand for both information and novelty. Between 1688 and 1745, then, while printed works served largely to consolidate British cultural memory, they also stored counter-memories that remained as fault lines in that memory. The affordances of print served both to highlight and to amplify the knottedness of cultural memory in Britain.

I would like to conclude this book by briefly gesturing toward the fate of British cultural memory in the decades after the period I have examined, during which the print marketplace continued to expand and Britain faced further challenges as a nation and as an empire. While the analysis of British cultural memory in the latter half of the eighteenth century could cover a range of diverse subjects and easily fill several additional books, I want to focus on the life of the printed memories that I have considered here after 1745, when they continued to circulate in functional memory in the developing disciplines of history and literature. I examine first how the multi-volume histories of the nation that were published at the end of the century represented a British cultural memory disturbed occasionally by the inclusion of traces of counter-memories. I conclude by considering how, in the hands of Walter Scott, the historical novel became an effective genre for acknowledging the interaction of memories and counter-memories. Scott framed the two together within a narrative of media succession in such as way as to diminish the power of those counter-memories.[2]

Cultural Memories and Feeling Histories

Richard Sher and Mark Towsey have remarked on the development of history as both a popular and a commercially successful subject area in the growing market for print in the latter half of the eighteenth century.[3] As Towsey notes, polite histories were "a central part of the rhythm of everyday life for men, women and children in genteel families across the

---

[2] On the development of disciplinarity in the eighteenth century, see Clifford Siskin, *The Work of Writing: Literature and Social Change in Britain, 1700–1830* (Baltimore: Johns Hopkins University Press, 1998).

[3] Richard B. Sher, *The Enlightenment and the Book: Scottish Authors and Their Publishers in Eighteenth-Century Britain, Ireland, and America* (Chicago: University of Chicago Press, 2007); Mark Towsey, *Reading History in Britain and America, c.1750–c.1840* (Cambridge: Cambridge University Press, 2019).

English-speaking world," earning writers like Edward Gibbon, David Hume and William Robertson considerable sums.[4] Within the general interest in history as a subject area, there was a growing appetite for histories specifically of the British nation, and authors, often in collaboration with publishers, competed with each other to satisfy that appetite. Advertisements for and prefaces to these national histories describe their works' attempts to appeal not only to readers' desires for specific content, but also their concerns regarding affordability and aesthetics. In his fifty-volume *A New History of England, from the Descent of the Romans, to the Demise of His Late Majesty* (1761–64), William Rider excuses himself for mentioning the "cheapness" of his edition by suggesting its benefit for society. As he asserts, more people will be able to purchase his less expensive volumes, leading to "an increase in the number of readers" who will have a "more extensive knowledge of the interests and constitutions of the kingdom."[5] The *Plan of a Complete History of England* by Tobias Smollett (1757), published by James Rivington and James Fletcher, notes the intended work's superiority because it will be the only history currently available to bring the topic "home to our own times and observations"; further enticement to readers is offered by the fact that the three-volume edition will be printed "in quarto" and include "three frontispieces, and a map."[6] Other works capitalized on visual technologies associated with print to attract readers. William Henry Montague's *A New and Universal History of England, from the Earliest Authentic Accounts, to the Present Time* (1771) advertises that it is "embellished and illustrated with upwards of one hundred and twenty copper-plates, from original drawings made on purpose for this work, by the celebrated Wale, and engraved by those eminent artists, Grignion and Walker," while John Newbery's *A New History of England; from the Invasion of Julius Caesar to the End of George the IId* (1781) hoped to capture the market of young readers by offering "cuts of all the Kings and Queens."[7]

The number of histories of England available in the marketplace grew even more after the 1750s. The *Plan of a Complete History of England* by

---

[4] Towsey, *Reading History*, 4–5.
[5] William Rider, *A New History of England, from the Descent of the Romans, to the Demise of His Late Majesty, George II*, 50 vols. (London, 1761–64), 1: xii.
[6] Tobias Smollett, *Plan of a Complete History of England* (London, 1757), 2–3. The *Plan* was published separately and then also included in volume 1 of Smollett's *A Complete History of England*, 4 vols (London, 1757–58).
[7] See William Henry Montague's *A New and Universal History of England, from the Earliest Authentic Accounts, to the Present Time* (London: J. Cooke, 1771) and John Newbery, *A New History of England; from the Invasion of Julius Cæsar to the End of George the IId* (London, 1781).

Smollett ended with a comparison between the price, size and numbers of volumes of his projected *History* and the handful of other histories available in the marketplace: those by Paul de Rapin de Thoyras, William Guthrie and Thomas Carte.[8] By the end of the century, such an attempt would have filled up many pages. The circulation of volumes of British history in quartos, octavos, weekly installments and expensive folios, frequently adorned with engravings and "cuts," ensured the consumption of British history by all literate levels of society. Moreover, whether leaning toward Tory or Whig interpretations, these histories participated in the steady reinscription of earlier sites of memory on a historical timeline of the nation dating back to its earliest era. Instead of providing documentary evidence in the manner of a number of histories examined in previous chapters, these longer-scale histories include an editorial presence that converts the documentary evidence into a seamless narrative.

As it was evolving into a polite subject and a potentially lucrative business for authors and publishers, British historiography was also changing, becoming more concerned with creating what Karen O'Brien describes as "a new social narrative that could stand beside and even subsume the conventional account of political action."[9] The printed works produced at the end of the eighteenth century both reflected and contributed to this growing interest in a more socially oriented history, explaining the 1745 Rising, for example, by noting that Scottish Highland and Irish society followed a model that pre-dated the more civilized state of the rest of Britain. Writers of histories after 1745 further explored the social fabric of not just of Scotland's Highlands and Gaelic Ireland but of the British Isles in general, becoming "increasingly preoccupied with the rise of civil society in Britain, including the legal regimes, political and religious identities, and social customs that formed the public framework for individual lives."[10] As has been noted, the fact that many of these historians were Scottish suggests how individuals from that nation in particular sought to recover from the negative consequences of the recent Jacobite Rising by writing their nation into modernity.

---

[8] See Paul Rapin de Thoyras, *The History of England. Written in French by Mr. De Rapin Thoyras. Done into English*, ed. Nicolas Tindal (London, 1725); William Guthrie, *A General History of England from the Invasion of Julius Cæsar to 1688* (London, 1744); Thomas Carte, *A General History of England* (London, n.d.).

[9] Mark Salber Phillips, *Society and Sentiment: Genres of Historical Writing in Britain, 1740–1820* (Princeton, NJ: Princeton University Press, 2000), xii.

[10] Karen O'Brien, "History and the Novel in Eighteenth-Century Britain," *Huntington Library Quarterly* 68, nos. 1–2 (2005): 402.

Mark Salber Phillips argues that as a consequence of this changing focus of historiography, "For the first time, evocation became an important goal of historical narrative, and sympathetic identification came to be seen as one of the pleasures of historical reading."[11] Beginning with David Hume's *History of Great Britain*, he asserts, historians experimented with and discussed cultivating readerly sympathy. As Charles Coote expressed it in his own attempt to rival Hume's *History*: "Our passions take part in the narration: we are alternately soothed into complacency, dissolved into pity, and roused into resentment."[12] In the thriving market for print in post-1745 Britain, writers and publishers jostled with each other to produce a comprehensive history that would provide the nation with a firm ideological footing in the present as well as cultivate readerly feeling toward it – and that would sell copies. The multi-volume histories of two of these writers, David Hume and Tobias Smollett, both begun in the decade following Culloden, represent different attempts to shape individual sites of national memory into a long narrative arc and to direct readers' sentiments within that narrative. While Hume invites sympathy for the Stuarts in his portrayal of Charles I in *The History of Great Britain*, he also tempers that sympathy through adopting a reflective narrative attitude which affirms the constitutional importance of 1688. Smollett, however, offers no such mediating historical distance. Instead, his *Complete History of England* re-activates counter-memories by re-inscribing traces from earlier Jacobite texts.

In the Introduction, I discussed Hume's contribution in *A Treatise of Human Nature* to the reconceptualizing of memory as a series of "impressions" as well as his discussion in *Essays, Moral and Political* of the "sympathy or contagion of manners" between individuals in a nation. In his *History of Great Britain* (1754–62; later pointedly renamed *The History of England*), Hume took on the project of marking the development of the "sympathy or contagion of manners" in the British Isles from the conquest by Julius Caesar to the 1688 Revolution, at the same time turning his observations into comments that would create a new series of "impressions" on readers in the present. Significantly, however, he began writing that history not in chronological order but starting with the moment that he felt was most significant for a Britain now emerging from the Jacobite civil wars: the time of the Stuart monarchs whose ousting was the direct

---

[11] Phillips, *Society and Sentiment*, xii.
[12] Charles Coote, *The History of England, from the Earliest Dawn of Record to the Peace of MDCCLXXXIII*, 9 vols. (London, 1796), 1: ii.

cause of the recent disturbance. For Hume, the endpoint of his history, 1688, represented a fundamental shift for the nation. William of Orange himself had characterized his arrival in Britain as a restoration of the "Laws and Liberties" of the three nations. Early influential histories such as those of de Rapin, who had in fact accompanied William on his expedition and fought for him in Ireland, had represented the Revolution as a reinstatement of the nation's Constitution, which had been "essentially unchanged since the ancient Saxons."[13] Hume, however, characterizes the British past as consisting of a constant struggle between "Liberty" and "Authority." The reign of the Stuarts, he suggests, was only the most recent manifestation of the monarchical absolutism and political tyranny that had been features of this chequered past. Hume depicts the 1688 Revolution as a conclusive break with Britain's earlier struggles between "the crown and the people: Privilege and Prerogative," as it led to the establishment of an incontrovertible constitution:[14]

> The revolution forms a new epoch in the constitution; and was attended with consequences much more advantageous to the people, than the barely freeing them from a bad administration. By deciding many important questions in favor of liberty, and still more, by that great precedent of deposing one King, and establishing a new family, it gave such an ascendant to popular principles, as has put the nature of the English Constitution beyond all controversy. And it may safely be affirmed, without any danger of exaggeration, that we in this island, have ever since enjoyed, if not the best system of government, at least the most entire system of liberty, that ever was known amongst mankind. (2: 443)

The Prince of Orange's *Declaration* gets pride of place in Hume's *History*, with Hume noting that it was "dispersed all over the kingdom" (2: 425). Hume also summarizes the *Declaration*'s contents as a way of indicating the many grievances of the nation's subjects under James. Of the *Declaration of Rights*, which was based on the Prince's *Declaration*, Hume announces that it "finally determined" all the points which had "of late years been disputed between King and people" (2: 442). In shaping the memory of the Revolution, of the Prince's *Declaration* and of the

---

[13] See Simon Kow, "Politics and Culture in Hume's History of England," in *A Companion to Enlightenment Historiography*, ed. Sophie Bourgault and Robert Sparling (Leiden and Boston: Brill, 2013), 67, 64.
[14] David Hume, *The History of England, from the Invasion of Julius Cæsar to the Revolution in 1688*, 6 vols. (London: A. Millar, 1762), 2: 442.

resulting *Declaration of Rights* at mid-century, Hume also comments obliquely on the recent struggles in Britain.[15]

Hume himself suggested that his *History* incorporates both Tory and Jacobite counter-memories. In his autobiographical sketch prefaced to a posthumous edition of his *History*, he indicated that "I was assailed by one cry of reproach, disapprobation, and even detestation; English, Scotch, and Irish, Whig and Tory, churchman and sectary, freethinker and religionist, patriot and courtier, united in their rage against the man, who had presumed to shed a generous tear for the fate of Charles I. [sic] and the earl of Strafford."[16] The representation of Charles I during his trial and final days is indeed positive. Hume represents the compassion that both individuals and the nation as a whole have for the condemned monarch. After Charles is tried, "the people ... pour forth their wishes" for the King and honour him with their "generous tears," while a soldier in the crowd is "seized by contagious sympathy" to utter a prayer for Charles (5: 455). The reader is engaged with Charles in his final actions as he avows his fidelity to his wife, sits his son on his knee and forgives those who have condemned him. But, although it contains such moments of sympathy, the narrative of Hume's *History* also encourages summative reflection. After seemingly getting caught up in "contagious sympathy" himself, Hume analyzes the "character of this Prince," objectively weighing his positive and negative traits and concluding that "his fate threw him into a time" when his "want of suppleness and dexterity" caused him to make fatal mistakes (5: 458–59). *The History* finishes with the celebratory moment of 1688, moving the reader to see the eradication of the Stuarts as necessary for the transformation of the nation into a state of constitutional freedom.

Mark Towsey suggests that Hume's *History* "quickly became an important means by which readers ... accumulated historical information" about what made their nation so "special."[17] In inscribing the Revolution as the moment when "the English" become truly exceptional by establishing "the most perfect and most accurate system of liberty that was ever found compatible with government," Hume helped keep the Revolution in the functional memory of the nation.[18] Even though debated, and, as Towsey points out, interpreted by readers in different

---

[15] Phillips suggests that "Hume's Stuart volumes can be read as seeking a kind of historical distance that would allow the turbulent epoch that closed in 1688 ... to be both accepted and transcended" (*Society and Sentiment*, 34).
[16] David Hume, *The History of England, from the Invasion of Julius Cæsar to the Revolution in 1688*, 8 vols. (London: T. Cadell, 1778), 1: xi.
[17] Towsey, *Reading History*, 104.   [18] Hume, *History of England* (1762), 2: 446.

ways, Hume's *History* dominated the landscape of British historiography for the rest of the eighteenth century and into the early nineteenth century, appearing in new editions, abridgements and, as we will see, mixed editions. The debates about the 1688 Revolution that took place during the discourse on the French Revolution, for example, re-activated Hume's views of the former and of the English nation even in the midst of contesting their actual impact on British freedom.[19]

Avoiding direct commentary on recent events, Hume ends his *History* at a time period early enough for him to achieve not just "sympathetic engagement" but also "a kind of reflective detachment" on the past.[20] In *A Complete History of England*, Tobias Smollett also begins with Julius Caesar but brings the historical record nearer to the present: to the Treaty of Aix-La-Chapelle in the works' initial four-volume form (1757–58). Whereas Hume sought to train readers to alternate between sympathetic focus and reflective distance, Smollett aims to make readers want to read "what every person ought to know" by making a "History of our own country" which is "succinct, candid and complete" as well as more affordable, more "agreeable" to peruse and "less burthensome to the memory."[21] In order to facilitate this process, he notes in his *Plan of a Complete History of England* that he has stripped out all "useless disquisitions" which serve merely to increase the size of the volume, "interrupt the thread of the narrative" and "perplex the reader" (n.p.). He asserts that he has also "waved [*sic*] all remarks of his own, except such as seemed absolutely necessary" in his hopes that his readers will themselves do the work of "reflection" and "judgement" (n.p.). As Richard Jones notes, instead of presenting "disquisitions" as Hume did, Smollett uses connotative phrases, "beacon" words, to guide readers' affective responses to the events which he represents.[22] When he comes to the discussion of Culloden, however, Smollett totally abandons his plan to avoid "all remarks of his own" that might "forestall" the judgement of his readers. Instead, he presents a scathing criticism of the actions of the Duke of Cumberland's troops after the battle, deliberately attempting to generate readerly sympathy through including both his own remarks and remarks that are drawn from texts of Jacobite counter-memory.

---

[19] See Anthony Jarrells, *Britain's Bloodless Revolutions: 1688 and the Romantic Reform of Literature* (Basingstoke: Palgrave Macmillan, 2005).
[20] Phillips, *Society and Sentiment*, 57.
[21] "Plan of the Complete History of England" in Smollett, *A Complete History of England*, 1: n.p.
[22] Richard J. Jones, "Continued Continuations of Complete Histories: Tobias Smollett and the Work of History," *Journal for Eighteenth-Century Studies* 41, no. 3 (2018): 396.

Smollett's description of the action on the battlefield itself is presented with an air of objectivity and appears based in part on the *Particulars of the Victory*, discussed in the Introduction. But whereas the *Particulars* indicated that "the Rebels lost 2000 men upon the Field of Battle, and in the Pursuit" (3), Smollett suggests that "three thousand Rebels were slain on the field, and in the pursuit" (4: 673). He excoriates the government troops for their behaviour off the battlefield, noting that "the glory of the victory" was "sullied by the barbarity of the soldiers" (4: 673). Crucially, he indicates that atrocities were not just carried out by the common soldiers: their military leaders not only took part but also encouraged barbaric behaviour: "not contented with the blood which was so profusely shed in the heat of action, they traversed the field after the battle, and massacred those miserable wretches who lay maimed and expiring; nay, some officers acted a part in this cruel scene of assassination: the triumph of low illiberal minds, uninspired by sentiment, untinctured by humanity" (4: 673). Suggesting that the soldiers and officers were lacking feeling for those they slew, Smollett is concerned to train his readers to experience "sentiment" and a feeling of "humanity" for the Jacobites. His language rises to a crescendo of outrage when he reflects on how government troops were given orders by Cumberland to "lay waste the country with fire and sword" (4: 674), representing in prose some of the same scenes that he had described in the poem he composed shortly after Culloden, *The Tears of Scotland*.[23] In order to further activate his readers' sentiments, he describes in gruesome detail the fate of not only the men, but their families and communities:

> the men were either shot upon the mountains like wild beasts, or put to death in cold blood, without form of trial; the women, after having seen their husbands and fathers murdered, were subjected to violation, and then turned out naked, with their children, to starve on the barren heath .... Those ministers of vengeance were so alert to the execution of their office, that in a few days there was neither house, cottage man, nor beast to be seen in the compass of fifty miles; all was ruin, silence and desolation. (4: 674)

Rather than suggesting that the body politic was purged with the punishment of the Jacobite prisoners, as the trial and execution pamphlets published after 1745 had, Smollett condemns the treatment of the Jacobites, noting that all the gaols in London and the north were full and that many captives were "crowded together" on the prison ships, where they perished "for want of air and exercise" (4: 674).

---

[23] Tobias Smollett, *The Tears of Scotland* (Edinburgh, 1746).

Smollett offers a "disquisition" on the aftermath of Culloden which elicits sympathy for the Jacobites. But his account goes further than just mobilizing his readers' compassion, for he also reactivates Jacobite counter-memories. In particular, he invites identification with the Jacobite leader's own sense of devastation after Culloden, suggesting that if "the humane reader cannot reflect upon such a scene without genuine horror; what then must have been the sensation of the fugitive prince, when he beheld these spectacles of woe?" (4: 674). Smollett's subsequent account of the adventures of the "fugitive prince" Charles Edward Stuart reiterates the language and sentiments of the "Chevalier" narratives when he comments: "sometimes he lurked in caves and cottages, without attendants, or any other support but that which the poorest peasant could supply. Sometimes he was rowed in fisher-boats from isle to isle, among the Hebrides, and often in sight of his pursuers" (4: 674). Repeating the providential perspective common to such Jacobite narratives, Smollett suggests that "In the course of these peregrinations, [Charles Edward Stuart] was more than once hemmed in by his pursuers, in such a manner as seemed to preclude all possibility of escaping; yet, he was never abandoned by his hope and recollection" (4: 674). Charles Edward Stuart stands out as one of the remarkable individuals of his *History*, as Smollett, repeating sentiments found in *Alexis, Ascanius* and other post-1745 narrative accounts, comments on his commendable character, noting that Charles "maintained the most amazing equanimity and good humour" through "the whole course of his distresses" (4: 675). Although Smollett himself claims that his *History* has merely "explained the rise, progress and extinction of the rebellion," the affective tone in this passage inscribes sympathetic feeling for the Jacobites into his account of British history while breathing new life into Jacobite counter-memories.

Smollett's *Complete History* was much more immediately popular than Hume's *History* had been, selling approximately ten thousand copies per week in 1758 as well as being sold in weekly installments.[24] Finding his efforts successful, Smollett wrote an additional five volumes as a *Continuation of the Complete History of England* (1760–65) to bring his account up to the beginning of the reign of George III.[25] Hume's and Smollett's separate accounts were linked after the deaths of both authors,

---

[24] Jones, "Continued Continuations," 392. Smollett's *History*, unlike Hume's, had also included engraved plates to give it additional readerly appeal.
[25] Tobias Smollett, *Continuation of the Complete History of England*, 5 vols. (London: Printed for Richard Baldwin 1760–65).

however, when, in 1782, an advertisement announced the publication by Thomas Cadell of Hume's *History of England, with Portraits* in weekly installments to be followed by "Dr. SMOLLETT's History from the Revolution to the Death of George the Second"; together, announced the advertisement, the works would "form a complete HISTORY of ENGLAND from the Invasion of Julius Caesar to the Death of George the Second." The installments of the two different histories were designed to look like one work, however, for they were produced using the same "Paper, Print, and Portraits."[26] Cadell published all of Hume's *History* and Smollett's post-Revolution chapters together again in book form in *The History of England from the Revolution to the Death of George the Second* (1785), and the idea that Smollett's *History* was a "continuation" of Hume's spread after this point. In 1793 Charles Cooke advertised a "Pocket Edition" that added "Dr SMOLLETT's" version of events after 1688 to the entirety of Hume's *History*, also including a further "Continuation, to the present Time" by Thomas Lloyd. In Philadelphia, Robert Campbell's *The History of England, from the Revolution to the End of the American War and Peace of Versailles in 1783* (1796–98) also advertised "Smollett's Continuation to Hume's *History of England*."[27] What initially began as a marketing opportunity came to set a standard for the history of Britain. As Jones indicates, "the suggestion that Smollett wrote a continuation to David Hume's *The History of England* (1754–62) still influences readers today."[28] In terms of the impact on cultural memory, the yoking together of Hume's volumes with the latter chapters of Smollett's *History* re-activated and re-arranged earlier printed memories, integrating the strong promotion of the Revolution as the birth of British freedom with an equally strong sympathetic perspective on the Jacobites. The combined *History* represented a British cultural memory that promoted the English constitution as "the most perfect and most accurate system of liberty that was ever found compatible with government" (2: 446), but it also included traces of counter-memories of those who had recently borne the brunt of the violence of those upholding that constitution.

---

[26] Ibid.; Jones, "Continued Continuations," 391.
[27] Advertisement on final page of David Hume, *The History of England, from the Invasion of Julius Caesar to the Revolution*, 6 vols. (Philadelphia: Robert Campbell, 1796).
[28] Jones suggests that this combining of all of Hume's but only part of Smollett's work encouraged the representation of "Smollett as a similar but lesser writer to Hume" ("Continued Continuations," 391).

Late eighteenth-century British historiography emphasized the importance of feeling in consolidating national memory, but works such as Smollett's *History* and the combined *History* with Hume also re-activated some of the counter-memories considered in earlier chapters of this book. The idea of feeling history would be further employed by Walter Scott in consciously drawing official memories and counter-memories together in the form of the historical novel. Scott's novels acknowledge the affective power of the counter-memories, but also contain them within a consciously mediated framework.[29] While Scott was not the inventor of the genre of the historical novel, he was the one who best understood the principle that Belsey discusses of thinking about "the past not simply as it was," but "as it will turn out to have been" in consequence of having been remembered.[30]

Framed Knots of Memory in Walter Scott's *Waverley*

In *The Afterlives of Walter Scott: Memory on the Move*, Ann Rigney analyzes the power and popularity of Scott's *oeuvre*, suggesting that he "provided a blueprint for imagining a relationship to the past that was eminently suitable to conditions of life in the nineteenth century, characterized as it was by increasing mobility, the growing power of the media, urbanization, and mass migration."[31] Rigney asserts that Scott's success lay in the fact that he represented moments of change to a British population that was conscious of living in a time of change. Scott, she argues, "opened up the past as an imaginative resource, inspiring a fashion for history as a key to collective identity that continues down to the present time."[32] In discussing Scott's extension and adaptation of affective history, I want to focus particularly on *Waverley* because, while it established what Rigney refers to as a "blueprint" for the rest of Scott's *oeuvre*, it also represents a conscious reworking of the texts that I examined in Chapter 5.

Scott drew on a vast number of historical materials, printed works, manuscripts and oral testimonies in the course of writing *Waverley*. As the *Catalogue of the Library at Abbotsford* indicates, he collected Ray's *A Compleat History of the Rebellion* and Henderson's *The History of the Rebellion, 1745 and 1746*, as well as *Alexis; or, the Young Adventurer*.

---

[29] Walter Scott himself credits Maria Edgeworth and Elizabeth Hamilton for paving the way for *Waverley* (*Waverley*, ed. Susan Kubica Howard [Peterborough: Broadview, 2010], 483).
[30] Belsey, "Remembering as Re-inscription," 4.   [31] Rigney, *Afterlives of Walter Scott*, 4.
[32] Ibid.

A Novel, Young Juba: or, the History of Young Chevalier and *The Wanderer, or Surprizing Escape*, among others. He owned four versions of *Ascanius*, two in English and two in French.[33] He borrowed material from these popular narratives for *Waverley*, even, like Smollett, echoing their rhetoric at times. Unlike the popular narratives written after the 1745 Rising or the longer historiographical accounts of the later eighteenth century, however, *Waverley* consciously turns these knotted frictions of memory into fiction, allowing the counter-memories affective weight, but at the same time consciously highlighting how they are mediated into memory.

As numerous critics have noted, *Waverley* merges the individual *Bildungsroman* with the development of political loyalty to the British state, following the adventures of Edward Waverley as he shifts from his early infatuation with Flora MacIvor and the Jacobite cause to love for Rose Bradwardine and recognition of the benefits of the Hanoverian regime.[34] *Waverley* flirts with the temptations of counter-memories of the "primitive and brave race" of Highlanders (433), but ultimately reinforces a consolidated British cultural memory. What is crucial to note for purposes of this book is that part of the effectiveness of *Waverley*'s promotion of official British cultural memory stems from the fact that Scott consciously draws attention to the mediated construction of that memory. In his last conversation with Edward, for example, Fergus MacIvor indicates his understanding of the way in which official cultural memory works by erasing elements that do not fit its narrative. Fergus remarks about his gruesome sentence of execution according to English law for high treason: "I suppose one day or other – when there are no longer any wild Highlanders to benefit by its tender mercies – they will blot it from their records, as levelling them with a nation of cannibals" (435). Fergus suggests that the English law is more barbaric than any "wild" Highland customs and that the forging of official cultural memory will involve "blotting" out not only the counter-memories but also any memories that would reflect negatively on the government in power.

---

[33] John George Cochrane, *Catalogue of the Library at Abbotsford* (Edinburgh: Maitland Club, 1838), 89.
[34] Criticism concerning *Waverley* and Scott is extensive. See, for example, Ian Duncan, *Scott's Shadow: The Novel in Romantic Edinburgh* (Princeton, NJ: Princeton University Press, 2007); Carolyn McCracken-Flesher, *Possible Scotlands: Walter Scott and the Story of Tomorrow* (Oxford: Oxford University Press, 2005); Penny Fielding, *Writing and Orality: Nationality, Culture, and Nineteenth-Century Scottish Fiction* (Oxford: Oxford University Press, 1996); Juliet Shields, *Sentimental Literature and Anglo-Scottish Identity, 1745–1820* (Cambridge: Cambridge University Press, 2010) and Rigney, *Afterlives of Walter Scott*.

But in his description of the way in which the trauma of Fergus's fate is blotted out within Edward's own consciousness, Scott also contains Fergus's bitter comments within a narrative that demonstrates how such counter-memories are also transformed through inscription. As he performs the "task of writing to Rose" about Fergus's execution, Edward notices that he "suppresses his own feelings of calamity" and that, as a result, he is able to replace "his first horrible sensations" with more cheerful reflections on "the prospects of peace and happiness which lay before them" (438). In this initial inscription by Edward, the memory of the execution becomes altered, and, over time, the altered representation takes the place of the original "horrible sensations" in his consciousness. As Scott indicates, "the picture which [Edward] drew for [Rose's] benefit" became "gradually familiarized to his own mind" (438). Although the horrors are downplayed for Rose's "benefit," this replacement is subsequently internalized by Edward. By the time Edward reaches his "native country," his replacement of the original memory with one less difficult is complete, and Edward is able to "look round for enjoyment upon the face of nature" (435). Crucially, Scott emphasizes the changing affect that accompanies the replacement of "the first horrible sensations" by later more pleasant memories. The passage also draws attention to a grammatical shift in which Edward changes from being subject to "sensations" to being a subject in his own right able to "look round for enjoyment" in the external world. The memory of Fergus is inscripted a second time when it is represented by the portrait that hangs on the wall at Tully-Veolan of Edward and Fergus together in Highland dress.[35] The complex manner in which remembering interweaves with forgetting in Edward's consciousness also reflects the way in which memories are "plucked," changed and then returned to the official record in a more acceptable form from where they can be re-circulated. As the memory of "horror" subsides for an individual, the passage suggests, so painful memories of national fissures will also subside in the process of representation. In Scott, counter-memories are represented as powerful, but through being acknowledged, they can be integrated into a progressive narrative and lose their power to stimulate action. By focusing the reader's attention on the process whereby cultural memory is formed through initial inscription and then re-circulation in an altered form, Scott also comments on the work of *Waverley* itself in fixing the cultural memory of the past: his own

---

[35] Silke Stroh, *Gaelic Scotland in the Colonial Imagination: Anglophone Writing from 1600 to 1900* (Evanston, IL: Northwestern University Press, 2017), 180.

novelization of the story of Fergus represents yet another layer in the complex process of remediating the horrors of the Jacobite Rising.

Mediating Memory in *Waverley*

Scott also lends weight to an incorporating British modernity by linking it with a narrative of media progression. While, as suggested in Chapter 5, the popular narratives of the 1745 Rising demonstrated a new consciousness of their own processes of mediation, *Waverley* demonstrates a hyper-consciousness of the affordances of mediation and their connection to memory. As someone who was both artistically involved in the collection and dissemination of ballads (for the *Minstrelsy of the Scottish Border*) and professionally interested in the economics of the publishing industry, Scott was attuned to the affordances of both old and new media.[36] *Waverley* confirms the important role that oral and manuscript culture play in the articulation and circulation of sites of memory, but it also makes a point of representing those mediations as antiquated or ineffectual in contrast to the modernity of print culture. In this manner, Scott connects his progressive history of the nation with a progressive history of media.

Scott initially indicates the important roles that song plays in Highland culture in his depiction of the song sung by Mac-Murrough, the MacIvor family *bhairdh*. The song performed by Mac-Murrough serves several purposes: "to recite many proper names, to lament the dead, to apostrophize the absent, to exhort, and entreat, and animate those who were present" (171). The clan respond accordingly to Mac-Murrough's song as they are moved out of their individual selves into one passionate unit: "Their wild and sun-burnt countenances assumed a fiercer and more animated expression; all bent forward towards the reciter, many sprung up and waved their arms in ecstasy, and some laid their hands on their swords" (171). Flora's later English remediation of Mac-Murrough's song still captures some of the essence of the original performance: even though she is performing for Edward alone, she suggests the original community role of song by substituting "a lofty and uncommon Highland air, which had been a battle-song in former ages" for "the measured and monotonous recitative" of the bard's original performance" (182). By the end of the novel, however, the MacIvor clan, which has been held together and

---

[36] Walter Scott, *Minstrelsy of the Scottish Border* 2 vols. (Kelso: James Ballantyne, 1802) and 3 vols. (Edinburgh: James Ballantyne, 1803). See Davis, *Acts of Union*, chapter 5, and Jane Millgate, *Walter Scott: The Making of the Novelist* (Toronto: University of Toronto Press, 1984).

animated by song, has been subdued. Although Edward has pledged to help the members of the clan financially, their leader has been executed. In his final words to Edward, Fergus hints at the way his memory will move into the oral and legendary realm, suggesting that, after his death, Flora will think of him "as of the heroes of our race, upon whose deeds she loved to dwell" (435). Oral counter-memories of the Highlands in *Waverley* are represented as affective, but they are also effectively removed from the realm of action to the realm of sentiment.

Scott also offers a representation of the ineffectuality of Lowland oral culture in the character of Davie Gellatley. Davie is associated right from his initial appearance in the novel with song when he makes his ungainly way toward Edward at Tully-Veolan, gesturing oddly and singing an old "Scottish ditty" (9). Davie is a repository of Lowland cultural memories, but he is a limited kind of repository. As Rose explains, he has a "prodigious memory, stored with miscellaneous snatches and fragments of all tunes and songs" (121). He is a fragmented character who combines "the simplicity of the fool" with "the extravagance of a crazed imagination" (99), and as a "half-crazed simpleton" he is able to circulate only fragments of song (120). While Davie stores memories, then, he is not capable of translating them to the functional memory of the present. Moreover, the memories of "old Scottish poetry" that he does store have been combined in his mind with other materials such as the "fragments of songs and music unlike those of this country" that he has learned from his educated brother (121). Where the archive of the Highland memory is reduced to sentimental reflections on the past, the archive of Lowland culture is both fragmentary and unreliable.

Scott also carves out a place for manuscript culture in a less distant past, connecting it specifically with early eighteenth-century English Jacobite networks. Sir Everard, a "High-church" supporter of the "house of Stewart," Scott notes, subscribes to "Dyer's Weekly Letter," and first learned of the political successes of his brother through the "cool and procrastinating alembic" of that manuscript newsletter (61–62). Edward's tutor, Mr. Pembroke, pens Jacobite manuscripts which he gives to Edward and which are subsequently interpreted as evidence of Edward's Jacobite politics when he is arrested in Cairnvreckan after accidentally shooting the blacksmith. Edward's own early effusions in manuscript are associated with Jacobitism, too, for Mr. Pembroke passes on the "fragments of irregular verse" that he finds in Edward's room to his Aunt Rachel, who translates them "to her common-place book," where they join "choice receipts for cookery and medicine, favourite texts, and portions from High-church divines, and a few songs, amatory and jacobitical" (80). While oral culture is associated with Highland nostalgia and Lowland fragmentation in *Waverley*, manuscript culture is the stuff of more recent Jacobite culture, circulating among antiquated schoolmasters and old maids.

In *Waverley*, Scott suggests that the vanishing oral mediations of the Highlands, the fragmented songs of the Lowlands and the scribblings of English Jacobites have given way to the complex apparatuses of mass media in the present. He consciously compares the "slow succession of intelligence" of the weekly manuscript newsletter of the early eighteenth century, for example, with the modern transport of newspapers in his own time "by means of which every mechanic at his six-penny club may nightly learn from twenty contradictory channels the yesterday's news of the capital" (62). While he critiques modern mass media for being overly democratic as well as "contradictory," Scott nevertheless represents the communications media of the present age as a progression from the media of the past. Highland and Lowland orality and Jacobite manuscript culture, although colourful, are relegated to earlier stages of an evolutionary model as print comes to dominate.

Moreover, in Scott's hands the historical novel itself serves to highlight print's power, as it is capable of absorbing and re-presenting oral and manuscript culture within the pages of a book. In the final chapter of *Waverley*, "A Postscript, which should have been a Preface," Scott's narrator indicates how he has incorporated the oral testimony of those "folks of the old leaven" among whom he spent some of his boyhood into the novel's pages. The narrator also conveys to the reader the manuscript materials to which he has access. In discussing Aunt Rachel's commonplace book, for example, he notes that "the volume itself, with other authentic records of the Waverley family, were exposed to the inspection of the unworthy editor of this memorable history" who subsequently copied out Edward's fanciful poem (80). In *Waverley*, Scott suggests that British cultural memory is created not by excising but by incorporating the memory and the media of counter-memories into the fabric of print. In *The Break-Up of Britain*, Tom Nairn famously asserted that Scott's "essential point is that the past really is gone. The heart may regret this, but never the head ... For all its splendour, his panorama of the Scottish past is valedictory in nature."[37] In contrast to Nairn's comment, however, I suggest that the power of the *Waverley* novels lies in the fact that Scott

---

[37] Tom Nairn, *The Break-Up of Britain: Crisis and Neonationalism* (London: NLB and Verso Editions, 1981), 105.

indicates that the past is never really gone. To try to negate the past only allows for the re-activation of counter-memories. Instead, Scott acknowledges and includes counter-memories within the national consciousness, but at a safe remove. Although works on the 1745 Rising like *Ascanius* were in fact still circulating when Scott was writing *Waverley*, it was important for Scott that he create a break with the past. Notably, he suggests, *Waverley* takes place from a position "Sixty Years Hence."

In the course of writing his many other novels, Scott further developed the template he had created in *Waverley*, re-activating memorable events from Scottish and British history, including those of 1688, 1715 and 1745 examined in this book, embedding those variously mediated memories within compelling narratives that engaged readers' sentiments. By self-consciously drawing attention to the complexity of cultural memory and by connecting British cultural memory to a narrative of media succession leading up to print, Scott did not resolve the knots that constitute British cultural memory, but he framed them in such a way as to lessen their inherent power to disrupt in the present while drawing attention to the important role of memory in culture.

Conclusion

In her perceptive discussion of Scott in *The Afterlives of Walter Scott*, Rigney identifies a critical blind spot in Memory Studies in general when she suggests that "The dynamics of collective remembrance over a longer period has not yet received the sustained attention it deserves, whether in theoretical reflection or in the form of empirical studies demonstrating the extent to which modern societies are capable, or not, of transmitting memories over a longer period."[38] This book has provided a perspective on the "dynamics of collective remembrance" over a period of roughly sixty years, examining how the technologies of remembrance changed between 1688 and 1745 and suggesting that the conceptualization of memory also shifted in relation to those technological shifts. Where Rigney reads Scott as a pioneer of using the past in a process of "collective identity," I have examined him instead as an endpoint for the representations of cultural memory in texts that I have explored. In writing the history of cultural memory over a "longer period" and focusing on knots rather than sites of memory, I have drawn on but also questioned Nora's theories regarding *lieux de mémoire*. By returning to the era of the early

[38] Rigney, *Afterlives of Walter Scott*, 9.

eighteenth century, a time when print culture was becoming more pervasive and more naturalized, this study has introduced a historical and media perspective into the discourse on cultural memory. By analyzing the initial inscription of the 1688 Revolution, the War of the Two Kings, the Darien expedition and the uprisings of 1715 and 1745 through a combination of media, *Mediating Cultural Memory* has also contributed to a questioning of what Monica Juneja has described as Nora's "overly consensual conjunction of collective memory and national identity."[39] Nora imagined events being "plucked out of the flow of history" and then returned to it in a different form as condensed sites of memory. In contrast, I have suggested that the meaning that is invested in a site of memory is connected to the initial mediation of the event as well as its subsequent storage and reactivation. Moreover, that which Nora refers to as the "sea of living memory" is itself constituted through a complex mixture of oral, manuscript and print mediations mixing past and present even as far back as the early eighteenth century.

My focus on the complexities of memory and forgetting in the first half of the eighteenth century may seem remote, but, in fact, I suggest it can serve the present moment in important ways. By putting the founding memories of the British nation under the microscope, considering how they were initially inscripted and calling attention to the specific agents who were served in the process of creating, storing and reactivating these memories, *Mediating Cultural Memory* has aimed to question how events of national memory are produced and perpetuated. In addition, by drawing attention to the ways in which print participated in the creation of those memories as it was gaining prominence, this book also points to the need to attend to the way in which the current media landscape privileges certain memories and ways of remembering over others.

In our current polarized political climate, it is salutary to remember that *lieux de mémoire* are not "fixed entities or finished products,"[40] but ever-changing processes; they can be recalled and remediated in different ways for different interest groups – not only to amplify differences but also to generate empathetic connections. As Mieke Bal suggests, "Art – and other cultural artifacts such as photographs and published texts of all kinds – can mediate between the parties to the traumatizing scene and between these

---

[39] Monica Juneja, "Architectural Memory between Representation and Practice: Rethinking Pierre Nora's *Les lieux de mémoire*," in *Memory, History, and Colonialism: Engaging with Pierre Nora in Colonial and Postcolonial Contexts*, ed. Indra Sengupta (London: German Historical Institute London, 2009), 35.
[40] Rigney, *Afterlives of Walter Scott*, 19.

and the reader or viewer. The recipients of the account perform an act of memory that is potentially healing, as it calls for political and cultural solidarity in recognizing the traumatized party's predicament."[41] If, as Nikulin argues, "memory" has now come to replace reason as a way of explaining "a historical, political, or social phenomenon,"[42] then the activities of studying the creation and re-inscription of memories and engaging empathetically with those that have been forgotten have never been as important as they are in the present moment.

---

[41] Mieke Bal, Jonathan V. Crewe and Leo Spitzer, *Acts of Memory: Cultural Recall in the Present* (Hanover, NH, and London: University of New England Press, 1999), x.
[42] Nikulin, *Memory: A History*, 5.

Bibliography

Manuscripts

British Library. Hardwicke Papers, vol. 541. Add. MS 35889, fol. 346 recto and verso. Letter from William Stanhope, Lord Harrington, to Thomas Robinson, Whitehall, April 25, 1746.
British Library. Add. MS 45731, fol. 83. Newsletter to Edmond Poley, December 14, 1688.
British Library. Sloane MS 900. "The Fingallian Travesty, or the Sixt Book of Virgill's Ænæids."
Folger Library. MS L.c.1–3950. Newdigate Family Collection of Newsletters.
National Library of Scotland. Adv. MS 32.6.16–26. Robert Forbes, "The Lyon in Mourning."
National Library of Scotland. Adv. MSS 83.7.4. Darien papers.

Newspapers and Periodicals

Daily Courant
The Flying-Post
The General Advertiser
The London Evening Post
The Orange Gazette
The Penny London Post or the Morning Advertiser
The Post Boy
The Post-Man
The Scots Magazine, Containing, a General View of the Religion, Politicks, Entertainment, &c. in Great Britain
St. James's Evening Post

Primary and Secondary Printed Materials

A Brief Character of Ireland with Some Observations of the Customs &c. of the Meaner Sort of the Natural Inhabitants of that Kingdom. London, 1692.

A Candid and Impartial Account of the Behaviour of Simon Lord LOVAT. London, 1747.

A Collection of State Tracts, Publish'd on Occasion of the Late Revolution in 1688. Vol. 1. London, 1705.

A Compleat and Authentic History of the Rise, Progress and Extinction of the Late Rebellion. London, 1747.

A Compleat History of the Late Rebellion. London, 1716.

A Complete and Authentick History of the Rise, Progress and Extinction of the Late Rebellion. London, 1746.

"A Dialogue between a Loyal Addressor, and a Blunt Whiggish Clown." In *Lampoons*. London, 1687. English Broadside Ballad Archive, http://ebba.english.ucsb.edu.

A Faithful Register of the Late Rebellion. London, 1718.

A Full and Authentic History of the Rebellion MDCCXLV and MDCCXLVI. London, n.d.

A Full Description of These Times; or the Prince of ORANGE's March from EXETER to LONDON. London, 1689. English Broadside Ballad Archive, http://ebba.english.ucsb.edu.

A Gentleman Lately Arriv'd. *The History of Caledonia: or, the Scots Colony in Darien in the West Indies*. London, 1699.

A Genuine Account of the Behaviour, Confession, and Dying Words, of Francis Townly [sic], (Nominal) Colonel of the Manchester Regiment, Thomas Deacon, James Dawson, John Barwick, George Fletcher and Andrew Blood, Captains in the Manchester Regiment. London, 1746.

A Genuine Narrative of the Life, Behaviour, and Conduct of Simon, Lord Fraser, of Lovat. London, 1747.

A Journey through Part of England and Scotland. Along with the Army under the Command of His Royal Highness the Duke of Cumberland. London, 1746.

A Letter from a Gentleman in Exeter to His Friend in London. London, 1688.

A Letter from a Gentleman in the Country to His Friend at Edinburgh. Edinburgh, 1696.

A Letter from the Commission, of the General Assembly, of the Church of Scotland; to the Honourable Council and Inhabitants of the Scots Colony of Caledonia in America. Glasgow, 1699.

A Letter, Giving a Description of the Isthmus of Darian. Edinburgh, 1699.

A Letter Writ by Mijn Heer Fagel, Pensioner of Holland to Mr. James Stewart, Advocate, Giving an Account of the Prince and Princess of Orange's Thoughts Concerning the Repeal of the Test and the Penal Laws. London, 1688.

"A New Catch, in Praise of the Reverend Bishops." In *A Collection of the Newest and Most Ingenious Poems, Songs, Catches &c. against Popery Relating to the Times*, 20. London, 1689.

"A New Song." In *A Collection of the Newest and Most Ingenious Poems, Songs, Catches &c. against Popery Relating to the Times*, 9. London, 1689.

A New Touch of the Times, OR, the Nations Consent, for a Free Parliament. London, 1689. English Broadside Ballad Archive, http://ebba.english.ucsb.edu.

A Pindarick Ode upon His Most Sacred Majestie's Late Gracious Indulgence. London, 1687. English Broadside Ballad Archive, http://ebba.english.ucsb.edu.

A Relation of the Bloody Massacre in Ireland Acted by the Instigation of the Jesuits, Priests, and Friars. London, 1689.

A Review of the Two Late Rebellions, Historical, Political and Moral. London, 1747.

A Short Account from, and Description of the Isthmus of Darien, Where the Scots Collony Are Settled. Edinburgh, 1699.

A Short View of the Methods Made Use of in Ireland for the Subversion and Destruction of the Protestant Religion and Interest. London, 1689.

A True Account from Colonel Kirke, of the Relieving of London-Derry, Brought by Mr. Beale the Messenger, in an Express to the Court. Edinburgh, 1689.

Addison, Joseph. *The Free-Holder: or, Political Essays.* London, 1716.

Aeneas, and His Two Sons. A True Portrait. London: J. Oldcastle, 1746.

Alexis; or, the Young Adventurer. A Novel. London, 1746.

Alker, Sharon, and Holly Nelson. *Besieged: Early Modern British Siege Literature, 1642–1722.* Montreal: McGill-Queens University Press, 2021.

An Act of Parliament for Encourageing the Scots Affrican and Indian Company. Edinburgh, 1695.

An Account of the Behaviour, and Conduct, of Simon Lord Fraser, of Lovat. London, 1747.

An Account of the Proceedings and Transactions That Have Happened in the Kingdom of England, since the Arrival of the Dutch Fleet, and the Landing of the Prince of Orange's Army. London, 1688.

An Address to His Grace the Lord Archbishop of Canterbury, and the Right Reverend the Bishops. London, 1688.

An Alphabetical List of the Knights and Commissioners of Shires, Citizens and Burgesses. London, 1711.

An Answer to a Dangerous Pamphlet Entitled A Candid and Impartial Account of the Behaviour of Simon Lord LOVAT. London, 1747.

An Answer to a Paper, Intitled, Reflections on the Prince of Orange's Declaration. London, 1688.

An Apology for the Failures Charged on the Reverend Mr. George Walker's Account of the Late Siege of Derry. London, 1689.

An Authentick Narrative of the Whole Proceedings of Court at St. Margaret's Hill, Southwark. London, 1746.

An Exact Account of the Affairs in Ireland, and the Present Condition of London-Derry. London, 1689.

An Honest Man's Wish for the Prince of Orange. London?, 1688.

An Officer of the Royal Army. *The History of the Wars in Ireland, between Their Majesties Army, and the Forces of the Late King James.* London: Benjamin Johnson, 1690.

An Ode Made on the Welcome News of the Safe Arrival and Kind Reception of the Scottish Collony at Darien in America. Edinburgh, 1699.

Anderson, Benedict. *Imagined Communities: Reflections on the Origin and Spread of Nationalism*. Rev. ed. London: Verso, 2006.

Andrews, Alexander. *The History of British Journalism: From the Foundation of the Newspaper Press in England to the Repeal of the Stamp Act in 1855*. London: R. Bentley, 1859.

Andrews, J. H. "Land and People, c. 1685." In *A New History of Ireland*, vol. 3, *1534–1691*, edited by T. W. Moody, F. X. Martin and F. J. Byrne, 458–76. Oxford: Oxford University Press, 2009.

Argyll, Earl of (Archibald Campbell). *The Declaration and Apology of the Protestant People* and *The Declaration of Archibald Earl of Argyle*. Campbell-Town, 1685.

The Declaration and Apology of the Protestant People and *The Declaration of Archibald Earl of Argile*. Edinburgh, 1685.

Armitage, David. *The Ideological Origins of the British Empire*. Cambridge: Cambridge University Press, 2000.

"The Scottish Vision of Empire: The Intellectual Origins of the Darien Venture." In *A Union for Empire: Political Thought and the British Union of 1707*, edited by John Robert, 97–118. Cambridge: Cambridge University Press, 1995.

Articles of Union. Edinburgh, 1706.

Ascanius; or the Young Adventurer, a True History. London: Printed for G. Smith, 1746.

Ascanius: or, the Young Adventurer; a True History. London: Printed for T. Johnstone, 1746.

Assmann, Aleida. *Cultural Memory and Western Civilization: Functions, Media, Archives*. Cambridge: Cambridge University Press, 2011.

Assmann, Aleida, and Linda Shortt. "Memory and Political Change: Introduction." In *Memory and Political Change*, edited by Aleida Assmann and Linda Shortt, 1–14. London: Palgrave Macmillan, 2012.

Assmann, Jan. *Moses the Egyptian: The Memory of Egypt in Western Monotheism*. Boston, MA: Harvard University Press, 1997.

Atherton, Ian. "The Itch Grown a Disease: Manuscript Transmission of News in the Seventeenth Century." *Prose Studies* 21, no. 2 (1998): 39–65.

"The Press and Popular Political Opinion." In *A Companion to Stuart Britain*, edited by Barry Coward, 88–110. Oxford: Oxford University Press, 2007.

Auffenberg, Thomas. "Church–State Philanthropy: English Charity Briefs and the Relief of Persecuted Continental Protestants." *A Journal of Church and State* 21, no. 2 (1979), 287–303.

Bal, Mieke. *Travelling Concepts in the Humanities: A Rough Guide*. Toronto: University of Toronto Press, 2002.

Bal, Mieke, Jonathan V. Crewe and Leo Spitzer. *Acts of Memory: Cultural Recall in the Present*. Hanover, NH, and London: University of New England Press, 1999.

Ball, F. Elrington. *The Judges in Ireland, 1221–1921*. 2 vols. London: J. Murray, 1926; reprinted Clark, NJ: The Lawbook Exchange, 2005.

Bannet, Eve Tavor. *Empire of Letters: Letter Manuals and Transatlantic Correspondence*. Cambridge: Cambridge University Press, 2005.

Barber, Alex. "'It Is Not Easy What to Say of Our Condition, Much Less to Write It': The Continued Importance of Scribal News in the Early 18th Century." *Parliamentary History* 32, no. 2 (2013): 293–316.

Barker, Hannah. *Newspapers, Politics, and Public Opinion in Late Eighteenth-Century England*. Oxford: Oxford University Press, 1998.

Barnard, Tony. "The Uses of 23 October 1641 and Irish Protestant Celebrations." *The English Historical Review* 106, no. 421 (October 1991): 889–920.

Bartlett, Thomas. *Ireland: A History*. Cambridge and New York: Cambridge University Press, 2010.

Belsey, Catherine. "Remembering as Re-inscription – with a Difference." In *Literature, Literary History, and Cultural Memory*, edited by Herbert Grabes, 3–18. Tübingen: Gunter Narr Verlag, 2005.

Benedict, Barbara M. "Encounters with the Object: Advertisements, Time, and Literary Discourse in the Early Eighteenth-Century Thing-Poem." *Eighteenth-Century Studies* 40, no. 2 (2007): 193–207.

Black, Fischer. "Noise." *The Journal of Finance* 41, no. 3 (1986): 529–43.

Black, Jeremy. *The English Press: A History*. London: Bloomsbury Academic, 2019.

The English Press in the Eighteenth Century. London and Sydney: Croom Helm, 1987.

Maps and Politics. Chicago: University of Chicago Press, 1997.

Bloom, Lillian. "Joseph Addison (1 May 1672–17 June 1719)." In *Dictionary of Literary Biography*, vol. 101, *British Prose Writers, 1660–1800*, 1st ser., edited by Donald T. Siebert, 2–28. Detroit, MI, and London: Gale Research, 1991.

Bohun, Edmund. *The History of the Desertion*. London, 1689.

Borlase, Edmund. *The History of the Execrable Irish Rebellion Trac'd from Many Preceding Acts, to the Grand Eruption the 23 of October, 1641*. London, 1680.

Bowie, Karin. *Public Opinion in Early Modern Scotland, c. 1560–1707*. Cambridge: Cambridge University Press, 2020.

Scottish Public Opinion and the Anglo-Scottish Union, 1699–1707. Woodbridge: Boydell Press, 2007.

Boyer, Abel. *History of King William the Third. In III Parts*. 3 vols. London: A. Roper, 1702–03.

Boyer, Richard. "English Declaration of Indulgence of 1687 and 1688." *The Catholic Historical Review* 50, no. 3 (1964): 332–71.

Brewer, John. *The Sinews of Power: War, Money and the English State, 1688–1783*. Cambridge, MA: Harvard University Press, 1990.

Briggs, Asa, and Peter Burke. *A Social History of Media: From Gutenberg to the Internet*. Malden, MA: Blackwell, 2001.

Bullard, Rebecca. *The Politics of Disclosure, 1674–1725: Secret History Narratives*. London: Pickering and Chatto, 2009. "Secret History, Politics and the Early

Novel," in *The Oxford Handbook of the Eighteenth-Century Novel* edited J. A. Downie (Oxford: Oxford University Press, 2016).
Burnet, Gilbert. *Bishop Burnet's History of His Own Time.* 2 vols. London, 1724–34.
A Collection of Eighteen Papers Relating to the Affairs of Church & State during the Reign of King James the Second. London, 1689.
A Compleat Collection of Papers in Twelve Parts Relating to the Great Revolutions in England and Scotland. London, 1689.
A Review of the Reflections on the Prince of Orange's Declaration. London, 1688.
The Expedition of His Highness the Prince of Orange for England. London, 1688.
Burton, John. *A Genuine and True Journal of the Most Miraculous Escape of the Young Chevalier.* London, 1749.
Burton, John Hill, ed. *The Darien Papers: Being a Selection of Original Letters and Official Documents Relating to the Establishment of a Colony at Darien.* Edinburgh: Thomas Constable, 1849.
Butler, Jemmy. *The Strolling Hero, or* Rome's *Knight-Errant.* London, 1744.
Campbell, John. *Lives of the Admirals, and Other Eminent British Seamen.* 4 vols. London, 1742–44.
Canny, Nicholas. *Making Ireland British, 1580–1650.* Oxford: Oxford University Press, 2003.
Care, Henry. *An Answer to a Paper Importing a Petition of the Archbishop of Canterbury; and Six Other Bishops.* London, 1688.
Carleton, William. *The Life of William Carleton; Being His Autobiography and Letters.* London: Downey and Co., 1896.
Carnell, Rachel. *Realism, Partisan Politics, and the Rise of the British Novel.* New York and Houndmills: Palgrave Macmillan, 2006.
Carpenter, Andrew. *Verse in English from Eighteenth-Century Ireland.* Cork: Cork University Press, 1998.
Carpenter, Andrew, ed. *Verse Travesty in Restoration Ireland: 'Purgatorium Hibernicum' (NLI MS 470) and "the Fingallian Travesty" (BL, Sloane MS 900).* Dublin: Irish Manuscripts Commission, 2013.
Carroll, Clare. "Barbarous Slaves and Civil Cannibals." In *Circe's Cup: Cultural Transformation in Early Modern Ireland,* 11–27. Cork: Cork University Press, 2002.
Carte, Thomas. *A General History of England.* London, n.d.
Cesari, Chiara de, and Ann Rigney, eds. *Transnational Memory: Circulation, Articulation, Scales.* Berlin: De Gruyter, 2014.
Chaghafi, Elisabeth. "The Newsy Baronet: How Richard Newdigate (Per)used His Newsletters." The Collation: Research and Exploration at the Folger, September 19, 2019, https://collation.folger.edu/2019/09/newsy-baronet/.
Chandler, James, Arnold I. Davidson and Adrian Johns. "Arts of Transmission: An Introduction." *Critical Inquiry* 31, no. 1 (2004): 1–6.
Claydon, Tony. "Daily News and the Construction of Time in Late Stuart England, 1695–1714." *Journal of British Studies* 52, no. 1 (2013): 55–78.
William III and the Godly Revolution. Cambridge: Cambridge University Press, 1996.

Cochrane, John George. *Catalogue of the Library at Abbotsford*. Edinburgh: Maitland Club, 1838.
Cockburn, J. S. *A History of English Assizes 1558–1714*. Cambridge: Cambridge University Press, 1972.
Colley, Linda. *Britons: Forging the Nation 1707–1837*. New Haven, CT: Yale University Press, 1992.
  Captives: Britain, Empire and the World, 1600–1850. New York: Anchor Books, 2004.
Collier, Jeremy. *The Desertion Discuss'd. In a Letter to a Country Gentleman*. London, 1689.
Coltman, Viccy. *Art and Identity in Scotland: A Cultural History from the Jacobite Rising of 1745 to Walter Scott*. Cambridge: Cambridge University Press, 2019.
Company of Scotland Trading to Africa and the Indies. *Act for a Company Trading to Affrica [sic] and the Indies*. Edinburgh, 1695.
  Advertisement. Edinburgh, the 9th of July 1696. Edinburgh, 1696.
  An Express from the African and Indian Scots Company's Fleet. Edinburgh, 1699.
  A Full and Exact Collection of All the Considerable Addresses, Memorials, Petitions, Answers, Proclamations, Declarations, Letters and Other Publick Papers, Relating to the Company of Scotland Trading to Africa and the Indies, since the Passing of the Act. Edinburgh, 1700.
  A List of the Subscribers to the Company of Scotland Trading to Africa and the Indies: Taken in Edinburgh, &c. until the 21 of April Inclusive 1696. Edinburgh, 1696.
  The Original Papers and Letters, Relating to the Scots Company Trading to Africa and the Indies. Edinburgh, 1700.
  Scotland's Right to Caledonia (Formerly Called Darien). Edinburgh, 1700.
Coolahan, Marie-Louise. "Whither the Archipelago? Stops, Starts, and Hurdles on the Four Nations Front." *Literature Compass* 15, no. 11 (2018): 1–12.
Coote, Charles. *The History of England, from the Earliest Dawn of Record to the Peace of MDCCLXXXIII*. 9 vols. London, 1796.
Coote, Richard, Earl of Bellomont. *A Proclamation*. New York, 1699.
Cope, Esther S. "The King's Declaration Concerning the Dissolution of the Short Parliament of 1640: An Unsuccessful Attempt at Public Relations." *Huntington Library Quarterly* 40, no. 4 (August, 1977): 325–31.
Cowan, Brian. *The Social Life of Coffee: The Emergence of the British Coffeehouse*. New Haven, CT: Yale University Press, 2005.
Cox, Richard. *Aphorisms Relating to the Kingdom of Ireland Humbly Submitted to the Most Noble Assembly of Lords & Commons at the Great Convention at Westminster*. London, 1689.
  Autobiography of the Rt. Hon. Sir Richard Cox, Bart. Edited by Richard Caulfield. London: J. Russell Smith, 1860.
  Hibernia Anglicana; or, the History of Ireland, from the Conquest Thereof to This Present Time. London, 1689.

Cranfield, Geoffrey. *The Development of the Provincial Newspaper, 1700–1760*. Oxford: Clarendon Press, 1962.
Crawford, George. *The Peerage of Scotland*. Edinburgh, 1716.
Crownshaw, Richard, Jane Kilby and Antony Rowland. *The Future of Memory*. New York and London: Berghahn Books, 2010.
Cruickshanks, Eveline. *The Glorious Revolution*. New York: St. Martin's Press, 2000.
Cullen, Edward. *The Isthmus of Darien Ship Canal*. 2nd ed. London: Effingham Wilson, 1852.
Cunningham, Bernadette. "Historical Writing, 1660–1750." In *The Irish Book in English, 1550–1800*, edited by Raymond Gillespie and Andrew Hadfield, 264–81. Oxford: Oxford University Press, 2006.
Dale, Richard. *The First Crash: Lessons from the South Sea Bubble*. Princeton, NJ: Princeton University Press, 2004.
Danziger, Kurt. *Marking the Mind: A History of Memory*. Cambridge: Cambridge University Press, 2008.
Darcy, Eamon. *The Irish Rebellion of 1641 and the Wars of the Three Kingdoms*. Woodbridge: Boydell Press, 2013.
Darnton, Robert. "An Early Information Society: News and the Media in Eighteenth-Century Paris." *The American Historical Review* 105, no. 1 (2000): 1–35.
Davis, Leith. *Acts of Union: Scotland and the Literary Negotiation of the British Nation, 1707–1830*. Stanford, CA: Stanford University Press, 1998.
——— "The Aftermath of Union." In *The Cambridge Companion to Scottish Literature*, edited by Gerard Carruthers and Liam McIlvanney, 56–70. Cambridge: Cambridge University Press, 2012.
——— "Cultural Memory and Cultural Amnesia: Ireland and the 'Glorious Revolution.'" *Studies in Eighteenth-Century Culture* 47 (2017): 185–205.
——— "Imagining the Miscellaneous Nation: James Watson's *Choice Collection of Comic and Serious Scots Poems*." *Eighteenth-Century Life* 35, no. 3 (2011): 60–80.
——— "Mediating the 'Sudden & Surprising Revolution': Official Manuscript Newsletters and the Glorious Revolution." In *After Print: Eighteenth-Century Manuscript Cultures*, edited by Rachael Scarborough King, 148–74. Charlottesville: University of Virginia Press, 2020.
——— "Memory Studies and the Eighteenth Century." *Literature Compass* 16, no. 2, January 17, 2019, https://doi.org/10.1111/lic3.12504.
——— *Music, Postcolonialism, and Gender: The Construction of Irish National Identity, 1724–1874*. Notre Dame, IN: University of Notre Dame Press, 2005.
Daybell, James, and Andrew Gordon. "Introduction: The Early Modern Letter Opener." In *Cultures of Correspondence in Early Modern Britain*, edited by James Daybell and Andrew Gordon, 1–26. Philadelphia: University of Pennsylvania Press, 2016.
The Declaration of His Highnes William Henry. The Hague, 1688.
The Declaration of James Duke of Monmouth &; the Noblemen, Gentlemen & Others, Now in Arms, for Defence & Vindication of the Protestant Religion,

& *the Laws, Rights, & Privilieges of England, from the Invasion Made upon Them & for Delivering the Kingdom from the Usurpation & Tyranny of James Duke of York*. London, 1685.

Defoe, Daniel. *Caledonia, &c: A Poem in Honour of Scotland, and the Scots Nation*. Edinburgh, 1706.

The History of the Union of Great Britain. Edinburgh, 1709.

Letters of Daniel Defoe. Edited by George Harris Healey. Oxford: Clarendon Press, 1955.

DeMaria, Robert, Jr. "The Eighteenth-Century Periodical Essay." In *The Cambridge History of English Literature, 1660–1780*, edited by John Richetti, 527–48. Cambridge: Cambridge University Press, 2005.

Digby, Lettice, Lady. *A Full and True Account of the Inhumane and Bloudy Cruelties of the Papists to the Poor Protestants in Ireland in the Year 1641*. London: Peter Richman, 1689.

Donald, Diana. *The Age of Caricature: Satirical Prints in the Reign of George III*. New Haven, CT: Yale University Press, 1996.

Donaldson, William. "Forbes, Robert (bap. 1708, d. 1775), Jacobite Annalist and Scottish Episcopal Bishop of Ross and Caithness." *Oxford Dictionary of National Biography*, September 20, 2019, www.oxforddnb.com/view/10.1093/ref:odnb/9780198614128.001.0001/odnb-9780198614128-e-9845.

Dooley, Brendan. "The Down Survey of Ireland: Mapping a Century of Change." Trinity College Dublin, 2013, http://downsurvey.tcd.ie.

"Preface." In *The Dissemination of News and the Emergence of Contemporaneity in Early Modern Europe*, edited by Brendan Dooley, xiii–xiv. Farnham: Ashgate, 2010.

Duncan, Ian. *Scott's Shadow: The Novel in Romantic Edinburgh*. Princeton, NJ: Princeton University Press, 2007.

Echard, Laurence. *The History of the Revolution, and the Establishment of England in the Year 1688*. London: Jacob Tonson, 1725.

Edinburgh, the 12th Day of March 1698. Edinburgh, n.d.

Eisenstein, Elizabeth. *The Printing Press as an Agent of Change: Communications and Cultural Transformations in Early-Modern Europe*. Cambridge: Cambridge University Press, 1979.

Ellis, George Agar, ed. *Letters Written during the Years 1686, 1687, 1688, and Addressed to John Ellis, Esq*. 2 vols. London: Henry Colburn and Richard Bentley, 1831.

Erll, Astrid. "Literature, Film, and the Mediality of Cultural Memory." In *Cultural Memory Studies: An International and Interdisciplinary Handbook*, edited by Astrid Erll and Ansgar Nünning, 389–98. Berlin: De Gruyter, 2008.

Memory in Culture. Houndmills: Palgrave Macmillan, 2011.

"Travelling Memory." *Parallax* 17, no. 4 (2011): 4–18.

Evelyn, John. *Diary and Correspondence of John Evelyn, F.R.S.* Edited by William Bray. 4 vols. London: Henry Colburn, 1850.

Exquemelin, Alexandre. *The History of the Bucaniers of America*. London, 1699.

Ezell, Margaret J. M. *Social Authorship and the Advent of Print.* Baltimore: Johns Hopkins University Press, 1999.
Farewell, James. *The Irish Hudibras, or, Fingallian Prince.* London, 1689.
Ferguson, Robert. *A Brief Justification of the Prince of Orange's Descent.* London, 1689.
Ferris, Ina. "Printing the Past: Walter Scott's Bannatyne Club and the Antiquarian Document." *Romanticism* 11, no. 2 (2005): 143–60.
Fielding, Henry. *The True Patriot and Related Writings.* Edited by W. B. Coley. Middleton, CT: Wesleyan University Press, 1987.
Fielding, Penny. *Writing and Orality: Nationality, Culture, and Nineteenth-Century Scottish Fiction.* Oxford: Oxford University Press, 1996.
Fletcher, Andrew. *A Short and Impartial View of the Manner and Occasion of the Scots Colony's Coming Away from Darien in a Letter to a Person of Quality.* Edinburgh, 1699.
Speeches by a Member of the Parliament, Which Began at Edinburgh the 6th of May 1703. Edinburgh, 1703.
Flint, Christopher. *The Appearance of Print in Eighteenth-Century Fiction.* Cambridge: Cambridge University Press, 2011.
Forbes, Robert. *The Lyon in Mourning.* 3 vols. Edinburgh: Printed by T. and A. Constable for the Scottish History Society, 1895–96.
Foster, Elizabeth. "Petitions and the Petition of Right." *Journal of British Studies* 14, no. 1 (1974): 21–45.
Foster, James. *An Account of the Behaviour of the Late Earl of Kilmarnock.* London, 1746.
Foucault, Michel. *Discipline and Punish: The Birth of the Prison.* Translated by Alan Sheridan. 2nd ed. New York: Vintage, 1995.
"Nietzsche, Genealogy, History." In *Language, Counter-Memory, Practice: Selected Essays and Interviews*, edited by Donald Bouchard, 139–64. Ithaca, NY: Cornell University Press, 1977.
Fox, Adam. "Remembering the Past in Early Modern England: Oral and Written Tradition." *Transactions of the Royal Historical Society* 9 (1999): 233–56.
"Sir William Petty, Ireland, and the Making of a Political Economist, 1653–87." *Economic History Review* 62, no. 2 (2009): 388–404.
Fox, Adam, and Daniel Woolf, eds. *The Spoken Word: Oral Culture in Britain, 1500–1850.* Manchester: Manchester University Press, 2003.
Fraser, Peter. *The Intelligence of the Secretaries of State and Their Monopoly of Licensed News 1660–1688.* Cambridge: Cambridge University Press, 1956.
Fries, Udo. "Newspapers from 1665–1765." In *News as Changing Texts: Corpora, Methodologies and Analysis*, edited by Roberta Facchinetti, Nicholas Brownlees, Birte Bös, and Udo Fries, 49–89. 2nd ed. Newcastle upon Tyne: Cambridge Scholars, 2015.
Gallup-Diaz, Ignacio. *The Door of the Seas and Key to the Universe: Indian Politics and Imperial Rivalry in the Darien, 1640–1750.* New York: Columbia University Press, 2004.
Gillespie, Raymond. "The Irish Protestants and James II, 1688–90." *Irish Historical Studies* 28, no. 110 (1992): 124–33.

Gitelman, Lisa. "Introduction: Media as Historical Subjects." In *Always Already New: Media, History and the Data of Culture*, 1–22. Cambridge, MA, and London: MIT Press, 2006.
   Paper Knowledge: Towards a Media History of Documents. Durham, NC: Duke University Press, 2014.
Goldie, Mark. "The Revolution of 1689 and the Structure of Political Argument." *Bulletin of Research in the Humanities* 83 (1980): 473–564.
Greenblatt, Stephen. *Cultural Mobility: A Manifesto*. Cambridge: Cambridge University Press, 2010.
Guthrie, Neil. *The Material Culture of the Jacobites*. Cambridge: Cambridge University Press, 2013.
Guthrie, William. *A General History of England from the Invasion of Julius Cæsar to 1688*. London, 1744.
Hadfield, Andrew, and John McVeagh. *Strangers to That Land: British Perceptions of Ireland from the Reformation*. Gerrards Cross: Colin Smythe, 1994.
Hagan, Anette. "The Spread of Printing." In *The Edinburgh History of the Book in Scotland*, vol. 2, *Enlightenment and Expansion, 1707–1800*, edited by Stephen Brown and Warren MacDougall, 112–17. Edinburgh: Edinburgh University Press, 2012.
Hamilton, John, second Lord Belhaven. *Lord Beilhaven's Speech in Parliament the Second Day of November 1706*. Edinburgh, 1706.
Harding, Nick. *Hanover and the British Empire, 1700–1837*. Woodbridge: Boydell Press, 2007.
Harris, Bob. "England's Provincial Newspapers and the Jacobite Rebellion of 1745–1746." *History* 80, no. 258 (1995): 5–21.
   "'A Great Palladium of Our Liberties': The British Press and the 'Forty-Five.'" *Historical Research* 68, no. 165 (1995): 67–87.
Harris, Michael. "London Newspapers." In *The Cambridge History of the Book in Britain*, vol. 5: *1695–1830*, edited by Michael F. Suarez, S. J. and Michael Turner, 413–33. Cambridge: Cambridge University Press, 2010.
   London Newspapers in the Age of Walpole: A Study of the Origins of the Modern English Press. Rutherford, NJ: Fairleigh Dickinson University Press, 1987.
Harris, Tim. *Revolution: The Great Crisis of the British Monarchy, 1685–1720*. London: Penguin, 2006.
Haslett, Moyra. "Introduction." In *Irish Literature in Transition, 1700–1780*, edited by Moyra Haslett, 1–28. Cambridge: Cambridge University Press, 2020.
Hayton, David. *Ruling Ireland, 1685–1742: Politics, Politicians and Parties*. Woodbridge: Boydell Press, 2007.
Henderson, Andrew. *The History of the Rebellion, 1745 and 1746. Containing, a Full Account of Its Rise, Progress and Extinction*. London: Reprinted from the Edinburgh Edition and sold by Ralph Griffiths, 1748.
Herries, Walter. "Epistle Dedicatory." In *A Defence of the Scots Abdicating Darien Including an Answer to the Defence of the Scots Settlement There*. Edinburgh, 1700.
   The Historian's Guide, or, Britain's Remembrancer. London, 1690.

The History of the Present Rebellion in Scotland. From the Departure of the Pretender's Son from Rome, Down to the Present Time. London, 1745.
The History of the Rebellion Raised against His MAJESTY KING GEORGE II. From Its Rise in August 1745, to Its Happy Extinction, by the Glorious Victory at Culloden, on the 16th of April, 1746. Dublin, 1746.
Ho Tai, Hue-Tam. "Remembered Realms: Pierre Nora and French National Memory." *The American Historical Review* 106, no. 3 (2001): 906–22.
Hoak, Dale. "The Anglo-Dutch Revolution of 1688–89." In *The World of William and Mary: Anglo-Dutch Perspectives on the Revolution of 1688–89*, edited by Dale Hoak and Mordechai Feingold, 1–26. Stanford, CA: Stanford University Press, 1996.
Hodges, James. *The Rights and Interests of the Two British Monarchies.* London, 1703.
Holland, Karen. "Disputed Heroes: Early Accounts of the Siege of Londonderry." *New Hibernia Review* 18, no. 2 (2014): 21–41.
Holmes, Geoffrey, and Daniel Szechi. *The Age of Oligarchy: Pre-industrial Britain 1722–1783.* London: Routledge, 2014.
Home, John. *History of the Rebellion in the Year 1745.* London: A. Strahan, 1802.
Hume, David. *The History of England, from the Invasion of Julius Cæsar to the Revolution in 1688.* 6 vols. London: A. Millar, 1762.
The History of England, from the Invasion of Julius Cæsar to the Revolution in 1688. 8 vols. London: T. Cadell, 1778.
The History of England, from the Invasion of Julius Caesar to the Revolution in MDCLXXXVIII. 6 vols. Philadelphia: Robert Campbell, 1796.
History of Great Britain Volume 2 Containing the Commonwealth and the Reigns of Charles II and James II. London, 1757.
A Treatise of Human Nature. 3 vols. London, 1739–40.
Essays, Moral and Political. 3rd ed. London, 1748.
Hutchby, Ian. "Technologies, Texts and Affordances." *Sociology* 35, no. 2 (2001): 441–56.
Innis, Harold A. *Empire and Communications.* Toronto: Dundurn Press, 2007.
Insh, George Pratt. *Papers Relating to the Ships and Voyages of the Company of Scotland Trading to Africa and the Indies, 1696–1707.* Edinburgh: Edinburgh University Press by T. and A. Constable for the Scottish History Society, 1924.
Insignia Praelustris Societatis Scoticanae ad Africam & Indias. Edinburgh, n.d.
Israel, Jonathan, ed. *The Anglo-Dutch Moment: Essays on the Glorious Revolution and Its World Impact.* New York: Cambridge University Press, 1991.
J.A. *Princely Excellency: or, Regal Glory.* London, 1702.
Jackson, Clare. *Restoration Scotland, 1660–1690: Royalist Politics, Religion and Ideas.* Rochester, NY: Boydell, 2003.
James II/VII. *By the King, a Declaration. As We Cannot Consider This Invasion of Our Kingdoms without Horror.* London and Edinburgh, 1688.
By the King, a Proclamation against Spreading of a Traiterous Declaration. London, 1685.
By the King a Proclamation for the Speedy Calling of a Parliament. London, 1688.

By the King. A Proclamation. To Restrain the Spreading of False News. London, 1688.
By the King, a Proclamation. Whereas the Prince of Orange and His Adherents. London, 1688.
His Majesties GRACIOUS DECLARATION to All His Loving Subjects for Liberty of Conscience Establishing Religious Toleration in England. London, 1688.
His Majesties Gracious Declaration. James R. Our Conduct Has Been Such in All Times. London, 1688,
Jardine, Lisa. *Going Dutch: How England Plundered Holland's Glory*. London: Harper Press, 2008.
Jarrells, Anthony. *Britain's Bloodless Revolutions: 1688 and the Romantic Reform of Literature*. Basingstoke: Palgrave Macmillan, 2005.
Jarvis, Rupert C. *Collected Papers on the Jacobite Rising*. 2 vols. Manchester: Manchester University Press, 1972.
Johns, Adrian. *The Nature of the Book: Print and Knowledge in the Making*. Chicago: University of Chicago Press, 1998.
Jones, Richard J. "Continued Continuations of Complete Histories: Tobias Smollett and the Work of History." *Journal for Eighteenth-Century Studies* 41, no. 3 (2018): 391–406.
Jordan, Charles Jacob. *A Treatise on Anastatic Printing, or the Art of Reprinting from Prints on Paper*. London, 1853.
Journal of the Pretender's Expedition to North Britain. London, 1745.
The Journals of the House of Commons, vol. 11. London: Printed for the House of Commons, 1803.
Joyfull Newes from Captain Marro in Ireland. London, 1642.
Juneja, Monica. "Architectural Memory between Representation and Practice: Rethinking Pierre Nora's *Les lieux de mémoire*." In *Memory, History, and Colonialism: Engaging with Pierre Nora in Colonial and Postcolonial Contexts*, edited by Indra Sengupta, 11–36. London: German Historical Institute London, 2009.
Kelly, James. "'The Glorious and Immortal Memory': Commemoration and Protestant Identity in Ireland 1660–1800." *Proceedings of the Royal Irish Academy* 94, no. 2 (1994): 25–52.
Kenny, Kevin. *Ireland and the British Empire*. Oxford: Oxford University Press, 2004.
Kernan, Alvin. *Print Technology, Letters, and Samuel Johnson*. Princeton, NJ: Princeton University Press, 1987.
Kerrigan, John. *Archipelagic English: Literature, History, and Politics, 1603–1707*. Oxford: Oxford University Press, 2008.
Keymer, Thomas, and Peter Sabor. Pamela *in the Marketplace: Literary Controversy and Print Culture in Eighteenth-Century Britain and Ireland*. Cambridge: Cambridge University Press, 2015.
Kidd, Colin. "North Britishness and the Nature of Eighteenth-Century British Patriotisms." *History Journal* 39, no. 2 (1996): 361–82.
King, Rachael Scarborough. "The Manuscript Newsletter and the Rise of the Newspaper, 1655–1715." *Huntington Library Quarterly* 79, no. 3 (2016): 411–37.

Writing to the World: Letters and the Origins of Modern Print Genres. Baltimore: Johns Hopkins University Press, 2018.

The Kings Letter TO THE Earl of Feversham. London, 1688.

Knapp, Lewis M. "Ralph Griffiths, Author and Publisher, 1746–1750." *The Library*, 4th ser., 20, no. 2 (1939): 197–213.

Knight, Charles. "The Spectator's Generalizing Discourse." In *Telling People What to Think: Early Eighteenth Century Periodicals from* The Review *to* The Rambler, edited by J. A. Downie and Thomas N. Corns, 44–57. London: Routledge, 1993.

Kow, Simon. "Politics and Culture in Hume's History of England." In *A Companion to Enlightenment Historiography*, edited by Sophie Bourgault and Robert Sparling, 61–99. Leiden and Boston: Brill, 2013.

Lamont, Craig. *The Cultural Memory of Georgian Glasgow*. Edinburgh: Edinburgh University Press, 2021.

Landsberg, Alison. *Prosthetic Memory: The Transformation of American Remembrance in the Age of Mass Culture*. New York: Columbia University Press, 2004.

Latour, Bruno, *Reassembling the Social: An Introduction to Actor-Network Theory*. New York: Oxford University Press, 2005.

Lenman, Bruce. *The Jacobite Risings in Britain: 1689–1746*. London: Eyre Methuen, 1980.

Levack, Bruce. *The Formation of the British State: England, Scotland, and the Union, 1603–1707*. Oxford: Clarendon Press, 1987.

Levy, Michelle. *Literary Manuscript Culture in Romantic Britain*. Edinburgh: Edinburgh University Press, 2020.

The Life, Adventures, and Many and Great Vicissitudes of Fortune of SIMON, Lord LOVAT. London, 1746.

The Life of Arthur Lord Balmerino, from the Time of His Birth to That of His Execution on Tower-Hill. London, 1746.

Lloyd, David. *Anomalous States: Irish Writing and the Post-colonial Moment*. Durham, NC: Duke University Press, 1993.

Locke, John. *An Essay Concerning Human Understanding*. London, 1695.

Lord, Evelyn. *The Stuarts' Secret Army: The Hidden History of the English Jacobites*. Abingdon and New York: Routledge, 2014.

Lucas, Stephen E. "The Rhetorical Ancestry of the Declaration of Independence." *Rhetoric & Public Affairs* 1, no. 2 (1998): 143–84.

Lupton, Christina. *Knowing Books: The Consciousness of Mediation in Eighteenth-Century Britain*. Philadelphia: University of Pennsylvania Press, 2011.

Luttrell, Narcissus. *A Brief Historical Relation of State Affairs from September 1678 to April 1714*. 6 vols. Oxford: Oxford University Press, 1857.

Macaulay, Thomas Babington. *History of England from the Accession of James the Second*. 5 vols., vol. 5 edited by Lady Hannah Trevelyan. London: Longman, Brown, Green, Longmans, 1848–61.

MacEachren, Alan M. *How Maps Work: Representation, Visualization, and Design*. New York and London: Guilford Press, 1995.

MacFarlane, Alasdair Cameron. "'A Dream of Darien': Scottish Empire and the Evolution of Early Modern Travel Writing." PhD diss., Durham University, 2018.
MacGillivray, Royce. *Restoration Historians and the English Civil War*. The Hague: Martinus Nijhoff, 1974.
Mackenzie, George. *Lives and Characters of the Most Eminent Writers of the Scots Nation*. Vol. 1. Edinburgh, 1708.
MacKenzie, John. *A Narrative of the Siege of Londonderry*. London, 1690.
Dr. Walker's Invisible Champion Foyl'd. London, 1690.
MacQueen, Jack. "From Rome to Ruddiman: The Scoto-Latin Tradition." In *The Edinburgh History of Scottish Literature*, vol. 1, *From Columba to the Union (until 1707)*, edited by Thomas Owen Clancy and Murray Pittock, 184–208. Edinburgh: Edinburgh University Press, 2006.
MacQueen, John, and Winifred MacQueen, eds. and trans. *Archibald Pitcairne: The Latin Poems*. Assen and Tempe: Royal Van Gorcum and Arizona Center for Medieval and Renaissance Studies, 2009.
The Manifestation of Joy, or, the Loyal Subjects Grateful Acknowledgment. Occasionally Written upon the Publication of His Majesties Most Gracious Declaration, Allowing LIBERTY of CONSCIENCE. 1687. English Broadside Ballad Archive, http://ebba.english.ucsb.edu.
Mann, Alastair J. *The Scottish Book Trade, 1500–1720: Print Commerce and Print Control in Early Modern Scotland; An Historiographical Survey of the Early Modern Book in Scotland*. East Linton: Tuckwell Press, 2000.
Marchant, John. *The History of the Present Rebellion: Collected from Authentick Memoirs, Letters and Intelligences*. London, 1746.
Maxwell, Richard. *The Historical Novel in Europe, 1650–1950*. Cambridge: Cambridge University Press, 2009.
McCormick, Ted. *William Petty and the Ambitions of the Political Arithmetic*. Oxford: Oxford University Press, 2009.
McCracken-Flesher, Carolyn. *Possible Scotlands: Walter Scott and the Story of Tomorrow*. Oxford: Oxford University Press, 2005.
McDowell, Paula. *The Invention of the Oral: Print Commerce and Fugitive Voices in Eighteenth-Century Britain*. Chicago: University of Chicago Press, 2017.
———. "'The Manufacture and Lingua-Facture of Ballad-Making': Broadside Ballads in Long Eighteenth-Century Ballad Discourse." *The Eighteenth Century* 47, nos. 2–3 (2006): 151–71.
McGrath, C. I. "Mitchelburne [Michelborne], John (1648–1721), Army Officer and Military Governor." *Oxford Dictionary of National Biography*, September 23, 2004, https://doi.org/10.1093/ref:odnb/18652.
McIntosh, Carey. *The Evolution of English Prose, 1700–1800*. Cambridge: Cambridge University Press, 2009.
McKenzie, Andrea. "Martyrs in Low Life? Dying 'Game' in Augustan England." *Journal of British Studies* 42, no. 2 (2003): 167–205.
McKenzie, D. F. *Bibliography and the Sociology of Texts*. Cambridge: Cambridge University Press, 1999.

McKitterick, David. *Print, Manuscript and the Search for Order, 1450–1830.* Cambridge: Cambridge University Press, 2005.
McLynn, Frank. *The Jacobites.* London: Routledge and Kegan Paul, 1988.
McNeil, Kenneth. *Scottish Romanticism and Collective Memory in the British Atlantic.* Edinburgh: Edinburgh University Press, 2021.
Memoirs of the Life of Lord Lovat. London, 1746.
Mendle, Michael. "Preserving the Ephemeral: Reading, Collecting, and the Pamphlet Culture of Seventeenth-Century England." In *Books and Readers in Early Modern England: Material Studies,* edited by Jennifer Andersen and Elizabeth Sauer, 201–16. Philadelphia: University of Pennsylvania Press, 2001.
Millgate, Jane. *Walter Scott: The Making of the Novelist.* Toronto: University of Toronto Press, 1984.
Mitchelburne, John. *Ireland Preserv'd: or the Siege of London-Derry.* London, 1705.
Monod, Paul. *Jacobitism and the English People: 1688–1788.* Cambridge: Cambridge University Press, 1989.
Montague, William Henry. *A New and Universal History of England, from the Earliest Authentic Accounts, to the Present Time.* London: J. Cooke, 1771.
More Newes from Ireland, or, the Bloody Practic[e]s and Proceedings of the Papists in That Kingdome at This Present. London, 1641.
Morley, Vincent. *The Popular Mind in Eighteenth-Century Ireland.* Cork: Cork University Press, 2017.
Morrill, John. "Thinking about the New British History." In *British Political Thought in History, Literature and Theory, 1500–1800,* edited by David Armitage, 23–46. Cambridge: Cambridge University Press, 2006.
Mr. John Mackenzyes Narrative of the Siege of London-Derry a False Libel. London, 1690.
Multigraph Collective. *Interacting with Print: Elements of Reading in the Era of Print Saturation.* Chicago: University of Chicago Press, 2018.
Nairn, Tom. *The Break-Up of Britain: Crisis and Neonationalism.* London: NLB and Verso Editions, 1981.
Nelson, Carolyn, Matthew Seccombe and Maureen Bell. "The Creation of the Periodical Press 1620–1695." In *The Cambridge History of the Book in Britain,* vol. 4, *1557–1695,* edited by John Barnard and D. F. McKenzie, 533–50. Cambridge: Cambridge University Press, 2002.
Nenadic, Stana. "Print Collecting and Popular Culture in Eighteenth-Century Scotland." *History* 82, no. 266 (1997): 203–22.
Neufeld, Matthew. *The Civil Wars after 1660: Public Remembering in Late Stuart England.* Woodbridge: Boydell Press, 2013.
Newbery, John. *A New History of England; From the Invasion of Julius Cæsar to the End of George the IId.* London, 1781.
Newdigate, Richard. *An Alphabetical List of the Knights and Commissioners of Shires, Citizens and Burgesses.* London, 1711.
The Case of an Old Gentleman, Persecuted by His Own Son. London, 1707.

Nicholson, Eirwen E. C. "Consumers and Spectators: The Public of the Political Print in Eighteenth-Century England." *History* 81, no. 261 (1996): 5–21.
Nikulin, Dmitri. *Memory: A History*. Oxford: Oxford University Press, 2015.
Nora, Pierre. "Between Memory and History: *les lieux de mémoire*." *Representations* 26 (1989): 7–25.
Nora, Pierre, and Lawrence D. Kritzman, eds. *Realms of Memory: Rethinking the French Past*. Translated by Arthur Goldhammer. New York: Columbia University Press, 1996.
O' Ciardha, Éamonn. *Ireland and the Jacobite Cause, 1685–1766: A Fatal Attachment*. Dublin: Four Courts Press, 2002.
O'Brien, Karen. "History and the Novel in Eighteenth-Century Britain." *Huntington Library Quarterly* 68, no. 1–2 (2005): 397–413.
O'Quinn, Daniel. *Entertaining Crisis in the Atlantic Imperium, 1770–1790*. Philadelphia: University of Pennsylvania Press, 2011.
Ohlmeyer, Jane. *Ireland from Independence to Occupation, 1641–1660*. Cambridge: Cambridge University Press, 1995.
Oldmixon, John. *The British Empire in America*. 2 vols. London, 1708.
Orr, Julie. *Scotland, Darien and the Atlantic World, 1698–1700*. Edinburgh: Edinburgh University Press, 2018.
Patten, Robert. *The History of the Late Rebellion*. London: Printed for J. Baker and T. Warner, 1717.
The History of the Late Rebellion. 3rd and 4th eds. London, 1717.
The History of the Rebellion in the Year 1715. London, 1745.
Paul, Helen Julia. "Risks and Overseas Trade: The Way in Which Risks Were Perceived and Managed in the Early Modern Period." Working Papers 7017. Economic History Society, 2007.
Peacey, Jason. *Print and Public Politics in the English Revolution*. Cambridge: Cambridge University Press, 2013.
Pennecuik, Alexander. *Caledonia Triumphans: A Panegyrick to the King*. Edinburgh, 1699.
Percy, Thomas. *Reliques of Ancient English Poetry*. 3 vols. London, 1765.
Perkins, Pam. "The 'Candour, Which Can Feel for a Foe': Romanticizing the Jacobites in the Mid-Eighteenth Century." *Lumen: Selected Proceedings from the Canadian Society for Eighteenth-Century Studies* 31 (2012): 131–43.
The Petition of William Sancroft, Archbishop of Canterbury and Six Other Bishops. London, 1688.
The Petition of the LORDS Spiritual and Temporal for the Calling of a Free Parliament Together, with His Majesty's Gracious Answer to Their Lordships. London, 1688.
Pettegree, Andrew. *The Invention of News: How the World Came to Know about Itself*. New Haven, CT: Yale University Press, 2014.
Phillips, Mark Salber. *Society and Sentiment: Genres of Historical Writing in Britain, 1740–1820*. Princeton, NJ: Princeton University Press, 2000.
Philo-Caledon. *A Defence of the Scots Settlement at Darien with an Answer to the Spanish Memorial against It*. 1699.

Pincus, Steven. *1688: The First Modern Revolution*. New Haven, CT: Yale University Press, 2009.
Pinkerton, John. *The Medallic History of England to the Revolution, with Forty Plates*. London, 1790.
Pinkham, Lucile. *William III and the Respectable Revolution: The Part Played by William of Orange in the Revolution of 1688*. Cambridge, MA: Harvard University Press, 1969.
Pittock, Murray. "Charles Edward Stuart." *Études écossaises*, no. 10 (2005): 57–71.
Culloden (Cùil Lodair). Oxford: Oxford University Press, 2016.
Material Culture and Sedition, 1688-1760: Treacherous Objects, Secret Places. Houndmills: Palgrave Macmillan, 2013.
The Myth of the Jacobite Clans: The Jacobite Army in 1745. 2nd ed. Edinburgh: Edinburgh University Press, 2009.
Poetry and Jacobite Politics in Eighteenth-Century Britain and Ireland. Cambridge: Cambridge University Press, 1994.
Plank, Geoffrey. *Rebellion and Savagery: The Jacobite Rising of 1745 and the British Empire*. Philadelphia: University of Pennsylvania Press, 2006.
Pollard, Mary. *Dublin's Trade in Books, 1550–1800*. Oxford: Oxford University Press, 1989.
Poole, Thomas. *Reason of State: Law, Prerogative, Empire*. Cambridge: Cambridge University Press, 2015.
Postman, Neil. *Amusing Ourselves to Death: Public Discourse in the Age of Show Business*. London: Penguin, 2005.
Powell, Manushag. "Afterword: We Other Periodicalists, or, Why Periodical Studies?" *Tulsa Studies in Women's Literature* 30, no. 2 (2011): 441–50.
The Prince of Orange His Declaration Shewing the Reasons Why He Invades England: With a Short Preface, and Some Modest Remarks on It. London, 1688.
Private Occurrences, OR, the Transactions of the Four Last Years. London, 1688. English Broadside Ballad Archive, http://ebba.english.ucsb.edu.
Proposals for a Fond to Cary [sic] on a Plantation. Edinburgh, 1695.
Rae, Peter. *The History of the Late Rebellion; Rais'd against His Majesty King George, by the Friends of the Popish Pretender*. Dumfries, 1718.
The History of the Rebellion, Rais'd against His Majesty King George I. London, 1746.
Ramsay, Allan. *The Ever Green, Being a Collection of Scots Poems, Wrote by the Ingenious before 1600*. Edinburgh, 1724.
The Tea-Table Miscellany. Edinburgh, 1724.
Rapin de Thoyras, Paul de. *The History of England. Written in French by Mr. De Rapin Thoyras. Done into English*. Edited by Nicolas Tindal. London, 1725.
Ray, James. *A Compleat History of the Rebellion, from Its first Rise in 1745, to Its Total Suppression, at the Glorious Battle of Culloden, in April, 1746*. Manchester, 1747.
Raymond, Joad. *The Invention of the Newspaper: English Newsbooks, 1641–1649*. Oxford: Clarendon Press, 1996.

"The Newspaper, Public Opinion, and the Public Sphere in the Seventeenth Century." *Prose Studies* 21, no. 2 (1998): 109–40.

Pamphlets and Pamphleteering in Early Modern Britain. Cambridge: Cambridge University Press, 2003.

Raymond, Joad, ed. *News Networks in Seventeenth Century-Britain and Europe*. New York: Routledge, 2006.

R.B. *The History of the Kingdom of Ireland*. London: Nathaniel Crouch, 1693.

"RBS Heritage Hub: Company of Scotland Trading to Africa and the Indies," www.rbs.com/heritage/companies/company-of-scotland-trading-to-africa-and-the-indies.htm. Accessed July 16, 2019.

Reasons Why the Church of England, as Well as Dissenters Should Make Their Address of Thanks to the King's Majesty. London, 1687.

Reflections on a Paper Pretending to Be an Apology for the Failures Charged on Mr. Walker's Account of the Siege of Londonderry. London, 1689.

Reid, Steven J., and David McOmish. *Neo-Latin Literature and Literary Culture in Early Modern Scotland*. Leiden and Boston: Brill, 2017.

Reiman, Donald. *The Study of Modern Manuscripts: Public, Confidential and Private*. Baltimore: Johns Hopkins University Press, 1993. 39

Remarks upon the Scotch Act, in a Letter to a Friend. London, 1695.

Renan, Ernst. "What Is a Nation?" Translated by Martin Thom. In *Nation and Narration*, edited by Homi K. Bhabha, 8–22. London: Routledge, 1990.

Ricœur, Paul. *Memory, History, Forgetting*. Chicago: University of Chicago Press, 2004.

Rider, William. *A New History of England, from the Descent of the Romans, to the Demise of His Late Majesty, George II*. 50 vols. London, 1761–64.

Riding, Jaqueline. *Jacobites: A New History of the '45 Rebellion*. London: Bloomsbury, 2016.

Ridpath, George. *An Enquiry into the Causes of the Miscarriage of the Scots Colony at Darien*. Glasgow, 1700.

Rigney, Ann. *The Afterlives of Walter Scott: Memory on the Move*. Oxford: Oxford University Press, 2012.

"Plenitude, Scarcity and the Circulation of Cultural Memory." *Journal of European Studies* 35, no. 1 (2005): 11–28.

"Portable Monuments: Literature, Cultural Memory, and the Case of Jeanie Deans." *Poetics Today* 25, no. 2 (2004): 361–96.

Robertson, John. "Hume, David (1711–1776), Philosopher and Historian." *Oxford Dictionary of National Biography*, September 23, 2004, https://doi.org/10.1093/ref:odnb/14141.

Rothberg, Michael. "Introduction: Between Memory and Memory: From Lieux de Mémoire to Noeuds de Mémoire." *Yale French Studies*, nos. 118–19 (2010): 3–12.

Multidirectional Memory: Remembering the Holocaust in the Age of Decolonisation. Stanford, CA: Stanford University Press, 2009.

"The Royal Bank of Scotland Group Plc." In *International Directory of Company Histories*, edited by Jay P. Pederson, vol. 38, 392–99. Farmington Hills, MI: St. James Press, 2001.

R.P. *A Loyal Paper of Verses upon His Majesties Gracious Declaration*. London, 1687.
Sandrock, Kirsten. *Scottish Colonial Literature: Writing the Atlantic, 1603–1707*. Edinburgh: University of Edinburgh Press, 2021.
Sankey, Margaret. *Jacobite Prisoners of the 1715 Rebellion: Preventing and Punishing Insurrection in Early Hanoverian Britain*. Burlington, VT: Ashgate, 2005.
Schneider, Gary. *The Culture of Epistolarity: Vernacular Letters and Letter Writing in Early Modern England, 1500–1700*. Newark: University of Delaware Press, 2005.
Schwoerer, Lois G. *The Declaration of Rights, 1689*. Baltimore: Johns Hopkins University Press, 1981.
  "The Glorious Revolution as Spectacle: A New Perspective." In *England's Rise to Greatness, 1660–1763*, edited by Stephen Baxter, 109–50. Berkeley: University of California Press, 1983.
  "Liberty of the Press and Public Opinion, 1660–1695." In *Liberty Secured? Britain before and after 1688*, edited by J. R. Jones, 199–230. Stanford, CA: Stanford University Press, 1992.
  "Propaganda in the Revolution of 1688–89." *American Historical Review* 82, no. 4 (1977): 843–74.
Scott, Walter. *Minstrelsy of the Scottish Border*. 2 vols. Kelso: James Ballantyne, 1802. 3 vols. Edinburgh: James Ballantyne, 1803.
  Waverley. Edited by Susan Kubica Howard. Peterborough: Broadview, 2010.
Seasonable Considerations on the Present War in Scotland. London, 1746.
Seton, Bruce Gordon, and Jean Gordon Arnot. *The Prisoners of the '45*. Edinburgh: Printed by T. and A. Constable for the Scottish History Society, 1928.
Shapiro, Barbara. *Political Communication and Political Culture in England, 1558–1688*. Stanford, CA: Stanford University Press, 2012.
Sharpe, Kevin. *Rebranding Rule: The Restoration and Revolution Monarchy, 1660–1714*. New Haven, CT: Yale University Press, 2013.
Sher, Richard B. *The Enlightenment and the Book: Scottish Authors and Their Publishers in Eighteenth-Century Britain, Ireland, and America*. Chicago: University of Chicago Press, 2007.
Shields, Juliet. *Sentimental Literature and Anglo-Scottish Identity, 1745–1820*. Cambridge: Cambridge University Press, 2010.
Siskin, Clifford. *The Work of Writing: Literature and Social Change in Britain, 1700–1830*. Baltimore: Johns Hopkins University Press, 1998.
Siskin, Clifford, and William Warner. "This Is Enlightenment: An Invitation in the Form of an Argument." In *This Is Enlightenment*, edited by Clifford Siskin and William Warner, 1–34. Chicago and London: University of Chicago Press, 2010.
Slowey, Desmond. *The Radicalization of Irish Drama 1600–1900*. Dublin: Irish Academic Press, 2008.
Smollett, Tobias. *A Complete History of England, Deduced from the Descent of Julius Cæsar, to the Treaty of Aix La Chapelle, 1748*. 4 vols. London, 1757–58.

Continuation of the Complete History of England. 5 vols. London: Printed for Richard Baldwin, 1760–65.
Plan of a Complete History of England. London, 1757.
The Tears of Scotland. Edinburgh, 1746.
Smyth, Jim. *The Making of the United Kingdom, 1660–1800: State, Religion and Identity in Britain and Ireland.* Harlow and New York: Longman, 2001.
Smyth, William J. *Map-Making, Landscapes and Memory: A Geography of Colonial and Early Modern Ireland, c. 1530–1750.* Cork: Cork University Press, 2006.
Snyder, Henry L. "The Circulation of Newspapers in the Reign of Queen Anne." *The Library*, 5th ser., 23, no. 3 (1968): 206–35.
Some Considerations upon the Late Act of the Parliament of Scotland, for Constituting an Indian Company in a Letter to a Friend. London, 1695,
Some Matters of Fact, in Vindication of the King's Evidence from the Falsities, Calumnies, Equivocations, and Misrepresentations Set Forth in Mr. Gascoigne's Paper. London: J. Baker, 1716.
Some Reflections upon His Highness the Prince of Oranges Declaration. London, 1688.
Sommerville, C. John. *The News Revolution in England: Cultural Dynamics of Daily Information.* Oxford: Oxford University Press, 1996.
Sowerby, Scott. *Making Toleration: The Repealers and the Glorious Revolution.* Cambridge, MA: Harvard University Press, 2013.
The Speeches of the Six Condemn'd L[ords] at Their Tryals in Westminster-Hall. London, 1716?
State of the Papist and Protestant Proprieties in the Kingdom of Ireland in the Year 1641. London, 1689.
Steele, Richard. *The British Subject's Answer, to the Pretender's Declaration.* London, 1716.
 The Crisis, or, a Discourse Representing, from the Most Authentick Records, the Just Causes of the Late Happy Revolution. London, 1714.
 The Town Talk, the Fish Pool, the Plebian, the Old Whig, the Spinster, &c. London, 1790.
Stephens, Frederic George, ed. *Catalogue of Prints and Drawings in the British Museum: Division 1. Political and Personal Satires.* Vol. 1. London: Printed by order of the Trustees, 1870.
Story, George Warter. *A True and Impartial History of the Most Material Occurrences in the Kingdom of Ireland during the Two Last Years.* London, 1691.
Stroh, Silke. *Gaelic Scotland in the Colonial Imagination: Anglophone Writing from 1600 to 1900.* Evanston, IL: Northwestern University Press, 2017.
Suarez S. J., Michael F., and Michael Turner, eds. *The Cambridge History of the Book in Britain*, vol. 5, *1695–1830*. Cambridge: Cambridge University Press, 2010.
The Sun-Fire Office. *The Historical Register: Containing an Impartial Relation of All Transactions, Foreign and Domestick.* London, 1717.
Sutherland, James. *The Restoration Newspaper and Its Development.* Cambridge: Cambridge University Press, 1986.

Szechi, Daniel. *1715: The Great Jacobite Rebellion*. New Haven, CT: Yale University Press, 2006.
"The Jacobite Theatre of Death." In *The Jacobite Challenge*, edited by Eveline Cruickshanks and Jeremy Black, 57–74. Edinburgh: John Donald, 1988.
Temple, John. *The Irish Rebellion: or, an History of the Beginnings and First Progresse of the Generall Rebellion Raised within the Kingdom of Ireland*. London, 1646.
Terdiman, Richard. *Present Past: Modernity and the Memory Crisis*. Ithaca, NY, and London: Cornell University Press, 1993.
Towsey, Mark. *Reading History in Britain and America, c.1750–c.1840*. Cambridge: Cambridge University Press, 2019.
Trevelyan, George Macauley. *The English Revolution, 1688–1689*. London: T. Butterworth, 1938.
The Trials of William Earl of Kilmarnock, George Earl of Cromartie, and Arthur Lord Balmerino, for High Treason, before the House of Peers, at Westminster Hall, on the 28th and 30th of July, and the First of August, 1746. 3rd ed. London, 1746.
True Member of the Church of England. *The Dutch Design Anatomized*. London, 1688.
The Tryals of William, Earl of Kilmarnock, George, Earl of Cromertie [sic], and Arthur Lord Balmerino, for High Treason. London, 1746.
Twyman, Michael. "Printed Ephemera." In *The Cambridge History of the Book in Britain*, vol. 5, *1695–1830*, edited by Michael F. Suarez, S. J. and Michael Turner, 66–82. Cambridge: Cambridge University Press, 2010.
"UK Memory of the World," https://www.unesco.org.uk/portfolio/memory-of-the-world/. Accessed July 16, 2019.
The Union-Proverb. London, 1708.
Unesco in Scotland. London: UK National Commission for Unesco, 2016.
Verax, Philanax (Roderick MacKenzie). *A Letter from a Member of the Parliament of Scotland to His Friend in London*. London, 1695.
Wafer, Lionel. *A New Voyage and Description of the Isthmus of America*. London, 1699.
Walker, George. *A True Account of the Siege of London-Derry*. London, 1689.
A Vindication of the True Account of the Siege of Derry. London, 1689.
Walker, R. B. "The Newspaper Press in the Reign of William III." *The Historical Journal* 17, no. 4 (2013): 691–709.
The Wanderer, or Surprizing Escape. London, 1747.
Ward, James. *Memory and Enlightenment: Cultural Afterlives of the Long Eighteenth Century*. Houndmills: Palgrave Macmillan, 2018.
Warner, William. *Licensing Entertainment: The Elevation of Novel Reading in Britain, 1684–1750*. Berkeley: University of California Press, 1998.
Protocols of Liberty: Communication Innovation and the American Revolution. Chicago: University of Chicago Press, 2013.
Watson, James. *A Choice Collection of Comic and Serious Scots Poems Both Ancient and Modern*. Edinburgh, 1706–1711.

Watt, Douglas. *The Price of Scotland: Darien, Union and the Wealth of Nations*. Edinburgh: Luath Press, 2007.
Weber, Harold. *Memory, Print, and Gender in England, 1653–1759*. Houndmills: Palgrave Macmillan, 2008.
Whatley, Christopher. *The Scots and the Union: Then and Now*. Edinburgh: Edinburgh University Press, 2014.
Whitehall, April 26, 1746: This Afternoon a Messenger Arrived from the Duke of Cumberland, with the Following Particulars of the Victory Obtained by His Royal Highness over the Rebels, on Wednesday the 16th Instant Near Culloden. London, 1746.
Whitehead, Anne. *Memory*. The New Critical Idiom. London and New York: Routledge, 2008.
Whitelocke, Bulstrode. "The Publisher to the Reader." In *Memorials of the English Affairs*. London, 1682.
Whyte, Lawrence. *Poems on Various Subjects, Serious and Diverting*. Dublin, 1740.
Wilkinson, W. *A Compleat History of the Trials of the Rebel Lords in Westminster-Hall*. London, 1746.
Williams, Abigail. *Poetry and the Creation of a Whig Literary Culture, 1681–1714*. Oxford: Oxford University Press, 2005.
Williams, Raymond. *Keywords: A Vocabulary of Culture and Society*. Rev. ed. New York: Oxford University Press, 1985.
Wilson, Kathleen. *The Island Race: Englishness, Empire, and Gender in the Eighteenth Century*. London and New York: Routledge, 2006.
Wilson, Samuel. *Christ the Great Propitiation. A Sermon Preached at the Evening Lecture in Silver-Street, September 14, 1746*. London, 1746.
Woolf, Daniel. "News, History and the Construction of the Present in Early Modern England." In *The Politics of Information in Early Modern Europe*, edited by Brendan Dooley and Sabrina Baron, 80–118. London and New York: Routledge, 2001.
Yadav, Alok. "Nationalism and Eighteenth-Century British Literature." *Literature Compass* 1, no. 1 (2005): 1–14.
Young Juba: or, the History of the Young Chevalier, from His Birth, to His Escape from Scotland, after the Battle of Culloden. London, 1748.
Zaret, David. *Origins of Democratic Culture: Printing, Petitions and the Public Sphere in Early Modern England*. Princeton, NJ: Princeton University Press, 2000.
Zboray, Ronald J., and Mary Saracino Zboray. "Print Culture." In *The Handbook of Communication History*, edited by Peter Simonson, Janice Peck, Robert T. Craig and John P. Jackson, Jr., 181–95. New York: Routledge, 2013.
Zook, Melinda. *Radical Whigs and Conspiratorial Politics in Late Stuart England*. University Park: Pennsylvania State University Press, 1999.

Index

A Collection of State Tracts, Publish'd on Occasion of the Late Revolution in 1688 and Princely Excellency: or, Regal Glory, 65–66

A Compleat and Authentick History of the Rise, Progress and Extinction of the Late Rebellion, 204–5, 241–42, 244

A Compleat Collection of Papers in Twelve Parts Relating to the Great Revolutions in England and Scotland (*Publick Papers*), 23–24, 64–65, 186–92

A Compleat History of the Rebellion, from Its First Rise in 1745, to Its Total Suppression, at the Glorious Battle of Culloden, in April, 1746 (Ray), 245–46, 261–62

A Compleat History of the Trials of the Rebel Lords in Westminster-Hall; and the Rebel Officers and Others Concerned in the Rebellion in the Year 1745, 226–27, 261–62

A Declaration of James Duke of Monmouth, 37–38

A Defence of the Scots Abdicating Darien (Herries), 139–40

"A Dissertation on Italian and Irish Music, With Some Panegyrick on Carralan Our Late Irish Orpheus" (Whyte), 107

A Full and Authentic History of the Rebellion MDCCXLV and MDCCXLVI, 242–43

A Full and Exact Collection of All the Considerable Addresses, Memorials, Petitions, Answers, Proclamations, Declarations, Letters and Other Publick Papers, Relating to the Company of Scotland Trading to Africa and the Indies, 142–43

A Full and True Account of the Inhumane and Bloudy Cruelties of the Papists to the Poor Protestants in Ireland in the Year 1641 (Digby), 95–96

A Full Description of These Times; or the Prince of ORANGE's March from EXETER to LONDON (ballad), 52–53

A Genuine Account of the Behaviour, Confession, and Dying Words, of Francis Townly [sic], (Nominal) *Colonel of the Manchester Regiment, Thomas Deacon, James Dawson, John Barwick, George Fletcher and Andrew Blood, Captains in the Manchester Regiment*, 215–17

A Genuine Narrative of the Life, Behaviour, and Conduct of Simon, Lord Fraser, of Lovat, 223–24

A Journey through Part of England and Scotland. Along with the Army under the Command of His Royal Highness the Duke of Cumberland, 8–9

A Large Map of Ireland, in One Sheet (Morden), 76–77, 85–86

A Letter from a Gentleman in Exeter to His Friend in London, 52–53

A Letter from a Gentleman in the Country to His Friend in Edinburgh, 119–20

A Letter from a Member of the Parliament of Scotland to His Friend in London, 116–17

A Letter from the Commission, of the General Assembly, of the Church of Scotland; to the Honourable Council and Inhabitants of the Scots Colony of Caledonia in America, 127

A Letter, Giving a Description of the Isthmus of Darian, 128–31, 133–34

A Letter Writ by Mijn Heer Fagel, Pensioner of Holland to Mr. James Stewart, Advocate, Giving an Account of the Prince and Princess of Orange's Thoughts Concerning the Repeal of the Test and the Penal Laws, 45–46

A Loyal Paper of Verses upon His Majesties Gracious Declaration (pamphlet), 41

A Narrative of the Siege of Londonderry (Mackenzie), 92–94

A New and Exact Map of the Kingdom of Ireland, 77–78

A New and Universal History of England, from the Earliest Authentick Accounts, to the Present Time (Montague), 252

A New History of England, from the Descent of the Romans, to the Demise of His Late Majesty (Rider), 252
A New History of England; from the Invasion of Julius Caesar to the End of George the IId (Newbery), 252
A New Touch of the Times, OR, the Nat[i]ons Consent, for a Free Parliament (ballad), 52–53
A New Voyage and Description of the Isthmus of America, 132–33
A Pindarick Ode upon His Most Sacred Majestie's Late Gracious Indulgence (pamphlet), 40–43, 45–46
A Relation of the Bloody Massacre in Ireland Acted by the Instigation of the Jesuits, Priests, and Friars, 95–96
A Review of the Reflections on the Prince of Orange's Declaration (Burnet), 57
A Review of the Two Late Rebellions, Historical, Political and Moral, 198–99
A Short Account from, and Description of the Isthmus of Darien, Where the Scots Collony Are Settled, 133–34
A Short and Impartial View of the Manner and Occasion of the Scots Colony's Coming Away from Darien (Fletcher), 141
A Short View of the Methods Made Use of in Ireland for the Subversion and Destruction of the Protestant Religion and Interest, 96–99
A Short View of the Late Troubles (Dugdale), 60–61
A Treatise of Human Nature (Hume), 12–14, 254
A True Account from Coll. Kirke of the Relieving of London-Derry, Brought by Mr. Beale, a Messenger, in an Express to the Court, 87–88
A True Account of the Siege of London-Derry (Walker), 89–92
Act for Encouraging of Forraigne Trade, 110–12
Acton, Anne, 217–18
Acts of Union (1707), 1–2
  Jacobite Risings and, 23–24
Addison, Joseph
  Free-Holder under, 23–24, 157–58, 176, 181–85
  on Jacobite Rising (1715), 165–85
addresses of loyalty, newspaper publications of, 158–70
advertisements
  in newspapers, 75–86
  news stories connected to, 172–75
  reward for capture of Charles Edward Stuart in, 204–5
Aeneas, and His Two Sons. A True Portrait, 201–2, 209–10

Aeneid (Virgil), *Irish Hudibras* and, 82–86
Afterlives of Walter Scott: Memory on the Move, The (Rigney), 261, 267–69
Alexis; or, the Young Adventurer. A Novel, 229–33, 244, 261–62
Alker, Sharon, 99–100
Always Already New: Media, History and the Data of Culture (Gitelman), 17–18
Amusing Ourselves to Death: Public Discourse in the Age of Show Business (Postman), 10–11
An Account of the Behaviour of the Late Earl of Kilmarnock, since his Sentence (Foster), 221–22
An Account of the Proceedings and Transactions That Have Happened in the Kingdom of England, 51–52, 61–62
An Act of Parliament for Encourageing the Scots Affrican and Indian Company, 112n.16
An Answer to a Paper, Intitled, Reflections on the Prince of Orange's Declaration, 57
An Apology for the Failures Charged on the Reverend Mr. George Walker's Account of the Late Siege of Derry, 92–94
An Authentick Narrative of the Whole Proceedings of Court at St. Margaret's Hill, Southwark, in the Months of June, July and August, 1746, 215–28
An Enquiry into the Causes of the Miscarriage of the Scots Colony at Darien (Ridpath), 140–47
An Epitome of Sr. William Petty's Large Survey of Ireland (Lea), 76–77
An Essay Concerning Human Understanding (Locke), 12
An Exact Account of the Affairs in Ireland, 87–88
An Express from the African and Indian Scots Company's Fleet, Landed in New EDINBURGH IN CALEDONIA, 126–27
An Honest Man's Wish for the Prince of Orange, 60
An Ode Made on the Welcome News of the Safe Arrival and Kind Reception of the Scottish Collony at Darien in America, 127
Anderson, Benedict, 11
Anglo-Dutch Wars (1652–74), 55–57
Anglophone tradition, Gaelic-Irish contact with, 107
Anne (Queen of England)
  ascension of, 98–99
  death of, 157–58
  Scotland and, 143
Aphorisms Relating to the Kingdom of Ireland Submitted to the Most Noble Assembly of Lords & Commons at the Great Convention at Westminster (Cox), 78–79
Archipelagic English (Kerrigan), 84–85

Argyll, Duke of. *See* Campbell, Archibald (Earl of Argyll)
Ascanius; or the Young Adventurer; a True History, 8–9, 229–30, 233–36, 238–40, 244–45, 261–62, 267
Assmann, Aleida, 2–3, 9–10, 15–16
Assmann, Jan
  on cultural memory, 1–2
  on national memory, 3–4
The Athenian Gazette (Dunton), 176
Atherton, Ian, 160
authority, oral and print media and, 21–22
Autobiography (Carleton), 105

Baker, Henry, 87–88, 99
Bal, Mieke, 15–16, 268–69
ballads
  anti-Catholic sentiments in, 69n.3
  bishops' *Petition* in, 44
  Declaration by William of Orange in, 17–18, 52–53
  historical accounts of, 28–31
  James II/VII's political agenda in, 41
  Revolution of 1688 in, 66
  Scott's collection and dissemination of, 264–67
"The Banishment of Poverty," 147
Bannet, Eve Tavor, 114
Barber, Alex, 168
Barnard, Tony, 94–95
Belsey, Catherine, 3–4, 197–98
Benedict, Barbara, 75–76
Berrington, Edward, 169
Bibliography and the Sociology of Texts (McKenzie), 76–77
Bill, Charles, 40
Bill of Rights, 60
Black, Fischer, 118–19
Bohun, Edmund, 47, 56–57, 62–64, 70
Book History Studies, 17–18
  sites of cultural memory and, 18–19
Bowie, Karin, 109–10, 138n.102, 142–43
Boyd, William (Earl of Kilmarnock), 214–15, 218–22
Boyer, Abel, 50–51, 59, 65–66, 160–61
Bradshaw, James, 226–27
Brewer, John, 19–21
Brexit referendum, 25–26
A Brief Character of Ireland with Some Observations of the Customs &c. of the Meaner Sort of the Natural Inhabitants of That Kingdom, 97–98
British Civil Wars (1639–53), 33–34, 36, 38–39, 54–55, 60–61
  periodical essays during, 176

The British Empire in America (Oldmixon), 150–51
British Mercury, 185–86
British Parliament, newsletter accounts of, 164
British Studies, cultural memory and, 19–21
Buckley, Samuel, 176
Burnet, Gilbert (Bishop), 4–5, 29–31, 48–49, 52–53, 57, 66
Burton, John Hill, 151–55
Bury, Lord, 5–6
By the King, a Declaration. As We Cannot Consider this Invasion of Our Kingdoms without Horror (James II/VII), 53–54
By the King. A Proclamation. To Restrain the Spreading of False News (James II/VII), 49–50
By the King, a Proclamation. Whereas the Prince of Orange and His Adherents (James II/VII), 50–52

Cadell, Thomas, 259–60
Caledonia Triumphans: A Panegyrick to the King, 127
Caledonian Mercury, 202
Campbell, Archibald (Earl of Argyll), 35–39
Campbell, Colin, 135–37
Campbell, John, 150–51
Campbell, Robert, 259–60
Carleton, William, 105
Carnell, Rachel, 233
Carpenter, Andrew, 29, 89n.42
Carroll, Clare, 86, 92–94
Carte, Thomas, 252–53
Catalogue of the Library at Abbotsford, 261–62
Catholics
  British displacement in Ireland of, 76–77
  British mockery of, 29
  in Ireland, 69–70
  in *Irish Hudibras*, 82–86
  Jacobite Rising (1715) and, 158–59
  James II/VII's support for, 70
  in "Lillibullero" (song), 82–86
  in Mitchelburne's *Ireland Preserv'd*, 102, 105
  in siege of Derry, 92–94
  Walker's vilification of, 88
  War of Two Kings and polarization concerning, 97–98, 105–7
censorship
  under Charles II, 34–35
  of Jacobite Rising (1715) news coverage, 169
  under James II/VII, 35–36, 45–47
  lapse in Britain of, 109–10
  of print media, 33–34
  under William III/II, 73–77

Charles I (King of England, Ireland and Scotland), 48
Charles II (King of England, Ireland and Scotland)
   court spectatorship and performativity under, 34–35
   official documents of, 32n.17
'The Cherry and the Slae" (Montgomerie), 147
"Chevalier" narratives of Jacobite Rising (1745), 227–40, 247–48
Chiesley, Robert, 112–13
Choice Collection of Comic and Serious Scots Poems Both Ancient and Modern (Watson), 147
"Christ's Kirk on the Green" (James V?), 147
"Circular Letter read in the Churches, for animating the People to take Arms in Defence of his Majesty and the Constitution," 189–90
clans, challenge to monarchy from, 36–37
Clark, Joseph, 92–94
Claydon, Tony, 35, 166–67
coffee-house culture, print media and role of, 7–8
Coley, W. B., 204–5
Colley, Linda, 108–10
Collier, Jeremy, 62–64
colonialism and colonies
   cultural memory of, 108–10
   desertion and troubles in Darien, letters about, 134–38
   English presence in Ireland as, 99–107
   letters between directors and colonists in Darien, 122–26
   maps of Ireland as tools for, 85–86
   news sources and letter pamphlets and, 126–34
   War of Two Kings and legacy of, 97–98 *see also* specific colonies
Company of Scotland Trading to Africa and the Indies
   abandonment of Darien colony and, 137–38
   Articles of Union and, 146
   colonists' letters to directors of, 122–26
   communication leaks in letters to, 134
   compensation for directors and shareholders of, 149
   criticism of, 138–43
   cultural memory in letters of, 141–43
   Darien colony proposal and, 110–12
   digital preservation of letters from, 108–10
   foreign investment in, 120–22
   global commerce network and, 112–13
   letter pamphlets promoting Darien by, 114–18, 126–34
   letters of, 23, 110–20
   official public documents of, 141–43
   rediscovery of papers of, 151–56
   Scottish defense of, 138–43
   subscriptions to, 118–19
   William III/II's opposition to, 120–22, 142–43
consciousness of mediation, emergence of, 10–11
consumption of news, eighteenth-century concerns over, 205–6
Continuation of the Complete History of England (Smollett), 259–60
"Continuation, to the present Time" (Lloyd), 259–60
Cooke, Charles, 259–60
counter-memories
   Gaelic Catholic counter-memory in oral culture, 106
   in historical accounts, 261
   historical accounts and creation of, 189–90
   national identity and, 20–21
Court of Star Chamber, 34–35
Covenanters, 36–37
Cox, Richard, 22–23, 78–82
Cranfield, Geoffrey, 204–5
Crawford, George, 219–21
The Crisis, or, a Discourse Representing, from the Most Authentick Records, the Just Causes of the Late Happy Revolution (Steele), 65–66
Culloden, Battle of
   in cultural memory, 5–6, 200–1, 210–13
   in historical novels, 231–33
   printed works on, 24–25
   Smollett's description of, 258–59
cultural memory
   British imperialism and, 105–7
   of Darien colony, 138–43
   digital media and, 25–26
   historical accounts and creation of, 188–89, 198–99, 251–61
   in Ireland, 105
   Jacobite Rising (1715) and, 157–58
   Jacobite Rising (1745) and, 200–1, 247–48
   lieu de mémoire and, 2–3
   media shift of seventeenth to eighteenth centuries and, 1
   memory of culture and, 249–51
   periodical essays and, 165–85
   popular histories of Jacobite Rising (1745) and, 244
   print media and, 3–4, 9–10
   Revolution of 1688 in, 59–67
   in Scott's *Waverley*, 261–67
   sites of, 18–19
Cultural Memory and Western Civilization: Functions, Media, Archives (Assmann), 9–10, 15–16

Cultural Memory Studies, overview of, 15–21
cultural nationalism
　in Scottish pamphlets and poetry, 147–50
　Scottish Union and emergence of, 146–47
Cunningham, Bernadette, 106

The Daily Courant
　advertisements in, 172–75
　Jacobite Rising (1715), coverage in, 160–61, 167–71
　Spectator and, 176
Dalzell, Robert (Earl of Carnwath), 180–81, 190–92
Danziger, Kurt, 15–16
Darien colony
　abandonment of, 135–37
　books on, 150–51
　between Company of Scotland directors and colonists and, 122–26
　correspondence concerning, 23
　digital preservation of letters relating to, 108–10
　as economic and political disaster, 143
　English hostility linked to failure of, 138–43
　English writing on, 149–50
　erasure in cultural memory of, 148–50
　letter pamphlets from, 126–34
　proposals for, 110–12
　rediscovery of papers on, 151–56
　as Scottish colonial enterprise, 1–2
　Scottish Union of 1707 and, 143–51
　Spanish and French incursions in, 134–35
　William III/II's opposition to, 120–22, 134–35, 142–43
The Darien Papers: Being a Selection of Original Letters and Official Documents Relating to the Establishment of a Colony at Darien by the Company of Scotland Trading to Africa and the Indies, 151–56
Darnton, Robert, 18–19
Daybell, James, 124–25
Deacon, Thomas, 216–17
The Declaration and Apology of the Protestant People (Monmouth), 36–39, 48–49
The Declaration of Archibald Earl of Argyll, 36–39, 48–49
Declaration of His Highnes William Henry (William of Orange)
　Argyll and Monmouth declarations compared with, 36–39, 48–49
　in ballads, 17–18, 52–53
　Bohun's discussion of, 62–64
　in cultural memory, 59–67
　drafting of, 4–5, 48
　historical reproductions of, 64–66

Hume's discussion of, 255–56
James II/VII's opposition publications against, 53–59
James II/VII's suppression of, 50–52
　as official document, 21–22
　performances and public readings of, 51–52
　as political document, 47–53, 249–51
　popular culture references to, 17–18
　printing of, 6–7, 30–31
　Protestant fears addressed in, 71–72
Declaration of Rights, 60
　influences on, 6–7
Declaration of the Lords Spiritual and Temporal, 58
Defoe, Daniel, 149–50, 176
DeMaria, Robert Jr., 176
Derry, siege of (1689)
　conflicting accounts of, 92–94
　European context in Mitchelburne's *Ireland Preserv'd*, 104–5
　histories of, 22–23
　in Irish cultural memory, 105
　as media event, 86–99
　Mitchelburne's *Ireland Preserv'd* and, 99–107
　newspaper accounts of, 87–92
　pamphlet wars in narratives of, 92–94
　Protestant refugees from, 69–70
The Desertion Discuss'd (Collier), 62–64
"A Dialogue between a Loyal Addresser, and a Blunt Whiggish Clown," 46
Digby, Lettice (Lady), 95–96
digital media, cultural memory and, 25–26
Discipline and Punish (Foucault), 214
double authorship, archives of official papers and, 153–55
Down Survey (1656–58), 76–77
Dr. Walker's Invisible Champion Foyl'd (Mackenzie), 92–94
Drummond, Robert, 135–37
Drummond, William, 147
Dubh, Iain, 66
Dugdale, William, 60–61
Dumbarton, Earl of, 37–38
Dundee uprising, 75
Dunton, John, 176
duplicative powers, print media and, 9–10
The Dutch Design Anatomized (pamphlet), 55–57
Dyer, John, 161

East India Company, 113
Edinburgh Castle, Jacobite attack on, 175, 186–92
Edinburgh Evening Courant, 202
Edinburgh Gazette, 126–27
Eikon Basilike, 48
Eisenstein, Elizabeth, 9–10

Ellis, John, 58–59
Elphinstone, Arthur (Lord Balmerino), 214–15, 218–20, 222–23, 225–27
England
   power imbalance with Scotland of, 144–45
   see also Great Britain
The English Revolution, 1688–1689 (Trevelyan), 27–28
Episcopalian Church, Jacobite Rising (1715) and, 158–59
erasure of memory, national identity and, 20–21
Erll, Astrid
   on cultural memory, 25–26, 96, 198–99
   on *lieux de mémoire*, 3, 27–28
Essays, Moral and Political (Hume), 12–14, 254
Evelyn, John, 52–53
The Ever Green, Being a Collection of Scots Poems, Wrote by the Ingenious before 1600 (Ramsay), 148–49
Exclusion Crisis (1678–81), 33–34, 35n.27
executions
   of Jacobite Rising (1715), participants, 180–81, 190–92
   newspaper coverage of, 214
   of peers, 214–15
   sympathy for accused in accounts of, 218–28
The Expedition of His Highness the Prince of Orange for England (Burnet), 52–53

Fagel, Gaspar, 4–5, 45–46, 48–49
The Faithful Register of the Late Rebellion, 186–87, 193
Farewell, James, 22–23, 82–86
Fawkes, Guy, 52–53
Ferris, Ina, 153–55
Fielding, Henry, 204–6
Fletcher, Andrew, 141, 144–46
Fletcher, George, 217–18
Fletcher, James, 252
Floyd, George, 25–26
The Flying Post, 140–47, 159–61, 168–69
Fonvive, John, 160–61
Forbes, Robert, 210–12, 225–26, 230–31
Foster, James, 221–22
Foucault, Michel, 214–15
Fox, Adam, 47
Fraser, Simon (Lord Lovat), 214–15, 218–20, 223–25
The Free-Holder
   Addison as editor of, 23–24, 157–58, 176
   Jacobite Rising (1715), accounts in, 165–85
   launching of, 181–85
   Steele's comments on, 177
Fries, Udo, 75–76

Gaelic Jacobite poetic tradition, 106
Gascoigne, Richard, 193
General Advertiser, 218–20
George I (King of Great Britain and Ireland), 157–58, 182, 185
George II (King of Great Britain and Ireland), 5–6
Gibbon, Edward, 251–52
Gitelman, Lisa, 17–18, 31–33
"Glorious" Revolution. See Revolution of 1688 (England)
"Glorious" Revolution phenomenon, print media and creation of, 21–22
Goldie, Mark, 30–31
Gordon, Andrew, 124–25
Gordon, John, 193
Gordon, William (Viscount Kenmure), 180–81, 190–92
Graham, John (Viscount Dundee), 68–69
Great Britain
   newspaper proliferation in, 202–4
   Treaty of Union and formation of, 146
Great Northern War, 163–64
Greenblatt, Stephen, 137–38
Griffiths, Robert, 234–36, 238–40
Guthrie, Neil, 209–10
Guthrie, William, 252–53

Hague Gazette, 204–5
Hamilton, John (Lord Belhaven), 145–46
Hamilton, William, 124–25
Hanoverian monarchy
   ascendancy of, 5–6, 157–58
   counter-memory of Jacobite Rising (1745) and, 210–12
   in cultural memory, 24–25
   Jacobite opposition to, 158, 193–95, 203–4
   media legitimization of, 217
   support for, 8–9, 20–21, 173, 179–80, 182, 189–90
Harley, Robert, 149–50
Harris, Bob, 202–4
Harris, Tim, 70, 97–98
Haslett, Moyra, 107
Hay, John (Marquess of Tweeddale), 110–12
Hayton, David, 97–98
Henderson, Andrew, 234–35, 240–41, 244–45, 261–62
Herries, Walter, 139–40, 142–43
Hibernia Anglicana; or, the History of Ireland, from the Conquest Thereof to This Present Time (Cox), 22–23, 78–82, 85–86
Hills, Henry, 40, 59
His Majesties GRACIOUS DECLARATION to All His Loving Subjects for Liberty of Conscience (James II/VII, 1687)

bishops' opposition to oral delivery of, 43–45
Bohun's discussion of, 62–64
growing opposition to, 45–47
pamphlet versions of, 40–43
publication of, 39–40
republication of, 42–43
The Historian's Guide, or Britain's Remembrancer, 68–70
historical accounts
  counter-memories in, 261
  cultural memory and, 21–22, 25–26, 251–61
  Ireland as object of, 78–86
  of Jacobite Rising (1715), 185–99
  multi-volume histories, 25–26
  popular and commercial success of, 251–52
  popular histories of Jacobite Rising (1745), 240–47
  print media and rise of, 60–61
The Historical Novel in Europe (Maxwell), 229–30
historical novels
  cultural memory and, 25–26
  flight of Charles Edward Stuart in, 227–40
  political ideologies in, 233
  Scott's *Waverley*, 261–67
The Historical Register: Containing and Impartial Relation of All Transactions, Foreign and Domestic, 185–86
The History of Caledonia: or, the Scots Colony in Darian in the West Indies, 131–32
The History of England from the Accession of James the Second (Macaulay), 27–28
The History of England from the Revolution to the Death of George the Second (Smollett), 259–60
The History of England, from the Revolution to the End of the American War and Peace of Versailles in 1783 (1796–98) (Campbell), 259–60
The History of Great Britain (later *The History of England*) (Hume), 12–14, 254
History of His Own Time (Burnet), 29–30, 48
The History of King William III in Three Parts (Boyer), 65–66
The History of the Desertion (Bohun), 47, 62–64, 70
The History of the Kingdom of Ireland (R.B.), 96–99
The History of the Late Rebellion (Patten), 23–24, 186–87, 193–95
The History of the Late Rebellion; Rais'd against His Majesty King George, by the Friends of the Popish Pretender (Rae), 23–24, 195–97
The History of the Present Rebellion: Collected from Authentick Memoirs, Letters and Intelligences (Marchant), 204–8, 243–44

The History of the Rebellion, 1745 and 1746, Containing, a Full Account of Its Rise, Progress and Extinction (Henderson), 234–35, 240–41, 244–45, 261–62
History of the Rebellion in the Year 1745 (Home), 204–5, 246–47
The History of the Rebellion Rais'd against his Majesty King George I (Patten), 197–98
The History of the Rebellion Raised against His MAJESTY KING GEORGE II, 243
The History of the Rebellion Raised against His MAJESTY KING GEORGE II. From Its Rise in August 1745, to Its Happy Extinction, by the Glorious Victory at Culloden, on the 16th of April, 1746, 8–9, 241
History of the Union between England and Scotland (Dafoe), 149–50
The History of the Wars in Ireland, 96–99
Hodges, James, 144–46
Hogarth, William, 218–20
Home, John, 204–5, 246–47
House of Commons, newsletter accounts of, 164
Hume, David, 12–14, 25–26, 29, 251–52, 254–57, 259–60

imagined communities, print media and, 11
Indigenous peoples, in Scottish colonial letters, 131
information
  gaps in accounts of Jacobite Rising (1715), 166–67, 170–72, 175
  gaps in accounts of Jacobite Rising (1745), 204–5
  historical accounts' consolidation of, 187–88
  management of coverage of Jacobite Rising, 176–85
Ireland
  British mockery of, 29
  cultural memory in, 105
  erasure in post-Revolution accounts of, 70–75, 99–107
  histories of, 78–86
  Jacobite Rising (1715) and, 158–59
  James II/VII's presence in, 68–69, 101
  under James II/VII's rule, 70–75
  maps as instrument of control in, 76–77
  media coverage of, 22–23, 69–70
  in newspaper advertisements, 75–86
  Protestant refugees from, 69–70, 73–77
  Revolution of 1688 and role of, 69–70, 96–99
  in William III/II's *Declaration*, 71–72
Ireland Preserv'd: or the Siege of London-Derry (Mitchelburne), 99–107
Irish Gaelic oral culture, 66

The Irish Hudibras, or Fingallian Prince, 22–23, 82–86
Irish Rebellion (1641)
  cultural memory of, 22–23, 94–99, 105–7
  histories of, 92–96
  siege of Derry compared with, 69–70, 76–77
  War of Two Kings and, 96–99
The Irish Rebellion (Temple), 93–94
Israel, Jonathan, 30–31

Jacobite poetry, 106, 147–50
Jacobite Prisoners of the 1715: Preventing and Punishing Insurrection in Early Hanoverian Britain (Sankey), 185
Jacobite Rising (1715), 1–2
  causes of, 158–61
  criticism in historical accounts of, 198–99
  cultural memory and role of, 157–58
  The Free-holder's coverage of, 176–78, 181–85
  historical accounts of, 185–99
  information management about, 176–85
  in manuscript newsletters, 161–67
  newspaper accounts of, 24–25, 167–72
  political goals of, 249–51
  printed accounts of, 23–24, 159–61
  sympathy for accused in, 180–81, 190–92
  The Town-Talk's coverage of, 176–81
Jacobite Rising (1745), 1–2
  British exceptionalism and, 249–51
  "Chevalier" narratives of, 227–40
  cultural memory and, 200–1
  in historical novels, 227–40
  knots of memory and, 247–48
  media support for, 226–27
  news accounts of, 24–25, 201–10
  pamphlet coverage of, 215–17
  popular histories of, 240–47
  printed accounts of, 23–24
  prisoners' narratives of, 213–28
Jacobitism and the English People (Monod), 229–30
James I/VI (King of England, Ireland and Scotland), 52–53
James II/VII (King of England, Ireland and Scotland), 4–5
  Addison's comments on, 182
  Argyll's and Monmouth's declarations against, 36–39
  bishops' opposition to, 43–45, 57–58
  in Bohun's *History of the Desertion*, 62–64
  Catholicism and, 29–30
  censorship under, 35–36, 50–52
  Charles II and, 34–35
  conflict with William, 69–70
  documents against William of Orange published by, 53–59

documents published by, 4–5, 10, 39–40, 49–50
flight to France by, 58–59
in Ireland, 68–69, 101
Ireland during reign of, 70–75
in Jacobite poetry, 147
opposition to, 45–47
pamphlets critical of, 30–31, 45–47
political agenda, promotion in pamphlets by, 40–43, 45
progresses for propaganda of, 41–42
Protestant clergy's resistance against, 43–45
support for, 110–12
William of Orange's campaign against, 47–53
Jardine, Lisa, 4–7
Johns, Adrian, 10
Jones, Richard, 257
Journal of the Pretender's Expedition to North Britain, 207–9

Kelly, James, 94
Kerrigan, John, 84–85
King, Rachel, 114
"King Charles's Lament," 147
Kings Letter TO THE Earl of Feversham, 58–59
Kneller, Godfrey, 89–90
Knight, Charles, 182
knots of memory (*noeuds de mémoire*)
  in historical accounts, 25–26
  Jacobite Rising (1715) and, 24–25, 157–58, 193
  Jacobite Rising (1745) and, 247–48
  printed media as, 25–26
  remembering and forgetting in, 69–70
  Rothberg on, 20–21

Làmh-sgrìobhainn Fheàrnaig (Fernaig manuscript) poetry, 66
"lampoons" (anti-government pamphlets), 46
land ownership in Ireland
  British displacement of, 97–98, 130
  Irish Rebellion of 1641 and issue of, 94
Lea, Phillip, 76–77
Letter to a Country Gentleman (Collier), 45–46
letters
  as bridge genre, 114
  between Company of Scotland directors and colonists, 122–26
  cultural memory and, 21–22
  on Darien colony, abandonment, 138–43
  Darien colony and cultural memory of, 108–10, 141–43
  on Darien troubles and desertion, 134–38
  foreign investors in Company of Scotland and, 120–22

Index

global commerce and, 112–13
history of events through, 23
letter pamphlets, 114–20, 126–34
support for Company of Scotland in, 141
William of Orange's arrival described in, 52–53
see also pamphlets
Levack, Bruce, 143
Licensing Acts (1662, 1679 and 1685), 7–8, 23, 34–35
James II/VII and renewal of, 35–36
lapse of, 34–35, 159–61
lieu de mémoire
defined, 2–3
memory and forgetting and, 14, 267–69
national identity and, 19–21
sites of cultural memory and, 18–19
The Life, Adventures, and Many and Great Vicissitudes of Fortune of SIMON, Lord LOVAT, 223
"The Life and Death of the Piper of Kilbarchan" (Sempill), 147
"Lilliburlero" (song)
Irish Hudibras and influence of, 82–86
national identity linked to, 28–31
Revolution of 1688 and, 66
literacy
letteracy and, 114
in Scotland, 109–10
The Lives and Characters of the Most Eminent Writers of the Scots Nation (Mackenzie), 148
Lives of the Admirals, and Other Eminent British Seamen (Campbell), 150–51
Lloyd, Thomas, 259–60
Locke, John, 12, 233
Lodge, Daniel, 117–18
London Courant, 175
London Evening Post, 204–5, 213–14
flight of Charles Edward Stuart in, 227–30
Lovat's execution in, 224–25
London Gazette
advertisements in, 78–86
Charles II's sanctioning of, 34–35
flight of Charles Edward Stuart in, 227–30
Ireland, coverage in, 69–70, 73–77
Irish Rebellion discussed in, 22
Jacobite Rising (1745) in, 204–5, 213
James II/VII's *Declaration* in, 40
promotion of James II/VII in, 56
siege of Derry, coverage in, 86–88
Steele as editor of, 176
Walker's *True Account* in, 87–92
war coverage in, 22–23
William supported by, 58, 61–62, 73–77
London Livery companies, 100–1

London Post, on Darien colony failure, 137
Lupton, Christina, 10–11, 203–4, 243
Luttrell, Narcissus, 44–47, 57–58
"The Lyon in Mourning" (Forbes), 210–11, 225–26, 230–31, 247–48

Mac Cairteáin, Uilliam, 66
Mac Cuarta, Séamas Dall, 66
Macaulay, Thomas Babington, 27, 60
MacDonald, Alexander, 230–31
Mackenzie, George (author of *Most Eminent Writers*), 148–49
Mackenzie, George (Earl of Cromartie), 215, 219–22
Mackenzie, John, 92–94
MacKenzie, Roderick ("Philanax Verax"), 116–17
MacRath, Donnchadh (Duncan Macrae), 66
The Manifestation of Joy, or, the Loyal Subjects Grateful Acknowledgment (ballad), 41
"Manifesto by the Noblemen, Gentlemen, and others" (Mar), 189–90
manuscript newsletters
confidentiality of, 166
decline of, 202
information gaps in, 171–72, 175
Jacobite Rising (1715) in, 157–58, 160–67
opposition to James II/VII in, 47 *see also* newsletters
maps
of Ireland, 76–78, 85–86
mediation of events and, 22–23
Marchant, John, 204–6, 243–44
Marking the Mind: A History of Memory (Danziger), 15–16
Maxwell, Richard, 229–30
Maxwell, William (Earl of Nithsdale), 180–81, 190–92
McDowell, Paula, 10–11
McKenzie, D. F., 76–77
media
cultural shift in Britain and Ireland, 1, 6–7
epistemologies linked to, 10–11
Jacobite Rising (1745) in, 201–10
official documents distribution and, 32–33
politics and role of, 7–8, 32–33
siege of Derry, coverage in, 86–99
transitions and cultural memory and, 17–18
mediation
Company of Scotland, creation and role of, 119–20
consciousness of, 10–11
in coverage of Culloden, 210–13
Cultural Memory Studies and role of, 15–16
of Darien expedition, 108–10

mediation (cont.)
  Irish news coverage, and, 69–70
  Jacobite codedness and secrecy and, 209–10
  material practices of, 7–8
  of memory in Scott's *Waverley*, 264–67
  memory's constructedness and precariousness and, 21
  in popular histories of Jacobite Rising (1745), 241–42
  print media and awareness of, 3–4
  in transatlantic communication, 137–38
Memoirs of the Life of Lord Lovat, 223–25
Memorials of the English Affairs (Whitelocke), 60–61
memory
  of culture, cultural memory and, 249–51
  as Enlightenment concept, 14
  Hume on, 12–14
  Locke's discussion of, 12
  past vs. modern memory, 18–19
  in Scott's *Waverley*, mediation of, 264–67
Memory (Whitehead), 15–16
Memory, Print and Gender in England, 1653–1759 (Weber), 16–17
Mendle, Michael, 60–62
Mitchelburne, John, 87–88, 99–107
Mobility Studies: A Manifesto (Greenblatt), 137–38
Monmouth, Duke of. *See* Scott, James (Duke of Monmouth)
Monod, Paul, 229–30
Montague, William Henry, 252
Montgomerie, Alexander, 147
monthly periodicals, *Particulars of the Victory* published in, 8–9
Morden, Robert, 76–77, 85–86
More Newes from Ireland, or, the Bloody Practic[e]*s and Proceedings of the Papists in That Kingdome at This Present*, 93–94
Morley, Vincent, 106
Morphew, John, 169
Mr. John Mackenzyes Narrative of the Siege of London-Derry a False Libel (Clark), 92–94
Muddiman, Henry, 34–35
multi-volume histories, cultural memory and, 25–26
Murray, John, 223–24
Murray, William (Lord Nairne), 180–81, 190–92
music and song
  cultural memory and, 82–86
  Gaelic Irish and Anglophone traditions, 107
  national identity and, 28–31
  Revolution of 1688 in, 66
  in Scott's novels, 264–67 *see also* specific songs

national identity
  Battle of Culloden linked to, 200–1
  cultural memory and, 249–51
  Darien colony (Company of Scotland) linked to, 141
  erasure of memory and, 20–21
  historical accounts and creation of, 188–89, 197
  Hume's discussion of, 5–6
  in *Irish Hudibras*, 84–85
  memory and, 14
  print media and consolidation of, 9–10
  Scottish Union and emergence of, 146–47
  in Scott's *Waverley*, 262
  state expansion and, 19–21
Navigation Acts, 143
Nelson, Holly, 99–100
New British Studies, 19–21
Newbery, John, 252
Newcomb, Thomas, 40
Newdigate, Richard, 161
Newdigate, Richard (second Baronet), 161n.16
Newdigate family newsletters, 23–24, 160–67
The News Revolution in England: Cultural Dynamics of Daily Information (Sommerville), 71–72
newsletters
  Charles II's use of, 34–35
  flight of James II/VII and arrival of William of Orange in, 58–59
  historicity of, 60–61
  information gaps in, 166–67, 170–71, 201–10
  see also manuscript newsletters
newspapers
  advertisements in, 21–22, 75–86
  Company of Scotland, coverage in, 113–15
  Culloden, coverage in, 210–13
  detailed information in, 171–72
  discontinuities of form and content in, 172–75
  flight of Charles Edward Stuart in, 227–30
  historical criticism of, 185–86
  historicity of, 60–61
  information management of Jacobite uprising in, 176–85
  Ireland, coverage in, 69–75
  Jacobite Rising (1715) in, 24–25, 157–61, 167–75
  Jacobite Rising (1745) in, 201–10
  multiplicity of, 175
  Particulars of the Victory published in, 8–9
  peers' executions reported in, 214–15
  periodical essays and development of, 176
  placement of news in, 172–75
  prisoners of Jacobite Rising (1745) in, discussion of, 213–28

proliferation of, 202–4
War of the Two Kings (Ireland), coverage in,
    22–23
see also pamphlets
Nichols, John, 165–85
Nikulin, Dmitri, 268–69
noise trading, Company of Scotland and, 118–19
Nora, Pierre
    cultural memory and, 2–3, 15–16
    on national identity, 21, 201
    on sites of cultural memory, 18–19, 267–69

Ó Ruairc, Brian na Múrtha (Brian O'Rourke), 107
O'Brien, Karen, 253
official public documents
    of Company of Scotland, 141–43
    cultural memory and, 21–22
    Declaration of William of Orange as, 60–61
    double authorship in rediscovery of, 153–55
    as historical source, 31–33
    James II/VII's use of, 45, 53–59
    manuscript newsletters as, 166
Ogilvy, James (Marquis of Tullibardine), 120–22
Oldmixon, John, 150–51
"On the Lord Lovat's Execution," 224–25
O'Quinn, Daniel, 174–75
oral culture
    Gaelic Catholic counter-memory in, 106
    Jacobite Rising (1715) in, 160
    opposition to James II/VII and, 47
    Revolution of 1688 and impact of, 30–31, 66
    Scott's novels and, 264–67
Orange Gazette, 22–23
    Ireland, coverage in, 71–72
The Original Papers and Letters Relating to the Scots Company Trading to Africa and the Indies, 141–43
Orr, Julie, 134
Ottoman–Venetian War, 163–64
Otway, Thomas, 99

pamphlets
    Argyll and Monmouth declarations circulated as, 36–39
    Culloden battle, coverage in, 6, 210–13
    flight of Charles Edward Stuart in, 229–30
    Jacobite Rising (1745), trials and executions of prisoners in, discussion of, 218–28
    Jacobite Rising (1745) in, 209–10, 215–17
    Jacobite Risings in, 24–25
    James II/VII's political agenda promoted in, 40–43
    letter pamphlets, 114–20, 126–34
    in opposition to James II/VII, 45–47
    Particulars of the Victory published in, 8–9
    political discourse in, 30–31

Scottish Union, debate in, 143
siege of Derry, coverage in, 92–94
support for Jacobites in, 226–27
"Panurgi Philocaballi Scoti Grameidos" (James Philip [Philp] of Almerieclose), 66
Paper Knowledge: Toward a Media History of Documents (Gitelman), 31–33
Particulars of the Victory
    drafting of, 6
    news pamphlet distribution of, 8–9
Paterson, William, 110–13, 117–18, 120–22, 135–37
Patten, Robert, 23–24, 193–95, 197–98
Paul, Helen Julia, 118–19
Peacy, Jason, 33–34
The Peerage of Scotland (Crawford), 219–21
Penny London Post or Morning Advertiser, 214
    flight of Charles Edward Stuart in, 227–30
Penny Post, printed media distribution and, 35n.28
The People of Scotland's Groans and Lamentable Complaints (Watson), 147
Percy, Thomas, 30–31
performativity, of Restoration monarchy, 34–35
periodical essay
    cultural memory and, 165–85
    Jacobite Rising (1715) in, 157–58, 176–85
    origins of, 176
Perkins, Pam, 229–30
The Petition of the LORDS Spiritual and Temporal for the Calling of a Free Parliament Together, with His Majesty's Gracious Answer to Their Lordships, 57–58
The Petition of William Sancroft, Archbishop of Canterbury and Six Other Bishops, 43–45
Petty, William, 76–77, 97–98
Philip (Philp), James, of Almerieclose, 66
Phillips, Mark Salber, 254
Pincus, Steven, 37–38
Pinkham, Lucile, 41–42, 45–46
Pitcairne, Archibald, 66
Pittock, Murray, 5n.17, 66n.138, 198, 200n.1, 198–99, 209–10, 210, 213n.42, 224n.68, 233, 236, 240
Plank, Geoffrey, 217
Plan of a Complete History of England (Smollett), 8–9, 252, 257–60
"Pléaráca na Ruarcach" (Aodh Mac Gabhráin [Hugh McGauran]), 107
Poemata selecta (Pitcairne), 66
poetry
    oral culture and, 30–31, 66
    Scottish national identity and, 147–50
Poetry and Jacobite Politics in Eighteenth-Century Britain and Ireland (Pittock), 198–99

"Polemo-Middinia" (Drummond), 147
political agendas
  demand for print media and, 33–45
  James II's promotion of, 35–36, 40–43
  official documents in, 31–33
  pamphlets' role in, 30–31
Political Economy of Ireland (Petty), 97–98
Pollard, Mary, 106
popular culture
  in ballads, 29–30
  Declaration (William of Orange) in, 17–18
  memory and narrative in, 21–22
  see also music and song
portability of print media, 10–11
postal service, printed media distribution and, 35n.28
Post Boy, 113–15, 159–61
The Post-Man, 159–61, 173, 175, 177
Postman, Neil, 10–11
The Prince of Orange His Declaration Shewing the Reasons Why He Invades England: With a Short Preface, and Some Modest Remarks on It, 56–57
Print Culture Studies, 17–18
print media
  British culture of, 7–8
  Catholic issue in, 97–98
  censorship of, 34–35
  cultural memory and, 3–4
  dominance in mid-eighteenth century of, 203–4
  elevated status of, 10
  imagined communities and, 11
  Ireland, coverage in, 69–70, 85–86
  Jacobite Rising (1715) and role of, 159–61
  Jacobite Rising (1745) in, 201–10
  memory and, 14
  national identity consolidation and, 9–10, 14
  official documents and, 32–33
  portability of, 10–11
  pre-1688 evolution of, 33–45
  Protestant–Catholic polarization and, 105–7
  retrospective narratives of historical events, 61–62
  in Scott's novels, 264–67
  William of Orange's campaign and role of, 47–53
prisoners' narratives of Jacobite Rising (1745), 213–28
Private Occurrences, OR, the Transaction of the Four Last Years, 50–51
propaganda
  Argyll and Monmouth declarations as, 37–38
  Company of Scotland's letter pamphlets as, 119–20
  James II/VII's management of, 35–36, 39–42, 45
  official documents as tool for, 31–33
  pamphlets as tool for, 31
  William of Orange's campaign of, 47–53, 55–57
Proposals for a Fond to Cary [sic] on a Plantation (Paterson), 110–12
Protestants
  cultural memory in, 105–7
  declarations in support of, 36–39
  in Ireland, 69–70
  Irish Protestant refugees in England, 69–70, 73–77
  Jacobite Rising (1715) and, 158–59
  in Mitchelburne's *Ireland Preserv'd*, 102, 105
  siege of Derry and role of, 92–94
  War of Two Kings and polarization concerning, 97–98, 105–7
  William of Orange and, 29–30
public credit, William III/II's use of, 110–12
public opinion
  official documents and, 34
  pamphlets and, 31
  print media and development of, 33–34
Pyke, Thomas, 57–58

Radclyffe, James (Earl of Derwentwater), 180–81, 190–92
Rae, Peter, 23–24, 186–87, 195–97
Ramsay, Allan, 148–49
Rapin de Thoyras, Paul de, 252–55
Ray, James, 245–46, 261–62
Raymond, Joad, 30–31, 54–55, 174–75
reading practices
  Jacobite Rising (1745), impact on, 200–1
  promotion in popular histories of, 242–43
  self-conscious discourse on, 10–11
Realms of Memory: Rethinking the French Past (Nora), 2–3
Reasons Why the Church of England, as Well as Dissenters Should Make Their Address of Thanks to the King's Majesty, for His Late Gracious Declaration for Liberty of Conscience (pamphlet), 40–43
Reflections upon His Highness the Prince of Orange's Declaration, 54–55, 57
Reflexions on a Paper Pretending to Be an Apology for the Failures Charged on Mr. Walker's Account of the Siege of Londonderry, 92–94
Reiman, Donald, 166
religious tolerance, James II/VII's advocacy of, 39–40
Reliques of Ancient English Poetry (Percy), 30–31
Remarks upon the Scotch Act, in a Letter to a Friend, 114–18

"Remembering as Re-inscription – with a Difference" (Belsey), 3–4
Renan, Ernst, 20–21
retrospective narratives of historical events, 61–62
Review of the British Nation (Defoe), 176
Revolution of 1688, 1–2
  cultural memory and amnesia concerning, 21–22, 27–28, 249–51
  erasure of Ireland in accounts of, 69–70, 96–107
  print narrative of, 10
  retrospective narratives of, 59–67
  Scottish national division and, 110–12
  War of the Two Kings (Ireland) and, 20–21
"The Revolution of 1689 and the Structure of Political Argument" (Goldie), 30–31
rhetoric of epistolarity, 128
Rider, William, 252
Ridpath, George, 140–47
Rigney, Ann, 10–11, 18–19, 261, 267–69
Rivington, James, 252
Robertson, William, v, 252
Rothberg, Michael, 20–21
Royal Bank of Scotland, Company of Scotland's metamorphosis into, 108–10
rumour, political role of, 47
Rycaut, Paul, 120–22

St James's Evening Post, 160–61, 168–69
  censorship of, 169
Sandrock, Kristen, 127
Sankey, Margaret, 185
Schneider, Gary, 128
Schwoerer, Lois, 6–7, 30–31, 33–34, 60
Scotland
  Darien expedition, impact in, 1–2, 23, 143
  English power imbalance with, 144–45
  Jacobite Rising (1715) and, 158–59
  newspapers, proliferation in, 202
  pamphlet war over Union in, 143
  political impact of Union in, 146–47
  print media, growth in, 109–10
  Union of 1707 and, 143–51
Scotland's Right to Caledonia (Formerly Called Darien), 125n.60
Scots Gaelic oral culture, 66
Scots Magazine, 212–13, 247
Scott, James (Duke of Monmouth), 35–39
Scott, Walter (Sir), 25–26, 261–67
Scottish Parliament
  Company of Scotland, debate in, 117–18
  opposition control of, 138n.102
  Union and loss of, 146–49

Seasonable Considerations on the Present War in Scotland, 206–9
self-awareness
  in popular histories of Jacobite Rising (1745), 241, 245–46
  proliferation of print culture and, 203–4
Sempill, Robert, 147
Sher, Richard, 251–52
Shortt, Linda, 2–3
siege dramas, siege of Derry in, 99–107
siege of Derry. *See* Derry, siege of (1689)
Sileas na Ceapaich (Cicely Macdonald of Keppoch), 66
Siskin, Clifford, 21–22
Slowey, Desmond, 99–100
Smollett, Tobias, 8–9, 25–26, 252, 257–60
Smyth, James, 117–18
Snyder, Henry L., 160–61
social narrative, history as, 253
Some Considerations upon the Late Act of the Parliament of Scotland, for Constituting an Indian Company In a Letter to a Friend, 115–16
Sommerville, C. John, 71–72, 175
Sophia of Hanover, 143
Sowerby, Scott, 42–43
The Spectator, 176
spectatorship, Restoration monarchy's use of, 34–35
Speech in Parliament, the Second Day of November 1706 (Hamilton, Lord Belhaven), 145–46
Stamp Act (1712), 159–61
state expansion
  maps as instrument of, 76–77
  national identity and, 19–21
State of the Papist and Protestant Proprieties in the Kingdom of Ireland in the Year 1641, 95–96
Steele, Richard
  on Jacobite Rising (1715), 165–85
  as *Town-Talk* editor, 23–24, 157–58, 176
Story, George Warter, 68–69
Strange, John, 218–28
The Strolling Hero, or Rome's Knight-Errant (Butler), 202
Stuart, Charles Edward, 5–6
  "Chevalier" escape narratives about, 227–40
  escape of, 24–25, 200–1, 212–13, 227–30
  newspaper information about, 204–5
  reliance on print information, 209–10
Stuart, James Francis Edward, 4–5, 163–64, 178–80
Stuart monarchy
  end of, 157–58
  execution of Charles I and, 190–92
  support for, 209–10, 216–17

Stuart monarchy (cont.)
  threat of, 5–6, 158–59, 182
Suarez, S. J., Michael F., 7–8
Sun Fire Office, 185–86
Swift, Jonathan, 107
Szechi, Daniel, 158–59, 166–67

Talbot, Richard (Earl of Tyrconnell), 29, 70
The Tatler, 176
The Tears of Scotland (Smollett), 258–59
The Tea-Table Miscellany (Ramsay), 148–49
Temple, John, 93–94
theatre
  Declaration in, 17–18
  Mitchelburne's *Ireland Preserv'd* as siege drama, 99–107
Towneley, Francis, 216–17
The Town-Talk
  Jacobite Rising (1715), accounts in, 165–85
  Steele as editor of, 23–24, 157–58, 176
Towsey, Mark, 251–52, 256–57
transatlantic communication, mediation in, 137–38
transmedia phenomena, cultural memory and, 27–28
"Travelling Memory" (Eril), 25–26, 96
Treaty of Limerick (1691), 97–98
Treaty of Union (1707), 146
Trevelyan, G. M., 27, 31n.14, 60
trials of Jacobite Rising (1715), participants, 180–81, 190–92
  visual images of, 226–27
trials of Jacobite Rising (1745), participants
  newspaper coverage of, 214
  of peers, 214–15
  sympathy for accused in accounts of, 218–28
  see also executions
The Trials of William Earl of Kilmarnock, George Earl of Cromartie, and Arthur Lord Balmerino, for High-Treason, before the House of Peers, at Westminster-Hall, on the 28th and 30th of July, and the 1st of August, 1746, 218–20, 222–23, 226–27
True Copies of the Papers Wrote by Arthur Lord Balmerino, 226–27
The True Patriot (periodical), 205–6
truth-telling, evolution of print media and, 10–11
Turner, Michael, 7–8
typographical fixity, print media and, 9–10

UK Memory of the World Register, 108–10
UNESCO's Memory of the World project, 108–10

Vanderbanc, Peter, 89–90
Venice Preserv'd (Otway), 99
The Vindication of the True Account of the Siege of Derry, by Mr. George Walker (Walker), 92–94
visual culture, trial and execution narratives and rise of, 226–27

Wafer, Lionel, 132–33
Walker, George, 22–23, 87–92
  Mitchelburne and, 99
The Wanderer, or Surprizing Escape, 236–40, 261–62
War of the Two Kings (Ireland), 1–2
  cultural memory of, 96, 105–7
  erasure of memory of, 20–23
  legacy of, 97–98
  political goals of, 249–51
  print media coverage of, 69–70 *see also* Derry, siege of (1689)
Ward, James, 14
Warner, William, 21–22, 32–33
Watson, James, 147
Watt, Douglas, 118–19, 138–39, 148–51
Waverley (Scott), 25–26, 261–67
Weber, Harold, 16–17
The Weekly Packet, 175
weekly periodicals, *Particulars of the Victory* published in, 8–9
Whatley, Christopher, 144, 146–47
Whigs
  Revolution of 1688 and, 65
  Scottish national division and, 110–12, 147
White, Robert, 82
Whitehead, Ann, 15–16
Whitelocke, Bulstrode, 60–61
Whyte, Lawrence, 107
Widdrington, William (Baron Widdrington), 180–81, 190–92
William, Duke of Cumberland, 5–6
William III/II (King of England, Ireland and Scotland), 5–6, 147
  see also William of Orange
William and Mary
  acknowledgment of royal status, 6–7, 64–66, 68–70
  Declaration of Rights and, 60
  engravings of, 82
  in Fagel's *Letter*, 45–46
  in post-Revolution histories, 62–64
  Scottish national division and reign of, 110–12
  Walker's meeting with, 88
  see also William of Orange

William of Orange
    arrival in London of, 58–59
    in ballads, 17–18, 52–53
    conflict with James II/VII, 69–70
    Cox's support for, 78–79
    Darien colony opposed by, 120–22, 134–35, 142–43
    death of, 98–99
    documents published by, 4–7, 10
    historical defense of, 29–30
    James II/VII's opposition campaign against, 53–59
    multi-media propaganda campaign by, 47–53
    news coverage of arrival in England, 52–53
    pamphlets in support of, 30–31
    political goals of, 254–55
women, Addison on national role of, 183–84
Woolf, Daniel, 166
Wye, William, 161

Young Juba: or, the History of the Young Chevalier, from His Birth, to His Escape from Scotland after the Battle of Culloden, 236–39, 261–62

Zaret, David, 33–34, 38–39
Zook, Melinda, 35n.27

For EU product safety concerns, contact us at Calle de José Abascal, 56–1°, 28003 Madrid, Spain or eugpsr@cambridge.org.

www.ingramcontent.com/pod-product-compliance
Ingram Content Group UK Ltd.
Pitfield, Milton Keynes, MK11 3LW, UK
UKHW022247220326
469255UK00019B/408